CIVIL JURISDICTION
IN
SCOTLAND

CIVIL JURISDICTION
IN
SCOTLAND

by

A. E. ANTON
C.B.E., M.A., LL.B., F.R.S.E., F.B.A.
Solicitor
Visiting Professor, University of Aberdeen

EDINBURGH
W. GREEN & SON LTD
1984

First Published in 1984

ISBN 0 414 00736 0

Printed in Great Britain by
Thomson Litho Ltd, East Kilbride, Scotland

PREFACE

THIS book is designed as a comprehensive guide to the application in Scotland of the Civil Jurisdiction and Judgments Act 1982 and of the European Judgments Convention, to which the Act will give the force of law. The book deals with jurisdiction and the recognition and enforcement of judgments in matters within the scope of the Act and of the Convention. It does not deal with matters outwith their scope, notably jurisdiction and recognition of judgments in matters relating to status.

When the 1982 Act becomes fully operative it will, in matters within its scope, completely change the Scottish rules for the assumption of jurisdiction and will materially change those relating to the recognition and enforcement of foreign judgments. In relation to jurisdiction, both where the defender is domiciled in another State party to the Convention and in a few special cases, the rules of the Convention will apply directly and have the force of law; by virtue of the 1982 Act, substantially the same rules will apply where the defender is domiciled in another part of the United Kingdom; and the same rules will form the core of those applicable where the defender is domiciled elsewhere. In relation to judgments within the scope of the Convention—essentially judgments in patrimonial matters—emanating from the courts of a State party to the Convention, a new scheme set out in the Convention becomes applicable, permitting of the recognition and enforcement of such judgments with a minimum of formality throughout the States parties to the Convention. The 1982 Act introduces a similar scheme to facilitate the reciprocal enforcement of the judgments of the courts of one part of the United Kingdom in its remaining parts. Significant changes, moreover, are made to the general rules applicable to the recognition and enforcement of other external judgments.
introduces a similar scheme to facilitate the reciprocal enforcement of the judgments of the courts of one part of the United Kingdom in its remaining parts. Significant changes, moreover, are made to the general rules applicable to the recognition and enforcement of other external judgments.

It need hardly be insisted, therefore, that the 1982 Act is of primordial importance for Scottish practitioners. The object of this book is to assist them in applying it. While the Act itself is a model of clarity, reflecting the considerable skills of its draftsman and of those who instructed him, the same can less easily be said of the Convention. Its apparent simplicity is illusory and conceals a variety of problems. The manner of its interpretation, therefore, becomes a matter of crucial importance. The 1982 Act requires the Convention to be interpreted in accordance with the principles laid down by, and the relevant decisions of, the Court of Justice of the European Communities. Even where the Convention is not applicable as such, the Scottish courts are required to have regard to the European Court's precedents when considering rules in the Act derived to any extent from Title II of the Convention. Special attention, therefore, is paid in this book to the interpretative techniques developed by the European Court and to the decisions of that Court in issues arising from the Convention.

Careful account is also taken of existing commentaries, official and unofficial, on the Convention with a view to throwing light on questions not so far the subject of decision or commentary by the European Court. While it is an invidious task to select for mention individual writings, it would be out of place not to refer to Professor G. A. L. Droz's commentary on the Convention, *Compétence Judiciaire et Effets des Jugements dans le Marché Commun* (Paris, 1975). Without that commentary the task of those in the United Kingdom concerned with the negotiations on the Accession Convention and with the legislation designed to implement the Judgments Convention would have been immeasurably more difficult. Mr. Lawrence Collins' *The Civil Jurisdiction and Judgments Act 1982* (London, 1983) will be found to be an admirable independent commentary from an English standpoint upon the Act and the Convention.

It had been hoped to print as appendices to this book, and to refer in the text to, the Acts of Sederunt which were understood to be in preparation supplementing in matters of detail the provisions of the Act and of the Convention. Unfortunately, these Acts of Sederunt were not available as the book went to press, a fact which may help to explain certain gaps in the numbering of the footnotes.

Mrs. Moira Johnston cheerfully and efficiently transformed an illegible manuscript into typescript. I am most grateful to her. Thanks are also due to the many colleagues and friends who allowed me to discuss with them troublesome points. More specifically, thanks are due to Mr. Hugh Macdiarmid, of the Office of the Solicitor to the Secretary of State, for his encouragement and assistance. The Hon. Lord Maxwell kindly read pilot versions of the central parts of this book: his friendly criticism and balanced advice helped to mould its final shape. For this, and for much else, I am deeply indebted to him. Mr. Paul R. Beaumont, of the University of Aberdeen, generously read successive drafts of the text and helped with the tedious task of proof-reading. I am grateful to him for this and for his perceptive advice both on matters relating to the Convention and on matters of general Community law.

Finally, I express my thanks to Miss Iris Stewart of W. Green & Son Ltd. for her patience, efficiency, and ready comprehension of problems in an alien field. In this context readers should be aware that W. Green & Son Ltd. propose to publish in the *Scots Law Times* Notes prepared by Mr. Paul R. Beaumont and the writer which annotate past and future decisions of the European Court relating to the Judgments Convention. These Notes should be of material assistance to readers in keeping up to date with the subject-matter of this book.

1 March 1984 A. E. ANTON

Publishers' Note
Since this book went to press it has been announced that, since Belgium's ratification of the Judgments Convention has been delayed, the Government's intention to bring the provisions of the 1982 Act relating to the Convention into force in the course of 1984 will not be realised.

CONTENTS

		PAGE
Preface	. . . .	v
Table of Statutes	. . . .	xi
Table of 1968 Convention and its associated instruments	. . .	xiii
Table of Cases (Alphabetical order)	. . . . .	xv
Table of Cases (Chronological order)	. . . . .	xix
References	. . . .	xxi

PARA.

CHAPTER 1 INTRODUCTION
The purposes of the 1982 Act . . . 1.01
The 1968 Convention and its associated instruments 1.05
Background to the 1968 Convention . . 1.09
Salient features of the Convention . . . 1.16
Scheme of the 1982 Act 1.31
Arrangement of this book 1.37

CHAPTER 2 THE INTERPRETATION OF THE CONVENTION
Introduction 2.01
The Protocol on interpretation . . . 2.04
Authority of the European Court's judgments 2.09
Principles applied by the European Court in the interpretation of the Conventions . . 2.12

CHAPTER 3 SCOPE OF THE 1968 CONVENTION AND OTHER ASPECTS OF ITS APPLICATION
Scope 3.01
Territorial application 3.42
Temporal application 3.47

CHAPTER 4 DOMICILE AND SEAT UNDER CONVENTION AND 1982 ACT
Introduction 4.01
Domicile of individuals under the Convention 4.06
Domicile of individuals under 1982 Act . . 4.12
Seat of corporations and associations under Convention 4.22
Seat of corporations and associations under 1982 Act 4.26

[vii]

PARA.

CHAPTER 5 PRINCIPAL JURISDICTIONAL RULES UNDER THE
           CONVENTION
                Introduction 5.01
                Domicile: the general principle . . . 5.04
                Special jurisdictions in Article 5 . . . 5.12
                Special jurisdictions in Articles 6 and 6A . . 5.59

CHAPTER 6 JURISDICTION IN INSURANCE AND CONSUMER
           CONTRACTS UNDER CONVENTION
                Introduction 6.01
                Insurance contracts 6.07
                Consumer contracts 6.25

CHAPTER 7 OTHER RULES OF JURISDICTION UNDER THE
           CONVENTION
                Introduction 7.01
                Exclusive jurisdictions 7.02
                Prorogation and submission 7.23
                Verification of jurisdiction and due service . 7.29
                Lis pendens and related actions . . . 7.38
                Provisional and protective measures . . 7.44

CHAPTER 8 RECOGNITION AND ENFORCEMENT UNDER THE
           CONVENTION
                Introduction 8.01
                Judgments to which scheme applies . . . 8.05
                Recognition 8.07
                Enforcement 8.30
                Specialities in relation to maintenance orders . 8.53
                Enforcement of Scottish judgments under the
                     Convention 8.56
                Authentic instruments and court settlements . 8.57
                Interest and currency of payment . . 8.67
                Legal aid and security for costs . . . 8.69

CHAPTER 9 UNITED KINGDOM SCHEME FOR JURISDICTION AND
           ENFORCEMENT
                Jurisdiction 9.01
                Reciprocal recognition and enforcement under
                     the 1982 Act 9.33

CHAPTER 10 JURISDICTION OF THE SCOTTISH COURTS
                Introduction 10.01
                Interpretation of Schedule 8 . . . . 10.03
                Scope of Schedule 8 . . . . . 10.06
                Relationship of Scottish rules to other rules 10.10
                Scottish rules of jurisdiction 10.14

CHAPTER 11 MISCELLANEOUS MATTERS
                Introduction 11.01
                Provisions directly affecting Scots law . . 11.02
                Provisions not directly affecting Scots law . . 11.20

Table of Contents

			PAGE
APPENDIX	1.	CIVIL JURISDICTION AND JUDGMENTS ACT 1982 .	211
	2.	CONVENTION ON THE ACCESSION TO THE 1968 CONVENTION (with its associated instruments) OF THE HELLENIC REPUBLIC SIGNED ON 25TH OCTOBER 1982	281
	3.	CONVENTION ON THE SERVICE ABROAD OF JUDICIAL AND EXTRAJUDICIAL DOCUMENTS IN CIVIL OR COMMERCIAL MATTERS CONCLUDED 15TH NOVEMBER 1965	286
Index		. . . .	299

TABLE OF STATUTES

[This table of selected references points to the paragraph numbers of the text]

Administration of Justice Act 1920 9.36(6), 11.10–11.11
s.10...11.11
Administration of Justice Act 1956 ...... 3.35
Administration of Justice Act 1977 ...... 8.68
Administration of Justice (Scotland) Act 1972
  s.1 .... 7.47, 11.04
  s.3 ....10.48
  Part II 8.16
Arbitration Act 1975........................3.23
  s.1 ....10.13
Arbitration (Scotland) Act 1894
  ss.3, 4 and 5...............................10.48
Bankruptcy Act 1914
  s.121 .... 9.36(3)
Bankruptcy (Scotland) Act 1913
  s.170 .... 9.36(3)
Carriage by Air Act 1961..................3.35
Carriage by Air Act 1971..................3.33
Carriage by Air (Supplementary Provisions) Act 1962........................3.35
Carriage by Railway Act 1972.............3.35
Carriage of Goods by Road Act 1965 .. 3.35, 11.07
Children and Young Persons (Scotland) Act 1937
  s.91...10.31
Civil Evidence Act 1968 .... 8.42
Civil Jurisdiction and Judgments Act 1982
  s.2 .... 1.31, 5.01
    (1).......................... 2.01, 8.01, 10.10
    (2)..2.15
  s.3 ....1.31, 2.01–2.02, 2.12, 8.01
    (1).......................... 2.01, 2.11, 10.04
    (2).................................2.01, 2.15
    (3).................................2.02, 2.18
  s.4 .... 8.36(6)
    (1)...8.46
    (3)...8.46
  s.5 ....8.55
  s.6
    (1)...............................8.49, 8.51
    (3)...8.55
  s.7 ....8.46
  s.9
    (1)...3.34
    (2)...3.40
  s.10
    (2)...5.53
    (3).............................. 9.24, 10.58
  s.11...............................8.41, 8.42
  s.12...8.56
  s.13...8.59
  s.15...8.02
  s.16.....................5.01, 9.05, 9.06, 9.41
    (3)...9.06
    (4)..................7.19–7.21, 9.26, 10.51
  s.17...............................9.05, 9.06, 9.10
    (1).............................. 9.11, 10.07

s.18............................. 9.35, 9.36, 9.42
s.19....................1.32, 9.04, 9.34, 9.43
s.20................................. 5.01, 10.10
  (1).......1.34, 1.35(3), 3.01, 10.01, 10.20
  (3)...10.01
  (5)..............................10.03, 10.05
s.21.............................9.11, 10.07–10.08
s.22...10.12
  (1)...................4.32, 5.09, 10.01, 10.77
  (2)...10.13
  (4)..............................7.05, 10.09, 10.51
s.24................................. 7.47, 11.02
s.27.........2.28, 7.47, 8.47, 11.03, 11.04
s.28.......................... 4.25, 8.47, 11.04
s.30................................. 3.03, 11.21
s.31...............................3.04, 11.05, 11.19
  (3).............................. 3.04, 11.07
s.32............... 3.26, 11.08–11.09, 11.19
s.33.............................. 11.19, 11.22
s.34............................... 8.32, 11.23
s.35
  (1)...11.10
  (2)...11.11
s.37...11.12
s.38...11.15
s.39...11.16
s.40
  (2)...11.17
s.41............... 4.10, 4.14, 9.06, 10.16
  (1).............................. 4.14, 4.15
  (2).............................. 4.16, 10.20
  (3)...4.16
  (4)...4.19
  (5).............................. 4.18, 10.20
  (6)...4.18
  (7)...4.21
s.42.............................. 4.26–4.33
s.43............... 4.33–4.34, 7.17, 9.06, 10.66
s.44..............................6.10, 6.11, 6.31
s.45............................ 5.52, 9.06, 10.35(2)
s.46..............................4.35, 9.06
s.47.............................. 2.01, 9.04, 10.02
s.48.. 8.46
s.49.............................. 4.32, 9.31, 10.12
s.50..............................8.02, 9.08
s.52...3.43
s.53...............................11.18, 11.23
Sched. 1. *See* TABLE OF 1968 CONVENTION.
Sched. 2. *See* TABLE OF 1968 CONVENTION (1971 PROTOCOL).
Sched. 3. *See* TABLE OF 1968 CONVENTION (1978 ACCESSION CONVENTION).
Sched. 4................................. 9.01 *et seq.*
  Art. 2...............................9.15
  Art. 3...............................9.16
  Art. 4...............................9.17
  Art. 5..................5.27, 5.35, 9.18
  Art. 5A 9.19, 10.46

Art. 6............................9.20
Art. 6A 9.21
Art. 13 ....9.23
Art. 14 ....9.24
Art. 15 ....9.25
Art. 16 ....9.26, 9.29
Art. 17 ....9.27
Art. 18 ....9.28
Art. 19 ....9.29
Art. 20 ....9.30
Arts. 21–23.....................9.31
Art. 24 ....9.32
Sched. 5....................1.32, 9.10, 9.12
Sched. 6...........................9.35–9.39
Sched. 7 ....9.35–9.39
Sched. 8...........................10.01 *et seq.*
r.1 ....10.14–10.17
r.2 ....10.18 *et seq.*
(1) 10.19–10.20, 10.50
(2) 10.21–10.23
(3) 5.35, 10.24–10.25
(4) 10.26–10.28, 10.46
(5) 5.27, 10.29–10.31
(6) 10.32–10.33
(7) 10.34–10.35
(8) 1.34, 10.12, 10.36–10.40
(9) 10.41–10.42
(10)....................5.35, 10.43
(11)..................10.44–10.45
(12)..................10.46–10.47
(13)..................10.48–10.50
(14)............................10.51
(15) 10.50, 10.52–10.56
r.3 ....10.57–10.60
r.4 1.18, 10.46, 10.51, 10.61–10.63
(1)
(a)................ 10.64–10.65
(b) 4.34, 10.66–10.68
(c)................ 10.69–10.70
(d) 10.71
(2) 10.69–10.70
(3) 10.62
r.5 .... 10.49, 10.72–10.79
(1) 10.75
(2) 10.73
(3) 10.76
(4) 10.77
r.6 ....10.78
r.7 ....10.79
r.8 .... 10.80–10.81
Sched. 9...............................10.08
Sched. 10 ....11.10
Sched. 11 ....11.12–11.14
Sched. 13 ....9.41–9.43
Companies Act 1948
s.276 ....9.36(3)
ss.399 and 400 ....7.15
Consumer Credit Act 1974
s.141(3)..................... 10.59–10.60
Continental Shelf Act 1964................9.12
County Courts Act 1959
s.139 ....9.35

Criminal Justice (Scotland) Act 1980
ss.58–67 ....5.41
European Communities Act 1972
s.3(1)............................2.01
s.3(2)............................2.15
Evidence Act 1851 ....8.42
Foreign Judgments (Reciprocal Enforcement) Act 1933 ... 3.29, 8.16, 11.10
s.1 ....8.02, 8.03, 8.35
s.2 ....8.68
s.4 ....3.25, 8.03, 8.13, 8.17, 8.51, 11.08
s.8 ....3.29, 8.09
Inferior Courts (Judgments Extension)
Act 1882 ....9.02
s.8 ....9.02
Judgments Extension Act 1868...........9.02
Law Reform (Jurisdiction in Delict)
(Scotland) Act 1971....................10.25
Law Reform (Miscellaneous Provisions) (Scotland) Act 1940
s.4..................................10.59
Law Reform (Miscellaneous Provisions) (Scotland) Act 1968
s.10............................8.25
s.12............................8.25
Maintenance Orders Act 1950............9.18,
9.36(5), 10.31,
11.13
Maintenance Orders (Reciprocal En-
forcement) Act 1972.. 5.34, 8.54, 10.31,
11.12–11.14
Matrimonial Proceedings (Children)
Act 1958
s.17...............................10.31
Merchant Shipping Act 1974...............3.36
Merchant Shipping (Liability of Shipowners and Others) Act 1958
Part VIII.............................5.70
Merchant Shipping (Oil Pollution) Act
1971
s.13..............................3.36
Mobile Homes Act 1975....................9.11
Nuclear Installations Acts 1965 and
1969 ....3.36
Policy-holders Protection Act 1975
s.7 ....6.14
Protection of Trading Interests Act
1980 ....8.16, 9.12, 11.15
Sheriff Courts (Scotland) Act 1907... 1.35(4)
s.6 ....10.01
(a)................... 5.61, 10.53
(b) 10.32
(c)..................... 5.09, 10.38
(d) 10.39, 10.64
(e)...........................10.43
(f)............................10.22
(g)...........................10.41
(h) 5.69, 10.56
State Immunity Act 1978   3.04, 11.05, 11.06
Third Parties (Rights against Insurers)
Act 1930 ....6.14
Trusts (Scotland) Act 1921
s.24A .... 10.34, 10.35(6)

TABLE OF 1968 CONVENTION, ANNEXED PROTOCOL, 1971 PROTOCOL, 1978 ACCESSION CONVENTION AND 1982 ACCESSION CONVENTION

[These selected references are to paragraph numbers]

1968 Convention
Preamble...**3.05**
Art. 1 .....2.28–2.29, **3.01–3.36**, 8.05, 9.09,
10.06
(1) 2.28–2.29, **3.07–3.12**
(2)   3.13–3.26, 5.31, 5.32, 5.56, 6.04
Art. 2..... 2.30, **5.04–5.08**, 5.15, 5.16, 7.20
(1) 4.04, **5.04–5.08**, 5.26–5.28, 5.32,
5.50
(2) **5.07**
Art. 3 ....**1.24–1.26**, 4.01, 5.16, 8.04
(1) 2.01, 5.02, **5.08–5.09**
(2) 2.01, 4.21, 5.02, 10.41
Art. 4 .... 1.26, 3.37, 4.02, 4.20, 4.21, **5.10,**
6.08, 6.10, 6.30
(1) 5.01, **5.10**, 5.15
(2) 5.01, **5.11**
Art. 5 ....**5.12–5.16**, 5.62, 6.04, 9.18, 10.18
(1) **5.17–5.25**, 5.50, 5.51, 5.62,
7.26(7), 10.04, 10.21
(2) 3.14, **5.26–5.34**, 9.18,
10.29–10.31
(3) **5.35–5.39**, 7.20, 9.18,
10.24–10.25, 10.43
(4) 3.06, **5.40–5.43**, 10.26–10.27
(5) **5.44–5.49**, 6.04, 6.08, 6.10, 10.32
(6) 4.04, 5.14, **5.50–5.56,**
10.34–10.35
(7) **5.57**
Art. 6 ....**5.59**, 9.20, 10.52
(1) 4.14, **5.60–5.64**, 10.53
(2) **5.65–5.68**, 10.54
(3) **5.69**, 10.55
Art. 6A..**5.70**
Art. 7 ....6.08, **6.10**, 9.04, 10.11
Art. 8
(1) 5.06, 6.08, **6.11**
(2) 4.05, 4.14, 6.05, 6.08, 6.10, **6.11,**
6.12
Art. 9 ....6.11, **6.12**, 6.13
Art. 10............................6.11, **6.13–6.14**
(1) 6.08, **6.13**
(2) 6.08, **6.14**
(3) 6.08, **6.14**, 6.15
Art. 11..............................6.08, **6.15**
Art. 12.......... 3.50, 4.13, 5.10, 5.54, 6.04,
6.16–6.17, 6.32,
7.23, 7.27
Art. 12A 6.02, **6.18–6.24**
Art. 13...............**6.25–6.32**, 10.57–10.58
(1) **6.24–6.29**, 9.23, 10.12
(2) 4.05, 6.05, **6.30–6.31**, 9.23
(3) **6.25**
Art. 14...............**6.32**, 9.24, 10.57–10.58
Art. 15.......... 3.50, 4.13, 5.04, 5.10, 5.54,
6.16, 6.31, **6.32,**
7.23, 7.27, 9.25,
10.57–10.58

Art. 15 (cont'd)
(3).................................4.13
Art. 16... 4.02, 4.10, 5.02, 5.62, **7.02–7.06,**
7.27, 8.03, 9.07,
9.26, 10.12,
10.61–10.71
(1).......2.28, 5.09, 5.50, **7.07–7.11,**
9.04, 9.26, 10.42
(2).............4.25, 4.26, 4.33, 4.34,
7.12–7.17, 10.46,
10.47, 10.66, 10.68
(3)...............**7.18**, 10.69, 10.70
(4)............. **7.19–7.21**, 9.26, 10.51
(5)....................**7.22**, 10.71
Art. 17.......2.31, 3.05, 3.50, 4.02, 5.02(4),
5.26, 6.16, 6.33,
7.23–7.25, **7.26,**
8.26, 9.27,
10.72–10.76,
11.08
(1)...... **7.26(2)**, **7.26(4)**, 9.27, 10.73
(2).......... 5.54, 7.26(2), **7.27**, 10.76
(3)..................................**7.27**
(4)............................**7.26(12)**
Art. 18..........2.21, 6.33, **7.28**, 9.28, 10.78
Art. 19...**7.04–7.05**, **7.29–7.30**, 9.29, 10.79
Art. 20 **7.29–7.36**, 7.39, 9.30, 10.80–10.81
(1).....**7.29–7.30**, 7.39, 10.80–10.81
(2)..............**7.31–7.36**, 7.39, 9.30
(3)..............**7.31–7.36**, 7.39, 9.30
Art. 21..................5.02(5), **7.38–7.40**, 9.31
Art. 22.....................5.02(5), **7.40–7.42**
Art. 23.............................**7.17**, 7.43, 9.31
Art. 24.... 3.02, **7.43–7.48**, 8.17, 8.47, 9.32
Art. 25....................**8.02–8.05**, 8.12, 8.34
Art. 26........................**8.07–8.11**, 9.34
Art. 27.... 1.12, 1.29, 3.02, **8.12–8.21**, 8.44
(1)..............................**8.13–8.16**
(2)....................7.32, **8.17–8.18**
(3)..............................**8.19–8.20**
(4)............................1.14, **8.21**
(5)..............................**8.19–8.20**
Art. 28... 1.12, 1.29, 3.02, 3.37, 7.04, 7.17,
8.22–8.27
Art. 29.............................1.13, **8.21**
Art. 30......................................**8.28–8.29**
Art. 31..**8.37**
Art. 32..8.43
Art. 33.......................................**8.39–8.40**
Art. 34...................7.32, 8.26, 8.44
Art. 35..**8.49**
Art. 36.......................................**8.50–8.51**
Art. 37.....................2.08, **8.51–8.52**
Art. 38..8.52
Art. 39.......................................8.46, **8.51**
Art. 40..**8.49**
Art. 41..**8.49**
Art. 42.....................................8.12, **8.45**

Art. 43.................................**8.36**
Art. 44...................8.31, 8.41, **8.69–8.71**
Art. 45..............................8.31, **8.70**
Art. 46..............................8.39, 8.42
Art. 47.......................**8.39–8.42**, 8.44
Art. 48............................8.42, **8.44**
Art. 49................................**8.42**
Art. 50....................7.22, **8.57–8.60**
Art. 51....................7.22, **8.61–8.65**
Art. 52.... 1.23, **4.06–4.11**, 4.15, 4.21, 7.21
    (1)..............4.07, 4.10, **4.12–4.14**
    (2)............4.07, **4.09**, 4.15, 4.21
    (3)............4.07, **4.08, 4.15**, 4.21
Art. 53   1.23, 2.03, **4.22–4.25**, 5.50–5.52,
                 7.12–7.13, 7.21
    (1).....................**4.23–4.25**, 7.17
    (2)...................4.04, **5.50–5.52**
Art. 54................................**3.49–3.51**
Art. 55..............................1.15, **3.29**
Art. 56................................**3.29–3.30**
Art. 57...........3.26, **3.31–3.36**, 3.41, 5.09,
                5.16, 5.34, 5.58,
                5.70, 6.25, 7.20,
                7.26(14),
                8.05(6), 8.27,
                10.08
    (1)...............................**3.31–3.36**
    (2)...........................**3.41**, 5.16
Art. 59.....**3.37–3.40**, 4.21, 8.03, 8.22–8.24

Art. 60................................**3.42–3.46**
Art. 62..................................3.47
Art. 63..................................1.07
Art. 68..................................2.15
Annexed Protocol
  General **1.07**
  Art. I
    (1)................................**5.23**
    (2)............................**7.26(13)**
  Art. II 2.20, 5.43, **8.25**
  Art. III **8.31**
  Art. IV **7.31**
  Art. V **5.68**
  Art. VA..................... 5.26, **8.05(2)**
  Art. VB **5.24**
  Art. VC................................**7.21**
  Art. VD................................**7.21**
1971 Protocol 1.07, **2.04–2.08**, 2.10, 2.28,
                10.05

1978 Accession Convention
  General 1.07
  Art. 8 ....6.17
  Art. 11................... 7.26(6), 7.27
  Art. 25........................5.58, 8.27
  Art. 29................................5.24
  Art. 35................................7.24
  Art. 39................................3.48
1982 Accession Convention
  General 1.07
  Art. 9 ....5.24

TABLE OF CASES

(Alphabetical order)

[References are to paragraph numbers]

Abidin Daver [1984] 1 All E.R. 470 (H.L.) 4.32, 5.09
Allen & Leslie (International) Ltd. v. Wagley, 1976 S.L.T. (Sh.Ct.) 12 ....10.43
Almacoa v. Ets. Moteurs Cérès, Tribunal de Grande Instance, Troyes, October 4,
1978, Digest I–27.1 – B.4, 1979 Clunet p.623, note Huet and Kovar.................8.13
Argyllshire Weavers Ltd. v. A. Macaulay (Tweeds) Ltd., 1962 S.C. 388 ....7.38 (1)
Atlantic Star [1974] A.C. 436..5.09
Att-Gen. v. Prince Augustus of Hanover [1957] A.C. 436.....................................2.23

Baccini v. Office National de l'Emploi (238/82) [1983] 3 C.M.L.R. 572......................2.06
Bavaria Fluggesellschaft and Germanair v. Eurocontrol (9 & 10/77) [1977] E.C.R.
1517; [1980] 1 C.M.L.R. 566 ....2.04, 2.10, 2.13, 2.27, 2.28, 3.07, **3.30**, 10.05
Bergman v. Grows-Farm (114/76) [1977] E.C.R. 1211...7.44
Bertrand v. Ott (150/77) [1978] E.C.R. 1431; [1978] 3 C.M.L.R. 499 ...2.23, 2.28, 2.31, 6.03,
6.27
Bier v. Mines de Potasse d'Alsace (21/76) [1976] E.C.R. 1735; [1977] 1 C.M.L.R. 284;
[1978] Q.B. 708 ....2.24, 2.28, 5.12, **5.37–5.39**, 6.08 (5), 6.12, 10.25
Black-Clawson International Ltd. v. Papierwerke Waldhof-Aschaffenburg A.G.
[1975] A.C. 591 ....3.29, 8.11, 9.34
Blanckaert & Willems v. Trost (139/80) [1981] E.C.R. 819; [1982] 2 C.M.L.R. 1 ...2.30, 5.46
Blasquez (Raymond) v. Levy and Son (1893) 1 S.L.T. 14 ....7.24
Bowman v. Wright (1877) 4 R. 322 ....10.41
Bresciani Case (87/75) [1976] E.C.R. 129 ....2.24
British South Africa Co. v. Companhia de Moçambique [1893] A.C. 602 ....11.21
Bruce v. British Motor Trading Corporation, 1924 S.C. 908 ....4.31
Buchanan (James) & Co. Ltd. v. Babco Forwarding and Shipping (UK) Ltd. [1978]
A.C. 141 ....2.12
Bulmer v. Bollinger [1974] Ch. 401 ....2.21

Caledonian Stores v. Allard Hewson, 1970 S.L.T. 195 ....10.40
Campins v. Campins, 1979 S.L.T. (Notes) 41 ....3.14
Carse v. Coppen, 1951 S.C. 233 ....4.27
C.H.W. v. G.J.H. (25/81) [1982] E.C.R. 1189; [1983] 2 C.M.L.R. 125 3.02, 3.17, **3.18**, 7.28,
7.45
C.I.L.F.I.T. v. Italian Ministry of Health (283/81) [1983] 1 C.M.L.R. 472............2.08, 2.11
Clark's Trustee, 1966 S.L.T. 249 ....5.52
Clausen-Werft KG and Clausen v. Internationale Stoombootdiensten, Vredegerecht,
Antwerp February 15, 1977, Digest I–51 – B.1 ....8.10, 8.66
Colzani v. RÜWA. *See* Estasis Salotti v. RÜWA.
Commerzbank A.G. v. Large, 1977 S.L.T. 219 ....8.68
Commissioners of Customs and Excise v. Cure and Deeley [1962] 1 Q.B. 340..............2.23
Continental Can (6/72) [1973] E.C.R. 215 ....2.26
Continental Pharma v. Labuz, Brussels Court of First Instance, February 28, 1978,
Digest I–38 – B.3 ....8.28
Cooper & Co. v. Jessop Brothers (1906) 8 F. 714..10.49
Crédit Chimique v. James Scott Engineering Group Ltd., 1979 S.C. 406, 1982 S.L.T.
131..4.32, 5.09
Cristini (32/75) [1975] E.C.R. 1085 ....2.26

Da Costa en Shaake v. Nederlandse Belastingadministrie (28–30/62) [1963] E.C.R. 31 ...2.10
De Bloos v. Bouyer (14/76) [1976] E.C.R. 1497; [1977] 1 C.M.L.R. 60........2.16, 2.18, 2.27,
2.28, **5.19**, **5.46**,
5.62
De Cavel v. De Cavel (No. 1) (143/78) [1979] E.C.R. 1055; [1979] 2 C.M.L.R. 547 .....2.29,
3.02, 3.14, **3.17**,
5.31, 7.45,
8.05(6)

Table of Cases

De Cavel v. De Cavel (No. 2) (120/79) [1980] E.C.R. 731; [1980] 3 C.M.L.R. 1...2.09, 3.03, 3.14, 5.20, **5.29–5.30**, 7.45

Denilauler v. Couchet Frères (125/79) [1980] E.C.R. 1553; [1981] 1 C.M.L.R. 62........ 1.28, 2.24, 8.03, 8.17, 7.44, **7.46**

De Wolf v. Cox (42/76) [1976] E.C.R. 1759; [1977] 2 C.M.L.R. 43..............2.16, **8.10**, 8.32

Distillers Co. (Biochemicals) Ltd. v. Thompson [1971] A.C. 458...............................5.39

Doohan v. National Coal Board, 1959 S.L.T. 308 ....8.70

Effer v. Kantner (38/81) [1982] E.C.R. 825; not yet reported in C.M.L.R. 2.27, 5.18, 7.10

Elefanten Schuh v. Jacqmain (150/80) [1981] E.C.R. 1671; [1982] 3 C.M.L.R. 1...2.15, 2.21, 2.27, **7.28**, 7.41, 9.28, 10.78

Estasis Salotti v. RÜWA (24/76) [1976] E.C.R. 1831; [1977] 1 C.M.L.R. 345   2.18, 2.28, 2.31, **7.25**, 7.26(5), 7.26(6)

Føroya Fiskasola, L/F v. Charles Mauritzen Ltd., 1977 S.L.T. (Sh.Ct.) 76 and 1978 S.L.T. (Sh.Ct.) 27.. 8.68

Garland v. British Rail Engineering [1982] 2 All E.R. 402 ....2.11

Gasque v. Inland Revenue Commissioners [1940] 2 K.B. 80....................................4.27

General Trading Corporation v. James Mills (Montrose) Ltd., 1982 S.L.T. (Sh.Ct.) 30... 8.70

Gerling v. Italian State (201/82) Judgment of July 14, 1983 (unreported)... 6.16, **7.26(5)**, 7.28

Goderbauer v. Syndic in Bankruptcy of B.V. Schroefboutenfabriek (288/82) Judgment of November 15, 1983 (unreported) **7.19**, 7.30

Gourdain v. Nadler (133/78) [1979] E.C.R. 733; [1979] 3 C.M.L.R. 180 2.28, **3.03**, 3.21, 8.05

Hallais v. Kunz, November 25, 1977, Cour d'Appel, Paris, Digest I–51 – B.2 ....8.65

Hamlyn & Co. v. Talisker Distillery (1894) 21 R. (H.L.) 21 ....10.13, 10.49

Henry v. Geoprosco International Ltd. [1976] Q.B. 726 ....11.22

Hesperides Hotels Ltd. v. Aegean Turkish Holidays Ltd. [1979] A.C. 508 ....11.21

Hollandia [1982] 3 W.L.R. 1111; [1982] 3 All E.R. 1141............................2.01, 2.12, 2.26

Humblet v. Belgian State (6/60) [1960] E.C.R. 559..2.22

Industrial Diamond Supplies v. Riva (43/77) [1977] E.C.R. 2175; [1978] 1 C.M.L.R. 349...2.18, 2.24, **8.28**

Ivenel v. Schwab (133/81) [1982] E.C.R. 1891; [1983] 1 C.M.L.R. 538 2.09, 2.18, 2.25, 5.12, **5.20**

Kirkpatrick v. Irvine (1836) 16 S. 1200...10.40

Klomps v. Michel (166/80) [1981] E.C.R. 1593; [1982] 2 C.M.L.R. 773 .... 1.28, 7.36(4), **8.17–8.18**

Las Mercedes (Owners) v. Abidin Daver (Owners) [1984] 1 All E.R. 740 ....5.09

Llewellyn v. Hebbert, 1983 S.L.T. 370 (O.H.) 10.40

LTU v. Eurocontrol (29/76) [1976] E.C.R. 1541; [1977] 1 C.M.L.R. 88 ....2.13, 2.23, 2.28, 3.02, 3.07, **3.11**, 7.44, 8.05

McArthur v. McArthur (1842) 4 D 354 ....10.40

MacShannon v. Rockware Glass Ltd. [1978] A.C. 705 ....4.32, 5.09

Manghera Case (59/75) [1976] E.C.R. 100..2.24

Mattheus v. Doego (93/78) [1978] E.C.R. 2203...2.07

Mauritzen Ltd. v. Baltic Shipping Co., 1948 S.C. 646; 1948 S.L.T. 300.....................10.13

Meeth v. Glacetal (23/78) [1978] E.C.R. 2133; [1979] 1 C.M.L.R. 520............. 2.32, 7.26(9)

Munzer Case, Cass. Civ. I, January 7, 1964; (1964) 53 *Revue Critique* 344, note Batiffol... 1.14

Netherlands State v. Rüffer (814/79) [1980] E.C.R. 3807; [1981] 3 C.M.L.R. 293 .... 2.09, 2.13, 2.28, 2.29, 3.06, **3.11**, 5.35

Onnen v. Nielen, Gerechtshof Amsterdam, February 19, 1976, Digest I–27.4 – B.1 ...... 8.21

Pendy Plastic *v.* Pluspunkt (228/81) [1982] E.C.R. 2723; [1983] 1 C.M.L.R. 665 .... 7.36, **8.17**
Perry *v.* Wright [1908] 1 K.B. 441 .... 10.04
Peters *v.* Zuid Nederlandse Annemers Vereniging (34/82) [1983] E.C.R. 987 **5.17**, 5.22, 5.35
Ponder *v.* Ponder, 1932 S.C. 233 .... 3.14
Porta-Leasing *v.* Prestige International (784/79) [1980] E.C.R. 1517; [1981] 1
     C.M.L.R. 135 .... 2.18, **7.26(13)**
Portelange *v.* Smith Corona (10/69) E.C.R. 309 .... 2.06

Radoyevitch *v.* Radoyevitch, 1930 S.C. 619 .... 3.14
Raulin *v.* Fischer [1911] 2 K.B. 93 .... 5.41
R. *v.* Bouchereau (30/77) [1977] E.C.R. 1999 .... 8.14
R. *v.* Chapell, The Times, May 26, 1984 .... 5.42
R. *v.* Henn and Darby [1981] A.C. 850 .... 2.09, 2.12
Rinkau (157/80) [1981] E.C.R. 1391; [1983] 1 C.M.L.R. 205 .... 2.18, 2.20, **8.25**
Rohr *v.* Ossberger (27/81) [1981] E.C.R. 2431; [1982] 3 C.M.L.R. 29 .... 2.15, 2.18, 2.21,
                                            2.27, **7.28**, 9.28,
                                             10.78
Russell *v.* F. W. Woolworth & Co. Ltd., 1982 S.L.T. 428 .... 10.25

S. A. Consortium General Textiles *v.* Sun and Sand Agencies [1978] Q.B. 279 .... 8.16
Sanders *v.* Van der Putte (73/77) [1977] E.C.R. 2383; [1978] 1 C.M.L.R. 331 ...... 2.18, 2.28,
                                             5.18, 7.03, 7.08,
                                             7.10
Sanderson & Son *v.* Armour & Co., 1922 S.C. (H.L.) 117 .... 10.49
Sanicentral *v.* Collin (25/79) [1979] E.C.R. 3423; [1980] 2 C.M.L.R. 164 ..... 1.18, 2.03, 3.12,
                                             3.50
Sargeant *v.* Sargeant, 1973 S.L.T. (Notes) 27 .... 3.14
Scotmotors (Plant Hire) Ltd. *v.* Dundee Petrosea Ltd., 1980 S.C. 351; 1982 S.L.T. 181 ... 7.25
Segoura *v.* Bonakdarian (25/76) [1976] E.C.R. 1851; [1977] 1 C.M.L.R. 361 2.18, 2.31, 7.25,
                                             7.26(6)
Sgarlata (40/64) [1965] E.C.R. 227 .... 2.20
Shah *v.* Barnet London B.C. [1983] A.C. 309 .... 2.26, 4.13
Smith *v.* Stewart & Co., 1960 S.C. 329 .... 4.11
Société du Gaz de Paris *v.* Armateurs Français, 1926 S.C. (H.L.) 13 .... 4.32, 5.09
Somafer *v.* Saar-Ferngas (33/78) [1978] E.C.R. 2183; [1979] 1 C.M.L.R. 490 .... 2.13, 2.28,
                                             2.30, 5.04, 5.12,
                                             5.13, 5.46–5.48,
                                             7.44
Sotgiu (152/73) [1974] E.C.R. 153 .... 2.26
Stag Line Ltd. *v.* Foscolo Mango & Co. Ltd. [1932] A.C. 328 .... 2.12
Stauder *v.* Ulm (29/69) [1969] E.C.R. 419 .... 2.15, 2.17

Tessili *v.* Dunlop (12/76) [1976] E.C.R. 1473; [1977] 1 C.M.L.R. 26 .... 2.13, 2.16, 2.21, 2.27,
                                             2.28, 5.04, **5.21**
Textielindustrie *v.* General Accident, September 13, 1977, Digest I–8 – B.1 .... 6.10
Tracomin S.A. *v.* Sudan Oil Seeds Co. Ltd. [1983] 1 W.L.R. 662; [1983] 1 Lloyd's Law
     Reports 560 and [1983] 2 Lloyd's Law Reports 384 .... 3.26, 11.08, 11.19

United Creameries Co. *v.* Boyd & Co., 1912 S.C. 617 .... 10.49

Van Duyn *v.* Home Office (41/74) [1974] E.C.R. 1337 .... 8.14
Vassen *v.* Beambtenfonds Mijnbedrijf (61/65) [1966] E.C.R. 261 .... 8.05
Vervaeke *v.* Smith [1981] 1 All E.R. 55 and [1983] A.C. 145 .... 3.29
Vidlocker *v.* McWilliam, 1964 S.L.T. (Notes) 6 .... 8.70

Wall's Trustees *v.* Drynan (1888) 15 R. 359 .... 7.30

Zelger *v.* Salinitri (56/79) [1980] E.C.R. 89; [1980] 2 C.M.L.R. 635 .... 2.30, **5.22**, 7.26(7)
Zelger *v.* Salinitri (No. 2) (129/83), Judgment of June 7, 1984 (unreported) ...... 2.28, 7.38(1)

TABLE OF CASES

(Chronological order)

24.10.1975	Landgericht Aachen, Digest I–16.1 – B.1	7.10
30.10.1975	Landgericht Trier, Digest I–17.3 – B.2	7.26(12)
16.1.1976	Landgericht Aachen, January 16, 1976, Digest I–57 – B.2	7.26(14)
9.12.1977	Oberlandesgericht Düsseldorf, Digest I–26 – B.1	8.11
2.6.1977	Oberlandesgericht Celle, Digest I–27.1 – B.1	8.03(6)
24.2.1978	Landgericht Mainz, Digest I–17.3 – B.1 and B.2	7.26(12)

REFERENCES

In the interest of uniformity this book adopts, so far as practicable, the vocabulary of the Civil Jurisdiction and Judgments Act 1982[1] and of the 1968 Convention. The following abbreviated references are commonly used:

1. "1968 Convention"
   The Convention on jurisdiction and the enforcement of judgments in civil and commercial matters signed at Brussels on 27 September 1968.[2] Unless the context otherwise requires, this expression refers to the 1968 Convention as amended by the 1978 and 1982 Accession Conventions.

2. "Annexed Protocol"
   The Protocol annexed to and signed contemporaneously with the 1968 Convention.[3]

3. "1971 Protocol"
   The Protocol on the interpretation of the 1968 Convention by the European Court signed at Luxembourg on 3 June 1971.[4]

4. "1978 Accession Convention"
   The Convention on the Accession to the 1968 Convention (with its Annexed Protocol) and the 1971 Protocol of Denmark, the Republic of Ireland and the United Kingdom, signed at Luxembourg on 9 October 1978.[5]

5. "1982 Accession Convention"
   The Convention on the accession to the 1968 Convention (with its Annexed Protocol), the 1971 Protocol and the 1978 Accession Convention of the Hellenic Republic signed on 25 October 1982.[6]

6. "Jenard Report"
   The reports by Mr. P. Jenard on the 1968 Convention and the 1971 Protocol.[7]

---

[1] C. 27.
[2] The 1968 Convention, its Annexed Protocol, and the 1971 Protocol were all amended by the Accession Conventions of 1978 and 1982. An English version of the 1968 Convention, its Annexed Protocol, and the 1971 Protocol was published in the Official Journal of the European Communities, O.J. 1978, L. 304/36. The 1968 Convention appears as Sched. 1 to the 1982 Act and the 1971 Protocol as Sched. 2. A consolidated version of the English text of the Convention, its associated Protocols and the Accession Conventions of 1978 and 1982 is to be found in O.J. 1983, C97/1.
[3] See footnote 2.
[4] See footnote 2.
[5] See footnote 2.
[6] O.J. 1982, L 388/1.
[7] Reproduced in O.J. 1979, C59/1-70 (references are to the page numbers).

7. "Schlosser Report"
   The report by Professor Peter Schlosser on the 1978 Accession Convention.[8]

8. "1982 Act"
   The Civil Jurisdiction and Judgments Act 1982.

9. "European Court"
   The Court of Justice of the European Communities.

10. "E.C.R."
    The official "Reports of Cases Before the Court of Justice of the European Communities." The references to these cases in this book include references to the names of the parties, to the serial number of the case, and to the year and page number of the European Court Reports, *e.g. Tessili* v. *Dunlop* (12/76) [1976] E.C.R. 1473.

11. "C.M.L.R."
    The *Common Market Law Reports*—an unofficial series of case reports on Community Law.

12. "O.J."
    The Official Journal of the European Communities. It will be cited as O.J. 1979, C59/1 or [1980] O.J. L266/1.

13. "Obligations Convention"
    The Convention on the law applicable to contractual obligations signed at Rome on 19 June 1980.[9]

14. "Obligations Report"
    The Report on the Obligations Convention by Professors Mario Guiliano and Paul Lagarde.[10]

15. "Maxwell Report"
    The Report of the Scottish Committee on Jurisdiction and Enforcement (Lord Maxwell, Chairman) (Edinburgh 1980).

16. "1868 Act"
    The Judgments Extension Act 1868.

---

[8] Reproduced in O.J. 1979, C59/71-151 (references are to the page numbers).
[9] O.J. 1980, L266/1.
[10] O.J. 1980, C282/1.

17. "1882 Act"
    The Inferior Courts (Judgments Extension) Act 1882.

18. "1907 Act"
    The Sheriff Courts (Scotland) Act 1907.

19. "1933 Act"
    The Foreign Judgments (Reciprocal Enforcement) Act 1933.

20. "Anton"
    A. E. Anton, *Private International Law* (Edinburgh, 1967).

21. "Dicey and Morris"
    Dicey and Morris, *The Conflict of Laws* (10th edn., London, 1980).

22. "Droz"
    The study by M. Georges A. L. Droz of the 1968 Convention entitled
    *Compétence Judiciaire et Effets des Judgments dans le Marché
    Commun* (Paris, 1972).

CHAPTER 1

INTRODUCTION

THE PURPOSES OF THE 1982 ACT

1.01 THE Civil Jurisdiction and Judgments Act 1982[1]—the 1982 Act—radically changes the law of the United Kingdom, and especially that of Scotland, in matters relating to the jurisdiction of courts and tribunals and to the recognition and enforcement of external judgments. The primary purpose of the 1982 Act[2] is to give the force of law within the United Kingdom to the Convention on jurisdiction and the enforcement of judgments in civil and commercial matters signed at Brussels on September 27, 1968[3]— the European Judgments Convention or the 1968 Convention—and to its several associated instruments.[4] In turn, the primary object of the 1968 Convention was to facilitate among the Member States of the European Communities the reciprocal recognition and enforcement of judgments. It does so by specifying what rules of jurisdiction may be applied within Contracting States in actions directed against persons domiciled in other Contracting States and by requiring each Contracting State to recognise freely judgments given in other Contracting States and to enforce them with a minimum of formality.

1.02 At the risk of considerable over-simplification,[5] it may be said that, in relation to the United Kingdom, the 1968 Convention requires its courts to entertain actions on any matter coming within the scope of the Convention directed against defenders domiciled in the United Kingdom. The Convention also entitles and requires those courts to entertain such actions when directed against defenders domiciled in another Contracting State in accordance with, and only in accordance with, a standard set of jurisdictional rules. Though in some cases these rules are based on mere procedural convenience, for the most part they take account of connections between the subject-matter of the proceedings and the United Kingdom or of connections between the parties involved in them and the United Kingdom or its legal systems. The Convention also requires the United Kingdom to recognise and enforce judgments given in the other Contracting States in terms of a relatively simple and summary scheme. In these matters the 1982 Act requires United Kingdom courts to apply any relevant principles laid down by the European Court of Justice,[6] and the Act assumes[7] that

---

[1] c. 27.

[2] The 1982 Act, however, has other important purposes, which are summarised in para. 1.03 below.

[3] An English version of the 1968 Convention (as subsequently amended) is printed as Sched. 1 to the 1982 Act. For the "authentic" English text see para. 2.15 below.

[4] These are described in para. 1.07 below.

[5] In particular, no account is taken of the rules for prorogation in Arts. 12, 15 and 17 of the Convention, of the rules creating "exclusive" jurisdictions regardless of domicile in Art. 16, nor of the provisions in Art. 57 of the Convention relating to other Conventions on particular matters.

[6] s. 3.

[7] Also in s. 3.

rulings on the interpretation of the Convention may or shall be sought by United Kingdom courts from the European Court in accordance with a Protocol on the interpretation of the 1968 Convention signed at Luxembourg on June 3, 1971—the 1971 Protocol.[8]

1.03 The 1982 Act goes further than the Convention strictly requires. It makes provision for the recognition and enforcement in one part of the United Kingdom of judgments given in another part of that country and it makes further provision for the recognition and enforcement in the United Kingdom of judgments given in countries outside the EEC. The 1982 Act accepts the broad scheme of jurisdiction set out in the 1968 Convention as the basis of a new set of rules for the allocation of jurisdiction among the courts of different parts of the United Kingdom in cases where the courts of some part of the United Kingdom are entitled to assume jurisdiction under the Convention. In relation to Scotland, moreover, the 1982 Act introduces a new set of rules of jurisdiction applicable when neither the jurisdictional rules of the 1968 Convention nor those of the scheme for allocation of jurisdiction within the United Kingdom fall to be applied. This new set of rules is largely, but not exclusively, derived from the rules of the 1968 Convention. In the application of these sets of rules the 1982 Act[9] provides that regard shall be had to any relevant principles and decisions of the European Court on the interpretation of the corresponding provisions of the 1968 Convention.

1.04 It is evident that an understanding of the nature and characteristics of the 1968 Convention and of the way in which it is interpreted by the European Court is the key to the understanding of the central features of the 1982 Act. It seems inevitable, therefore, that this introduction should attempt to describe briefly the origins of the 1968 Convention, as well as its legal background and its main features.

THE 1968 CONVENTION AND ITS ASSOCIATED INSTRUMENTS

1.05 The 1968 Convention historically derives from the inclusion in the EEC Treaty, Art. 220(4), of a requirement that Member States[10] should:

> "enter into negotiations with each other with a view to securing for the benefit of their nationals . . . the simplification of formalities governing the reciprocal recognition and enforcement of judgments of courts or tribunals and of arbitration awards."

In consequence, in a note dated October 22, 1959 the Commission of the EEC pointed to the obstacles within the original Member States to the recognition and enforcement of judgments and argued that a true internal market could not be achieved unless these obstacles were removed.[11] This

---

[8] The Protocol entered into force on September 1, 1975. An English version of the 1971 Protocol (as subsequently amended) is printed as Sched. 2 to the 1982 Act.

[9] ss. 16(3) and 20(5).

[10] At that time Belgium, the Federal Republic of Germany, France, Italy, Luxembourg and the Netherlands.

[11] An extract from the note appears in the Jenard Report, p.3.

proposition might occasion surprise, but the descriptions in the then current literature[12] of the prevailing chaos in these matters among the Member States suggest that the Commission's case was a stateable one.[13]

1.06   On February 18, 1960 the Committee of Permanent Representatives appointed a Committee of Experts who on December 11, 1964 produced a draft Convention accompanied by an Explanatory Report[14] from its Rapporteur, M. P. Jenard, an experienced international lawyer and a director in the Belgian Ministry of Foreign Affairs. Following the Extraordinary Session in April 1966 of the Hague Conference on Private International Law, the Committee of Experts met again in July of that year to take account of the reactions of other States to the draft Convention and, in particular, of their forcibly expressed comments on the fact that the Convention would give wider effect to unacceptable assumptions of jurisdiction on the part of Member States.[15] The draft was only slightly amended and was thereafter transmitted to the governments of the six Member States. It was signed by them on September 27, 1968 and became effective as between those States on February 1, 1973.

1.07   The 1968 Convention must be read along with a variety of ancillary instruments. In the first place, a Protocol—the Annexed Protocol—was issued with the Convention and is declared by Art. 65 of the Convention to form an integral part of it. This Annexed Protocol deals with a few minor matters, especially derogations from its provisions in favour of particular Member States. In the second place, following a joint Declaration relating to the conferring of an interpretative role upon the European Court, a separate Protocol on the interpretation of the 1968 Convention was prepared and, as already mentioned, signed at Luxembourg on June 3, 1971—the 1971 Protocol.[16] Its provisions are described in Chapter 2.[17] In the third place, Art. 63 of the 1968 Convention envisaged that any new Member State of the European Communities would accept that Convention as the basis for any negotiations between that State and the Contracting States necessary to ensure the implementation of Article 220(4) of the EEC Treaty. A similar provision appeared in the 1971 Protocol.[18] In the context of the entry of Denmark, Ireland and the United Kingdom into the Communities substantial adjustments were agreed and embodied in a separate Convention on the accession of these States to the 1968 Convention and to the 1971 Protocol signed at Luxembourg on October 9, 1978—the 1978 Accession Convention.[19] In 1982 an additional Accession Convention was negotiated with Greece following the entry of that country

---

[12] .The literature on this topic is immense, but reference may be made in particular to P. Bellet, (1965) 92 *Clunet* 833–870; P. Mercier, *Effets internationaux des jugements dans les Etats membres du Marché commun* (Lausanne, 1965), *passim*; M. Weser, (1959) 48 *Revue critique*, 613–659; (1960) 49 *Revue critique* 21–41, 151–172, 313–333, 533–556; and (1961) 50 *Revue critique*, 105–129.

[13] See paras. 1.09–1.15 below.

[14] O.J. 1979, C59/1–70.

[15] See K.H. Nadelmann, (1967) 67 *Col. Law Rev.* 995–1023; id. 1967–68 C.M.L.Rev. 409–420; id. (1969) 82 Harv.L.R. 1282–1292. For other views, see Mercier, 1967 *Cahiers de droit européen* 367–387 and 513–531 and de Winter, (1968) 17 I.C.L.Q. 706–719.

[16] See 1982 Act, Sched. 2.

[17] paras. 2.04–2.08

[18] Art. 9.

[19] An English version was published in the United Kingdom in Cmnd. 7395 (1978): European Communities No. 46 (1978).

into the European Communities and signed on October 25, 1982—the 1982 Accession Convention.[20]

1.08   The 1968 Convention (with its Annexed Protocol), the 1971 Protocol, and the two Accession Conventions introduce in matters within their scope a novel scheme of jurisdictional rules and a multilateral system for the recognition and enforcement of judgments. To appreciate the originality and importance of this scheme and, indeed, to understand many of its individual provisions, it is necessary to place the 1968 Convention into the legal context against which it was elaborated.

BACKGROUND TO THE 1968 CONVENTION

1.09   At the time when the 1968 Convention was drafted there were two principal obstacles to the creation of a liberal system for the recognition and enforcement of judgments within the six EEC Member States. The first was that màny of them adopted internationally unacceptable grounds of jurisdiction and the second, which arose partly as a reaction to the first, was that most of these States refused to recognise and enforce foreign judgments unless they were subjected to rigorous "controls," which included the examination of the basis of jurisdiction of the court which had given the judgment—the court of origin—but which might go far beyond such examination.

1.10   Many legal systems adopt internationally unacceptable—or exorbitant—grounds of jurisdiction. Several of those identified as unacceptable by the Supplementary Protocol of February 1, 1971 to the Hague Convention on the recognition and enforcement of foreign judgments in civil and commercial matters were in common use among Member States.[21] In the Federal Republic of Germany, for example, the presence of property or of the subject-matter of the dispute within the territory of a court clothes that court with jurisdiction in actions of a patrimonial nature where no other German court has jurisdiction over the defender. Like the Scottish jurisdiction based on arrestment, there need be no connection between the subject-matter of the action and the asset founding jurisdiction, and the value of the asset has no bearing on the matter.[22] In France and Luxembourg the nationality of the pursuer is a ground of jurisdiction, and this ground is available to nationals who are not resident in those countries and where the dispute has no connection with those countries.[23] The nationals of those countries, conversely, might be sued in their courts even in respect of obligations contracted abroad and with foreigners.[24] In Belgium and Holland the exercise of jurisdiction on the basis of the pursuer's nationality had been dropped in favour of a jurisdiction based on the pursuer's

---

[20] O.J. 1982, L.388/1. A consolidated and updated version of all these instruments is published in O.J. 1983, C97/1.

[21] The writer has relied heavily on the writings of Bellet and Weser cited in n. 12 above for the details of these jurisdictions.

[22] Code of Civil Procedure, Art. 23; K.H. Nadelmann in *XXth Century Comparative and Conflicts Law* (Leiden, 1961), pp. 328–330.

[23] French Civil Code, Art. 14; Luxembourg Civil Code, Art. 14. This jurisdiction, however, is inapplicable to real rights in immoveables abroad or in relation to the enforcement of decrees abroad.

[24] French Civil Code, Art. 15; Luxembourg Civil Code, Art. 15.

domicile or residence in those countries.[25] The Belgian courts also exercised jurisdiction in any proceedings against their nationals.[26] In the Netherlands, moreover, a non-resident defender may be sued in the Netherlands courts in respect of obligations which he has contracted towards a Netherlands national, whether in the Netherlands or in another country.[27] In Italy, jurisdiction on the basis of the pursuer's nationality had been dropped but, essentially as a riposte to the exercise of unacceptable jurisdictions elsewhere, it was possible to sue a foreigner in Italy on any basis which would have been available to that foreigner under his national law.[28] Italy, it may be added, has provisions permitting of the exercise of jurisdiction notwithstanding the existence of prorogation or arbitration agreements.[29]

1.11   The other, and related, feature of the legal scene in the original EEC countries was the existence of serious practical obstacles to the enforcement of foreign judgments.[30] Though probative force might be given to foreign judgments in legal proceedings in the Netherlands, in the absence of treaty provisions a foreign judgment as such was not enforced.[31] In the Federal Republic, unless in terms of a treaty, foreign judgments were enforced only on the basis of reciprocity.[32] In the Member States, moreover, other than the Netherlands—where the question did not arise in the same form—judgments were not always recognised and were never enforced unless, following an appropriate procedure, a judicial authority had authorised this by what was called an *exequatur*.

1.12   The conditions for the grant of *exequatur* varied in their rigour from State to State. In some, these conditions were specifically provided for by legislation.[33] In others, they were essentially aspects of *ordre public*—or public policy in a broad sense—the contravention of which was invariably a ground of refusal. Though the courts of some countries, particularly of France, tended to narrow the scope of this ground of refusal by distinguishing between *ordre public interne* and *ordre public international*, it was often wide enough to cover procedural defects, including fraud, going to the assumption of jurisdiction, and certain matters of substance. This may help to explain why Art. 27 of the 1968 Convention, while admitting public policy as a ground of refusal of recognition, makes no express reference to fraud and why it is provided in Art. 28(3), not only that the jurisdiction of the court of origin may not be reviewed, but that the test of public policy may not be applied to the rules relating to jurisdiction. Whether or not as an aspect of public policy, the original Member States were accustomed to

---

[25] For Belgium, see Law of March 25, 1876, Arts. 53 and 54. A foreigner, however, is not subject to this jurisdiction if he can show that in his own country a similar rule is not applied to Belgians. See Weser, (1959) 48 *Revue Critique* 615 at p. 626. For Holland, see Code of Civil Procedure, Art. 126(3) and de Winter, (1968) 17 I.C.L.Q. 706 at p.707.

[26] Civil Code, Art. 15.

[27] Code of Civil Procedure, Art. 127.

[28] Code of Civil Procedure, Art. 4(4); M. Cappelletti and J.M. Perillo, *Civil Procedure in Italy* (The Hague, 1965), pp. 367–394; L. Marmo, in *De Conflictu Legum*, (Leiden, 1962), pp. 324–330.

[29] Code of Civil Procedure, Art. 2; Cappelletti and Perillo, above, p. 374.

[30] The present description is based preponderantly on Mercier's essay, cited in n. 12 above.

[31] Jenard Report, p. 6.

[32] Code of Civil Procedure, Art. 328.

[33] For Belgium, see the Judicial Code contained in the Law of October 10, 1967, cited in the Jenard Report, p. 4. For Germany, see Code of Civil Procedure, Art. 328, cited in the Jenard Report, p. 4. For Italy, see Code of Civil Procedure, Art. 797 and Cappelletti and Perillo, above, pp. 370–384.

review the "international competence" of the court of origin and they all verified whether the court of origin had respected the rights of the defence. Some checked also the "internal" jurisdictional competence of the court of origin and the observance by it of its own procedural requirements, including rules relating to service and notice.

1.13   Two conditions for *exequatur*, however, may be referred to less summarily since they are the object of specific prohibitions in the 1968 Convention. In some systems the court of *exequatur* virtually transformed itself into a court of appeal and examined the acceptability of the foreign judgment on the merits. This form of review—called *révision au fond*—was abandoned in France in 1964 in the celebrated *Munzer* case[34] on the ground that it seemed to question the authority and competence of the foreign court. *Révision au fond*, however, remained applicable in Belgium[35] and Luxembourg. This helps to explain why Art. 29 of the Convention expressly provides that under no circumstances may the substance of a foreign judgment be reviewed.

1.14   In France, moreover, despite the decision in the *Munzer* case, the courts continued to decline to enforce a foreign judgment when the court of origin had applied a law other than that applicable under the French choice of law rules unless the same result would have been reached by the application of the latter.[36] This rule was not applied in terms in Belgium or Germany, but in those countries the court of *exequatur* would verify whether the court of origin, in dealing with preliminary questions affecting status, had applied rules consistent with their own choice of law rules. These rules may help to explain the existence and terms of Art. 27(4) of the Convention.[37] In Germany, too, the court of *exequatur* verified whether the foreign decision was consistent with German rules conceding exclusive jurisdiction to particular courts, for example, in relation to immoveable property. This rule throws some light on the "exclusive jurisdiction" in Art. 16(1).

1.15   The existence of these practical obstacles to the reciprocal enforcement of judgments within the Member States of the European Communities when coupled with the continued exercise within these States of exorbitant rules of jurisdiction may help to put into perspective the views expressed by the Commission in its note of October 22, 1959 that, in what was designed to become a common market, efficacious solutions to the problem of the reciprocal enforcement of judgments were required. These obstacles to enforcement had already induced the Member States to enter into a network of bilateral conventions on the reciprocal recognition and enforcement of judgments listed in Art. 55 of the 1968 Convention. But this network was not complete and, since the Conventions differed widely in their general approach and in detail, in the view of one particularly well-qualified observer[38] they tended to complicate rather than to facilitate the task of practitioners and the courts.

---

[34] Cass. Civ. I, January 7, 1964, (1964) 53 *Revue Critique* 344, note Batiffol.

[35] Though it has been described as largely theoretical there. See Bellet, n. 12 above, p.834.

[36] Bellet, n. 12 above, p. 838 suggests, however, that the principle is in practice applied only in matters of status.

[37] See para. 8.21 below.

[38] Bellet, n. 12 above, p. 835.

SALIENT FEATURES OF THE CONVENTION

A. Concern with International Legal Relationships of a Community Character

1.16   It is a feature of the 1968 Convention that it is designed, as its preamble states, to affect legal relationships within the Contracting States only where an international element is involved. This concept[39] is not defined, since the international element in a legal relationship will depend upon the facts of the case. The element appears clearly enough in the Convention at the stage of recognition and enforcement, since the scheme relates only to the recognition and enforcement in one Contracting State of judgments[40] given in another Contracting State. It appears less clearly in relation to jurisdiction. Here, however, the draftsmen of the Convention appear to have made an effort not to intervene in matters within the sphere of the domestic jurisdiction of a Contracting State.

1.17   The Jenard Report[41] states that:

> "Proceedings instituted in the courts of a Contracting State which involve only persons domiciled in that State will not normally be affected by the Convention; Article 2 simply refers matters back to the rules of jurisdiction in force in that State."

The same approach is adopted in other articles which employ domicile as a ground of jurisdiction.[42] It is left to the law of the State of the domicile to·specify the particular court in which the domiciliary may be sued. In terms of the Convention alone, indeed, persons domiciled in a Contracting State are not liable to be sued in that State by virtue, for example, of the special jurisdictions in Art. 5. These jurisdictions, as the wording of that provision makes clear, may be invoked against a domiciliary of one Contracting State only *in another Contracting State*. In Art. 16, again, jurisdiction is conceded to the courts of a specified Contracting State rather than to the court of the place within that State where the immoveable property is situated, the company has its seat, or the registers are kept. It is left to the law of that State to specify what particular court within it should exercise jurisdiction.

1.18   It is thought, moreover, that the scheme of the Convention may be better understood if it is kept in mind that, as a rule, the Convention is concerned only with international legal relationships of a Community character. The reasons, for example, which justify the exclusive jurisdictions in Art. 16 would seem to apply wherever in the world the property is situated, the company register is kept, and so on. This is recognised in the relevant Scottish rules in the 1982 Act.[43] Art. 16 of the Convention, however, is limited in its operation to the courts of *the Contracting State* where the property is situated, the register is kept, and so on. The desire of the draftsmen of the Convention to confine themselves to legal relation-

---

[39] As the Jenard Report explains, at p. 8. See also the Schlosser Report, at p. 81.
[40] And of "authentic instruments" and court settlements: Arts. 50 and 51.
[41] p. 8.
[42] *Cf.* Arts. 8(1)(1)–(3) and 14.
[43] Sched. 8, r. 4.

ships of a Community character[44] may also help to explain other aspects of the Convention, for example, their failure in Art. 17—before its amendment by the 1978 Accession Convention[45]—to deal with the effects or prorogation agreements between parties, none of whom is domiciled in a Contracting State. Their concern to confine the Convention to legal relationships of a Community character may also help to explain the existence of the crucial Art. 4 of the Convention, which leaves it to each Contracting State to apply its own rules of jurisdiction in cases where the defender is domiciled in none of the Contracting States.

B. A "DOUBLE" CONVENTION

1.19   For a United Kingdom lawyer perhaps the most unusual feature of the 1968 Convention is that, as well as providing a scheme for the recognition and enforcement of judgments given in a Contracting State, it prescribes directly when the courts, and often a court, of a Contracting State may assume jurisdiction in proceedings involving persons domiciled in another Contracting State or, in a few cases,[46] in proceedings intimately linked by their nature with a particular Contracting State. Since the Convention regulates both jurisdiction and enforcement, it is often referred to as a "double" convention.

1.20   The approach of the 1968 Convention contrasts with that adopted in the bilateral conventions on recognition and enforcement of judgments linking the United Kingdom with other States, including the six original Member States of the European Communities other than Luxembourg.[47] These conventions contain no rules regulating directly the assumption of jurisdiction by the courts of the Contracting States, but permit a court in which the recognition of a foreign judgment is sought to refuse to recognise that judgment if the court of origin assumed jurisdiction on grounds other than certain specified grounds. Such conventions, regulating recognition and enforcement only, could usefully be described as "single" conventions.

1.21   The Committee of Experts apparently devoted much time to considering which of these types of convention was to be preferred.[48] Their Report, however, justifies the adoption of a double convention in a relatively summary way. It states that:

> "the adoption of common rules of jurisdiction would allow increased harmonization of laws, provide greater legal certainty, avoid discrimination and facilitate the 'free movement' of judgments, which is after all the ultimate objective."

It is evident, as the Report infers, that only a double convention could strike directly and effectively at rules of jurisdiction which, being discriminatory, run counter to basic policies of the EEC Treaty.[49] A convention

---

[44] The European Court in *Sanicentral* v. *Collin* (25/79) [1979] E.C.R. 3423[5] spoke of the Convention seeking "to determine the jurisdiction of the courts of the Contracting States in the intra-Community legal order in regard to matters of civil jurisdiction."

[45] Art. 11.

[46] *Cf*. Arts. 5(6), 6A and 16.

[47] These conventions are specified in Art. 55 of the 1968 Convention and will be superseded by it. Under Art. 56, however, they continue to have effect in relation to matters to which the 1968 Convention does not apply. See paras. 3.29 and 3.30 below.

[48] Jenard Report. p. 7.

[49] *Cf*. EEC Arts. 7 and 220(1).

striking at discriminatory or exorbitant rules only at the stage of recognition would have afforded insufficient protection to persons who had assets within the State assuming jurisdiction or who might wish to conduct business there. More especially, however, only a "double" convention containing direct rules of jurisdiction and placing confidence in their application by the courts of each Contracting State would permit of the elimination or at least the drastic reduction of the controls customarily imposed at the phase of recognition and enforcement.[50]

C. TREATMENT OF EXORBITANT JURISDICTIONS

1.22 In relation to exorbitant jurisdictions, it may be noticed first that, although Art. 220(4) of the EEC Treaty refers to securing the benefits of the reciprocal enforcement of judgments for the nationals of Member States, the 1968 Convention abandons nationality as a test of international jurisdictional competence in favour of "domicile."[51] This choice is lucidly explained in the Jenard Report.[52] One important consideration, however, was the fact that the use of nationality as the criterion would have tended to extend within the Common Market the operation of exorbitant rules of jurisdiction. A judgment, for example, given in France on the basis of the French nationality of the defender[53] would have had to be recognised throughout the Community and even in the German courts of his domicile or habitual residence. Speaking more generally, the choice of nationality would have applied the jurisdictional scheme of the Convention to persons who had lost their social connections with the State of the forum and disapplied it to persons who, though possessing strong social connections with that State, were not among its nationals.

1.23 The choice by the Committee of Experts of "domicile" as an alternative to nationality might surprise an United Kingdom lawyer, but "domicile" was a common criterion of jurisdiction among Member States[54] and in their legal systems the concept bears little resemblance to the traditional concept of "domicile" in United Kingdom law.[55] It has closer affinities with the concepts of ordinary residence or of habitual residence, though in truth its meaning differs from legal system to legal system. For this reason, it is not defined in the Convention. Arts. 52 and 53 confine themselves to indicating to which legal system reference must be made for the ascertainment of a person's domicile.

1.24 The Convention strikes at the use by Contracting States of exorbitant jurisdictions both directly and indirectly. It does so directly by declaring in Art. 3 that certain specified rules of law in use in Member States may not be applied to found jurisdiction against a person domiciled in any Contracting State. Many of the specified rules have been referred to above.[56] The 1978 Accession Convention added to them a provision of Danish

---

[50] See paras. 1.27 to 1.30 below.
[51] The term is not to be understood in the sense traditional in the United Kingdom. Its meaning is summarily explained in the following paragraph and more fully in Chap. 4.
[52] p. 14.
[53] French Civil Code, Art. 15.
[54] See Jenard Report, p. 15. *Cf.* Art. 7 of the EEC Treaty, which states that: "Within the scope of application of this Treaty, and without prejudice to any special provisions contained therein, any discrimination on grounds of nationality shall be prohibited."
[55] See Chap. 4.
[56] para. 1.10.

law permitting a foreigner to be sued in the Danish court of a district in which he is resident at the time of the proceedings or possesses property, as well as certain provisions of the laws of Ireland and of the United Kingdom.[57]

1.25   The Convention also attacks indirectly the use of exorbitant jurisdictions by providing in Art. 3(1) that the rules of jurisdiction in the Convention and no other rules are to be applied in proceedings against persons domiciled in a Contracting State. Among these rules pride of place must be given to Art. 2 which states that, unless the rules of the Convention otherwise provide, persons domiciled in a Contracting State, whatever their nationality, are to be sued in the courts of that State. As explained above,[58] the choice of domicile rather than of nationality as the primary basis of international competence in the Convention should itself tend to reduce recourse to exorbitant jurisdictions. But the main barrier to their use is to be found in the principle that a person domiciled in any Contracting State may be sued in another Contracting State only by virtue of the special rules of jurisdiction contained in Sections 2 to 9 inclusive of Title II of the Convention. These were intended to be, and to a large extent are, acceptable bases of jurisdiction.

1.26   But the protection Art. 3(1) provides is not extended, as Art. 4 makes quite explicit, to persons who are not domiciled in one of the Contracting States. Except in a few specified cases,[59] Contracting States retain the right to apply to such persons any grounds of jurisdiction whatever, including the jurisdictions otherwise inapplicable in terms of Art. 3. The provisions in the Convention, moreover, for the recognition and enforcement of judgments envisage that judgments given in one Contracting State should normally[60] be recognised and enforced in the other Contracting States irrespective of their jurisdictional basis. Judgments, therefore, against persons who are not domiciled in a Contracting State may be enforced throughout the territories of the Contracting States even when based upon a discriminatory or exorbitant ground of jurisdiction. The combined effect, therefore, of these provisions is to widen considerably the area of effectiveness of the exorbitant jurisdictions of Member States in relation to non-EEC domiciliaries. While these provisions were still in draft, they became known to government officials and lawyers within the United Kingdom, and their concerns were articulated forcibly by United Kingdom representatives to the Extraordinary Session of the Hague Conference on Private International Law in April 1966.[61] The provisions were the object of vigorous criticism in the United States.[62] Although persons domiciled in

---

[57] See 1968 Convention, Art. 3. In relation to Ireland the rules specified are those which enable jurisdiction to be founded on the document instituting the proceedings having been served on the defender during his temporary presence in Ireland. The same rules are specified for the United Kingdom, though no such rules are applied in Scotland. The other rules specified for the United Kingdom are those which enable jurisdiction to be founded upon the presence within the United Kingdom of property belonging to the defender or upon the seizure by the pursuer of property situated in the United Kingdom. These last rules, of course, are familiar ones in Scots law.

[58] para. 1.22.

[59] See Arts. 8(2), 13(2), 16 and 17.

[60] Subject, that is, to the limited exception specified in Art. 28(1).

[61] L.I. de Winter, "Excessive Jurisdiction in Private International Law," (1968) 17 I.C.L.Q. 706 at p. 711.

[62] K.H. Nadelmann, (1967) 67 *Col. Law Rev.* 995–1023; *id.*1967–68 C.M.L.Rev. 409–420; *id.* (1969) 82 Harv. L.R. 1282–1292. For a reply, see P. Mercier, 1967 *Cahiers de droit européen*, 367–387 and 513–531.

non-Contracting States may secure protection in terms of conventions entered into with a view to taking advantage of Art. 59 of the Convention, none have been concluded to date.

D. JURISDICTIONAL CONTROL BY THE COURT OF ORIGIN

1.27 It is an important and novel feature of the Convention that it is generally left to the court of origin alone, on the basis of mutual trust between the courts of the Contracting States, to secure compliance with the jurisdictional rules of the Convention. Submission is a ground of jurisdiction under the Convention except where another court has exclusive jurisdiction under Art. 16.[63] Where, therefore, the defender has entered appearance it is left to him to challenge the jurisdiction of the court of origin in that court. Where the defender has not appeared, or in cases within the scope of Art. 16, the court of origin is required of its own motion to consider its own jurisdictional competence and to dismiss or to sist the action if it lacks it.[64] In either case the court of origin's decision on the matter must be accepted in courts where recognition or enforcement is sought, though exceptions are admitted in specified cases.[65] Despite these exceptions, it may be said that the examination of its own jurisdictional competence by the court of origin plays an important part in a scheme which is designed to reduce to a minimum the controls applied to external judgments at the stage of recognition and enforcement.

E. A SUMMARY SCHEME OF RECOGNITION AND ENFORCEMENT

1.28 The main object of the 1968 Convention was to facilitate the reciprocal recognition and enforcement of judgments in terms of Art. 220(4) of the EEC Treaty. Having struck directly at the operation of exorbitant jurisdictions in relation to persons domiciled in other Contracting States, having unified in relation to such persons the applicable grounds of jurisdiction, and having required the courts of the Contracting States to monitor their own jurisdictional competence, it was possible to adopt a liberal and simple system for the recognition and enforcement of judgments emanating from the Contracting States.[66] This system applies to all judgments in matters within the scope of the Convention and is not limited to judgments against a person domiciled in a Contracting State.[67] It applies to every species of judgment,[68] and is not limited to money judgments or to judgments which are final.

1.29 Judgments within the scope of the Convention emanating from a court or tribunal in a Contracting State are to be recognised in the other Contracting States "without any special procedure being required."[69] Procedural steps need be taken only when "any interested party . . . raises the

---

[63] Art. 18.
[64] Arts. 19, 20(1), 21 and 22.
[65] See Art. 28(1) and the discussion at para. 8.22 below.
[66] *Cf.* the remarks of the European Court in *Denilauler* v. *Couchet Frères* (125/79) [1980] E.C.R. 1553 [13] and *Klomps* v. *Michel* (166/80) [1981] E.C.R. 1593 [7].
[67] The implications of this are briefly discussed in para. 1.26 above.
[68] Art. 25.
[69] Art. 26(1).

recognition of a judgment as the principal issue in a dispute,''[70] usually, it may be presumed, when the right to found on the judgment is challenged. Recognition is the rule, and may be withheld only in the cases specified in Arts. 27 and 28. The merits of the judgment are never to be reviewed and *révision au fond* becomes incompetent.[71] Control by reference to the choice of law rules of the State in which recognition is sought is competent only in cases where the court of origin has decided certain preliminary questions relating to status, matrimonial property, or succession in a manner which conflicts with a rule of private international law of the State in which recognition is sought, and then only if the same result would not have been reached by applying that rule.[72] Control of the jurisdictional competence of the court of origin is in principle excluded, and is allowed only, apart from the cases provided for in Art. 59, in relation to the exclusive jurisdictions in Art. 16 and jurisdiction in matters relating to insurance and consumer contracts.[73] Even in those cases the other court is bound by the findings of fact of the court of origin. The test, moreover, of public policy may never be used as a means of controlling the jurisdictional competence of the court of origin.[74] The Convention, however, retains in Art. 27 such traditional grounds for refusing recognition as the defender's lack of opportunity to arrange for his defence (at least in judgments given in default of appearance), the existence of an incompatible judgment in a dispute between the same parties, and the fact that the recognition of the judgment would be contrary to public policy in the State where recognition is sought.

1.30   Where enforcement is sought a procedure is required, but it is designed to be of a summary nature. It involves an application by an interested party to a specified court in the Contracting State where enforcement is sought.[75] The court is required to give its decision without delay without the party against whom enforcement is sought being entitled to make any submissions on the application.[76] The court is apparently entitled to refuse the application on any of the grounds applicable to a refusal of recognition,[77] but it is difficult to see how at this stage of the procedure the court can often be in possession of the relevant facts. The decision is intimated to the applicant who, under the scheme in the Convention, serves it upon the party against whom enforcement is sought.[78] The latter may ask the court to set aside the judgment[79] and, until the period allowed for this has elapsed, only protective measures may be taken by the person seeking to enforce the judgment.[80] Rights of appeal are envisaged,[81] but the emphasis is upon a simple and expeditious procedure.

---

[70] Art. 26(2).
[71] Art. 29. *Cf.* Art. 34(3) and para. 1.13 above.
[72] Art. 27(4), and see para. 1.14 above.
[73] Art. 28(1).
[74] Art. 28(3).
[75] Arts. 31 and 32.
[76] Art. 34(1).
[77] Art. 34(2).
[78] Arts. 35 and 36(2).
[79] Arts. 36 and 37.
[80] Art. 39.
[81] Arts. 40 and 41.

SCHEME OF THE 1982 ACT

A. THE 1968 CONVENTION TO HAVE FORCE OF LAW

1.31   The 1982 Act gives effect to the 1968 Convention and its associated instruments by providing in sections 2 and 3 that they shall have the force of law in the United Kingdom, that judicial notice shall be taken of them, and that they are to be interpreted in accordance with the principles laid down by the European Court of Justice. The "associated instruments" include the 1971 Protocol on interpretation of the Convention by the European Court under which a Scottish court may, or may be bound to, seek an interpretative ruling from the European Court. The Convention is directly applicable in the Scottish courts and supersedes any rules of jurisdiction and any rules for the recognition and enforcement of foreign judgments, including common law rules, which might otherwise be applicable in matters within the scope of the Convention. It does not, however, override any Conventions which, on particular matters, contain provisions on jurisdiction or the recognition and enforcement of judgments; nor does it override statutory or other rules of law which implement those provisions.[82]

B. THE INTER-UNITED KINGDOM SCHEME FOR THE ALLOCATION OF JURISDICTION AND THE ENFORCEMENT OF JUDGMENTS

.32   In relation to defenders domiciled in the United Kingdom and in relation to cases in which the connecting factors in Art. 16 of the Convention point to the United Kingdom, the 1982 Act treats each part of the United Kingdom for jurisdictional purposes in much the same way as if it were a separate Contracting State under the 1968 Convention. Rules similar to those in the Convention are applied by Part II of, and Schedule 4 to, the Act to determine whether the courts of law of any part of the United Kingdom, or any particular court within that part have or has jurisdiction in proceedings whose subject-matter is within the scope of the 1968 Convention and is not specially excluded.[83] There are certain omissions— notably of the special rules of jurisdiction in relation to insurance in Section 3 of Title II of the Convention—and other modifications, but, by and large, the same rules of jurisdiction are applicable. Moreover, in determining any question as to the meaning and effect of these rules, the court is required to 'have regard to' any relevant decisions of the European Court.[84] The jurisdictional framework of the Convention was introduced to regulate the allocation of jurisdiction between the courts of the United Kingdom not by reason of any obligations arising from the Convention, but rather for reasons of convenience.[85] Moreover, the application of the jurisdictional rules of the Convention would serve to exclude the application by the courts of one part of the United Kingdom of exorbitant rules of

---

[82] 1968 Convention, Art. 57 and 1982 Act, s. 9(1).
[83] See s. 17 and Sched. 5.
[84] See 1982 Act, s. 16(3).
[85] The justification for this approach is given in para s. 9.02–9.05 below.

jurisdiction in relation to the domiciliaries of other parts of the United Kingdom. In consequence, a relatively automatic system for the reciprocal enforcement of United Kingdom judgments could be introduced. The 1982 Act assumes without specific prescription[86] that the judgments of the courts of one part of the United Kingdom will be recognised in the other parts. In relation to their enforcement, the Act provides a simple system of enforcement following registration applicable to a range of subject-matters rather wider than those covered by the 1968 Convention.[87]

C. THE SCOTTISH RULES OF JURISDICTION IN PATRIMONIAL MATTERS

1.33   In cases where neither the Convention nor the scheme for the allocation of jurisdiction within the United Kingdom applies, Part III of, and Schedule 8 to, the 1982 Act provide a set of rules of jurisdiction for the Scottish courts of general application in patrimonial matters—the Scottish rules of jurisdiction. Certain subject-matters are specifically excluded by section 21(1) and Sched. 9, notably proceedings relating to the status and capacity of natural persons, proceedings for regulating the custody of children, proceedings relating to the management of the affairs of incapable persons, and proceedings relating to bankruptcy and the liquidation of companies. The stress, however, is upon the generality of the application of the rules specified in Schedule 8, subject only to the qualification that they are not to affect "the operation of any enactment which confers jurisdiction on a Scottish court in respect of a specific subject-matter on specific grounds."[88]

1.34   The core of these rules of jurisdiction is once more derived from the rules contained in Title II of the 1968 Convention. The special rules of jurisdiction in relation to insurance in Section 3 of that Title are again omitted, and there are other modifications to those "derived rules." In relation to these "derived rules" the court is once again required to 'have regard to' any relevant decisions of the European Court. In contrast, however, with its provisions for the inter-United Kingdom allocation of jurisdiction, the 1982 Act supplements the rules of jurisdiction in Title II of the Convention with other rules which do not appear there and whose exercise in relation to domiciliaries of Contracting States may even be excluded by the 1968 Convention. In particular, the Scottish common law rules permitting jurisdiction to be founded upon the arrestment of moveables within Scotland or upon the ownership of heritage are preserved in rule 2(8) of Schedule 8. Though rule 2(8) is couched in terms which appear at first sight to exclude its application to United Kingdom domiciliaries only, the general primacy of the rules in the Convention means that these Scottish rules cannot be applied in relation to the domiciliaries of other Contracting States. In relation to persons domiciled in a Contracting State, Art. 3 of the Convention specifically and expressly prevents the assumption of jurisdiction upon the two common law grounds referred to above. Art. 3, however, also provides that:

---

[86] See s. 19.

[87] See 1982 Act, ss. 16–18 and Scheds. 5–7.

[88] s. 21(1)(*a*). This provision would seem to be designed mainly to preserve the operation of provisions implementing conventions which, in particular matters, contain provisions governing jurisdiction. See 1968 Convention, Art. 57 and 1982 Act, s. 9.

"Persons domiciled in a Contracting State may be sued in the courts of another Contracting State only by virtue of the rules set out in Sections 2 to 6 of this Title."

Art. 3 in principle excludes as against persons domiciled in another Contracting State recourse to the application of *any* Scottish rules of jurisdiction. In practice, however, a Scottish court when applying the rules of the Convention will often be applying rules identical in content with those of Schedule 8 to the 1982 Act. By virtue of section 20(1) of the 1982 Act a similar situation obtains in relation to persons domiciled in another part of the United Kingdom.

D. JUSTIFICATION FOR THE SCHEME OF JURISDICTION APPLICABLE IN SCOTLAND UNDER THE 1982 ACT

1.35 At first sight the scheme of jurisdiction applicable in Scotland by virtue of the 1982 Act may seem to be unnecessarily complex. It would have been open to the United Kingdom to retain the existing Scottish rules of jurisdiction save where this was impermissible under the Convention. This was the course adopted by the Act for England and Wales and for Northern Ireland except in relation to the scheme for the inter-United Kingdom allocation of jurisdiction. The Maxwell Committee, however, advised against this course in relation to Scotland, and recommended instead that the jurisdictional rules in the 1968 Convention should be taken as the norm both where the defender is domiciled in another part of the United Kingdom and where he is domiciled in Scotland or in a non-Contracting State. Their reasons for doing so are set out in full in their Report[89] but may be restated as follows:

(1) The rules of jurisdiction in the Convention were similar in character and in some respects in detail to those of Scots law. It would have been confusing for practitioners if, in relation to a subject-matter within the scope of the Convention, they had to apply separate and only slightly different rules of jurisdiction in cases where proceedings were directed respectively against persons domiciled in another part of the United Kingdom, against persons domiciled in another Contracting State, and against persons not domiciled in any Contracting State. It would have been still more confusing if they had to apply (possibly in relation to the same action) one set of rules of jurisdiction to matters within the scope of the Convention and another set of rules to matters outside its scope.

(2) It might not always be easy, moreover, to determine whether a defender was domiciled in another Contracting State or in another part of the United Kingdom nor to determine whether the subject-matter of the proceedings fell within the scope of the Convention or (it might be) within the scope of any scheme on similar lines for the inter-United Kingdom allocation of jurisdiction. Under the Convention the domicile of an individual may involve questions of foreign law.[90] The domicile of an individual in another Contracting State is a matter for the law of that State, and the national law of an individual is applied to determine a domicile of dependence. The provisions, moreover, relating to the scope of the Convention

---

[89] Report of the Scottish Committee on Jurisdiction and Enforcement (Chairman: The Hon. Lord Maxwell) (Edinburgh, 1980), pp. 16–19.
[90] Art. 52.

give rise to several difficulties. While the European Court has determined that a Community interpretation must be given to those provisions, its guidelines on the matter are not as yet fully developed.[91]

(3) The Maxwell Committee, therefore, thought it better if a set of rules were adopted which, to a greater rather than a lesser extent, would apply in all civil actions of a patrimonial nature, whatever the personal connections of the parties and whatever the subject-matter of the action. It seemed desirable, that is, to render otiose as far as practicable questions relating to the potential applicability either of the scheme of jurisdiction in the Convention or of that for the inter-United Kingdom allocation of jurisdiction. This might be of assistance to the court, as well as to pursuers, in so far as the court may have a duty in certain cases under Arts. 19 and 20(1) of the Convention to declare of its own motion that it has no jurisdiction. The committee recognised that, where the Convention did not apply, it might be desirable to discard some of the rules which it prescribed, notably those concerned with insurance contracts, and that it might be desirable, in relation to defenders not domiciled in any other Contracting State, to preserve in Scotland the operation of certain rules of jurisdiction which find no place in the Convention. The committee considered, however, that by and large the scheme for jurisdiction in the Convention could form the basis of the law of Scotland.

(4) Though the Maxwell Committee recognised that some of the jurisdictional rules in the Convention might not be ideal, others were preferable to the existing rules of Scots law. They were not unacceptable as a whole. Their adoption would permit not only the discarding of the unsatisfactory jurisdictional rules in the Sheriff Courts (Scotland) Act 1907, but the adoption of a single, coherent scheme which would serve at one and the same time to delimit the international jurisdiction of the Scottish courts and, as the committee proposed at the same time, both the allocation of jurisdiction among the courts of the United Kingdom and the internal allocation of jurisdiction among the Scottish courts.

1.36   The Maxwell Committee's views were accepted, it would appear, by the Government of the day and form the rational basis of the rules of jurisdiction in the 1982 Act relating to the inter-United Kingdom scheme of allocation of jurisdiction and to the Scottish rules of jurisdiction.

ARRANGEMENT OF THIS BOOK

1.37   The 1982 Act gives formal and practical primacy as a source of law to the provisions of the 1968 and 1978 Conventions and to the Protocols associated with the former by declaring in Part I of the Act that the Conventions should have the force of law in the United Kingdom,[92] by subordinating the effect of Part II (Jurisdiction, and Recognition and Enforcement of Judgments, within the United Kingdom) to the Provisions of the 1968 Convention, and by subordinating the effect of Part III of the Act (Jurisdiction in Scotland) to the provisions of both Parts I and II of the Act. It seems inevitable, therefore, that any discussion of the 1982 Act should

---

[91] See for example, paras. 3.08–3.12, 3.15–3.18 and 3.23–3.26 below.
[92] s. 2.

commence with the provisions of the Conventions and proceed with the scheme in Part II of the Act for the inter-United Kingdom allocation of jurisdiction and recognition of judgments before examining Part III of the Act relating to the jurisdiction of the Scottish courts. It is appreciated that the Scottish rules of jurisdiction will be of primary interest to Scottish practitioners, but, while some repetition is unavoidable, to depart from the order of the Act would considerably increase the amount of such repetition.

1.38   The order, therefore, of this book is as follows. After this introduction, Chapters 2 and 3 will deal with the interpretation of the Convention and with its scope. Chapter 4 deals with "domicile" in the perspectives both of the Convention and of the 1982 Act. Chapters 5, 6 and 7 deal with the rules of jurisdiction in the Convention and Chapter 8 with its provisions for the recognition and enforcement of judgments. That chapter completes the discussion of the Convention. Chapter 9 describes the schemes for the allocation of jurisdiction between the courts of different parts of the United Kingdom and for the reciprocal enforcement of judgments emanating from those courts. Chapter 10 deals with the Scottish rules of jurisdiction. It describes these rules in a relatively summary way. Where the rule is derived from those in the Convention it is briefly explained and the reader is referred back to the fuller discussion in Chapters 5, 6 or 7. Where the rule is derived from the existing rules of Scots law, it is explained with similar brevity and the reader is referred to the author's own book on *Private International Law*.[93] Chapter 11, the concluding chapter, deals with certain miscellaneous matters, several of which are essentially independent of the 1968 Convention.

---

[93] Edinburgh, 1967.

CHAPTER 2

THE INTERPRETATION OF THE CONVENTION

INTRODUCTION[1]

2.01 SECTION 2(1) of the 1982 Act declares that: "The Conventions[2] shall have the force of law in the United Kingdom, and judicial notice shall be taken of them." "Force of law" means no more or less than that they are to be treated "as if they were part of directly enacted statute law."[3] Following, moreover, the model of the European Communities Act 1972,[4] section 3(1) of the 1982 Act provides that:

> "Any question as to the meaning or effect of any provision of the Conventions shall, if not referred to the European Court in accordance with the 1971 Protocol, be determined in accordance with the principles laid down by and any relevant decision of the European Court."

Section 3(2) of the Act requires judicial notice to be taken of any decision of, or expression of opinion by, the European Court on any such question. In consequence, any question as to their meaning and effect must be treated in the United Kingdom as a question of law and not one of fact. Since the Act, and its Schedules, were necessarily prepared in the light of then current interpretations of the meaning of the provisions of the Conventions, section 47(1)(a) of the Act confers on the Crown power by Order in Council to make such provision as is thought appropriate for bringing "the law of any part of the United Kingdom into accord with the Conventions as affected by any principle laid down by the European Court in connection with the Conventions."[5]

---

[1] There is a well-documented discussion of interpretation in the context of the 1968 Convention by C. Kohler, "The Case Law of the European Court on the Judgments Convention," (1982) 7 E.L.Rev., pp. 3–18 and 103–113. An elegant summary is contained in L. Collins, *The Civil Jurisdiction and Judgments Act 1982* (1983), pp. 10–16. In the wider context of the primary European Treaties there is a profusion of writing on references to the European Court and the Court's own approach to interpretation. Excellent introductions will be found in L. Neville Brown and F. G. Jacobs, *The Court of Justice of the European Communities* (2nd ed. 1983), pp. 237–259 and in L. Collins, *European Community Law in the United Kingdom* (2nd ed., 1980). See also H. G. Schermers, *Judicial Protection in the European Communities* (3rd ed., 1983). The most detailed discussion is that of A. Bredimas, *Methods of Interpretation and Community Law* (1978). On precedent in European Law, see the authoritative article by T. Koopmans in *Essays in European Law and Integration* (D. O'Keefe and H. G. Schermers ed., 1982).

[2] This expression is defined to mean the 1968 Convention, the 1971 Protocol and the 1978 Accession Convention. It will be noticed, however, that the English texts of these instruments set out in Scheds. 1, 2 and 3 to the Act are annexed only "for convenience of reference." As will be explained in para. 2.15, all the different language texts are equally authentic, and it is this corpus of texts, rather than simply the English texts, which comprises "the Conventions."

[3] *The Hollandia* [1982] 3 W.L.R. 1111, *per* Lord Diplock at p. 1116.

[4] s.3(1).

[5] S. 47(1)(b) permits the modification *inter alia* of Scheds. 4 and 8 in the light of such a principle, but not necessarily to bring the relevant provisions "into accord" with the Conventions.

2.02   Section 3(3) of the 1982 Act authorises the courts, in ascertaining the meaning or effect of any provision of the Conventions, to consider and to give such weight as may be appropriate in the circumstances to the Reports of Mr. P. Jenard on the 1968 Convention and the 1971 Protocol and that of Professor P. Schlosser on the 1978 Accession Convention. These Reports have been published in the Official Journal of the European Communities,[6] so that judicial notice may be taken of them.[7] Section 3(3) of the 1982 Act is subordinated to Section 3(1), making it clear that the weight to be attached to these Reports is simply that which may be given to them by the European Court. This question is discussed later.[8]

2.03   Apart from the effect of sections 2 and 3 of the 1982 Act in relation to the law of the United Kingdom, within the legal order created by the Conventions the European Court assumes that the law which it lays down, at least in matters within their scope, takes precedence over the national laws of the Contracting States. In *Sanicentral* v. *Collin*,[9] after emphasising that the 1968 Convention does not seek to affect the rules of substantive law of the Contracting States, the Court declared that:

> "the national procedural laws applicable to the cases concerned are set aside in the matters governed by the Convention in favour of the provisions thereof."

Even in cases where, in a particular provision, the 1968 Convention refers a matter to the "internal law" of a Contracting State—as it does for the determination of the domicile of an individual in the country of the forum[10]—or to the rules of private international law of a Contracting State—as it does for determining the domicile of a trust or the seat of a corporation or association[11]—the construction of the provisions of the Convention making these references to national law is thought to be a matter for the general law of the Convention.

THE PROTOCOL ON INTERPRETATION

2.04   The risk that diverging interpretations of the 1968 Convention might prejudice its efficacy as a species of uniform law was one apparent to the draftsmen of the Convention and, in a Declaration signed contemporaneously with the Convention on September 27, 1968, the original EEC States expressed their willingness to attribute an interpretative jurisdiction to the Court of Justice of the European Communities. A Protocol to this effect, signed on June 3, 1971, entered into force on September 1, 1975. The Accession Conventions declare that the European Court shall have jurisdiction to give rulings on the interpretation of the 1968 Convention, the 1978 and 1982 Accession Conventions and the 1971 Protocol itself.[12] That, however, is the extent of its jurisdiction. It is thought that the terms

---

[6] O.J. 1979, C59/1 and C59/71.
[7] European Communities Act 1972, s. 3(2).
[8] Para. 2.18.
[9] (25/79) [1979] E.C.R. 3423 [5].
[10] Art. 52(1).
[11] Art. 53.
[12] 1978 Convention, Art. 30; 1982 Convention, Art. 10.

of the 1971 Protocol preclude a court or a competent authority in a Contracting State from requesting the European Court to give a ruling on the interpretation of national legislation,[13] including any provision derived from the 1968 Convention and applied by the 1982 Act in circumstances where the Conventions as such are inapplicable, notably in the situations envisaged by Schedules 4 and 8.

2.05   The 1971 Protocol is clearly modelled upon the procedure for obtaining a preliminary ruling under the primary European Community treaties.[14] There are, however, important differences. Under the 1971 Protocol, courts deciding an issue at first instance have no power to request the European Court to give a ruling and the ambit of the discretion of the appellate courts which have such a power is more clearly specified. A further novelty is that by virtue of Art. 4 of the Protocol a "competent authority" in a Contracting State may request the European Court to give a ruling on the interpretation of the Convention.[15] Such a ruling has no effect on the judgments which gave rise to the competent authority's request, but it settles the law for the future.[16]

2.06   Otherwise the system envisaged in the 1971 Protocol for the reference of questions of interpretation to the European Court is in essence that envisaged by Art. 177 of the EEC Treaty and the corresponding provisions of the Euratom Treaty. This appears from Art. 5(1) of the 1971 Protocol which states:

> "Except where this Protocol otherwise provides, the provisions of the Treaty establishing the European Economic Community and those of the Protocol on the Statute of the Court of Justice annexed thereto, which are applicable when the Court is requested to give a preliminary ruling, shall also apply to any proceedings for the interpretation of the Convention and the other instruments referred to in Article 1."

It would be impracticable in this context to describe in any detail the procedure for such references to the European Court, and the reader is referred to the literature on this subject.[17] It is worth noting, however, that the question whether the provisions of Community Law—and, presumably, of the Conventions—apply to a particular case is in principle a matter for the national court only.[18] As the Court recently remarked:

> "According to well-established case law, the court may not in the framework

---

[13] This is confirmed in *Bavaria Fluggesellschaft and Germanair* v. *Eurocontrol* (9 & 10/77) [1977] E.C.R. 1517 [5]. See also para. 10.05 below.

[14] EEC Treaty, Art. 177. *Cf.* Euratom Treaty, Art. 150. References to the European Court under these provisions are to be made by a Scottish court in the form of a "case" following a procedure prescribed by Rules of Court: see R.C. 1965, r. 296A; Act of Sederunt (Rules of Court Amendment No. 5) 1972 (S.I. 1972 No. 1981); Act of Sederunt (Sheriff Court Procedure Amendment No. 2) 1973 (S.I. 1973 No. 543).

[15] But only in respect of a judgment in its own State (a) which has become *res judicata* and (b) conflicts with the interpretation given either by the Court of Justice or by specified courts of another Contracting State.

[16] The procedure is clearly modelled on the *pourvoi dans l'intérêt de la loi* known to French law and to systems influenced by that law. See Jenard Report, p. 69.

[17] For an introduction, see Brown and Jacobs, above, pp. 151–178. For a helpfully practical approach see Collins, *European Community Law in the United Kingdom*, above. For a comprehensive study, see J.A. Usher, *European Court Practice* (1983). In relation to Scotland these authorities should be read in conjunction with the relevant Acts of Sederunt. of Sederunt).

[18] *Portelange* v. *Smith Corona* (10/69) [1969] E.C.R. 309.

of the procedure for a preliminary ruling give a ruling on the application of provisions of national law or the relevance of the request for a preliminary ruling. In the framework of the division of jurisdiction between the national court and the Court of Justice laid down in Article 177 of the Treaty, it is indeed for the national court to assess, with full knowledge of the facts of the case, the relevance of questions of law raised by the dispute which has been brought before it and the necessity for a preliminary ruling in order to enable it to give judgment."[19]

2.07   The provisions of the 1971 Protocol are thought to be mandatory in the sense that the parties to a contract cannot by agreement fetter the discretion of a national court to refer an issue between them to the European Court.[20] The terms of Arts. 2 and 4 of the 1971 Protocol indicate that it is for the national court or the competent authority concerned, and not for the parties, to present the request and to formulate the questions on which an interpretative ruling is sought. From the standpoint of European law the precise form in which the request is presented is relatively unimportant, but the question should be framed in the abstract and relate simply to issues which are within the competence of the European Court.

2.08   From the standpoint of the practitioner the most important procedure is clearly that specified in Art. 3(1) and (2) of the 1971 Protocol. Under Art. 3(1) of the Protocol, a court of last resort[21] *shall* request the European Court to give a ruling if it considers that a decision on a question of interpretation of the Conventions is necessary to enable it to give judgment. This last phrase[22] indicates that the national court of last resort has a discretion to assess the relevance of questions as to which it is asked to request a ruling from the European Court.[23] In the *C.I.L.F.I.T.* case,[24] a reference under Art. 177(3) of the EEC Treaty (where the court of last resort is not in terms conceded any discretion), the European Court indicated that a national court of last resort need not request a ruling if

(1) the question raised is irrelevant in the sense that the answer to it could have no possible bearing on the outcome of the proceedings;

(2) the rule in question has already been the subject of interpretation by the European Court, even if the circumstances were marginally different; and

(3) there is no reasonable doubt how the question should be answered, having regard to the characteristics of Community law and the special difficulties associated with the interpretation of multilingual texts.

Under Art. 3(2) of the Protocol any other court sitting in an appellate capacity—including a court hearing an "appeal" against a decision authorising enforcement under Art. 37(1) of the Convention—again subject to the condition that it considers that a decision on the question is necessary to enable it to give judgment, *may* request the European Court to give a ruling. Their discretion, that is to say, extends beyond the question of relevance to the general appropriateness of the reference.

---

[19] *Baccini* v. *Office National de L'Emploi* (238/82) [1983] 3 C.M.L.R. 572 [11].

[20] *Mattheus* v. *Doego* (93/78) [1978] E.C.R. 2203—decision on general Community law.

[21] The House of Lords or a court to which application has been made under Art. 37(2) (maintenance orders) or under Art. 41 (further appeal against a judgment refusing enforcement).

[22] The same phrase also appears in Art. 177(2) of the EEC Treaty but is applied to courts other than courts of last resort.

[23] Jenard Report, p. 69.

[24] *C.I.L.F.I.T.* v *Italian Ministry of Health* (283/81) [1983] 1 C.M.L.R. 472.

AUTHORITY OF THE EUROPEAN COURT'S JUDGMENTS[25]

2.09   The European Court is in the habit of referring to its own previous decisions, and utilises them as authorities in subsequent decisions.[26] The Court's judgment includes a ruling in answer to the questions put to it in the request by the national court and a statement of the grounds in law on which that ruling is based. The ruling itself often echoes the language of the grounds, which embody legal arguments and statements of principle. These statements of principle, once developed, are often repeated, not always with express reference to their source, from case to case. Such principles obviously have a degree of authority, but nothing analogous to the system of *stare decisis* exemplified in English law has yet been developed. Both in cases concerned with the primary European Treaties[27] and in cases concerned with the 1968 Convention[28] the Court has been prepared, though rarely, to depart from its previous decisions and to do so for reasons which it does not always fully articulate. The techniques for elucidating the *ratio decidendi* of an earlier decision, and for following it or distinguishing it, are as yet in a relatively undeveloped state.[29]

2.10   The 1971 Protocol does not state affirmatively the effects of the rulings of the European Court as precedents in the national legal systems. The Protocol states negatively in Art. 4(2) that the interpretation given by the European Court in response to a request presented to it by a "competent authority" shall not affect the judgments which give rise to the request. The Protocol, however, was drafted against the background of the legal systems of the original Member States in which it is unusual for a court to be bound in any absolute or formal sense by an anterior decision. It is thought, therefore, that in principle at least, the rulings of the European Court are not formally binding in future cases in courts throughout the Community. Nevertheless, the Court's rulings possess a persuasive authority which is not significantly different in its effect. As the Jenard Report[30] explains in relation to rulings under Art. 4 of the 1971 Protocol, they will have "the greatest persuasive authority and will in future . . . constitute a decision of principle of the greatest importance for the future, and one which judges will generally follow." The European Court, not surprisingly, tends to emphasise the authority for national courts of its own rulings.[31] In a request under the 1971 Protocol, the second *Eurocontrol* case,[32] the Court declared:

----

[25] Brown and Jacobs, para. 2.01, n. 1 above, pp. 275–285; Koopmans, para. 2.01, n. 1 above, pp. 11–27.

[26] The Court's practice in the context of the primary treaties was referred to by Lord Diplock in *R. v Henn and Darby* [1981] A.C. 850 at p. 905. Its practice in the context of the 1968 Convention is illustrated, *e.g.* in *De Cavel v. De Cavel* (No.2) (120/79) [1980] E.C.R. 731; *Netherlands State v. Rüffer* (814/79) [1980] E.C.R. 3807 [7].

[27] Brown and Jacobs, above, p. 277.

[28] *Ivenel v. Schwab* (133/81) [1982] E.C.R. 1891.

[29] Koopmans, above, pp. 22–26.

[30] p. 70. It is hardly to be supposed that the authority of a ruling of the Court, unless for the parties themselves differs depending upon whether the request is made under Art. 3 or Art. 4 of the 1971 Protocol.

[31] See *Da Costa en Shaake v. Nederlandse Belastingadministratie* (28–30/62) [1963] E.C.R. 31.

[32] *Bavaria Fluggesellschaft and Germanair v. Eurocontrol* (9 & 10/77) [1977] E.C.R. 1517 [4].

"the principle of legal certainty in the Community legal system and the objectives of the Brussels Convention in accordance with Article 220 of the EEC Treaty, which is at its origin, require in all Member States a uniform application of the legal concepts and legal classifications developed by the Court in the context of the Brussels Convention."

2.11　From the standpoint of United Kingdom law the same result flows from the fact that questions as to the meaning and effect of the Conventions, if not referred to the European Court, are to be "determined in accordance with the principles laid down by and any relevant decision of the European court." A Scottish court, therefore, which is not sitting in an appellate capacity, must regard the European Court's rulings as authoritative, even when thought to be erroneous. It cannot simply disregard the ruling.[33] The same applies, in principle at least, to a court sitting in an appellate capacity. It may recall, however, that the European Court is not formally bound by its own previous decisions and, if it considers that an earlier ruling requires reconsideration, may request the European court for a ruling on a question of interpretation of the Convention. It will doubtless exercise restraint in practice, but in the last analysis may do so.[34] It may also be observed in this context that the Scottish courts would not appear to be bound by the earlier decisions of hierarchically superior courts in Scotland or even by those of the House of Lords on matters relating to the interpretation of the Convention as distinct from the provisions of the 1982 Act, including "derived" provisions. Their duty under section 3(1) of the 1982 Act is to apply "the principles laid down by and any relevant decision of the European Court."

PRINCIPLES APPLIED BY THE EUROPEAN COURT IN THE INTERPRETATION OF THE CONVENTIONS

A. GENERAL

2.12　The Conventions are in form and effect treaties and, in principle, apart from section 3 of the 1982 Act, the methods of interpretation applicable to internal United Kingdom legislation would not fall to be applied rigidly to the provisions of treaties but rather "broad principles of general acceptation."[35] That section, however, directs United Kingdom courts to interpret the Conventions in accordance with the principles adopted by the European Court. These principles are very different from those of Scots law, and Lord Diplock's remarks concerning the danger of an English court applying English canons of statutory interpretation to the interpretation of the EEC Treaty are equally apposite to a Scottish court in the interpretation of the 1968 Convention.[36]

---

[33] Brown and Jacobs, above, p. 283. In *Garland* v. *British Rail Engineering Ltd.* [1982] 2 All E.R. 402. Lord Diplock, at p. 415, referred to rulings of the European Court becoming "binding in all courts in England, including this House."

[34] See the *C.I.L.F.I.T.* case, referred to in para. 2.08 above.

[35] The words are those of Lord Macmillan in *Stag Line Ltd.* v. *Foscolo Mango Co. Ltd.* [1932] A.C. 328 at p. 350. They were repeated recently by Lord Wilberforce in *James Buchanan Co. Ltd.* v. *Babco Forwarding and Shipping (UK) Ltd.* [1978] A.C. 141 at p. 152 and by Lord Diplock in *The Hollandia* [1982] 2 W.L.R. 1111 at p. 1116.

[36] *R.* v. *Henn and Darby* [1981] A.C. 850 at p. 904.

2.13   In the first case in which it was called upon to interpret a provision of the 1968 Convention—the *Industrie Tessili* case[37]—the European Court showed its desire to integrate the Convention into the general body of Community law:

> "The Convention was established to implement Article 220 of the EEC Treaty and was intended according to the express terms of its preamble to implement the provisions of that Article ... Accordingly, the Convention must be interpreted having regard both to its principles and objectives and to its relationship with the Treaty."

Again, in the first *Eurocontrol* case[38] the Court referred in its ruling to "the general principles of law which stem from the *corpus* of national legal systems."[39] In other areas of Community Law the Court has frequently referred to "legal certainty" and "equality of rights" as being among those general principles. It has referred to them also in the context of the 1968 Convention.[40] The desire, however, of the European Court to integrate the Convention into the general body of European law is best illustrated by the decisions on the interpretation of the 1968 Convention where, as in its case law on the primary Treaties, the European Court makes constant reference to the scheme or system of the Convention and the policies to which it seeks to give effect.[41]

2.14   This tendency to integrate the Conventions into the mainstream of Community law makes it permissible, it is thought, to suppose that the European Court will tend to apply to the interpretation of the Conventions an approach similar to that which it has adopted in relation to the primary European treaties and subordinate EEC legislation. It is outwith the scope of this book to consider that approach in any detail, but its broad outlines may be sketched out.

B. MATERIALS AVAILABLE TO THE COURT

2.15   Allusion was made above[42] to the fact that "the Conventions" having the force of law under Art. 2 were not simply the English texts of the 1968 Convention and its associated instruments, but the whole corpus of texts drawn up in the official languages of the Contracting States concerned, each of which is declared to be "authentic."[43] This means that, in interpreting any provision of the Convention, a United Kingdom court, in principle at least, should consult the other language texts. In the context of

---

[37] *Industrie Tessili* v. *Dunlop* (12/76) [1976] E.C.R. 1473 [9].

[38] *LTU* v. *Eurocontrol* (26/76) [1976] E.C.R. 1541.

[39] It seems not unlikely that requests to the European Court for rulings on the interpretation of the 1968 Convention will give the Court an opportunity to develop these "general principles of law," but it would be premature to speculate further on the basis of the present case law.

[40] *Bavaria Fluggesellschaft and Germanair* v. *Eurocontrol* (9 & 10/77) [1977] E.C.R. 1517 [4] in a passage cited in para. 2.10 above; *Somafer* v. *Saar-Ferngas* (33/78) [1978] E.C.R. 2183 [8] (legal certainty); *Netherlands State* v. *Ruffer* (814/79) [1980] E.C.R. 3807 [14] (equality of rights).

[41] See the cases cited in para. 2.24.

[42] See para. 2.01, n. 2.

[43] 1968 Convention, Art. 68; 1971 Protocol, Art. 14; 1972 Accession Convention, Art. 41; 1982 Accession Convention, Art. 17.

a decision of the Commission under the EEC Treaty the European Court has remarked:

> "When a single decision is addressed to all the Member States, the necessity for uniform application and accordingly for uniform interpretation makes it impossible to consider one version of the texts in isolation but requires that it be interpreted on the basis of both the real intention of its author and the aim he seeks to achieve in the light, in particular, of the versions in [different] languages."[44]

The Court has adopted the same approach in cases under the 1968 Convention.[45] Only English texts of the 1968 Convention and of its associated instruments are annexed to the 1982 Act.[46] These English texts are not "authentic" texts: they are merely stated in section 2(2) to have been prepared from the authentic texts, which are to be found in the Official Journal of the European Communities,[47] of which judicial notice is to be taken in terms of section 3(2) of the European Communities Act 1972.

2.16   The primary European Treaties differ in their structure from United Kingdom statutes in that the former contain preambles, often lengthy, which state their legal basis and purpose and intent.[48] The substantive texts of the Treaties also contain references to policies to be attained and principles to be applied in their attainment.[49] The European Court has been accustomed to refer to all these materials when interpreting specific provisions of the primary European Treaties even when, *prima facie*, no ambiguity is involved. The Court adopts a similar approach in the interpretation of the 1968 Convention and, in elucidating its underlying policies, it is prepared to look to Art. 220 of the EEC Treaty, which is the formal and historical justification for the Conventions in the general law of the Communities, as well as to the preamble and the terms of the 1968 Convention.

2.17   In the context of the primary European Treaties the European Court has made little use of extrinsic materials as aids to interpretation, partly because the crucial *travaux préparatoirs*—in the primary Treaties the minutes of the meetings of the Foreign Ministers—have not been published.[50] This appears to have been a conscious decision on the part of those concerned,[51] no doubt because such *travaux* are likely to record individual points of view rather than the consensus embodied in the written text finally agreed. In the case of subordinate legislation under the Treaties, extrinsic materials, such as proposals by the Commission and opinions of the European Parliament, are available and are published in the Official

---

[44] *Stauder* v. *Ulm* (29/69) [1969] E.C.R. 419 [3].

[45] *Elefanten Schuh* v. *Jacqmain* (150/80) [1981] E.C.R. 1671; *Rohr* v. *Ossberger* (21/81) [1981] E.C.R. 2341.

[46] s. 2(2), and Scheds. 1, 2 and 3.

[47] For 1968 Convention, see O.J. 1972, L299/32 (Dutch, French, German and Italian) and O.J. 1978, L304 (Danish, English and Irish); for 1971 Protocol, see O.J. 1975, L204/28 (Dutch, French, German and Italian) and O.J. 1978, L304 (Danish, English and Irish); for 1978 Accession Convention, see O.J. 1978, L304 (all these languages); for 1982 Accession Convention, see O.J. 1982, L388/1 (these languages and Greek).

[48] For illustrations of the use of preambles see *Tessili* v. *Dunlop* (12/76) [1976] E.C.R. 1473 [9]; *De Bloos* v. *Bouyer* (14/76) [1976] E.C.R. 1497 [8]; *De Wolf* v. *Cox* (42/76) [1976] E.C.R. 1759 [15].

[49] *e.g.* EEC Arts. 2, 3, 39, 104 and 110.

[50] For details, see A. Bredimas, *Methods of Interpretation and Community Law* (1978), pp. 57–60

[51] R. Lecourt, *Le juge devant le Marché Commun* (1970), p. 64.

Journal. The Court has referred to such materials in elucidating the meaning of particular provisions,[52] but has done so rarely and with some discrimination. On the other hand Art. 190 of the EEC Treaty obliges the Council and Commission in the preparation of regulations, directives, and decisions to state their legal basis and to refer to any consultations or opinions which were necessary preliminaries to their enactment. The Court has frequently referred to these recitals.

2.18   Although section 3(3) of the 1982 Act permits United Kingdom courts to refer to the Jenard and Schlosser Reports on the 1968 and 1978 Conventions in ascertaining the meaning or effect of provisions of the Convention and to give them "such weight as may be appropriate in the circumstances," the European Court's use of extrinsic materials in the context of the primary Treaties does not throw much light upon what weight may appropriately be given to those Reports. The Jenard Report, however, has been referred to by the Court on one or two occasions,[53] though frequently by Advocates-General in their submissions to the Court.[54] It is no secret, however, and apparent from its terms that the Schlosser Report embodies the agreed understandings of the Council Working Party which drafted the Accession Convention concerning the effect of provisions both of the 1968 Convention and of the amendments to it introduced by the 1978 Accession Convention. It is thought, therefore, that these Reports are likely to have considerable persuasive authority. At the present stage, at least, of the development of case law on the Conventions they frequently facilitate the understanding of provisions whose apparent clarity of language often conceals serious problems of application.

C. APPROACHES TO INTERPRETATION

(a) Introduction

2.19   It is not uncommon in discussions of interpretation by the European Court to find references to its adoption of various specified methods of interpretation, such as the literal, historical, systematic, and teleological methods.[55] But the Court itself has refrained from discussing its own methods of interpretation. The term "methods of interpretation" is perhaps misleading in so far as it may suggest that such methods fall readily into categories rigorously distinct from one another of which only one may be appropriate to a particular phase in the process of interpretation. In practice they shade into one another: a court cannot adequately examine the text of a provision in isolation from its context or understand either

---

[52] *Stauder* v. *Ulm* (29/69) [1969] E.C.R. 419 [5].

[53] *Ivenel* v. *Schwab* (133/81) [1982] E.C.R. 1891 [11] and [12] where the Court also referred to the Report (O.J. 1980, C282/1) on the draft Obligations Convention (O.J. 1980, L266/1). *Rinkau* case (157/80) [1981] E.C.R. 1391 [6] and [8]. The Court occasionally uses the language of the Jenard Report without expressly citing it, *cf. Porta-Leasing* v. *Prestige International* (784/79) [1980] E.C.R. 1517 [6] and *Sanders* v. *Van der Putte* (73/77) [1977] E.C.R. 2383 [14].

[54] *De Bloos* v. *Bouyer* (14/76) [1976] E.C.R. 1497 *per* Adv.-Gen. Reischl at pp. 1515 and 1517: *Salotti* v. *RÜWA* (24/76) [1976] E.C.R. 1831, *per* Adv.-Gen. Capotorti at p. 1845; *Segoura* v. *Bonakdarian* (25/76) [1976] E.C.R. 1851 *per* Adv.-Gen. Capotorti at p. 1865; *Industrial Diamond Supplies* v. *Riva* (43/77) [1977] E.C.R. 2175 *per* Adv.-Gen. Reischl at pp. 2195 and 2198; *Rohr* v. *Ossberger* (27/81) [1981] E.C.R. 2431, *per* Adv.-Gen. Capotorti at p. 2443; etc., etc.

[55] *Cf.* H.G. Schermers, above, pp. 11 *et seq.*

without reference to the legal basis of the provision and the objectives which it seeks to secure. As in United Kingdom law, the provisions of a text are to be considered in their whole legislative context. The difference is that more emphasis is placed by the European Court upon the wider legislative context and, within that context, the purposes of the legislation are more often explicitly stated. With these words of warning, it may nevertheless be useful to arrange the examination of the European Court's approach to interpretation by reference to the overlapping categories of the literal approach, the contextual approach, and the purposive approach.

(b) The literal approach

2.20   In the context of the primary European treaties and their subordinate legislation the European Court has paid close attention to the words of any provision before it and, where these words are clear and unambiguous, normally gives effect to their natural meaning.[56] It is not, however, as likely as a United Kingdom court[57] to emphasise the literal meaning of a provision in its immediate and obvious context at the expense of its meaning in the wider context of the legislation as a whole. The European Court has adopted a similar approach when interpreting the 1968 Convention. In the *Rinkau* case,[58] for example, the Court was asked whether the right granted to an accused person under Art. II of the Annexed Protocol to be defended by persons qualified to do so, even if he does not appear in person, applies;

> "without restriction, or does the accused person have that right only where he has to defend himself against a civil claim made in the relevant criminal proceedings, or at any rate where the interests of the accused under civil law are affected by the outcome of the criminal proceedings?"

Art. II contains no express words restricting its application to criminal proceedings in which the accused's liability at civil law was or might be at issue, but the Court, having referred to the legislative history of Art. II and to the Jenard Report, concluded that it was necessary to look to "the actual intention behind the insertion in the Protocol of the provision in question."[59] On this basis the Court ruled that the right granted to an accused person by Art. II extended only to cases "in which the accused's liability at civil law, arising from the elements of the offence for which he is being prosecuted, is in question or on which such liability might subsequently be based."

2.21   The texts, however, presented to the European Court are less likely to be clear and unambiguous than legislation drafted in the United Kingdom. This arises partly from the greater generality of the terms used, partly from the tendency to use words and phrases without further definition,[60] and partly because concepts are used which turn out to have different meanings in the different Community legal systems.[61] In the case, moreover, of the 1968 Convention it appears that in some cases the draftsmen of the

---

[56] See *Sgarlata* case (40/64) [1965] E.C.R. 227.
[57] See Law Commissions' Report, *The Interpretation of Statutes* (1969) Law Com. No. 21, Scot. Law Com. No. 11, pp. 48–49.
[58] (157/80) [1981] E.C.R. 1391.
[59] [20].
[60] *Bulmer* v. *Bollinger* [1974] Ch. 401, *per* Lord Denning at p. 425(*G*).
[61] *Tessili* v. *Dunlop* (12/76) [1976] E.C.R. 1473 [10].

Convention intentionally left unamended a text, the imprecision of which they were aware, on the view that the ambiguity could be resolved at a later date by the European Court.[62] The risk of ambiguity is enhanced by the fact that it may be necessary to consult different language versions of the text, since each of them is declared to be equally authentic.[63] Though in some cases this may facilitate the task of a court which has access to these texts it may equally introduce uncertainty when there are minor differences between the texts. The European Court's construction of a text may surprise a practitioner who has relied merely upon the version in his own language. Art. 18, for example, of the 1968 Convention contains in the English and other texts the word "solely," which is absent in the French and Irish texts. The Court has construed the article in such a way as to deprive the word "solely" of any significance.[64]

2.22   When ambiguities emerge, the European Court, without disregarding the natural meaning of any provision which it is called upon to construe, is likely to pay careful attention both to the immediate and to the wider contexts in which that provision appears. In the *Humblet* case it declared:

> "it is not sufficient for the Court to adopt the literal interpretation and the Court considers it necessary to examine the question whether this interpretation is confirmed by other criteria concerning in particular the common intention of the High Contracting Parties and the *ratio legis*."[65]

(c) The contextual approach

2.23   It is said to be an elementary rule of United Kingdom law:

> "that no one should profess to understand any part of a statute or any other document before he has read the whole of it. Until he has done so he is not entitled to say that it or any part of it is clear or unambiguous."[66]

The European Court, however, arguably pays still closer attention to the wider context in which a provision appears and, in particular, to the "scheme"[67] or "system"[68] of the legislation. Part of the explanation for this may lie in the fact that in the European Treaties—and in the 1968 Convention—the relationship of one provision to another is not usually, as it is in United Kingdom statutes, made explicit in the text of the instrument, but is frequently left to inference from the place of the provision in the legislative scheme.

2.24   The considerable weight which the European Court is prepared to give to the legislative context of a provision is well illustrated in two cases concerned with the interpretation of the EEC Treaty. In the *Bresciani* case the Court declared:

> "The position of these Articles [Arts. 13 and 9 of the EEC Treaty] at the

---

[62] Art. 5(3) of the 1968 Convention is the most striking example. For its legislative history see the Jenard Report, p. 26 and paras. 5.35–5.38 below.

[63] See para. 2.15 above.

[64] *Elefanten Schuh* v. *Jacqmain* (150/80) [1981] E.C.R. 1671; *Rohr* v. *Ossberger* (21/81) [1981] E.C.R. 2341; *C.H.W.* v. *G.J.H.* (25/81) [1982] E.C.R. 1189. See also para. 7.28 below.

[65] *Humblet* v. *Belgian State* (6/60) [1960] E.C.R. 559 at p. 575 [2].

[66] *Att.-Gen.* v. *Prince Augustus of Hanover* [1957] A.C. 436, *per* Viscount Simonds at p. 463

[67] *LTU* v. *Eurocontrol* (29/76) [1976] E.C.R. 1541 [3].

[68] *Bertrand* v. *Ott* (150/77) [1978] E.C.R. 1431 [17]. *Cf. Commissioners of Customs and Excise* v. *Cure and Deeley* [1962] 1 Q.B. 340, where Sachs J. stressed the need "to examine the nature, objects, and scheme of the legislation as a whole."

beginning of that part of the Treaty reserved for the 'Foundations of the Community' is sufficient to indicate their crucial role in the construction of the Common Market."[69]

In the *Manghera* case the Court said that Art. 37(1) of the EEC Treaty had to be: "considered in its context in relation to the other paragraphs of the same article and in its place in the general scheme of the Treaty."[70] The weight which the European Court is prepared to give to the "scheme" or "system" of legislation is also illustrated in its interpretation of the 1968 Convention. In the *Reinwater* case the Court, referring to Art. 5(3), said:

'That provision must be interpreted in the context of the scheme for conferment of jurisdiction which forms the subject-matter of Title II of the Convention."[71]

Again, in the *Industrial Diamond Supplies* case the Court said:

"The meaning of the expression "ordinary appeal" may be deduced from the actual structure of Articles 30 and 38 and from their function in the system of the Convention."[72]

The same point is clearly, and indeed strikingly, illustrated by the Court's judgment in *Denilauler* v. *Couchet Frères*.[73]

2.25   When the Court, however, looks beyond the immediate context of a provision to the "system" of the Convention, it is looking to that "system" to elucidate the objectives or purposes of the Convention, or of a Title to it, as a guide to interpretation.[74] Although on one view this is merely an aspect of a contextual approach to interpretation, it deserves separate consideration.

(d) The purposive approach

2.26   As the preceding quotations incidentally illustrate, the European Court has frequently stressed the need, in elucidating the meaning of a particular provision, to have regard to the objectives or purposes of the legislation of which it is a component part. More often than has been customary in United Kingdom legislation these objectives or purposes are set forth not only in the extensive preambles to the text, which are virtually read as part of it, but in the substantive provisions of the text.[75] In the context, therefore, of the interpretation of the primary European Treaties and of the legislation subordinate to them, the Court has frequently used such phrases as "the system and objectives of the Treaty,"[76] "the fundamental nature, in the scheme of the Treaty, of the principles of freedom of movement and equality of treatment of workers,"[77] " . . . the purpose and

---

[69] (87/75) [1976] E.C.R. 129 [7].
[70] (59/75) [1976] E.C.R. 100 [6].
[71] *Bier* v. *Mines de Potasse d'Alsace* (21/76) [1976] E.C.R. 1735 [8].
[72] *Industrial Diamond Supplies* v. *Riva* (43/77) [1977] E.C.R. 2175 [29].
[73] (125/79) [1980] E.C.R. 1553 [11], [13] and [15].
[74] Occasionally, of course, the Court looks at both simultaneously. In the case of *Ivenel* v. *Schwab* (133/81) [1982] E.C.R. 1891 [10] the Court observed: "It is appropriate to examine that problem in the light of the objectives of the Convention and the general scheme of its provisions."
[75] *Cf.* EEC Arts. 1–9; ECSC Arts. 2–6; and Euratom Arts. 1–4.
[76] *Continental Can* (6/72) [1973] E.C.R. 215 [22–26].
[77] *Sotgiu* (152/73) [1974] E.C.R. 153 [4].

spirit of the Community rules on freedom of movement for workers"[78] etc., etc. This approach has sometimes been described as a teleological approach,[79] but the term seems a trifle grandiose[80] and is to be avoided because it suggests a possible severance between the texts and the "final ends" which may be taken into account by the Court. As Lord Mackenzie Stuart has said:"Once again may I emphasise that it is the text—including of course its expressed objectives—which dictates the approach of the Court."[81] He describes the approach of the court as a "purposive approach," and this term is adopted here. Similar language, and the same emphasis on the materials available to the court, appears in recent remarks by Lord Scarman made in the context of English law:

> "Judges may not interpret statutes in the light of their own views on policy. They may, of course, adopt a purposive interpretation if they can find in the statute read as a whole or in the material to which they are permitted by law to refer as aids to interpretation an expression of Parliament's purpose or policy."[82]

2.27   In its interpretation of the 1968 Convention the European Court has had regard to such general objectives or purposes as are expressed in the texts or may reasonably be inferred from the whole "legislative" materials before it. In *Tessili* v. *Dunlop*,[83] the first request presented to it for the interpretation of the 1968 Convention, the Court observed that "the Convention must be interpreted having regard both to its principles and objectives and to its relationship with the Treaty." In the second *Eurocontrol* case[84] the Court stressed the "objectives of the Brussels Convention in accordance with Article 220 of the EEC Treaty." In the *Elefanten Schuh*[85] case the Court justified its departure from the majority of the language texts of Art. 18 *inter alia* by stating that this "interpretation is more in keeping with the objectives and spirit of the Convention." Again, in the *De Bloos* case,[86] after referring to the purposes of the Convention as set out in its preamble, the Court said:

> "These objectives imply the need to avoid, as far as possible, creating a situation in which a number of courts have jurisdiction in respect of one and the same contract."

But these are only examples: the practice is well established.[87]

D. POLICIES OF INTERPRETATION SPECIFIC TO THE CONVENTION

2.28   In the course of its interpretation of the 1968 Convention the European

---

[78] *Cristini* (32/75) [1975] E.C.R. 1085 [16].

[79] Judge Pescatore in the *Van der Meersch Festschrift* (1972).

[80] See the not-too-serious comments of Lord Mackenzie Stuart in *The European Communities and the Rule of Law* (1977), at p. 76.

[81] Mackenzie Stuart, above, p. 77.

[82] *Shah* v. *Barnet London B.C.* [1983] A.C. 309 at pp. 347–348; see also *The Hollandia* [1982] 3 W.L.R. 1111, *per* Lord Diplock at p. 1116.

[83] (12/76) [1976] E.C.R. 1473 [9].

[84] *Bavaria Fluggesellschaft and Germanair* v. *Eurocontrol* (9 & 10/77) [1977] E.C.R. 1517 [4].

[85] *Elefanten Schuh* v. *Jacqmain* (150/80) [1981] E.C.R. 1671 [14], repeated in *Rohr* v. *Ossberger* (27/81) [1981] E.C.R. 2431 [7].

[86] *De Bloos* v. *Bouyer* (14/76) [1976] E.C.R. 1497 [9].

[87] *Cf. Effer* v. *Kantner* (38/81) [1982] E.C.R. 825[5].

Court has shown a disposition to place special emphasis upon certain principles or policies. In the second *Eurocontrol* case[88] the Court declared that the objectives of the 1968 Convention required, so far as their provisions permitted, their uniform interpretation. The uniform application of the Convention was the *raison d'être* of the 1971 Protocol, and the Court has made considerable efforts to secure it. In some cases, of course, the Convention expressly or by implication authorises or requires a "national" interpretation of its concepts and terms.[89] These cases, however, are rare. While the European Court may not have established a presumption in favour of a "Community" or independent interpretation of the provisions of the Convention[90] the Court has generally preferred to adopt an interpretation which will secure the uniform application of the law throughout the Community.[91] This is well illustrated in its approach to the scope of the Convention under Art. 1. In the first *Eurocontrol*[92] case the Court emphasised that:

"As Article 1 serves to indicate the area of application of the Convention it is necessary, in order to ensure, as far as possible, that the rights and obligations which derive from it for the Contracting States and the persons to whom it applies are equal and uniform, that the terms of that provision should not be interpreted as a mere reference to the internal law of one or other of the States concerned."

The same tendency to give a uniform interpretation to questions going to the scope of the Convention or of its provisions is illustrated in the *Société Bertrand* case[93] where the Court gave its own definition of "sale of goods on instalment credit terms" in Art. 13 of the Convention.

2.29   A further assertion of a general kind has been made in relation to the scope of the Convention:

"The drafters of the Convention intended its scope to be as wide as possible and the first paragraph of Article 1 to be so interpreted. The corollary of this is that the provisions of the second paragraph, setting out those civil and commercial matters specifically excluded from the scope of the Convention, must be construed narrowly."[94]

The authority cited for this proposition is the Jenard Report,[95] but the

---

[88] *Bavaria Fluggesellschaft and Germanair* v. *Eurocontrol* (9 & 10/77) [1977] E.C.R. 1517 [4]; *Netherlands State* v. *Rüffer* (814/79) [1980] E.C.R. 3807 [14].

[89] Arts. 52 and 53 are cases in point. See paras. 4.07–4.09 and 4.21–4.24 below. The reference to "public policy" in Art. 27 is thought to be a reference to the public policy of the state of recognition.In relation to Art. 16(1) it seems likely that it is for the law of the *situs* itself to determine whether property is immoveable.

[90] So far, the only cases in which it has not adopted an independent interpretation seem to be *Tessili* v. *Dunlop* (12/76) [1976] E.C.R. 1473 [9] and *Zelger* v. *Salinitri* (No. 2) (129/83) unreported.

[91] Cf. *Bier* v. *Mines de Potasse d'Alsace* (21/76) [1976] E.C.R. 1735 (Art. 5(3)); *De Bloos* v. *Bouyer* (14/76) [1976] E.C.R. 1497; *Somafer* v. *Saar-Ferngas* (33/78) [1978] E.C.R. 2183 (Art. 5(5)); *Sanders* v. *Van der Putte* (73/77) [1977] E.C.R. 2383 (Art 16(1)); *Salotti* v. *R Ü W A* (24/76) [1976] E.C.R. 1831 (Art. 17); *Meeth* v. *Glacetal* (23/78) [1978] E.C.R. 2133 (Art. 17); etc.

[92] *LTU* v. *Eurocontrol* (29/76) [1976] E.C.R. 1541 [3]. This opinion was confirmed in *Bavaria Fluggesellschaft* v. *Eurocontrol* (9 & 10/77 [1977] E.C.R. 1517; see also *Gourdain* v. *Nadler* (133/78) [1979] E.C.R. 733 [3].

[93] *Bertrand* v. *Ott* (150/77) [1978] E.C.R. 1431 [14]–[16].

[94] A. McCellan and G. Kremlis, (1983) 2 C.M.L.Rev. 529 at 533.

[95] p. 10.

relevant passage (cited below)[96] seems merely to stress the generality of the first paragraph where the second paragraph does not apply. It is submitted that it would be unfortunate if, as a general principle of interpretation, the exceptions in Art. 1(2) were to be narrowly construed. The exceptions have a practical justification which is explained in the Jenard Report and, for this reason, it is submitted that they should be applied fairly within the ambit of their rationale.[97]

2.30   As we have seen, the European Court has been accustomed to attach considerable importance to the place of particular provisions in the legislative scheme as a whole. It has placed the provisions for jurisdiction in Title II of the 1968 Convention in a species of heirarchy of general principles and exceptions, and has tended to construe the former more liberally than the latter. Primacy is given to the general jurisdiction based on the domicile of the defender stated in Art. 2:

" . . . it is in accord with the objective of the Convention to avoid a wide and multifarious interpretation of the exceptions to the general rule of jurisdiction contained in Article 2."[98]

2.31   Subsidiarily, and clearly subject to the primacy which it gives to the general jurisdiction under Art. 2, the court has tended to construe the provisions of Section 2 of Title II more generously than those provisions which derogate from its application. Thus the Court in the *Société Bertrand* case[99] declared that:

"the compulsory jurisdiction provided for in the second paragraph of Article 14 of the Convention must, because it derogates from the general principles of the system laid down by the Convention in matters of contract, such as may be derived in particular from Articles 2 and 5(1), be strictly limited to the objectives proper to Section 4 of the said Convention."

A similar approach was adopted in relation to the interpretation of Art. 17 in the *Salotti* and *Segoura* cases.[1] In both cases the Court said:

"The way in which that provision is to be applied must be interpreted in the light of the effect of the conferment of jurisdiction by consent, which is to exclude both the jurisdiction determined by the general principle laid down in Article 2 and the special jurisdictions provided for in Articles 5 and 6 of the Convention. In view of the consequences that such an option may have on the position of the parties to the action, the requirements set out in Article 17

---

[96] "The solution adopted implies that all litigation and all judgments relating to contractual or non-contractual obligations which do not involve the status or capacity of natural persons, wills or succession, rights in property arising out of a matrimonial relationship, bankruptcy or social security must fall within the scope of the Convention, and that in this respect the Convention should be interpreted as widely as possible."

[97] The European Court appears to have given no countenance to the suggested principle of interpretation in cases where it might have had some claim to consideration, such as *De Cavel* v. *De Cavel* (No.1) (143/78) [1979] E.C.R. 1055 and *Netherlands State* v. *Rüffer* (814/79) [1980] E.C.R. 3807.

[98] *Somafer* v. *Saar-Ferngas* (33/78) [1978] E.C.R. 2183 [7]. This case is considered in paras. 5.45–5.48 below. See also *Blanckaert and Willems* v. *Trost* (139/80) [1981] E.C.R. 819 [2]; *Zelger* v. *Salinitri* (56/79) [1980] E.C.R. 89 [3] [4].

[99] *Bertrand* v. *Ott* (150/77) [1978] E.C.R. 1431 [17].

[1] *Salotti* v. *R Ü W A* (24/76) [1976] E.C.R. 1831 [7]; *Segoura* v. *Bonakdarian* (25/76) [1976] E.C.R. 1851 [6].

regarding the validity of clauses conferring jurisdiction must be strictly construed."

It appears from these citations that the European Court has a distinct tendency—though no more than that—to construe quite strictly such provisions of the Convention (including even those relating to the prorogation of jurisdiction in Arts. 17 and 18)[2] as derogate from the more general provisions of Sections 1 and 2 of Title II of the Convention.

2.32   It is almost certainly premature as yet to seek to isolate other trends in the interpretation of the Conventions by the European Court. A persuasive case, however, has been made for the view that the Court always seeks to avoid superfluous procedures[3] and to prefer whatever approach will best give practical efficacy to the Conventions.[4]

---

[2] See the discussion at paras. 7.26–7.28 below.
[3] *Meeth* v. *Glacetal* (23/78) [1978] E.C.R. 2133 [8].
[4] See Kohler, "The Case Law of the European Court on the Judgments Convention" (1982) 7 E.L.Rev.3, esp. at pp. 14 and 17.

CHAPTER 3

SCOPE OF THE CONVENTION
AND
OTHER ASPECTS OF ITS
APPLICATION

SCOPE

A. INTRODUCTION

3.01 THE provisions of the 1968 Convention defining its scope are important
In specifying when the Convention applies, they delimit at the same time
the spheres of application both of the rules for the United Kingdom
allocation of jurisdiction in Schedule 4 and of the Scottish jurisdictional
rules in Schedule 8. Neither of these sets of rules applies where the
Convention applies.[1] It is also at least one of the conditions of the application of the inter-United Kingdom rules that the proceedings relate to
subject-matters within the scope of the Convention. When, moreover, the
inter-United Kingdom rules apply, the application of the Scottish rules is
excluded.

3.02 In earlier writings the question was much discussed whether, if a judgment emanating from another Contracting State related to a matter
outwith the scope of the 1968 Convention, it need be recognised or
enforced.[2] The fact that a judgment relates to a matter outwith the scope of
the Convention is not expressly specified in Arts. 27 or 28 as a ground for
refusing to recognise it. Does the court addressed, nevertheless, have a
power to decline to do so on the ground that Arts. 27 and 28 can themselves only apply to cases where the Convention itself applies? If, again,
the court possesses this power, should it apply its own characterisation of
the concept of "civil and commercial matters," or is it bound to apply that
of the court of origin or, indeed, an independent Community interpretation of the concept? The decision of the European Court in the first
Eurocontrol case to adopt[3] an independent characterisation of the concept
places those issues in a new perspective. If Art. 1 governs the whole
Convention,[4] a judgment on a matter outwith its scope according to
criteria established by the European Court cannot give rise to the obligations of recognition and enforcement in Title II of the Convention. As the
Court later said:

> "A national court must not apply the Brussels Convention so as to recognise
> or enforce judgments which are excluded from its scope as determined by the
> Court of Justice."[5]

---

[1] 1982 Act, ss. 16(4) and 20(1).
[2] See Bellet, (1965) 92 *Clunet* 833 at p. 850: Giardina, (1978) 27 I.C.L.Q. 263 at 268;
Goldman, 1971 *Rev. Trim. Droit Européen* 1 at 9.
[3] *LTU* v. *Eurocontrol* (29/76) [1976] E.C.R. 1541: see para. 3.07 below.
[4] Jenard Report, p. 42.
[5] *Bavaria Fluggesellschaft* v. *Germanair* (9 & 10/77) [1977] E.C.R. 1517 [5].

The point is not confined to issues of recognition and enforcement. It may arise in the context of an application for provisional measures under Art. 24 of the Convention, and here the European Court has declared:

> "That provision in fact has in view cases in which provisional measures are ordered in a Contracting State where 'under this Convention' a court in another Contracting State has jurisdiction as to the substance of the matter. Therefore, it may not be relied on to bring within the scope of the Convention provisional or protective measures relating to matters which are excluded from it."[6]

3.03   It has been explained in Chapter 2[7] that the European Court has adopted certain policies of interpretation in relation to Art. 1. These are encapsulated in the judgment of the European Court in *Gourdain* v. *Nadler*[8]:

> "As Article 1 serves to indicate the scope of the Convention it is necessary, in order to ensure, as far as possible, that the rights and obligations which derive from it for the Contracting States and the persons to whom it applies are equal and uniform, that the terms of that provision should not be interpreted as a mere reference to the internal law of one or other of the States concerned . . . The concepts used in Article 1 must be regarded as independent concepts which must be interpreted by reference, first, to the objectives and scheme of the Convention and, secondly, to the general principles which stem from the corpus of the national legal systems."

It was also argued above[9] that the exceptions to Art. 1 are not necessarily to be construed restrictively. It is right, however, to emphasise that a matter is excluded from the scope of the Convention, it would seem, only when it is the principal subject of the proceedings. On the other hand, the fact that the principal subject of proceedings is excluded from the scope of the Convention does not necessarily mean that an ancillary order made in the course of the proceedings cannot be enforced under the Convention.[10] The test is whether the ancillary order, if it had been made independently, might itself have been enforced.[11]

3.04   It may not be inappropriate to end this introduction with a word of warning. The express provisions of the 1968 Convention relating to scope are not necessarily exhaustive of the cases where jurisdiction may not be assumed in relation to natural or legal persons domiciled in a Contracting State nor of the cases where the recognition and enforcement of a judgment emanating from a Contracting State may be withheld. The Convention says nothing about the immunities of States, international organisations, and persons enjoying diplomatic status. Droz[12] concludes from this that the matter is left to the law of each Contracting State. Despite the terms of the Convention, the Scottish courts may not, it is thought, assume jurisdiction where this would be contrary to the terms of the State Immun-

---

[6] *C.H.W.* v. *G.J.H.* (25/81) [1982] E.C.R. 1189 [12], following language similar to that adopted by the Court in *De Cavel* v. *De Cavel* (143/78) [1979] E.C.R. 1055 [9].

[7] paras. 2.28–2.31.

[8] (133/78) [1979] E.C.R. 733 [3].

[9] para. 2.29.

[10] Bellet, (1965) 92 *Clunet* 833 at p. 851. This view is reflected in the drafting of s. 30 of the 1982 Act. S. 30 is now in force, but applicable to the courts of England and Wales and Northern Ireland only.

[11] *De Cavel* v. *De Cavel* (No. 2) (120/79) [1980] E.C.R. 731.

[12] p. 48.

ity Act 1978 or, indeed, to any residual rules of the common law relating to state or diplomatic immunities. Section 31 of the 1982 Act appears to be drafted on this assumption. It is concerned with the judgments of the courts of overseas countries ("any country or territory outside the United Kingdom")[13] against a state—other than the United Kingdom or the state to which the court belongs—and specified organs of such a state. Such a judgment is to be recognised and enforced in the United Kingdom if and only if:

> "(a) it would be so recognised and enforced if it had not been given against a state; and (b) that court [the court of origin] would have had jurisdiction in the matter if it had applied rules corresponding to those applicable to such matters in the United Kingdom in accordance with sections 2 to 11 of the State Immunity Act 1978."[14]

There is no saving for judgments to which Title III of the 1968 Convention applies.

B. CRITERION OF INTERNATIONALITY

3.05   The preamble to the 1968 Convention, as explained above,[15] indicates that the Convention is concerned only with the "international jurisdiction" of the courts of the Contracting States, but the extent to which this principle controls the detailed provisions of the Convention relating to scope is as yet unclear. It may be of some importance, for example, in connection with the interpretation of the provisions on choice of court agreements in Art. 17, to the discussion of which the reader is referred.[16]

C. NATURE OF COURT OR TRIBUNAL

3.06   Article 1 states that the Convention shall apply in civil and commercial matters "whatever the nature of the court or tribunal." What is relevant is the nature of the proceedings rather than of the court before which they are brought. The fact that, to recover the costs of removing a wreck, the Netherlands State adopted judicial proceedings in the civil courts rather than administrative procedures (as were then adopted in the other Member States) was not sufficient to bring the judicial proceedings within the scope of the Convention.[17] The fact, again, that a civil claim for damages is brought incidentally before a criminal court (for example in the context of a road accident) would not exclude any award which followed from recognition under the Convention.[18] The generality of the language of Art. 1, moreover, has the incidental effect of applying the Convention to proceedings in any court or tribunal, whatever its rank in the judicial hierarchy. No distinction, that is to say, is made between "superior" and "inferior" courts.[19]

---

[13] 1982 Act, s. 50.
[14] This provision must be read subject to s. 31(3), which excludes its application in cases where jurisdiction against States is contemplated by certain international conventions.
[15] para. 1.16.
[16] See para. 7.26(3) below.
[17] *Netherlands State* v. *Rüffer* (814/79) [1980] E.C.R. 3807.
[18] 1968 Convention, Art. 5(4) and Jenard Report, p. 9.
[19] Contrast 1933 Act, s. 1.

D. SUBJECT-MATTER OF PROCEEDINGS

(a) Civil and commercial matters

3.07   Article 1 declares that the Convention applies in "civil and commercial matters." This expression, though appearing in conventions to which the United Kingdom is a party [20] is not one familiar there. Though it is well-known within the legal systems of the original Member States, the precise field covered by "civil and commercial matters" differs slightly from system to system. [21] The question, therefore, arose whether it was to be construed simply in accordance with the law applicable in the court trying the case or in a uniform manner independent of the internal laws of the Member States. The latter solution, as we have seen, [22] was preferred by the European Court in the first *Eurocontrol* case. [23] It declared that the expression should be interpreted with reference:

> "first, to the objectives and scheme of the Convention and secondly, to the general principles which stem from the corpus of the national legal systems."

This solution was re-affirmed in the second *Eurocontrol* case, [24] where it was explained that:

> "This interpretation is based on the desire to ensure in relation to Community law that the Contracting States and parties concerned have equal and uniform rights and duties under the Brussels Convention."

3.08   How is the expression "civil and commercial matters" likely to be construed by the European Court? It assumes the existence of a distinction between public and private law central to the legal systems of the original Member States and which has practical effects within them, but which has no such effects within the legal systems of the United Kingdom. Although the boundaries between the respective domains of public law and of private law may differ even in those States which attribute legal effects to the distinction, there are two common ideas at its root, the idea that the principle of separation of powers prevents the judges in the civil courts concerning themselves with the activities of the administration and the idea that, in cases involving a conflict between the public interest and a private interest, the former has some claim to priority. [25] Over the years these ideas were translated into the principle that issues involving the public service, whether between public authorities *inter se* or between them and private persons, should be resolved *prima facie* in administrative courts applying rules of administrative law.

---

[20] *e.g.* the Hague Convention of November 15, 1965 on the Service Abroad of Judicial and Extrajudicial Documents in Civil or Commercial Matters, the Hague Convention of March 18, 1970 on the taking of evidence abroad, and the bilateral Conventions entered into by the United Kingdom under the Foreign Judgments (Reciprocal Enforcement) Act 1933. See para. 3.29 below.

[21] Schlosser Report, p. 83.

[22] para. 3.02

[23] *LTU* v. *Eurocontrol* (29/76) [1976] E.C.R. 1541 [3].

[24] *Bavaria Fluggesellschaft* v. *Germanair* (9 & 10/77) [1977] E.C.R. 1517 [5].

[25] See *inter alios* L. Neville Brown and J.F. Garner, *French Administrative Law* (3rd ed., 1983); G. Vedel, *Droit Administratif* (7th ed. 1980); de Laubadère, *Traité élémentaire de droit administratif* 3 Vols. (1975–1978); C. Turpin, "Public Contracts," in *International Encyclopedia of Comparative Law*, Vol. VII, Chap. IV, paras. 33–46.

3.09   The criteria indicative of "public service" vary from system to system, but a useful starting point is the idea that a public service consists in the activities of public authorities to fulfil public needs. The notion of "public authority" is a wide one, and is not confined to the administrative authorities of the State. It is likely to include public corporations and, in France at least, certain private organisations satisfying a public need. Even when contracting with private individuals, such bodies do so by administrative contracts subject to special principles developed in and applied by the administrative courts. The very width of these criteria and, consequently, of the scope of administrative law has tended to produce a reaction against this. It has come to be recognised that public corporations, when engaged in commercial or industrial activities, may enter into relations of a private law character with other public authorities or with private companies or individuals, especially where they act under a legal framework similar to that applying to an ordinary commercial enterprise. These relations are then governed by private law and may be the subject of proceedings in the ordinary civil courts. In some cases, indeed, the competence of the civil courts is prescribed by statute law. Thus in France the liability of a public authority to its employees for accidents sustained at work may be adjudicated, like that of private employers, in the civil courts. More recently, the same principle has been applied in France to motor-accident cases.[26]

3.10   Since the distinction between public and private law is even less clear in the legal systems of the United Kingdom, an attempt was made during the negotiations preliminary to the Accession Convention to give greater precision to the expression "civil and commercial matters" appearing in Art. 1 of the 1968 Convention. The only alteration agreed, however, was to add to that article the sentence: "It [the Convention] shall not extend, in particular, to revenue, customs or administrative matters." This addition is only of marginal assistance. Revenue and customs matters are clearly excluded, but the words "administrative matters" remain imprecise and the inclusion of the words "in particular" is a reminder that the enumeration is not intended to be exhaustive.

3.11   How has the European Court approached the problem? In the first *Eurocontrol* case[27] the Court utilised the distinction known to French law between a public authority acting "unilaterally" in the exercise of statutory powers and such an authority acting within the framework of private law obligations. Eurocontrol, an international body concerned with air traffic control, obtained in a Belgian court, a decree against LTU, a German air transport undertaking, finding that LTU should pay to it certain charges fixed by Eurocontrol itself by virtue of what were in effect statutory powers. In a reference made to it, the European Court declared that:

> "Although certain judgments given in actions between a public authority and a person governed by private law may fall within the area of application of the Convention, this is not so where the public authority acts in the exercise of its powers [as such].[28] Such is the case in a dispute which . . . concerns the recovery of charges payable by a person governed by private law to a national or international body governed by public law for the use of equipment and services provided by such body, in particular where such use is obligatory and exclusive."[29]

---

[26] Law of December 31, 1957.

[27] *LTU* v. *Eurocontrol* (29/76) [1976] E.C.R. 1541.

[28] For the inclusion of these words, see the observations of the Advocate-General (Warner) in *Netherlands State* v. *Rüffer* (814/79) [1980] E.C.R. 3807 at 3828.

[29] *LTU* v. *Eurocontrol*, above [4].

The same distinction was employed by the European Court in *Netherlands State* v. *Rüffer*[30] to exclude from the scope of the Convention proceedings for the recovery of costs incurred by a public authority in the Netherlands in the exercise of statutory powers for the removal of a wreck from a public waterway. The Court considered that it was immaterial that these costs were recoverable in Holland by an ordinary action in the civil courts.

3.12 In another case the European Court has accepted the view taken in the Jenard Report[31] that the expression "civil and commercial matters" is apt to cover proceedings, in whatever court, arising out of a contract of employment.[32] It is understood, however, that the Italian courts have taken a different view and that the Italian Supreme Court has declined in this context to comply with Art. 3 of the 1971 Protocol requiring the requesting of a ruling on issues concerning the interpretation of the Convention.[33]

(b) Matters specifically excluded

3.13 Not all civil and commercial matters fall within the scope of the Convention. Art. 1(2) provides that:

> "The Convention shall not apply to:
> (1) the status or legal capacity of natural persons, rights in property arising out of a matrimonial relationship, wills and succession;
> (2) bankruptcy, proceedings relating to the winding-up of insolvent companies or other legal persons, judicial arrangements, compositions and analogous proceedings;
> (3) social security;
> (4) arbitration."

It may be repeated that this provision applies only where the principal issue in the proceedings is an excluded matter.[34] The terms in which these exclusions are expressed are very general and the European Court has been called upon to interpret several of them. It seems best to consider them subject by subject.

(1)(a) "the status or legal capacity of natural persons"

3.14 The ambit of the phrase "proceedings concerning the status of a person" is also relevant in the context of Art. 5(2), which creates a special jurisdiction in matters relating to maintenance which are ancillary to proceedings concerning status. It has been explained above[35] that, in other issues relating to Art. 1 of the Convention, the European Court has exhibited a strong tendency to adopt a uniform or independent characterisation of the concepts used within it. It is thought that the Court would do so in relation to the meaning of status proceedings both in Art. 1 and in Art. 5(2). In relation to the latter, this is arguably implicit in the Court's ruling in the first *De Cavel* case.[36] It may be useful, therefore, to observe that the

---

[30] Above, fn. 28.

[31] p. 24.

[32] *Sanicentral* v. *Collin* (25/79) [1979] E.C.R. 3423: confirmed in *Ivenel* v. *Schwab* (133/81) [1982] E.C.R. 1891.

[33] McClellan and Kremlis, (1983) 20 C.M.L.Rev. 529 at 532.

[34] See para. 3.03 above.

[35] See paras. 2.28 and 3.03.

[36] *De Cavel* v. *De Cavel* (No. 1) (143/78) [1979] E.C.R. 1055.

concept of proceedings concerning status appears to cover a wider range of proceedings in many European legal systems than it would in Scots law.[37] In relation to Scottish proceedings it might well be held to include actions of divorce and separation, actions of declarator of marriage and of declarator of nullity of marriage, petitions for declaration of death,[38] and actions for the custody of children.[39] The Maxwell Report suggests that the concept might also cover actions for adherence and aliment and actions of affiliation and aliment, though neither of these would be regarded as proceedings concerning status in Scots law.[40] Art. 1(2)(1), on the other hand, is not designed to exclude proceedings for maintenance: any doubt on the matter is excluded by the terms of Art. 5(2). The European Court, indeed, has held that a maintenance order may be enforced under the Convention though made in proceedings—in the particular case proceedings for divorce—which were themselves excluded from the scope of the Convention.[41] The exclusion applies to proceedings relating to the status or legal capacity of individuals only: corresponding proceedings relating to legal persons are not excluded.[42] Indeed, in relation to certain classes of such proceedings an exclusive jurisdiction is specified in Art. 16(2).

(1)(b) "rights in property arising out of a matrimonial relationship"

3.15   This expression is not a term of art in English or in Scots law and its construction is not free from difficulty. The French text uses the term *"régimes matrimoniaux"* and the German text the term *"die Güterstände,"* both of which refer to rules regulating the ownership and administration of the assets of spouses during their marriage, rules which they may choose or which, failing their choice, may be imposed by the law. There is no true analogue to these rules in the legal systems of the United Kingdom, though an express marriage contract might fall within these terms.

3.16   It appears from the Schlosser Report[43] that it was not the intention of the draftsmen of the Convention to exclude from its scope rights arising between spouses in the application of the general law of contract, tort or property even if, in the system in which the right arose, special rules might apply in these fields as between spouses. It was rather their intention to exclude rights arising from the application of "legal institutions limited to the relations between spouses, and whose most important feature is a comprehensive set of rules governing property." More especially, that Report states:

> "The Convention does not apply to the assumption of jurisdiction by United Kingdom and Irish courts, nor to the recognition and enforcement of foreign judgments by those courts, if the subject-matter of the proceedings concerns

---

[37] See Maxwell Report, p. 26.

[38] *Cf.* Schlosser Report, p. 89.

[39] It is understood that these actions are generally considered to be status proceedings in European countries. This makes unimportant the somewhat arid controversy whether they are to be considered as status proceedings in Scots law. They were so described in *Radoyevitch* v. *Radoyevitch*, 1930 S.C. 619 at 624 and *Ponder* v. *Ponder*, 1932 S.C. 233 at 236, but this issue becomes of less importance following the new approach of the Scottish courts to custody jurisdiction exemplified in *Sargeant* v. *Sargeant*, 1973 S.L.T. (Notes) 27 and in *Campins* v. *Campins*, 1979 S.L.T. (Notes) 41.

[40] They are assimilated to patrimonial actions for the purposes of Sched. 8 to the 1982 Act.

[41] See *De Cavel* v. *De Cavel* (No. 2) (120/79) [1980] E.C.R. 731.

[42] See Jenard Report, p.11.

[43] pp. 87–88.

issues which have arisen between spouses, or exceptionally between a spouse and a third party, during or after the dissolution of the marriage, and which affect rights in property arising out of the matrimonial relationship. The expression 'rights in property' includes all rights of administration and disposal—whether by marriage contract or by statute—of property belonging to the spouses."[44]

.17 Here reference may be made to the decision of the European Court in the *De Cavel* (No.1) case[45]: A husband had instituted in a French court proceedings for divorce against his wife and, alleging collaterally that his wife had removed from his flat in Frankfurt valuables belonging to him, applied in these proceedings for protective measures. He obtained an order from the French court which he sought to have enforced in Germany under the 1968 Convention. For the wife it was argued that the Convention did not apply. In the course of a reference to it the European Court declared:

> "The enforced settlement on a provisional basis of proprietary legal rela-tionships between spouses in the course of proceedings for divorce is closely linked to the grounds for the divorce and the personal situation of the spouses or any children of the marriage and is, for that reason, inseparable from questions relating to the status of persons raised by the dissolution of the matrimonial relationship and from the settlement of rights in property arising out of the matrimonial relationship. Consequently, the term 'rights in property arising out of a matrimonial relationship' includes not only property arrange-ments specifically and exclusively envisaged by certain national legal systems in the case of marriage, but also any proprietary relationships resulting directly from the matrimonial relationship or the dissolution thereof.[46] Disputes relat-ing to the assets of the spouses in the course of proceedings for divorce may, therefore, depending on the circumstances, concern or be closely connected with:
> (1) questions relating to the status of persons; or
> (2) proprietary legal relationships between spouses resulting directly from the matrimonial relationship or the dissolution thereof; or
> (3) proprietary legal relations existing between them which have no connec-tion with the marriage.
> Whereas disputes of the latter category fall within the scope of the Conven-tion, those relating to the first two categories must be excluded therefrom."[47]

This ruling presents considerable problems both of interpretation and of application. In disputes relating to the assets of spouses it is not clear what cases would be covered by category (1) which would not at the same time fall within category (2). The distinction between categories (2) and (3) is, superficially at least, easy to understand but will be difficult to apply in practice. The court of origin will not itself necessarily require to make such a distinction and the basis on which it has decided particular claims will not necessarily appear in its judgment. The court, therefore, to which an application for enforcement is made may require to investigate the finan-cial arrangements of the spouses during the course of the marriage which, as the Advocate-General (Warner) pointed out, is inappropriate in the course of a summary application for enforcement.

---

[44] p. 89, para. 50.
[45] *De Cavel* v. *De Cavel* (No. 1) (143/78) [1979] E.C.R. 1055.
[46] These last words were repeated by the Court in *C.H.W.* v. *G.J.H.* (25/81) [1982] E.C.R. 1189 [6].
[47] *De Cavel* v. *De Cavel* (No. 1), above [7].

3.18   Proposition (2) above was confirmed in *C.H.W.* v. *G.J.H.*[48] The European Court, after referring to the fact that provisional measures under Art. 24 are available only where the courts of another Contracting State have jurisdiction as to the substance, declared that provisional measures designed to obtain delivery of a document to prevent it being used as evidence in an action by a wife concerning her husband's management of her property did not "fall within the scope of the Convention if such management is closely connected with the proprietary relationship resulting directly from the marriage bond."

(1)(c) "wills and succession"

3.19   The expression "wills and succession" is extremely general and the European Court has not yet been called upon to elucidate its meaning. In view, however, of its tendency to give an independent meaning to the provisions defining the scope of the Convention, it seems likely that it will do so also in the present context. The expression almost certainly excludes all questions relating to the administration of the estates of deceased persons, relating to the validity and interpretation of wills, or relating to prior rights and rights to succeed on intestacy. In relation to trusts created by a will, the following view is expressed in the Schlosser Report:[49]

> "The expression 'wills and succession' covers all claims to testate or intestate succession to an estate. It includes disputes as to the validity or interpretation of the terms of a will setting up a trust, even where the trust takes effect on a date subsequent to the death of the testator. The same applies to proceedings in respect of the application and interpretation of statutory provisions establishing trusts in favour of persons or institutions as a result of a person dying intestate. The 1968 Convention does not, therefore, apply to any disputes concerning the creation, interpretation and administration of trusts arising under the law of succession including wills. On the other hand, disputes concerning the relations of the trustee with persons other than beneficiaries, in other words the 'external relations'of the trust, come within the scope of the 1968 Convention."[50]

(2) Bankruptcy and similar proceedings

3.20   It appears from the Schlosser Report[51] that the terms in which bankruptcy and other similar proceedings were excluded from the scope of the Convention were intended to dovetail into the field of application of the proposed European Bankruptcy Convention. Annex 1 to the Schlosser Report[52] contains a list of the proceedings which at the relevant time were envisaged as coming within the scope of the Bankruptcy Convention. The Commission Working Group on the Bankruptcy Convention began a second reading of the text in April 1983, but it remains unclear whether and, if so, when this Convention is likely to come into force. It would seem, therefore, for the present at least, that Art. 1(2)(2) of the Convention falls to be interpreted without reference to the text of the proposed European Bankruptcy Convention. The specific reference in the English text to "the winding-up of insolvent companies or other legal persons" indicates that

---

[48] (24/81) [1982] E.C.R. 1189 [9].
[49] p. 89, para. 52.
[50] See also the discussion of jurisdiction in trusts at paras. 5.55–5.56 below.
[51] p. 90.
[52] p. 145.

it was not intended to exclude proceedings relating to a voluntary winding-up under the Companies Act 1948 nor, it is thought,[53] to a winding-up subject to the supervision of the Court.

.21 In the case of *Gourdain* v. *Nadler*[54] the European Court, after stressing the desirability of a uniform interpretation of Art. 1, concluded that an order by a French court that the German manager of an insolvent French company should contribute to the assets of that company available for division, was derived from the law relating to bankruptcy and winding-up for the purposes of the Convention. The Court, however, remarked that: "it is necessary, if decisions relating to bankruptcy and winding-up are to be excluded from the scope of the Convention, that they must derive directly from the bankruptcy or winding-up."

(3) Social security

.22 The exclusion of social security springs from the fact that in some Member States social security matters were regarded as coming within the sphere of public law while in others as being upon the border line between public and private law. This exclusion, however, is possibly to be interpreted narrowly since the Schlosser Report[55] suggests that legal proceedings by social security authorities against third parties, in the exercise of rights acquired by subrogation or operation of the law, do come within the scope of the Convention.

(4) Arbitration

.23 Article 1(2)(4) baldly states that the Convention shall not apply to arbitration. This exclusion seems surprising in view of the terms of Art. 220 of the Treaty of Rome.[56] The draftsmen of the 1968 Convention were concerned, however, about the possible overlap between it and other international agreements in this field, including the 1923 and 1927 Geneva Conventions and Protocols and the Convention of 1958 on the Recognition and Enforcement of Foreign Arbitral Awards (the New York Convention), to the latter of which the United Kingdom is a party.[57]

.24 But the precise scope of this exclusion is not clear. As the Jenard Report suggests,[58] it probably means that the 1968 Convention does not apply for the purpose of determining the jurisdiction of courts in respect of proceedings relating to arbitration (*e.g.* proceedings to set aside an arbitral award), to the recognition of judgments given in such proceedings, nor to the recognition and enforcement of arbitral awards. This explanation is amplified in the Schlosser Report which states[59]:

> "The 1968 Convention does not cover court proceedings which are ancillary to arbitration proceedings, for example the appointment or dismissal of arbitrators, the fixing of the place of arbitration, the extension of the time limit for

---

[53] Schlosser Report, p. 91.

[54] (133/78) [1979] E.C.R. 733 [4].

[55] p. 92, and see Bellet, (1965) 92 *Clunet* 833 at 851.

[56] By it Member States are required to enter into negotiations with a view to "the simplification of formalities governing the reciprocal recognition and enforcement of judgments of courts or tribunals and of arbitration awards."

[57] Implemented by Arbitration Act 1975.

[58] p. 13.

[59] p. 93, paras. 64 and 65. On the authority of the Jenard and Schlosser Reports, see para. 2.18 above.

making awards or the obtaining of a preliminary ruling on questions of substance as provided for under English law in the procedure known as ' statement of a special case' (section 21 of the Arbitration Act 1950). In the same
way a judgment determining whether an arbitration agreement is valid or not,
or because it is invalid, ordering the parties not to continue the arbitration
proceedings, is not covered by the 1968 Convention. Nor does the 1968
Convention cover proceedings and decisions concerning applications for the
revocation, amendment, recognition and enforcement of arbitration awards.
This also applies to court decisions incorporating arbitration awards—a
common method of recognition in United Kingdom law. If an arbitration
award is revoked and the revoking court or another national court itself
decides the subject-matter in dispute, the 1968 Convention is applicable."

3.25   There is nothing, however, in the 1968 Convention analogous to section
4(3)(*b*) of the 1933 Act, which provides that, unless the judgment debtor
acquiesced in the original proceedings, the jurisdiction of the court of
origin shall not be recognised if the bringing of the proceedings in that
court "was contrary to an agreement under which the dispute in question
was to be settled otherwise than by proceedings in the courts of the country
of that court." The Schlosser Report[60] indicates that the Council Working
Party were divided on the question whether it could be inferred from the
exclusion of arbitration from the scope of the Convention that a judgment
emanating from a Contracting State could be denied recognition on the
ground that it overlooked the existence of a valid arbitration agreement
between the parties or held (wrongly) that the arbitration agreement was
invalid. An affirmative answer would be consistent with the principle that
Art. 1 "governs the whole of the Convention"[61] but this question must
remain an open one until the European Court pronounces on the matter.

3.26   It is possible, however, that reliance could be placed upon Art. 57 of the
1968 Convention which preserves the effect of other conventions on particular matters which govern jurisdiction and the enforcement of judgments.
Most[62] of the EEC Member States, including the United Kingdom, are
parties to the New York Convention. Article II of this Convention provides:

> "Each Contracting State shall recognise an agreement in writing under
> which the parties undertake to submit to arbitration all or any differences
> which have arisen or which may arise between them in respect of a defined
> legal relationship, whether contractual or not, concerning a subject-matter
> capable of settlement by arbitration."

Whether relying on the view that the New York Convention is a convention on a particular matter[63] whose operation is preserved by Art. 57 of the
1968 Convention or relying upon the generality of its Art. 1, Parliament
has tackled the problem presented by the failure of a foreign court to
observe the terms of an arbitration agreement in the context of a more
general provision. Under section 32 of the 1982 Act[64] a judgment given by
a court of an overseas country in any proceedings is not to be recognised or

---

[60] pp. 92 and 93.
[61] Jenard Report, p. 42.
[62] At the time of the publication of the Schlosser Report (March 5, 1979) only Luxembourg
and Ireland were not parties to the New York Convention.
[63] See paras. 3.27 and 3.31–3.36 below.
[64] s. 32 came into force on August 24, 1982. See also para. 11.08 below.

enforced in the United Kingdom if the bringing of those proceedings was contrary to an agreement under which the dispute in question was to be settled otherwise than by proceedings in the courts of that (foreign) country.[65] Exceptions are provided, mainly catering for cases where the person against whom the judgment was given was personally barred, for example by submission, from contesting it. This provision is extremely general in its operation, and applies *inter alia* to judgments given in breach of arbitration agreements.[66] Section 32, however, excludes from its operation "a judgment which is required to be recognised or enforced in the United Kingdom under the 1968 Convention." This caters for the possibility that the European Court might hold that the State addressed has no right to review an assumption of jurisdiction by the court of origin contrary to the terms of an arbitration agreement.

E. MATTERS COVERED IN OTHER CONVENTIONS

(a) Introduction

.27   In relation to other international conventions Title VII of the 1968 Convention adopts two different approaches. The 1968 Convention, in matters within its scope, is intended to be an exhaustive specification of the cases where a person domiciled in a Contracting State may be sued in another Contracting State and of the rules, as between the Contracting States, for the mutual recognition and enforcement of judgments. The 1968 Convention, therefore, supersedes, in these matters and as between the parties to it, other conventions regulating *generally* questions of jurisdiction and the enforcement of judgments—"general" conventions.[67]

.28   The parties to the 1968 Convention at the same time were parties to a variety of international agreements *on particular matters* which might specify rules of jurisdiction and/or rules for the recognition and enforcement of judgments in relation to these matters. In so far as these "special" conventions[68] contain rules relating to jurisdiction—as do the Warsaw Convention on international carriage by air and the Brussels Convention relating to the arrest of sea-going ships—their rules, while possibly appropriate to their subject-matter, may differ considerably from those adopted by the 1968 Convention. In so far as those "special" conventions contain rules concerning the recognition and enforcement of judgments—as does the Hague Convention of April 15, 1958 on the recognition and enforcement of decisions relating to maintenance obligations towards children— these rules are likely to specify restrictions upon recognition and enforcement (including jurisdictional conditions) which go beyond the very limited grounds for non-recognition contained in the 1968 Convention. Being bound by such "special" conventions, often on a multilateral basis involving non-Member States, the draftsmen of the 1968 Convention had little alternative but to allow these conventions to remain in operation in relation to the particular matters to which they apply, thus, in effect, allowing them to prevail over the 1968 Convention.

---

[65] s. 32(1)(*a*). s. 54 and Sched. 14 to the 1982 Act repeal s. 4(3)(*b*) of the 1933 Act.
[66] *Tracomin S.A.* v. *Sudan Oil Seeds Co. Ltd.* [1983] 1 W.L.R. 662 at 670.
[67] Art. 55.
[68] These conventions are referred to in para. 3.35 below.

(b) The "general" conventions

3.29   Article 55 lists the general conventions which are superseded by the 1968 Convention as between the parties to them and in relation to matters governed by the 1968 Convention. These conventions include the bilateral reciprocal enforcement conventions entered into between the United Kingdom and France, Belgium, Germany, Italy and the Netherlands in terms of the Foreign Judgments (Reciprocal Enforcement) Act 1933.[69] These conventions, however, in terms of Art. 56 continue to have effect in relation to judgments given before the entry into force of the 1968 Convention and to judgments to which the 1968 Convention does not apply. The conventions, for example, with Belgium and Italy do not have subject-matter restrictions like those in Art. 1 of the 1968 Convention. The absence, however, of these exclusions is not always material, since under all the bilateral conventions enforcement is restricted to money judgments. The same restriction does not apply to *recognition* under those conventions, but it is still a matter of controversy what judgments are entitled to recognition under section 8 of the 1933 Act.[70]

3.30   Article 56 was applied in the second *Eurocontrol* case.[71] *Eurocontrol* had obtained a judgment against the petitioners in Belgium and sought to enforce it in Germany in reliance upon the Convention of June 30, 1958 between Germany and Belgium on the Mutual Recognition and Enforcement of Judgments, Arbitration Awards, and Authentic Instruments. The European Court ruled that it was entitled to do so and that the interpretation of the scope of the latter Convention must be a matter for the national courts only. This would be true even of concepts which are common to the two Conventions, such as that of "civil and commercial matters."

(c) Conventions on particular matters

3.31   To give effect to the policy described above with respect to conventions on particular matters, Art. 57(1) initially provided only that:

> "This Convention shall not affect any Conventions to which the Contracting States are or will be parties and which, in relation to particular matters, govern jurisdiction or the recognition and enforcement of judgments."

This provision, standing by itself, was unclear. It was not obvious whether the jurisdictional provisions of a special convention to which an EEC Member State is a party override or are subordinate to the jurisdictional provisions of the 1968 Convention in relation to the domiciliaries of Member States which are not parties to the special convention. Nor was it apparent, for example, when such a convention contains provisions for jurisdiction but not provisions for the recognition and enforcement of judgments, whether the provisions for recognition and enforcement contained in the 1968 Convention might be invoked in relation to a judgment of a

---

[69] S.R. & O. 1936 No. 609 (France); S.R. & O. 1936 No. 1169 (Belgium); S.I. 1961 No. 1199 (German F.R.); S.I. 1973 No. 1894 (Italy); and S.I. 1969 No. 1063, as amended by S.I. 1977 No. 2149 (The Netherlands).

[70] Dicey, p. 1075: Foreign Judgments (Reciprocal Enforcement) Committee, Cmd. 4213 (1932), para. 4; *Black-Clawson International Ltd.* v. *Papierwerke Waldhof-Aschaffenburg A.G.* [1975] A.C. 591, *per* Lord Reid at 617; *Vervaeke* v. *Smith* [1981] 1 All E.R. 55 and [1983] A.C. 145, *per* Lord Diplock at 159.

[71] *Bavaria Fluggesellschaft and Germanair* v. *Eurocontrol* (9 & 10/77) [1977] E.C.R. 1517.

Member State proceeding on a ground of jurisdiction contained in the special Convention.

.32   In an effort, therefore, to clarify the sense of Art. 57(1), the 1978 Accession Convention provides in Art. 25(2) that:

> "With a view to its uniform interpretation, paragraph 1 of Article 57 shall be applied in the following manner:
> (a) The 1968 Convention as amended shall not prevent a court of a Contracting State which is a party to a convention on a particular matter from assuming jurisdiction in accordance with that convention, even where the defendant is domiciled in another Contracting State which is not a party to that convention. The court shall, in any event, apply Article 20 of the 1968 Convention as amended.
> (b) A judgment given in a Contracting State in the exercise of jurisdiction provided for in a convention on a particular matter shall be recognised and enforced in the other Contracting States in accordance with the 1968 Convention as amended.
> Where a convention on a particular matter to which both the State of origin and the State addressed are parties lays down conditions for the recognition or enforcement of judgments, those conditions shall apply. In any event, the provisions of the 1968 Convention as amended which concern the procedures for recognition and enforcement of judgments may be applied."

33   Discovering the field of application of Art. 57 presents peculiar difficulties for United Kingdom lawyers. When a convention has been implemented in the United Kingdom by scheduling its text to an Act (as, for example, in the Carriage by Air Act 1971), the problem is merely that of recalling the existence of the Act. The problem becomes more serious, however, where a convention has been implemented indirectly by provisions in statute law or in statutory instruments to a similar effect. These do not necessarily make any allusion to the treaty obligations to which they relate. It may be, too that, in the decision whether or not to ratify a convention, reliance was placed on the common law as well as upon statutory provisions. It is not necessarily apparent, therefore, from the statute book that an Act or any provision of an Act was designed to implement an international obligation.

.34   The 1982 Act does not list the conventions or the legislative provisions which have potential relevance in the context of Art. 57, presumably because it would have been difficult to ensure its completeness and impossible to ensure that it remained up-to-date. The 1982 Act assumes that the relevant conventions may be ascertained and deals with the problems presented by the fact that the convention itself may not have become law in the United Kingdom by providing in section 9(1) that the relevant provisions of the 1968 Convention "shall have effect in relation to—(a) any statutory provision, whenever passed or made, implementing any such other convention in the United Kingdom; and (b) any rule of law so far as it has the effect of so implementing any such other convention, as they have effect in relation to that other convention itself."

.35   It would be rash to do more than indicate in general terms the matters which are thought to be excluded from the scope of the 1968 Convention by the combined effect of Art. 57 and the conventions to which it refers. Most matters relating to shipping and to the international transport of persons and goods will fall to be governed directly or indirectly by particular conventions rather than by the 1968 Convention. This result is implicitly recognised in the specific exclusion[72] of contracts of transport from Title II, Section 4 of the Convention, dealing with jurisdiction over consumer contracts. Though the remaining provisions of the Convention in principle apply, they will often be superseded by the existence of rules derived from other conventions. Among those to which the Schlosser Report[73] alludes, and to which the United Kingdom is a party, in the general field of transport are the following:

(1) The Warsaw Convention for the unification of certain rules relating to international carriage by air, signed on October 12, 1929.[74]

(2) The Guadalajara Convention, supplementary to the Warsaw Convention, for the unification of certain rules relating to international carriage by air performed by a person other than a contracting carrier.[75]

(3) The Brussels Convention for the unification of certain rules concerning civil jurisdiction in matters of collision signed on May 10, 1952.[76]

(4) The Brussels Convention for the unification of certain rules relating to the arrest of sea-going ships signed on May 10, 1952.[77]

(5) The Berne Convention concerning the carriage of goods by rail (CIM) and annexes, signed on October 25, 1952, and the Convention replacing it signed at Berne on February 25, 1961.[78]

(6) The Berne Convention concerning the carriage of passengers and luggage by rail (CIV) and annexes signed on February 25, 1961.[79]

(7) The Geneva Convention on the contract for the international carriage of goods by road (CMR) and Protocol signed on May 19, 1956.[80]

3.36   In addition to these conventions concerned with the international carriage of persons and goods, other conventions of a miscellaneous character may contain special rules relating to jurisdiction and/or the recognition and enforcement of judgments. These include:

(1) The Paris Convention on third-party liability in the field of nuclear energy signed on July 29, 1960, together with an additional Protocol signed at Paris on January 28, 1964, a Supplementary Convention signed at Brussels on July 29, 1960, an Annex signed at Brussels on January 31, 1963, and an additional Protocol to the Supplementary Convention signed at Paris on February 28, 1964.[81]

(2) The Brussels Convention on civil liability for oil pollution damage signed on November 29, 1969.[82]

(3) The Convention supplementary to the Convention of November 29,

---

[72] Art. 13(3).

[73] p. 150.

[74] This must be read with a supplementary Convention and with various Protocols. The Carriage by Air Act 1961, Sched. 1, Art. 28(1) gives effect to a jurisdictional rule in the 1929 Convention.

[75] Effect is given to this by the Carriage by Air (Supplementary Provisions) Act 1962. The Convention, which is scheduled to the Act, contains in Art. VIII a choice of jurisdiction clause.

[76] See Administration of Justice Act 1956, Pts. I and V.

[77] Also given effect to in Pts. I and V of the 1956 Act.

[78] See Carriage by Railway Act 1972, s. 6(1) and Sched., Art. 15.

[79] This Convention was supplemented by an additional Convention relating to the liability for the death of and personal injury to passengers signed at Berne on February 26, 1966, both of which are given effect to within the United Kingdom, so far as legislation is required, by the Carriage by Railway Act 1972.

[80] See Carriage of Goods by Road Act 1965, Sched., Art. 31(1).

[81] See Nuclear Installations Acts 1965 and 1969.

[82] See Merchant Shipping (Oil Pollution) Act 1971, s. 13.

1969 on the establishment of an international fund for oil pollution damage signed on December 18, 1971.[83]

F. CONVENTIONS UNDER ARTICLE 59

.37   The combined effect of Arts. 4 and 28 of the Convention, as explained above,[84] is to require the recognition and enforcement throughout all the Contracting States of judgments against the domiciliaries of other States even when these judgments proceeded upon a basis of jurisdiction unavailable against the domiciliaries of the Contracting States in terms of Art. 3 of the Convention, such as, in France, the nationality of the pursuer or, in Germany, the presence of property there belonging to the defender. This means, in practical terms, that a non-EEC domiciliary cannot ignore proceedings in an EEC country based on an "exorbitant" ground of jurisdiction on the view that he has no assets or few assets in that country if he has assets in any other EEC countries. Since the judgment following those proceedings may be enforced in those countries, all his assets within the EEC are at risk.

.38   While the United Kingdom still remained outside the EEC, its officials in the context of the discussions on the draft Hague Convention on Recognition and Enforcement sought to persuade the representatives of the original Member States that the approach adopted in the then current draft of the proposed EEC Judgments Convention was unacceptable and might well prevent the conclusion by EEC States of bilateral judgments conventions with non-EEC States or even occasion the denunciation of existing bilateral conventions. Expressions of concern in still stronger terms were made by representatives of the United States.[85]

.39   The response of the representatives of the EEC States was to indicate that they were prepared to introduce into the proposed Convention a formula, now embodied in the first paragraph of Art. 59, to the effect that:

> "This Convention shall not prevent a Contracting State from assuming, in a convention on the recognition and enforcement of judgments, an obligation towards a third State not to recognise judgments given in other Contracting States against defendants domiciled or habitually resident in the third State where, in cases provided for in Article 4, the judgment could only be founded on a ground of jurisdiction specified in the second paragraph of Article 3."

The 1978 Accession Convention, however, further limited the powers of Contracting States to exclude the operation of the 1968 Convention by providing that their obligations to a third State could not include an obligation not to recognise a judgment given in another Contracting State by a court which based its jurisdiction on the presence or seizure of property:

> "(1) if the action is brought to assert or declare proprietary or possessory rights in that property, seeks to obtain authority to dispose of it, or arises from another issue relating to such property, or, (2) if the property constitutes the security for a debt which is the subject-matter of the action."

---

[83] See Merchant Shipping Act 1974, s. 6.
[84] para. 1.26.
[85] See also para. 1.26 above.

3.40   No Conventions under Art. 59 have as yet been concluded, although negotiations have taken place with the United States (since broken off) and with Australia and Canada. If and when such Conventions are concluded, section 9(2) of the 1982 Act provides that:

> "Her Majesty may by Order in Council declare a provision of a convention entered into by the United Kingdom to be a provision whereby the United Kingdom assumed an obligation of a kind provided for in Article 59."

G. PROVISIONS IN EUROPEAN COMMUNITY INSTRUMENTS

3.41   Article 57(2) of the 1968 Convention provides that:

> "This Convention shall not affect the application of provisions which, in relation to particular matters, govern jurisdiction or the recognition or enforcement of judgments and which are or will be contained in acts of the Institutions of the European Communities or in national laws harmonised in implementation of such acts."

The EEC Treaty does not clothe the institutions of the Community with any general powers to lay down rules governing the jurisdiction of the courts of Member States or the recognition and enforcement of their judgments. It is understood, however, that it is the view of the legal service of the EEC Commission that Community institutions may have the power in the context of a directive or regulation on a particular matter to supplement its substantive provisions with rules on jurisdiction or the enforcement of judgments. Art. 57(2), therefore, clarifies the relationship between any such rules and the rules in the 1968 Convention. It is not known whether any such rules on particular matters at present exist.

TERRITORIAL APPLICATION

3.42   The basic principle, which is subject to modifications discussed later, is that the 1968 Convention applies to the European territories of the Contracting States,[86] and the same principle is applied in the 1971 Protocol,[87] and in the 1978 Accession Convention.[88] The original parties to the 1968 Convention were Belgium, the Federal Republic of Germany, France, Italy, Luxembourg and the Netherlands. The signatories of the 1978 Accession Convention were the parties to the 1968 Convention together with Denmark, Ireland and the United Kingdom. The 1982 Accession Convention envisages that Greece should become a party to the earlier Conventions and the 1971 Protocol.

3.43   The United Kingdom includes Northern Ireland, but it does not include the Channel Islands, the Isle of Man, Gibraltar or the Sovereign Base Areas of Akrotiri and Dhekelia. Art. 60, therefore, of the 1968 Convention (as amended) provides that the Convention shall not apply to:

---

[86] Art. 60(1).
[87] Art. 6.
[88] Art. 27.

"any European territory situated outside the United Kingdom for the international relations of which the United Kingdom is responsible, unless the United Kingdom makes a declaration to the contrary in respect of any such territory."

Section 52(2) of the 1982 Act empowers the Crown by Order in Council to direct that all or any provisions of that Act shall extend to these territories.

.44　　　Such declarations, however, would not suffice to regulate, as between the United Kingdom and any of these territories, the jurisdiction of their courts and the mutual recognition and enforcement of judgments. Section 39 of the 1982 Act empowers the Crown by Order in Council to make provisions for this purpose corresponding, with such modifications as may seem appropriate, to the provisions of the 1968 Convention. The modifications which would be required are likely to correspond with the "adjustments" referred to in paragraph 252 of the Schlosser Report.[89]

.45　　　Article 60 of the Convention extends it to Greenland, to the French overseas departments and territories, and to Mayotte. Greenland has now left the European Communities and provision for the disapplication to it of the 1968 Convention will no doubt be made. Art. 60 also empowers the Netherlands and the Kingdom of Denmark to make declarations applying the 1968 Convention respectively to the Netherlands Antilles, and to the Faroes.

.46　　　Proceedings brought on appeal to courts in the Contracting States from the courts of their overseas territories are deemed by Art. 60 to be proceedings taking place in the last-mentioned courts.

TEMPORAL APPLICATION

.47　　　Article 62 of the 1968 Convention provides:

> "This Convention shall enter into force on the first day of the third month following the deposit of the instrument of ratification by the last signatory State to take this step."

The 1968 Convention entered into force as between the original Contracting States on February 1, 1973.

.48　　　Article 39 of the 1978 Accession Convention declares:

> "This Convention shall enter into force, as between the States which shall have ratified it, on the first day of the third month following the deposit of the last instrument of ratification by the original Member States of the Community and one new Member State.
>
> It shall enter into force for each new Member State which subsequently ratifies it on the first day of the third month following the deposit of its instrument of ratification."

Similar provision is made in the 1982 Accession Convention,[90] but it is related to the Hellenic Republic and those States which have put into force the 1978 Convention.

.49　　　The effect of the transitional provisions of the 1968 Convention in its original form were usefully summarised in the Jenard Report:[91]

---

[89] p. 143.
[90] Art. 15.
[91] p. 58.

(1) The Convention does not apply if the proceedings were commenced and the judgment given before the entry into force of the Convention.

(2) The Convention applies to proceedings which are instituted—and in which, therefore, judgment is given—after the entry into force of the Convention.

(3) Subject to certain conditions, the Convention also applies to judgments given after its entry into force in proceedings instituted before its entry into force.

3.50   Proposition (1) does not call for comment other than to say that it will be equally applicable in the context of the 1978 and 1982 Accession Conventions.[92] The two remaining propositions are less simple than might at first sight appear. Proposition (2) restates Art. 54(1) of the 1968 Convention, which declares:

> "The provisions of this Convention shall apply only to legal proceedings instituted and to documents formally drawn up or registered as authentic instruments after its entry into force."

This provision is in consonance with the general principle that enforcement treaties have no retroactive effect, so as not to disturb the antecedent legal relationships of the persons concerned.[93] In *Sanicentral* v. *Collin*,[94] however, a contract of employment between an employee resident in France and the German company which employed him to work in Germany contained a provision prorogating the jurisdiction of a German court. The question arose whether this provision could be founded upon by the company to exclude the jurisdiction of a French court in proceedings by the employee against his employer. The contract of employment had been concluded before the Convention came into force, and the employee argued that, since the prorogation provision was void by French law at the time the contract was made, the prorogation agreement remained void. The employer, on the other hand, argued that since the proceedings had been instituted after the Convention entered into force, the court must apply Art. 17 which validated the prorogation agreement. This view was upheld by the European Court. It explained:

> "By its nature a clause in writing conferring jurisdiction and occurring in a contract of employment is a choice of jurisdiction; such a choice has no legal effect for so long as no judicial proceedings have been commenced and only becomes of consequence at the date when the judicial proceedings are set in motion. That is therefore the relevant date for the purposes of an appreciation of the scope of such a clause in relation to the legal rules applying at that time."[95]

The Court, therefore, answered the question submitted to it as follows:

> "Arts. 17 and 54 of the Convention . . . must be interpreted to mean that, in judicial proceedings instituted after the coming into force of the Convention, clauses conferring jurisdiction included in contracts of employment concluded prior to that date must be considered valid even in cases in which they would have been regarded as void under the national law in force at the time when the contract was entered into."[96]

---

[92] See 1978 Convention, Art. 34(1) and 1982 Convention, Art. 12(1).

[93] Jenard Report, p. 57, start of commentary on Art. 54.

[94] (25/79) [1979] E.C.R. 3423.

[95] *Sanicentral* v. *Collin* (25/79) [1979] E.C.R. 3423 [6].

[96] *Ibid.*, p. 3431.

It will be observed that the Court has been careful to confine its answer to *contracts of employment*, but the ratio on which it proceeded would appear to extend to prorogation provisions in any contract. It also appears to confine itself to utilising the ratio to support the *validity* of a prorogation agreement. The same reasoning, however, would appear to apply when the effect of Art. 17 (or, indeed, of Arts. 12 and 15) would be to retrospectively invalidate the prorogation agreement. The consequences, however, seem startling.

3.51   Proposition 3 above is a summary of the effect of Art. 54(2) of the 1968 Convention, which provides:

> "However, judgments given after the date of entry into force of this Convention in proceedings instituted before that date shall be recognised and enforced in accordance with the provisions of Title III if jurisdiction was founded upon rules which accorded with those provided for either in Title II of this Convention or in a convention concluded between the State of origin and the State addressed which was in force when the proceedings were instituted."

This provision was apparently introduced because, if Art. 54(1) had stood alone, it would have excluded for a considerable period the application of the provisions of the Convention for the recognition and enforcement of judgments to judgments issued in proceedings which had commenced before the Convention entered into force but had only been concluded after that date. A similar provision, adapted to the accession to the 1968 Convention of Denmark, Ireland and the United Kingdom, is contained in Art. 34(3) of the 1978 Accession Convention and in Art. 12(2) of the 1982 Accession Convention. It will be noticed, however, that the bilateral Conventions entered into between the United Kingdom and Member States of the Community do not contain rules for the assumption of jurisdiction.

CHAPTER 4

DOMICILE AND SEAT UNDER
CONVENTION AND 1982 ACT

INTRODUCTION

4.01   THE 1968 Convention, as already explained, gives primacy to the concept of domicile as a criterion of international jurisdictional competence. Art. 2 states positively that if a person is domiciled in a Contracting State he must in general be sued in the courts of that State. The reference to the courts of the State of the person's domicile rather than to those of the *place* of his domicile indicates that it is for the law of the State of the domicile to specify what rules of jurisdiction—which need not necessarily themselves utilise the concept of domicile—will be applied to its own domiciliaries. Art. 3 states negatively that if a person is domiciled in a Contracting State he cannot be sued in another Contracting State unless the courts of that State are competent under the special jurisdictional rules set out in Sections 2 to 6 and 9 of Title II of the Convention.

4.02   These rules are supplemented by Art. 4 which, in effect, states that if a person is not domiciled in a Contracting State, he may be sued in any Contracting State on the basis of any rules of jurisdiction available in that State, including rules which might otherwise be regarded as exorbitant. Art. 4 refers to one exception only. The exclusive jurisdictions specified by Art. 16 are applicable whatever the domicile of the defender. Another exception, however, arises where parties, none of whom is domiciled in a Contracting State, have entered into a prorogation agreement valid under Art. 17.

4.03   Although, therefore, the concept of domicile is central to the scheme of jurisdiction in the 1968 Convention, it is not defined in it. Instead, Title V sets out choice of law rules indicating which legal system is to be applied to ascertain the domicile of individuals, of corporations and associations, and of trusts. It may be convenient to consider, apart from the case of trusts, what these choice of law rules are and, where they point to the law of the United Kingdom, to consider how the domicile of each of these entities is to be ascertained under the 1982 Act.

4.04   This chapter does not deal with the "domicile" of trusts. Although it is assumed in Arts. 5(6) and 53(2) of the Convention that trusts may have a domicile, trusts are not legal persons for the purposes of Arts. 2 and 53(1) of the Convention[1] and, consequently, *trusts as such* do not fall under the general jurisdiction available against persons domiciled in a Contracting State in terms of Art. 2(1) of the Convention. The domicile of a trust is used as a connecting factor only in the context of the special jurisdiction in Art. 5(6) which was added by the Accession Convention. The discussion of the domicile of a trust, therefore, is deferred until that provision is examined.[2]

---

[1] See Schlosser Report, p. 106.
[2] See para. 5.52 below.

4.05   Nor does this chapter deal with the "deemed domicile" of persons within a Contracting State for the purposes of Sections 3 and 4 of Title II of the Convention (insurance and consumer contracts) by virtue of their possessing a branch, agency or other establishment in that State.[3] This matter is considered in the context of these Sections of the Convention.[4]

DOMICILE OF INDIVIDUALS UNDER THE CONVENTION

4.06   The draftsmen of the 1968 Convention were confronted with the fact that, although domicile or a close analogue to it was adopted in the codes of the original Member States as the principal criterion of jurisdiction over individuals,[5] different definitions of the concept were adopted in those States. Government replies to a questionnaire prepared by the Council of Europe[6] indicate that, while in some of the original Member States of the EEC emphasis is placed upon the existence of a principal establishment or abode, in the others the concept points to the principal centre of a person's affairs. The replies also disclose differences in the approach of those States to domiciles of dependence (*e.g.* in relation to married women and children), to the attribution of a domicile to persons on government service, to the possibility of having by election a special domicile for special purposes, and to the possibility of having more than one domicile. It also appears that, in contrast with the position in United Kingdom systems of private international law, where an individual's domicile in the traditional sense is taken to refer to a territory with a single system of law, in Germany domicile refers to a particular place, whether a town or district or a part of a town or district. In Belgium, France and Luxembourg, on the other hand, domicile is understood to refer to a person's precise address.[7]

4.07   Having regard to the fact of this diversity of approach and to the fact that the incorporation into the Convention of a special definition of domicile would have added to this diversity at an international level, the draftsmen of the Convention decided merely to state choice of law rules specifying what law is to be applied to determine the domicile of an individual.[8] Art. 52 provides that the courts of a Contracting State shall apply:

(1) to determine whether an individual[9] is domiciled in the territory of that State, the law of that State[10];

(2) to determine whether an individual is domiciled in another Contracting State, the law of that State[11]; and

(3) to determine the domicile of an individual under whose national law

---

[3] See Art. 8, para. 2 (insurance contracts) and Art. 13, para. 2 (consumer contracts).
[4] See paras. 6.10, 6.11, 6.30 and 6.31 below.
[5] Jenard Report, p. 15.
[6] Replies made by Governments of Member States of the Council of Europe to the questionnaire on "Residence" and "Domicile" submitted by the European Committee on Legal Co-operation (C.C.J.) (Council of Europe, 1975).
[7] Council of Europe Resolution (72) 1 on the standardisation of the legal concepts of "domicile" and "residence", and explanatory memorandum adopted by the Council of Ministers on January 18, 1972 (Strasbourg, 1972), para. 17.
[8] Jenard Report, p. 16.
[9] Although Art. 52 refers throughout to a "party," the fact that Art. 53 deals separately with corporations and associations indicates that Art. 52 is limited to natural persons.
[10] Art. 52(1).
[11] Art. 52(2).

his domicile depends on that of another person or the seat of an authority, his national law.[12]

The Jenard Report explains that:

> "Article 52 does not deal with the case of a person domiciled outside the Community. In this case the court seized of the matter must apply its rules of private international law."[13]

4.08　This scheme is at least as complicated as it looks. Logical precedence must be given to Art. 52(3) if, as the Jenard and Schlosser Reports suggest,[14] that paragraph qualifies both the preceding paragraphs and especially if, as might be argued, paragraph 3 applies whether or not the national law of the individual concerned is that of a Contracting State. Art. 52(3) presents other problems, such as the definition of the "seat of an authority" and the ascertainment of domicile where the individual concerned has more than one nationality, but the main problem is that of the delay and expense associated with proof of foreign law in systems like those of the United Kingdom where the content of foreign law is a question of fact and not, as in the legal systems of the Member States other than Ireland, a question of law. It is hardly an answer to this that women and children are rarely involved in international litigation and that, in relation to the former, the principle that a married woman has a domicile of dependence is gradually disappearing among Member States.[15]

4.09　In cases not involving persons with a dependent domicile the court, where the individual concerned is not domiciled in the United Kingdom, will require to ascertain whether he is domiciled in another Contracting State. Here the scheme of Art. 52 once again becomes complex. Departing from the traditional approach of United Kingdom systems of private international law under which connecting factors are defined by the *lex fori*, Art. 52(2) refers the question whether a person is domiciled in another Contracting State to the law of that State. There is a certain logic about this solution within the context of a Convention designed *inter alia* to protect the domiciliaries of the Contracting States against the exercise of exorbitant jurisdictions. This advantage, however, is more than counterbalanced by the fact that it may be necessary to examine the laws of several Contracting States to ascertain whether the person concerned is domiciled in any of them. In the context of the relevant laws, moreover, additional facts may require to be ascertained. The consequent uncertainty, delay and expense are not easily justified.

4.10　It is true, nevertheless, to say that in most cases not involving persons with a dependent domicile the court will require merely to consider

---

[12] Art. 52(3).

[13] p. 16.

[14] Jenard Report, p. 17; Schlosser Report, p. 96. The latter report indicates that a United Kingdom court, in ascertaining the domicile of a minor who has come to the United Kingdom from another Contracting State, must first apply the traditional concept of domicile to ascertain whether the minor, under the law of his previous domicile, had the capacity to acquire a domicile within the meaning of the Convention in that part of the United Kingdom. It can only be hoped that this view is incorrect. The requirement of a "capacity" to acquire a domicile has never figured in the private international law of United Kingdom legal systems. Its introduction would be particularly inappropriate in questions relating to jurisdiction, where the arguments for the ready ascertainment of the relevant criteria are particularly strong.

[15] Though it still appears to be observed in France, Luxembourg, and—with qualifications—in Italy.

whether the individual concerned (usually the defendant or defender) is domiciled in the United Kingdom. For this purpose it will look to section 41 of the 1982 Act and, if under its provisions the individual concerned is domiciled in the United Kingdom, the court (except where the exclusive jurisdictions specified by Art. 16 apply) will apply the relevant rules of jurisdiction under the 1982 Act. In the application of Art. 52(1) it is immaterial that the individual concerned may at the same time be domiciled in another Contracting State.

4.11   The Convention does not state the point of time at which the domicile of a party is to be ascertained. It is thought that, in accordance with customary practice, the domicile of a party is to be ascertained at the time when the proceedings commenced.[16]

DOMICILE OF INDIVIDUALS UNDER 1982 ACT

A. GENERAL

4.12   Article 52(1) may have left it open to the United Kingdom to utilise for the purposes of the Convention its traditional concept of domicile. That concept, however, while possessing merit as a criterion for the ascertainment of the appropriate system of law in matters of status and succession, seems out of place in questions relating to the assumption of jurisdiction. Domicile in the traditional sense would have been too extensive because it would have included persons with a United Kingdom domicile of origin who are not, and possibly never have been, resident there. At the same time the concept would have been too restrictive in the sense that the traditional concept of domicile would have excluded from the jurisdiction of the United Kingdom courts persons habitually resident in the United Kingdom who do not intend to remain there indefinitely. The emphasis on intention, moreover, has always introduced an element of uncertainty into the attribution of a domicile in the traditional sense, an uncertainty inappropriate in a criterion for the determination of jurisdiction in ordinary civil actions. These defects were recognised by all concerned and the Council Working Party concerned with the Accession Convention requested the United Kingdom and Ireland:

> "to provide in their legislation implementing the 1968 Convention . . . for a concept of domicile which would depart from their traditional rules and would tend to reflect more the concept of 'domicile' as understood in the original States of the EEC."[17]

A residence-based test, therefore, seemed to be required.

4.13   The type of residence test to be selected was doubtless a matter of debate. Before the decision of the House of Lords in *Shah* v. *Barnet London Borough Council*[18] it might well have been thought that the test of

---

[16] In Scotland, it can usually be said that, "The citation of the defender is the commencement of an action (Erskine, Inst., III, vi, 3)": *Smith* v. *Stewart Co.*, 1960 S.C. 329, *per* Lord President Clyde at p. 334.
[17] Schlosser Report, p. 96.
[18] [1983] 2 A.C. 309.

ordinary residence would not necessarily have given sufficient weight to the stability or the continuity of the residence.[19] The test of habitual residence would not have suffered from this defect, but its increasing use in contexts associated with questions of personal status, where considerable emphasis on stability of residence seems appropriate, was doubtless thought to make its adoption in the present context undesirable. Consideration may also have been given to the fact that "habitual residence" itself appears alongside "domicile" as a test in Arts. 5(2), 12(3), 15(3) and 59, in contexts suggesting that the two concepts have different meanings.

4.14   In the result the 1982 Act adopts specialised residence-based definitions of domicile for the purposes not only of the Convention but of the Act generally.[20] The formulation of these definitions was complicated by the fact that, while the Convention usually refers to domicile within a Contracting State, in Arts. 5(2), 6(1) and 8(2) it refers to domicile at a place within a Contracting State. Moreover, for purposes of the internal allocation of jurisdiction within the United Kingdom—both where the Convention formally applies and where it does not—it was clearly necessary to distinguish between domicile in the United Kingdom, domicile in a part of the United Kingdom (England and Wales, Scotland, and Northern Ireland),[21] and domicile at a particular place within the United Kingdom.[22]

4.15   No provision is made in the 1982 Act for ascertaining when an individual is domiciled in another Contracting State. That is left to Art. 52(2) and (3) of the Convention, whose operation is preserved in section 41(1). It would have been open to the United Kingdom to provide for the attribution of domiciles of dependence to particular classes of persons, notably to minors, who possess United Kingdom "nationality." In the traditional concept of domicile, however, the need to attribute a domicile of dependence to minors arose mainly because of the large element of intention involved in the attribution to a person of a domicile of choice. In the definition of domicile for the purposes of the 1982 Act intention plays a subordinate role. The court is concerned mainly with factual questions, whether the nature and circumstances of a person's residence indicate that he has a substantial connection with the country in question. No provision, therefore, is made for the attribution, for the purposes of the 1982 Act, of a domicile of dependence to minors or, indeed, to any other class of persons who possess United Kingdom "nationality." Art. 52(3), accordingly, applies only to persons who are nationals of other Contracting States.

B. DOMICILE IN UNITED KINGDOM OR IN A PART OF UNITED KINGDOM

4.16   An individual is domiciled in the United Kingdom or in a particular part of the United Kingdom in terms of section 41(2) and (3) of the 1982 Act if and only if (a) he is resident in the territory in question; and (b) the nature and circumstances of his residence indicate that he has a substantial connection with that territory.

---

[19] Dicey, p. 142; Scottish Law Commission, *Report on Jurisdiction in Consistorial Causes Affecting Matrimonial Status* (1972) Scot. Law Com. No. 25, p. 28.
[20] This is a broad generalisation only and must be read in the context of ss. 41(1), 42(2) and 43(1), 45 and 46 of the 1982 Act.
[21] *Cf.* 1982 Act, s. 50.
[22] The relevant rules are in Sched. 4, Arts. 5(2), 6(1), and 13(1)(3), and in Sched. 8, Rr. 2(5), 2(15)(*a*), and 3(3).

4.17   No attempt was made to give greater precision to the term "substantial connection" other than that implied by the reference to the nature and circumstances of the residence of the individual concerned. The length of the residence will be important, but even a short period of residence might be sufficient if coupled with other factors—such as his moving house into, or accepting employment near, the place of his residence—which indicate that the individual has a substantial connection with the place of his residence. Although the individual's intentions as to residence are clearly relevant, it is thought that less weight is likely to be given to these factors than in the ascertainment of domicile in the traditional sense. The definition in section 41(2) and (3)[23] applies to children as well as to adults and, in relation to the former, it seems clear that less weight would be given to their intentions than to those of their parents or guardians.

4.18   The need for the ready ascertainment of such substantial connection for jurisdictional purposes is recognised by the introduction of a rebuttable presumption that an individual who is resident in the United Kingdom or in a particular part of the United Kingdom is domiciled there if he has been resident there for three months or more.[24] The existence of this presumption should make it unnecessary in the ordinary case to examine in detail the circumstances of a person's residence, unless the averments relating to his domicile are challenged.

4.19   The special case where an individual can be said to have a substantial connection with the United Kingdom but not with any particular part of it is provided for by a rule treating him as being domiciled in the part of the United Kingdom in which he is resident.[25]

C. Domicile at a Particular Place in United Kingdom

4.20   Section 41(4) of the 1982 Act provides that an individual is domiciled at a particular place within the United Kingdom if, and only if (a) he is domiciled in the part of the United Kingdom in which that place is situated; and (b) he is resident in that place. It will be apparent that here the test of substantial connection is applied not to the particular place, but to the part of the United Kingdom in which that place is situated.

D. Domicile in a State other than a Contracting State

4.21   Under Art. 4 of the Convention, Contracting States (subject only to Arts. 16 and 17) are free to apply their own rules of jurisdiction to persons not domiciled in any Contracting State, including "exorbitant" rules whose application to the domiciliaries of Contracting States would be disallowed under Art. 3(2). This provision is couched negatively, and it does not seem to be necessary to establish affirmatively, in the usual case at least, whether a person is domiciled in any particular non-Contracting State. It may be necessary to do so, however, in the context of Art. 59. Section 41(7) of the 1982 Act, therefore, provides that an individual is domiciled in a State other than a Contracting State if and only if (a) he is resident in that State;

---

[23] As explained in para. 4.15 above.
[24] s. 41(6).
[25] s. 41(5).

and (b) the nature and circumstances of his residence indicate that he has a substantial connection with that State. It should be noticed, however, that this provision, like the rest of section 41, must be read subject to Art. 52 of the Convention.[26] "Exorbitant rules," therefore, cannot be applied to persons who, though domiciled in a non-Contracting State in terms of section 41(7), are nevertheless at the same time domiciled in a Contracting State in terms of Art. 52(2) or (3).

SEAT OF CORPORATIONS AND ASSOCIATIONS UNDER CONVENTION

4.22 It is possible in the legal systems of the original Member States, as it is in those of the United Kingdom,[27] to speak of the domicile and, more readily in the former systems, of the nationality of corporations and associations. But in the legal systems of the original Member States general jurisdiction over corporations and associations is conceded rather on the basis of their "seat"—*siège, sede, sitz*.[28] There were differences, however, among those legal systems in their approach to the definition of "seat."[29] Perhaps the clearest definition is that in German law which declares that, "unless it is otherwise provided, the place where the administration of a corporation is carried on is its seat." The main contrast is between legal systems like the French which emphasise the place where the effective administrative centre of the corporation is located and Dutch law which looks to the place designated as the seat of the company in its administrative documents. Italian law appears to offer a choice.[30]

4.23 These differences of approach are once again referred to in the Jenard Report[31] to justify the decision of the draftsmen of the Convention not to attempt to define the seat of a corporation but to allow the seat to be determined by the application of the choice of law rules of the forum. Art. 53(1) of the Convention states this rule and at the same time integrates the concept of seat into the domicile-oriented structure of the Convention by providing:

> "For the purposes of this Convention, the seat of a company or other legal person or association of natural or legal persons shall be treated as its domicile. However, in order to determine that seat, the court shall apply its rules of private international law."

4.24 This provision presents certain problems including, in the first place, the question, To which entities is it designed to apply? The French text simply uses the words, "*des sociétés et des personnes morales*." They are both wide terms and the former is not applied exclusively to bodies possessing legal personality. Wide formulae are also used in the other language texts. In relation to a provision intended to apply to a variety of legal institutions

---

[26] s. 41(1).

[27] Dicey and Morris, pp. 481–482; Anton, p. 252; *Gasque* v. *Inland Revenue Commissioners* [1940] 2 K.B. 80 at p. 84; *Carse* v. *Coppen*, 1951 S.C. 233 at p. 244.

[28] See Rigaux, *Droit international privé* (1968), p. 535; Dalloz, *Répertoire de droit international* (1969), Vol. II, pp. 856–857; Cappelletti and Perillo, *Civil Procedure in Italy* (1965), pp. 92–93.

[29] There is an excellent study of the matter in Droz, pp. 234–237.

[30] See Civil Code, Art. 46 and Code of Civil Procedure, Art. 19.

[31] p. 57.

within the Member States it would have been inappropriate to use words having a narrow or technical meaning. The English text adopts a similarly wide formula when it refers to "a company or other legal person or association of natural or legal persons." It is possible, therefore, that Art. 53(1) was designed to be applied to all entities, other than individuals, which may be a party to legal proceedings. The answer to the initial question, however, will ultimately be one for the European Court. The first sentence of Art. 53(1), arguably, leaves to national law only the determination of the seat of the bodies specified in the first part of that provision.

4.25   In the second place, by leaving it to the private international law of each State to determine the seat of the entity in question, Art. 53(1) leaves open the possibility of problems, both at the stage of the assumption of jurisdiction and at that of recognition of decrees. The Dutch and French courts, for example, might simultaneously be entitled to assume jurisdiction over a company, the former on the ground that its memorandum and articles provided for the establishment of its seat in Holland and the latter on the ground that the real and effective seat of the company was located in France. At the jurisdictional stage the possibility of conflict is minimised by the provisions for *lis pendens* in Arts. 21 and 22, but not wholly excluded. The problem becomes quite serious at the stage of recognition. If, for example, a French court assumed jurisdiction in proceedings designed to challenge the validity of the constitution of a company on the ground that its effective seat under Art. 16(2) was located in France, the decision of the French court, it is thought, need not be recognised in Holland if under Dutch law the company's seat had been fixed in Holland.[32]

SEAT OF CORPORATIONS AND ASSOCIATIONS UNDER 1982 ACT

A. Introduction

4.26   The 1982 Act adopts two set of rules for determining the seat of a corporation or association. One set applies generally, and the other applies for the purposes of the exclusive jurisdictions in Art. 16(2) and the associated provisions in Schedules 4 and 8. The different definitions of "seat" reflect the view that in matters relating to the constitution of a corporation or association, its dissolution, and the validity of the decisions of its organs, the need for rules pointing to a single forum is especially important. The fact that such a body might carry on business in a part of the United Kingdom, while relevant to the assumption of jurisdiction in business and other day-to-day transactions, is irrelevant to the assumption of jurisdiction in issues of a "constitutional" character.

---

[32] This flows from the application of Art. 28(1), which states that a judgment will not be recognised if, *inter alia*, it conflicts with the provisions of Art. 16. The Jenard Report, p. 46, indicates that the provisions of Art. 16 partake of the character of rules of public policy. The matter is lucidly explained by Droz at p. 240.

B. GENERAL DEFINITION OF SEAT

4.27   The general definition of the seat of a corporation or association in section 42 of the 1982 Act takes as its leading principle the idea that a corporation or association should have its seat (and, therefore, its domicile) in a State only if one or other of two conditions is fulfilled—(a) that it was incorporated or formed under the law of that State and has its registered office or some other official address[33] there; or (b) that its central management and control is exercised there.[34] The terms "official address" and "business" are defined for the purposes of section 42 in section 42(8). The latter term is defined to include "any activity carried on by a corporation or association." This wide definition suggests that the earlier case law[35] on the meaning of the term "business" may be of limited relevance in this context.

4.28   The leading principle referred to above is applied to determine whether a corporation or association has its seat in the United Kingdom[36] or in a State other than the United Kingdom.[37] Its implications for the United Kingdom are considered in the following paragraph. In relation to other States, the same rule is applied whether or not the relevant State is a Contracting State. In relation to Contracting States, it will be noticed that the domicile of a corporation or association is not, as it is in the case of individuals,[38] referred to the law of the State in which it is alleged to be domiciled. This approach avoids the need to refer serially to the laws of a number of States; it avoids also the real risk that a State, even one of the Contracting States, might adopt an unacceptably extensive definition of the domicile of a corporation or association. This approach does not avoid the risk of concurrent declinatures of jurisdiction. To meet this problem, it is provided[39] that a corporation or association shall not be regarded as having its seat in a Contracting State other than the United Kingdom if it is shown that the courts of that Contracting State would not regard it as having its seat there.

4.29   These rules, however, do not serve to locate jurisdiction in a part of the United Kingdom or at a particular place within such a part. Section 42 achieves this by providing[40] that a corporation or association has its seat in a particular part of the United Kingdom if it has its seat within the United Kingdom *and* one of the following additional conditions is satisfied, namely that—(a) it has its registered office or some other official address in that part; or (b) its central management or control is exercised in that part; or (c) it has a place of business in that part. A similar system is adopted[41] to determine when a company has its seat in a particular place within the United Kingdom.

4.30   A significant feature of both rules is that, provided that the corporation or association has its seat in the United Kingdom, it suffices for it to have a place of business in a part of the United Kingdom (including Scotland) or at a particular place within such a part for it to be deemed to have its seat in

---

[33] This term is defined in s. 42(8).
[34] s. 42(2) (United Kingdom) and s. 42(6) (other States).
[35] See Dicey, p. 188.
[36] s. 42(2).
[37] Subject to s. 42(7).
[38] 1968 Convention, Art. 52(2).
[39] s. 42(7).
[40] s. 42(4).
[41] s. 42(5).

that part or at that place for purposes other than those of Art. 16(2) and the analogous provisions in Schedules 4 and 8 of the 1982 Act. A rule of this kind was strongly pressed by the Maxwell Committee[42] since the organisation of business in the United Kingdom is such that without it many corporations and associations could have been sued on the basis of their domicile in the English courts, and in those courts alone.

4.31   It is evident from the fact that the words "place of business," replaced the expression "carrying on business" in an earlier version of the Bill,[43] that the emphasis is upon the existence of an established place of business in the relevant part of the United Kingdom rather than the mere carrying on of business in that part. This is consistent with the common law rule in Scotland where a company is subject to the jurisdiction when it has a place of business and carries on business in Scotland.[44]

4.32   In cases where a corporation or association has its seat somewhere in the United Kingdom, the operation of a rule that it has a seat in any part of the United Kingdom where it has a place of business might in some cases prove highly inconvenient for defenders. The rules, however, for the inter-United Kingdom allocation of jurisdiction are to be read, in Scotland, subject to the principle of *forum non conveniens*,[45] and, in England, to the corresponding principle of *forum conveniens*.[46] Where to do so would not be inconsistent with the 1968 Convention, section 49 of the 1982 Act expressly saves the powers of any United Kingdom court to stay, sist or dismiss proceedings on the ground of *forum non conveniens* or otherwise. For the purposes of Schedule 8 the operation in Scotland of the principle of *forum non conveniens* is expressly preserved in section 22(1) of the 1982 Act.

C. Definition of Seat for the Purposes of Article 16

4.33   A slightly different definition of seat is given in section 43 when the question relates to the domicile of a corporation or of an association for the purposes of Art. 16(2) and associated purposes. Its place of business is here irrelevant. The leading principle is that a corporation or association should in this context have its seat (and therefore, its domicile) in the United Kingdom or in another Contracting State only if one or other of two conditions is fulfilled—(a) that it was incorporated or formed under the law of that State, or (b) that its central management and control is exercised there.[47] These rules would not by themselves preclude the attribution for the purposes of Art. 16(2) of a seat to a corporation or association in more than one State at the same time but, where one of those States is the United Kingdom, section 43(7) declares—presumably to lessen the risk of negative conflicts of jurisdiction—that the corporation or association shall

---

[42] See Report, pp. 36–39.
[43] H.L. Deb., Vol. 426, col. 723 (January 21, 1982).
[44] Anton, pp. 98 and 99; *cf.* Sheriff Courts (Scotland) Act 1907, s. 6(4); *Bruce* v. *British Motor Trading Corporation* 1924 S.C. 908.
[45] *Société du Gaz de Paris* v. *Armateurs Français*, 1926 S.C. (H.L.) 13; *Crédit Chimique* v. *James Scott Engineering Group Ltd.*, 1979 S.C. 406; 1982 S.L.T. 131.
[46] *MacShannon* v. *Rockware Glass Ltd.* [1978] A.C. 795; *The "Abidin Daver"* [1984] 1 All E.R. 470 (H.L.)
[47] s. 43(2) and (6).

not be regarded as having its seat in a Contracting State other than the United Kingdom, if it has its seat in the United Kingdom in terms of section 43(2)(*a*) or if the courts of that other Contracting State would not regard it as having its seat in that State for the purposes of Art. 16(2).

4.34   It will be observed that, in contrast with the provisions attributing a domicile to individuals[48] or attributing a seat to a corporation or association[49] for the general purposes of the Convention, these rules do not answer the question when a corporation or association has its seat in a State other than the United Kingdom or another Contracting State. An answer is not required for the construction of Art. 16(2), but it does seem to be required for the construction of Schedule 8, Rule 4(1)(*b*). How this gap will be filled by the courts is a matter of speculation.

D. DOMICILE AND SEAT OF CROWN

4.35   The Crown, it is thought, falls within the wide ambit of Art. 53 of the Convention and section 46 of the 1982 Act provides that for the purposes of the Act the seat of the Crown shall be treated as its domicile. Subject to the provisions of any Order in Council providing that for particular purposes the Crown shall have its seat in a specified part of the United Kingdom, section 46(3) declares that, for the purposes of the Convention and of the 1982 Act, the Crown in right of Her Majesty's Government in the United Kingdom shall have its seat in every part of, and every place in, the United Kingdom.

---

[48] See s. 41(7) and para. 4.21 above.
[49] See s. 42(6).

CHAPTER 5

PRINCIPAL JURISDICTIONAL RULES
UNDER THE CONVENTION

INTRODUCTION

5.01   THE rules of jurisdiction set out in Title II of the 1968 Convention are of
particular importance for Scots law. They specify limitatively the cases
where persons domiciled in a Contracting State other than the United
Kingdom may be sued in the Scottish courts and, for this and for other
purposes, these rules have the force of law in Scotland.[1] They are also
important because modified versions of Title II, set out in Schedules 4 and
8 to the 1982 Act, determine respectively when a defender domiciled in
another part of the United Kingdom may be sued in Scotland[2] and when a
defender domiciled in Scotland or lacking a domicile in any of the Contracting States may be sued in Scotland.[3] The modifications to Title II by way
of omissions in these Schedules are relatively few and mainly concern the
provisions relating to insurance in Section 3 of Title II. Modifications by
way of substitution or addition are printed in heavy type in Schedules 4 and
8 to the 1982 Act. This makes it readily apparent that, while significant
departures from the provisions in Title II have been made, particularly in
Schedule 8, the core provisions of Title II remain largely unaffected.
Accordingly, these provisions, together with the relevant case law of the
European Court,[4] will be described in detail in this and the two following
chapters, but described mainly by reference in Chapters 9 and 10, dealing
respectively with inter-United Kingdom questions of jurisdiction and enforcement and with the Scottish rules of jurisdiction.

5.02   The general scheme of jurisdiction under the 1968 Convention may be
set out as follows:

1. Certain proceedings are channelled to the courts of one State and of
one State alone regardless of the domicile of the persons concerned. These
"exclusive jurisdictions" are set out principally in Art. 16 and include
certain proceedings relating to immoveable property, the constitution of
companies and the decisions of their organs, and proceedings relating to
the registration of patents, trade marks and designs. In addition, however,
Art. 17 concedes exclusive jurisdiction in certain cases of prorogation and
in certain proceedings relating to trusts.

2. In relation to a defender *not* domiciled in a Contracting State only the
rules referred to in the preceding paragraph are mandatory.[5] Apart from
these rules each Contracting State remains free to apply to such a defender

---

[1] 1982 Act, s. 2.
[2] 1982 Act, s. 16.
[3] 1982 Act, s. 20.
[4] Relevant to the interpretation respectively of Scheds. 4 and 8 to the 1982 Act by ss. 16(3)
and 20(5).
[5] 1968 Convention, Art. 4(1).

its own rules of jurisdiction, including rules whose application to persons domiciled in another Contracting State would be excluded.[6]

3. Though Art. 3(2) of the Convention lists certain provisions which may not be applied to persons domiciled in a Contracting State, the list is not exhaustive and persons domiciled in a Contracting State may be sued in the courts of another Contracting State by virtue of the jurisdictional rules specified in the Convention and of no other rules.[7]

4. The rules of jurisdiction specified in the Convention in relation to persons domiciled in a Contracting State may be summarised as follows:
(a) Subject to the rules creating exclusive jurisdictions contained in Arts. 16 and 17 and to certain rules relating to prorogation in Arts. 12 and 15, a defender may always be convened in the courts of the State of his domicile.[8]
(b) A defender may be sued in the courts of a Contracting State other than that of his domicile only where the Convention so provides. It makes such provision in a series of rules whose justification is often a connection between the place where the events took place and the territory of the court[9] (e.g. the jurisdictions in Art. 5 relating to contract, delict, etc.), sometimes the policy of favouring particular classes of litigants[10] (e.g. the special jurisdictions in Sections 3 and 4 of Title II of the Convention relating to insurance and consumer contracts), and sometimes considerations of procedural convenience[11] (e.g. the rules in Arts. 6 and 6A relating to co-defenders, third-party claims, counterclaims, and claims for limitation of liability).

5. Where a court has jurisdiction under the rules referred to in paragraphs 1 and 4 above, it must exercise its jurisdiction whenever required to do so. The court has no general discretion to decline jurisdiction on the principle of *forum non conveniens*. It has limited powers only to decline jurisdiction where proceedings concerning the same cause of action have already commenced, or where related actions have been brought, in the courts of another Contracting State.[12]

5.03   Although the rules of jurisdiction in the Convention are closely interrelated, it has been thought convenient to consider them in three separate chapters. The present Chapter considers the primary rules conceding jurisdiction to the courts of the State of the domicile of the defender and the principal alternative bases of jurisdiction available in one Contracting State against a person domiciled in another Contracting State—the "special" rules of jurisdiction contained in Arts. 5, 6 and 6A of the 1968 Convention. Chapter 6 considers the rules of jurisdiction in matters relating to insurance and consumer contracts. Chapter 7 considers the remaining rules of jurisdiction, notably those in Art. 16 creating exclusive jurisdictions, those in Arts. 17 and 18 relating to prorogation and submission, and those in Arts. 21 and 22 relating to *lis pendens* and related actions.

---

[6] 1968 Convention, Art. 4(2).
[7] 1968 Convention, Art. 3(1).
[8] 1968 Convention, Art 2.
[9] See para. 5.12.
[10] See paras. 6.01 and 6.02.
[11] See para. 5.62.
[12] 1968 Convention, Arts. 21 and 22. Schlosser Report, pp. 97–99.

DOMICILE: THE GENERAL PRINCIPLE

.04   Article 2(1) of the Convention gives effect to the general jurisdictional principle, designed to protect defenders, that one person should in general sue another in a court which suits the latter's convenience. The principle *actor sequitur forum rei*, familiar both to Scots law and to the laws of the original Member States,[13] is given pride of place in the Convention:

> "Subject to the provisions of this Convention, persons domiciled in a Contracting State shall, whatever their nationality, be sued in the courts of that State."[14]

It is clearly the primary rule because, as more than once emphasised by the European Court, any departure from it must be justified by the existence of a special exception.[15]

.05   The rule in Art. 2(1) has another claim to primacy: it is general in its application. It applies, in principle at least, irrespective of the subject-matter of the dispute and whatever the nature of the proceedings. But the qualifying words "in principle at least" are necessary since the rule is inapplicable both where the subject-matter of the proceedings is excluded from the scope of the Convention by Art. 1[16] and where the proceedings fall within an exclusive jurisdiction by virtue either of their subject-matter in terms of Art. 16 or by virtue of prorogation in terms of Art. 17. The rule, moreover, is overtaken by special rules, also containing within them jurisdictions based on the domicile of the defender, when the proceedings concern matters of insurance and consumer contracts.[17]

.06   It is clear from the way in which it is expressed that Art. 2(1) refers to the domicile of the defender alone. That of the pursuer is relevant only in a few special cases.[18]

.07   Article 2(1) merely indicates the *State* which possesses jurisdiction on the basis of the defender's domicile and leaves it to individual States to specify the particular court within their territories where proceedings should be taken.[19] Art. 2(2) goes on to provide that, in regulating this internal allocation of jurisdiction, Contracting States may neither favour nor discriminate against persons who are not nationals of the State of their domicile. Art. 2(2) has limited relevance for the United Kingdom since the nationality of the parties has been irrelevant for purposes of jurisdiction in matters within the scope of Convention.

.08   Article 3(1) states the converse to Art. 2(1) and provides that:

> "Persons domiciled in a Contracting State may be sued in the courts of another Contracting State only by virtue of the rules set out in Sections 2 to 6 of this Title."

Reference has already been made to this principle in the discussion of Art.

---

[13] Jenard Report, pp. 18–20.

[14] Art. 2(1).

[15] Art. 3(1); *Tessili* v. *Dunlop* (12/76) [1976] E.C.R. 1473 [12]; *Somafer* v. *Saar-Ferngas* (33/78) [1978] E.C.R 2183 [7] and [8].

[16] See Chap. 3 above.

[17] Sections 3 and 4 of Title II of the 1968 Convention.

[18] Art. 5(2) (maintenance creditors); Art. 8(1)(2) (policy-holders); Art. 14(1) (consumers).

[19] The same approach is not taken in Arts. 5(2) and 6(1), where direct reference is made to the courts for the place in which the defender is domiciled.

2(1).[20] The second paragraph of Art. 3 goes on to list—though not exhaustively—a series of grounds of jurisdiction to be found in the laws of the Contracting States whose operation in relation to the domiciliaries of other Contracting States is specifically excluded on the ground of fairness to the defender. Strictly speaking, this list would appear to be redundant, since these rules are not to be found in Sections 2 to 6 of Title II. The list, however, was doubtless included to publicise the more blatant examples of "exorbitant" rules of jurisdiction.[21]

5.09   The rules of United Kingdom law included in this list of "exorbitant" jurisdictions are:

> "the rules which enable jurisdiction to be founded on:
> (a) the document instituting the proceedings having been served on the defendant during his temporary presence in the United Kingdom; or
> (b) the presence within the United Kingdom of property belonging to the defendant; or
> (c) the seizure by the plaintiff of property situated in the United Kingdom."

In practice, none of these rules is necessarily unfair to defenders because their operation is subject to the principle of *forum non conveniens*.[22] Paragraph (a) primarily relates to the jurisdiction exercised in England and Wales and Northern Ireland on the basis of the presence of the defender at the time of service of the writ. It would seem to have little application to the Scottish rule allowing the Court of Session to assume jurisdiction over "itinerants" who have been personally cited within the territory. Since an itinerant is a person who has no fixed residence in Scotland *or elsewhere*,[23] he is unlikely to be domiciled in another Contracting State. Paragraph (b) relates primarily to the *general* jurisdiction hitherto exercised by the Court of Session in actions of a patrimonial character by reason of the mere fact that the defender is the owner or tenant of, or the holder of a beneficial interest in, heritable property in Scotland. That paragraph, however, is rather widely expressed and would appear to cover in terms the jurisdiction of the courts of the *situs* in actions brought to declare proprietary or possessory rights in property, or to obtain authority to dispose of property, which is not necessarily an exorbitant basis of jurisdiction.[24] Paragraph (c) is evidently primarily directed against the Scottish rule permitting the Court of Session to exercise jurisdiction in actions for damages or otherwise claiming a sum of money if moveable property belonging to the defender is arrested in Scotland to found jurisdiction. It would also appear to exclude the operation of the jurisdiction of the sheriff under section 6(c) of the Sheriff Courts (Scotland) Act 1907. In so far, however, as the

---

[20] Para. 5.04.

[21] These "exorbitant" rules of jurisdiction are briefly examined in para. 1.10 above. As the Jenard Report, p. 19, points out, the inclusion of this list also serves to simplify the drafting of Art. 59.

[22] See, for Scots law, *Société du Gaz de Paris* v. *Armateurs Français*, 1926 S.C.(H.L.)13; *Crédit Chimique* v. *James Scott Engineering Group Ltd.*, 1979 S.C. 406, 1982 S.L.T. 131; Anton, pp. 148–154. For English law see, in particular, *The Atlantic Star* [1974] A.C. 436; *MacShannon* v. *Rockware Glass Ltd.* [1978] A.C. 795; The *Abidin Daver* [1984] 1 All E.R. 470 (H.L.). S. 49 of the 1982 Act preserves the operation of the principle of *forum non conveniens* generally so far as not inconsistent with the 1968 Convention, and s. 22(1) preserves the operation of the principle specifically in relation to Sched. 8 to that Act—the Scottish rules of jurisdiction.

[23] Anton, p. 105.

[24] See, *e.g.* 1968 Convention, Art. 16(1) and Art. 59(2).

sheriff's jurisdiction relates to the arrest of a ship or vessel, it is thought to be preserved by Art. 57 of the 1968 Convention.[25]

5.10   Article 4(1) states what is little more than a corollary to Art. 3, that, subject to the provisions of Art. 16,[26] each Contracting State may apply its own rules of jurisdiction when the defender is not domiciled in a Contracting State. Under Art. 4(1) the United Kingdom was free to retain its existing rules of jurisdiction in relation to such defenders or to make any amendments to those rules which might be thought desirable. In the result the 1982 Act makes relatively few amendments to the existing rules of jurisdiction in England, Wales and Northern Ireland, though certain important changes are made by the Act, notably in sections 25 (interim relief) and 30 (foreign land). Other changes were effected by the Rules of the Supreme Court (Amendment No. 2) 1983.[27] In relation to Scotland, however, for reasons already explained, a new code of jurisdiction has been introduced by Sched. 8 to the 1982 Act. This code is closely modelled upon the jurisdictional rules of the 1968 Convention but, in relation to persons not domiciled in a Contracting State, advantage has been taken of Art. 4(1) to retain or to state certain rules of jurisdiction whose operation in relation to persons domiciled in a Contracting State is excluded by Art. 3.

5.11   Article 4(2) provides that any person domiciled in a Contracting State may avail himself in another Contracting State of the rules of jurisdiction there in force, including "exorbitant" rules, in the same way as nationals of that State. This rule has no application to the scheme of jurisdiction within the United Kingdom since the nationality of parties to proceedings is irrelevant for purposes of jurisdiction in matters within the scope of the Convention. The provision, however, is of some interest to persons domiciled in the United Kingdom, because it means that in other Contracting States such persons may invoke in relation to defenders not domiciled in any Contracting State the "exorbitant" jurisdictions which are known to the laws of some at least of those Contracting States. They would be able to invoke, for example, Art. 14 of the French Civil Code,[28] which founds jurisdiction on the French nationality of the pursuer.

SPECIAL JURISDICTIONS IN ARTICLE 5

A. GENERAL

5.12   Apart from a general jurisdiction based on the domicile of the defender, the Convention provides in Sections 2 to 6 of Title II for a number of "special" jurisdictions. Here the nature of the proceedings or their subject-matter was thought to justify departures from the general principle *actor sequitur forum rei*. In the words of the European Court in the *Reinwater* case[29] the optional jurisdictions provided for in Art. 5 were introduced:

---

[25] See the Brussels Convention of May 10, 1952, referred to in para. 3.35.
[26] Though Art. 4(1) expressly refers only to Art. 16, account must also be taken of the provisions for prorogation in Art. 12, Art. 15 (though this is far from clear), and Art. 17.
[27] S.I. 1983 No. 1181 (L.21).
[28] See para. 1.10 above.
[29] *Bier* v. *Mines de Potasse d'Alsace* (21/76) [1976] E.C.R. 1735 [11]. This language was repeated in *Ivenel* v. *Schwab* (133/81) [1982] E.C.R. 1891 [11] and in *Somafer* v. *Saar-Ferngas* (33/78) [1978] E.C.R. 2183 [11].

> "having regard to the existence in certain clearly defined situations, of a particularly close connecting factor between a dispute and the court which may be called upon to hear it, with a view to the efficacious conduct of the proceedings."

The rules embodying the special jurisdictions are in some cases reformulations of traditional exceptions to the general principle *actor sequitur forum rei*. Others are relatively novel in character, giving effect, especially in matters of insurance and consumer contracts, to the desire to give special protection to one of the parties thereto.

5.13   The justification referred to above for the creation of special jurisdictions has led the European Court to adopt a relatively restrictive interpretation of the scope of these exceptions. In the *Somafer* case[30] the Court declared:

> "The scope and limits of the right given to the plaintiff by Article 5(5) must be determined by the particular facts which either in the relations between the parent body and its branches, agencies or other establishments or in relations between one of the latter entities and third parties show the special link justifying, in derogation from Article 2, the option granted to the plaintiff . . . The need to ensure legal certainty and equality of rights and obligations for the parties as regards the power to derogate from the general jurisdiction of Article 2 requires an independent interpretation, common to all Contracting States, of the concepts of Article 5(5) which are the subject of the reference for a preliminary ruling."

5.14   The special jurisdictions provided for in Art. 5 are formulated in terms which point to the courts of the particular place where the relevant event occurred rather than to the courts in general of the State connected with that event. It was presumably intended that these jurisdictions should be capable of being invoked by litigants as they are formulated in the Convention in those countries (such as the original Member States) where treaties are directly applicable. The one exception to this approach is to be found in Art. 5(6) and is possibly to be explained by the view that the domicile of a trust must reflect a connection with a legal system rather than with a particular place.

5.15   The initial words "a person domiciled in a Contracting State may, in another Contracting State, be sued . . . "are common to all the provisions of Art. 5. They serve to emphasise the fact that the provisions of Art. 5 are inapplicable where the defender is domiciled in the State of the forum or is not domiciled in any Contracting State. In the former case the jurisdictions relevant in terms of Art. 2 are available. In the latter case Art. 4(1) applies and the court before which the proceedings are brought is free to apply its own rules for the assumption of jurisdiction. In either case a Scottish court is free to apply the rules in the 1982 Act, Sched. 4 or, as appropriate, Sched. 8.

5.16   It is clear from the language of Art. 3 of the Convention that the rules in Sections 2 to 6 of Title II were intended to constitute an exhaustive list of the exceptions to Art. 2. These rules, however, must be read subject to Art. 57(2) which provides that the 1968 Convention is not to affect the application of provisions of other Conventions or of European Community legislation which, in relation to particular matters, govern jurisdiction or

---

[30] See *Somafer*, above, [8], and the Court's ruling.

the recognition and enforcement of judgments. The applicability of such other Conventions explains what would otherwise appear to be the alarmingly inadequate provisions relating to jurisdiction in admiralty matters.

B. ARTICLE 5(1)—CONTRACT

5.17 Article 5(1) provides that a person domiciled in a Contracting State may in another Contracting State be sued:

> " . . . in matters relating to a contract, in the courts for the place of performance of the obligation in question."

Art. 5(1) applies only to "matters relating to a contract." The Convention itself does not indicate when an issue is to be regarded as being of a contractual kind nor what law should determine the matter. It does not seem appropriate to apply the proper law of the contract or putative contract where the question is one whether the issue is contractual, quasi-contractual or quasi-delictual. The matter came before the European Court in the *Peters* case[31] where a Dutch association of building contractors, relying on Art. 5(1), sued a German construction company in the Dutch courts for the payment of a sum of money due to be paid by the company by virtue of their membership of the association and in terms of its rules. The German company claimed that the Dutch court had no jurisdiction under Art. 5(1) since under both Dutch and German law its relationship with the association was not of a contractual character. The European Court rejected this argument on the grounds that the characterisation of an obligation as being contractual or otherwise was a matter for Community rather than for national law and that, though the obligations of the members of the association to the association itself might not be of a contractual character under the laws of the relevant legal systems, their voluntary nature made it appropriate to look upon them as having a contractual character for the purposes of Art. 5(1).

5.18 The question has also arisen whether Art. 5(1) applies where the defender denies the existence of the contract upon the basis of which the pursuer's claim is based. The European Court has answered this question affirmatively, stressing that, if it were otherwise, a defender who sought to avoid the application of Art. 5(1) need merely assert that the contract founded upon by the pursuer did not exist.[32]

5.19 The Article refers not to the place of performance of the contract, but to the place of performance of the obligation in question. In the *De Bloos* case[33] the European Court was asked to decide whether the word "obligation" referred to any obligation arising out of or under the contract or simply to the obligation forming the basis of the proceedings. It preferred the latter approach declaring, as part of its answer to the first question put to it:

> " . . . in disputes in which the grantee of an exclusive sales concession charges the grantor with having infringed the exclusive concession, the word 'obliga-

---

[31] *Peters* v. *Zuid Nederlandse Aannemers Vereniging* (34/82) [1983] E.C.R. 987.
[32] *Effer* v. *Kantner* (38/81) [1982] E.C.R. 825 [7]. The Court reached a similar conclusion in the context of Art. 16(1) in *Sanders* v. *Van der Putte* (73/77) [1977] E.C.R. 2383.
[33] *De Bloos* v. *Bouyer* (14/76) [1976] E.C.R. 1497 [15].

tion' contained in Article 5(1) of the Convention . . . refers to the obligation forming the basis of legal proceedings, namely the contractual obligation of the grantor which corresponds to the contractual right relied upon by the grantee in support of the application."

5.20   Doubt, however, is thrown on this proposition by the Court's subsequent decision in the *Ivenel* case.[34] A French commercial traveller (Ivenel) had raised an action in France against his employer (Schwab), who resided in Germany, alleging breach of the contract of employment between them and sought to recover commission, compensation for loss of goodwill, and damages in lieu of notice. Schwab argued that, since the obligations founded upon were prestable only in Germany, the German courts alone possessed jurisdiction over him. In a reference by the French *Cour de Cassation* to the European Court the latter pointed out that the reason for the existence of the special grounds of jurisdiction in Art. 5 was the existence of:

"a close connecting factor between the dispute and the court with jurisdiction to resolve it."[35]

It added that:

"in the case of a contract of employment the connection lies particularly in the law applicable to the contract"[36]

The Court in this context referred to the provisions for contracts of employment in the Obligations Convention, Art. 6 of which provides that a contract of employment, in the absence of a choice of the applicable law, is to be governed:

"by the law of the country in which the employee habitually carries out his work in performance of the contract . . . unless it appears from the circumstances as a whole that the contract is more closely connected with another country."[37]

This line of reasoning led the Court to conclude that, in a contract of employment, the obligation characterising the contract is normally the obligation to carry out work. On this basis the Court ruled:

"The obligation to be taken into account for the purposes of the application of Article 5(1) of [the 1968 Convention] in the case of claims based on different obligations arising under a contract of employment as a representative binding a worker to an undertaking is the obligation which characterises the contract."

By stressing the obligation which characterises the contract as a whole rather than the obligation whose breach the pursuer founded upon, the Court has materially diverged from the stance it took in the *De Bloos* case. It may possibly be looking to the doctrine of characteristic performance not merely to determine questions of choice of law, but questions of jurisdiction under Art. 5(1).

5.21   The next issue arising is which law determines "the place of performance

---

[34] *Ivenel* v. *Schwab* (133/81) [1982] E.C.R. 1891.
[35] [11].
[36] [15].
[37] [13].

of the obligation in question." The argument was advanced in the *Tessili* case[38] that, in the interests of uniformity in the application of the Convention, the words should be given an independent meaning. The European Court, however, rejected this approach:

> "It is for the court before which the matter is brought to establish under the Convention whether the place of performance is situated within its territorial jurisdiction. For this purpose it must determine in accordance with its own rules of conflict of laws what is the law applicable to the legal relationship in question and define in accordance with that law the place of performance of the contractual obligation in question."

The Court went on to point out that the determination of the place of performance of obligations depends on the contractual context to which these obligations belong, in other words, that the place of performance will depend upon the terms of the contract in the light of the rules from time to time of the legal system governing it. This ruling has attracted some criticism.[39] It certainly requires the court at the stage of jurisdiction to consider questions, and not necessarily simple questions, relating to the applicable law and to its content. On the other hand, an alternative "Community" approach would require the court to develop its own law—a species of substantive law of contract—in a notoriously difficult area.

.22   The parties to a contract may themselves provide that an obligation under it is to be performed at a place which is not the place of performance otherwise indicated by the law, and the question has arisen whether such a clause is effective to confer jurisdiction upon the courts for the place of performance under Art. 5(1). The argument that such a stipulation is in effect a prorogation of jurisdiction agreement and, consequently, subject to the formalities of Art. 17 has been rejected by the European Court.[40] The clause, however, must be a valid one under the law applicable to the contract.[41]

.23   In relation to Art. 5(1) two exceptions and one transitory provision of a supplementary character must be noticed. A special rule displacing Art. 5(1) applies to persons who are domiciled in Luxembourg. Art. I(1) of the Annexed Protocol provides that:

> "Any person domiciled in Luxembourg who is sued in a court of another Contracting State pursuant to Article 5(1) may refuse to submit to the jurisdiction of that court. If the defendant does not enter an appearance the court shall declare of its own motion that it has no jurisdiction."

This special exemption was insisted upon by the representatives of Luxembourg in the course of the negotiations leading to the 1968 Convention. They argued that without such a rule the economic ties between Luxembourg and Belgium were likely to lead to an excessive transference of cases involving citizens of Luxembourg to the courts of Belgium.[42] The generalisation of this rule, however, seems excessive and likely to be a trap for the unwary.

---

[38] *Tessili* v. *Dunlop* (12/76) [1976] E.C.R. 1473 [13].
[39] Droz, 1977 *Dalloz-Sirey*, Chron. p. 287; Bischoff and Huet, 1977 *Clunet* 714. For a different view see Gothot and Holleaux, (1977) 66 *Revue Critique* 761.
[40] *Zelger* v. *Salinitri* (56/79) [1980] E.C.R. 891; *Peters* v. *Zuid Nederlandse Aannemers Vereniging* (34/82) [1983] E.C.R. 987.
[41] *Zelger* v. *Salinitri*, above, [5] and [6].
[42] See Jenard Report, p. 23.

5.24   Another exception is contained in Article VB of the Annexed Protocol. This provides that:

> "In proceedings involving a dispute between the master and a member of the crew of a sea-going ship registered in Denmark, in Greece or in Ireland, concerning remuneration or other conditions of service, a court in a Contracting State shall establish whether the diplomatic or consular officer responsible for the ship has been notified of the dispute. It shall stay the proceedings so long as he has not been notified. It shall of its own motion decline jurisdiction if the officer, having been duly notified, has exercised the powers awarded to him in the matter by a consular convention, or in the absence of such a convention has, within the time allowed, raised an objection to the exercise of such jurisdiction."[43]

5.25   A further provision of a transitional character may be noticed. Where a contract by its terms or by implication is governed by English law, in claims arising out of that contract service of the writ out of the jurisdiction has been permissible with the leave of the court to the effect of founding its jurisdiction.[44] A similar rule applies in Northern Ireland and in the Republic of Ireland. Art. 35 of the 1978 Accession Convention provides, therefore, that:

> "If the parties to a dispute concerning a contract had agreed in writing before the entry into force of this Convention that the contract was to be governed by the law of Ireland or of a part of the United Kingdom, the courts of Ireland or of that part of the United Kingdom shall retain the right to exercise jurisdiction in the dispute."

C. ARTICLE 5(2)—MAINTENANCE

5.26   Until it was amended by the 1978 Accession Convention, Art. 5(2) merely provided that a person domiciled in a Contracting State might be sued in matters relating to maintenance obligations[45] in the courts[46] for the place where the maintenance creditor is domiciled or is habitually resident. This ground of jurisdiction subsists. It is an alternative ground and nothing prevents the maintenance debtor being sued in the courts of his or her domicile[47] or in courts whose jurisdiction has been prorogated.[48] It is notorious, however, that the courts of the domicile of the maintenance debtor, assuming that he may be located, are not always convenient for the maintenance creditor or in a good position to judge his or her needs. It was decided, therefore, to allow the maintenance creditor to sue in his or her

---

[43] This provision was added by Art. 29 of the 1978 Accession Convention as amended by Art. 9 of the 1982 Accession Convention.

[44] R.S.C. Order 11, and 1(1)(f) which, however, did not apply to a defendant domiciled or ordinarily resident in Scotland. When s. 2 of the 1982 Act comes into force this rule will be replaced by Order 11, 1(1)(d)(iii)—S.I. 1983 No. 1181 (L.21), Rr. 1 and 7, which must be read subject to the Convention and to Sched. 4 to the 1982 Act.

[45] The French text refers to *obligations alimentaires*, which is translated as maintenance obligations. Though this translation is not wholly satisfactory, the term "maintenance" is retained in this book to conform with the vocabulary of the 1982 Act and of the English version of the Convention.

[46] In this context the term "court" is deemed to include the Danish administrative authorities—Annexed Protocol, Art. VA.

[47] 1968 Convention, Art. 2(1).

[48] 1968 Convention, Art. 17 (prorogation) and Art. 18 (submission).

own courts,[49] an idea which Art. 5(2) translates into the courts of his or her domicile or habitual residence. The "habitual residence" alternative was apparently introduced to ensure coherence with the Hague Convention of April 15, 1958, now replaced by the Hague Convention of October 2, 1973,[50] but it helpfully deals at the same time with the problem presented by the fact that in the original Contracting States children invariably, and married women usually, had a dependent domicile.[51]

5.27   The reference in Art. 5(2) to "the courts for the place where the maintenance creditor is domiciled or habitually resident" indicates that this is a "direct" rule of jurisdiction under which a maintenance creditor domiciled in a Contracting State may initiate proceedings for maintenance in the courts of his or her own State. A maintenance creditor, for example, who is domiciled or habitually resident in Scotland may sue a maintenance debtor domiciled in another Contracting State[52] either in the Court of Session (assuming that that court is otherwise competent) or in the sheriff court of the place of his own domicile or habitual residence. The maintenance creditor may also sue the maintenance debtor in terms of Art. 2(1) in the courts of the Contracting State of the latter's domicile

5.28   The grounds of jurisdiction relating to maintenance specified in the 1968 Convention in its original form presented difficulties for the United Kingdom. Art. 5(2), even when supplemented by grounds available under Art. 2(1), would not necessarily cover grounds of jurisdiction utilised in divorce and other status proceedings. Yet many, if not most, maintenance orders are made in the course of status proceedings. Accordingly, the 1978 Accession Convention[53] added to the text of Art. 5(2) in its original form a provision that, if the claim for maintenance is ancillary to proceedings concerning the status of a person, a court which under its own law has jurisdiction to entertain those proceedings has also jurisdiction to deal with the claim for maintenance. This rule, however, does not apply when the court's jurisdiction is based solely on the nationality of one of the parties.

5.29   What is a maintenance claim for the purposes of Art. 5(2)? One of the central problems has been discussed above,[54] that of distinguishing between a claim for maintenance—included in the Convention—and a claim for a share of matrimonial property on the rupture or dissolution of a marriage. The approach of the European Court is to regard as relatively unimportant the terms used to describe the claim: what matters is the practical result the order sought is designed to achieve. Thus, in the *De Cavel* (No.2) case,[55] the court assimilated to an award of maintenance a French judgment ordering a payment designed:

> "to compensate, as far as possible, for the disparity which the breakdown of the marriage creates in the parties' respective living standards. Article 271 [of the French Civil Code] provides further that the compensatory payment is to

---

[49] Jenard Report, p. 25.

[50] See para. 5.34 below.

[51] See para. 4.06 above.

[52] He or she may sue on the same basis a maintenance debtor domiciled or habitually resident in England or Northern Ireland under the 1982 Act, Sched. 4, Art. 5(2) and maintenance debtors domiciled or habitually resident elsewhere under the 1982 Act, Sched. 8, R. 2(5).

[53] Art. 5.

[54] Paras. 3.16–3.18.

[55] *De Cavel* v. *De Cavel* (No. 2) (120/79) [1980] E.C.R. 731 [3].

be fixed according to the needs of the spouse to whom it is paid, and the means of the other, having regard to the position at the time of divorce and its development in the foreseeable future."

5.30   This somewhat extensive view of the meaning of maintenance tends to confirm the similar approach indicated in the Schlosser Report.[56] The Convention includes maintenance claims on the part of adults as well as of children. It is not necessarily restricted to periodic claims and may extend to claims for lump sum payments. It is immaterial, too, whether the maintenance order is of an interim or final nature, so that a maintenance order pending divorce is included.[57]

5.31   Article 5(2) on the other hand, does not apply to claims for maintenance which emerge in a branch of the law—other than family relations— excluded from the scope of the 1968 Convention by Art. 1(2). This certainly excludes claims for periodic payments arising out of the law of matrimonial property[58] and is thought to exclude similar claims in the context of the law of succession. It is, moreover, an inference from the terms of the Schlosser Report[59] that it was thought that Art. 5(2) does not apply to orders for periodic payments made in the context of contractual or delictual obligations unless, in the former case, the order "merely crystallises an existing maintenance obligation which originated from a family relationship."

5.32   It is thought that the European Court would apply a "Community" interpretation to the words "proceedings concerning the status of a person" in Art. 5(2) and construe them in the same way as the corresponding words in Art. 1(2)(1).[60] The particular proceedings, therefore, which will be classified as status proceedings are not necessarily those which would be so classified by Scots law. It is not certain, for example, whether the European Court would exclude from the category of status proceedings actions of adherence and aliment or actions of affiliation and aliment.[61] In the present context only those status proceedings will be relevant in the course of which a maintenance order may be made. The law on this matter is fully and clearly explained by Dr Clive in his *The Law of Husband and Wife in Scotland*.[62]

5.33   Read along with the introductory words of Art. 5, the language of Art. 5(2) suggests that it may be founded upon only by the maintenance creditor. This may be important where the maintenance debtor seeks to have the original order rescinded or varied. He may found only upon Art. 2 and, in consequence, must initiate proceedings in the courts of the domicile of the maintenance creditor. While in the United Kingdom the court which issues a maintenance order usually has power to rescind or vary it, the Schlosser Report[63] indicates that under the legal systems of the original EEC Member States the courts of the State of origin lose their power to rescind or vary a maintenance order if they no longer have jurisdiction to issue a maintenance order. An attempt by the United Kingdom to secure an adjustment to the 1968 Convention to allow the court of origin to retain

[56] pp. 101–102.
[57] *De Cavel*, above, [10].
[58] *De Cavel* v. *De Cavel* (No. 1)(143/78) [1979] E.C.R. 547 [7].
[59] p. 102.
[60] See para. 3.14 above.
[61] Maxwell Report, pp. 47–48.
[62] (2nd ed., 1982), Chap. 12.
[63] p.105.

jurisdiction to rescind or vary its orders was rejected.[64] Nevertheless, although a maintenance order made in another Contracting State falls to be recognised and enforced in Scotland, it is thought that the Scottish courts could not be bound by such an order in all time coming. The maintenance creditor may request in Scotland provisional or protective measures under Art. 24 and may apply to the Scottish courts for a new order if those courts have jurisdiction over the maintenance debtor on the basis of his own domicile or habitual residence under Art. 5(2) or on the basis of the domicile of the maintenance debtor under Art. 2(1). The maintenance debtor may also invoke Art. 24 in Scotland, but is otherwise limited to following the maintenance creditor to the courts of the latter's domicile under Art. 2(1).

.34   Finally, it may be asked whether Art. 57 of the 1968 Convention may be of relevance in relation to the assumption of jurisdiction in matters relating to maintenance. The United Kingdom is a party to the United Nations Convention on the Recovery Abroad of Maintenance[65] and to the 1973 Hague Convention on the Recognition and Enforcement of Decisions relating to Maintenance Obligations.[66] The former is a system whereby the national authorities assist foreign applicants in proceedings in their courts and the latter, as its title indicates, is a convention relating to the recognition and enforcement of decisions. Neither contains any rules for the assumption of jurisdiction. The latter contains rules controlling the assumption of jurisdiction by foreign courts. These rules—Arts. 7 and 8— help to explain the introduction in Art. 5(2) of a reference to the habitual residence of the maintenance creditor, but are of no further relevance in the present context. The system of "provisional maintenance orders" envisaged by sections 3 and 4 of the Maintenance Orders Act 1972 applies only to "reciprocating countries" designated under section 1 of that Act. These are essentially "Commonwealth" countries[67] and, as far as the writer is aware, do not include any EEC Member States. Most of these[68] are parties to the 1973 Hague Convention and the procedure envisaged by the Reciprocal Enforcement of Maintenance Orders (Hague Convention Countries) Order 1959[69] envisages simply the recognition and enforcement of absolute and final orders going to or coming from a Contracting State.

D. ARTICLE 5(3)—DELICT[70]

.35   Under Art. 5(3) a person may be sued:

"in matters relating to tort, delict or quasi-delict, in the courts for the place where the harmful event occurred."

The provision neither defines its central terms nor indicates what law should determine whether an issue may properly be regarded as a delictual one. As we have seen, a similar problem arose in the context of Art. 5(1)

---

[64] See Schlosser Report, pp. 103–105.

[65] New York, June 20 to December 30, 1956, Cmnd. 6084 (T.S. 85 of 1975).

[66] Concluded October 2, 1973, Cmnd. 7939 (T.S. 49 of 1980).

[67] See S.I. 1974 No. 556; S.I. 1975 No. 2188, etc.

[68] As at October 24, 1983 ratifications were made by France, Italy, Luxembourg, the Netherlands and the United Kingdom.

[69] Which came into operation on March 1, 1980.

[70] See P. R. Beaumont, "Jurisdiction in Delict in Scotland" (1983) 28 J.L.S. 528.

and, in the *Peters* case[71] the European Court opted for a Community interpretation of the words "matters relating to a contract." This decision, and the arguments presented by Advocate General Warner in *Netherlands State* v. *Rüffer*[72] for a Community interpretation of the corresponding words in Art. 5(3), suggest that the Court may well elect to give a uniform or Community meaning to the words "tort, delict, or quasi-delict." The issue may arise in the context of threatened wrongs, since it is by no means clear that such wrongs are covered by the wording of Art. 5(3).[73] The language of Art. 5(3) is perfectly general. It appears, therefore, to be applicable whether the defender is himself the author of the damage or a person who is vicariously liable for it in respect of the actings of another.

5.36   Article 5(3) uses the expression, "the courts for the place where the harmful event occurred." No test in precisely the same terms was utilised as a criterion of jurisdiction in the legal systems of the original Member States, but the place of the delict was admitted as a criterion of jurisdiction in the laws of France and Germany and was admitted indirectly by the laws of the other Member States.[74] In these systems there had been some controversy as to whether the words "place of the delict" referred to the place where the wrongful act was committed or the place where the prejudice was sustained. The slightly different formula adopted by the draftsmen of the Convention does not really resolve this ambiguity. In the words of the Jenard Report[75]:

> "Article 5(3) uses the expression 'the place where the harmful event occurred.' The Committee did not think it should specify whether that place is the place where the event which resulted in damage or injury occurred or whether it is the place where the damage or injury was sustained. The Committee preferred to keep to a formula which had already been adopted by a number of legal systems, (Germany, France)."

5.37   In effect, therefore, it was left to the European Court to resolve the problem. The issue arose in the *Reinwater* case,[76] where Bier B.V., a market gardening firm in the Netherlands, and the Reinwater Foundation, a body which seeks the enhancement of the quality of the water in the Rhine basin, sought compensation in a Rotterdam court from a French undertaking, the Mines de Potasse d'Alsace SA, for damage caused to the pursuer's business by the alleged discharge of saline waste by the defenders into the Rhine. The defenders argued that the Dutch court lacked jurisdiction on the ground that the place where the harmful event occurred was in France, not in the Netherlands. The Gerechtshof at The Hague asked the Court of Justice for a ruling on the interpretation of the words "place where the harmful event occurred."

---

[71] *Peters* v. *Zuid Nederlandse Aannemers Vereniging* (34/82) [1983] E.C.R. 987.

[72] (814/79) [1980] E.C.R. 3807.

[73] In Sched. 4 to the 1982 Act the wording of Art. 5(3) is adopted in relation to the inter-United Kingdom allocation of jurisdiction with the significant addition of the words "or in the case of a threatened wrong is likely to occur." The same addition does not appear in R. 2(3) of Sched. 8 to the 1982 Act, presumably by reason of the special jurisdiction in interdict provided in Sched. 8, R. 2(10).

[74] Droz, p. 64.

[75] p. 26.

[76] (21/76) [1976] E.C.R. 1735.

.38   The European Court, after referring to the history and justification of Art. 5(3) above and the fact that the issue had been left open by the draftsmen of the Convention, explained that in its view both the place of the event at the origin of the damage and the place where the damage occurred constituted significant connecting factors with regard to jurisdiction. It would be inappropriate, therefore, to opt for one of them to the exclusion of the other:

> "To exclude one option appears all the more undesirable in that, by its comprehensive form of words, Article 5(3) of the Convention covers a wide diversity of kinds of liability. Thus the meaning of the expression 'place where the harmful event occurred' must be established in such a way as to acknowledge that the plaintiff had an option to commence proceedings either at the place where the damage occurred or at the place of the event giving rise to it."[77]

The Court's ruling, therefore, upon the question put to it was as follows:

> "Where the place of the happening of the event which may give rise to liability in tort, delict or quasi-delict and the place where that event results in damage are not identical, the expression 'place where the harmful event occurred' in Article 5(3) of the Convention . . . must be understood as being intended to cover both the place where the damage occurred and the place of the event giving rise to it. The result is that the defendant may be sued, at the option of the plaintiff, either at the courts for the place where the damage occurred or in the courts for the place of the event which gives rise to and is at the origin of that damage."

.39   The European Court's ruling in the *Reinwater* case still leaves certain questions unresolved. The words, "the place of the event which gives rise to and is at the origin of the damage," seem reasonably clear, but problems might arise, for example in a products liability case, where two or more events occurring in different countries were at the origin of the damage.[78] Nor are the words, "the place where the damage occurred," quite free from ambiguity. Are they apt to cover any place where *any* damage occurred, or do they cover only that place where the most substantial effects of the wrong were felt? The words presumably include "injury," but do they cover questions of consequential loss?

E. ARTICLE 5(4)—CIVIL CLAIMS IN CRIMINAL PROCEEDINGS

.40   Article 5(4) creates a special jurisdiction in relation to civil claims for damages or restitution made in the course of criminal proceedings. To the extent that the criminal court is competent under its own law to entertain such a claim, Art. 5(4) clothes it with jurisdiction in the civil claim for the purposes of the Convention. The rule was apparently thought necessary because the criminal action may be tried in a place other than the place of the harmful event, notably the place of arrest.[79]

.41   What is generally called a "conjoined civil action" is competent under the laws of the original Member States. It enables, for example, a person who has been injured in an action involving a motor-vehicle to intervene in

---

[77] The *Reinwater* case, above, [18] and [19].
[78] *Cf. Distillers Co. (Biochemicals) Ltd.* v. *Thompson* [1971] A.C. 458.
[79] Jenard Report, p. 26.

France and other EEC countries to claim civil damages in criminal proceedings against the person responsible for the accident. It is thought that awards of damages made in the course of such proceedings would be enforceable in the United Kingdom under the common law.[80] While there is nothing equivalent to a "conjoined civil action" in Scots law, the courts have jurisdiction under particular enactments to make orders for compensation, restitution, or delivery of property. Under sections 58 to 67 of the Criminal Justice (Scotland) Act 1980, where a person is convicted of an offence, the court may make a "compensation order" requiring him to pay compensation for any personal injury, loss or damage caused (whether directly or indirectly) by the acts which constituted the offence. No compensation order, however, may be made in respect of either:

(a) loss suffered in consequence of the death of any person; or

(b) injury loss or damage due to the presence of a motor vehicle on the road unless in the special situation envisaged in section 58(2) of the 1980 Act.

Section 67 of the 1980 Act prescribes the effect of a compensation order upon a subsequent award of damages in civil proceedings.

5.42   It is thought, nevertheless, that Art. 5(4) has no jurisdictional implications for the Scottish courts for the reason that compensation orders under the 1980 Act cannot be said to have been made by a criminal court *in the exercise of a civil jurisdiction*. The language of sections 58 to 67 of that Act, especially the relationship of compensation orders and fines and the fact that the means of the convicted person are to be taken into account, seem to exclude the inference that the orders are made in pursuance of "a civil claim for damages or restitution." If this reasoning is correct, and it is supported by the terms of the Maxwell Report,[81] such compensation orders would not fall to be enforced in other Contracting States under the 1968 Convention nor in other parts of the United Kingdom by virtue of sections 16 to 18 of, and Schedule 4 to, the 1968 Act.

5.43   Incidental reference may be appropriate here to Art. II of the Annexed Protocol to the 1968 Convention. This provides *inter alia* that if a defender in criminal proceedings fails to appear:

> "a judgment given in the civil action without the person concerned having had the opportunity to arrange for his defence need not be recognised or enforced in the other Contracting States."

This provision is discussed below.[82]

F. ARTICLE 5(5)—BRANCH, AGENCY OR ESTABLISHMENT

5.44   A further exception to the domicile rule is contained in Art. 5(5). A defender domiciled in a Contracting State may be convened, in disputes arising out of the operations of a branch, agency or other establishment, in the courts for the place where the establishment is situated. A similar provision existed in German and Italian law and was embodied in bilateral judgments conventions between EEC Member States.[83]

5.45   The wording of Art. 5(5) suggests that it may be founded upon only by

---

[80] *Raulin* v. *Fischer* [1911] 2 K.B. 93.
[81] p. 216. See also *R.* v. *Chapell*, The Times May 26, 1984.
[82] See para. 8.25 below.
[83] Jenard Report, p. 26.

the pursuer.[84] The defender may be an individual, a company or another body, but he or it must be domiciled in one Contracting State and have a branch, agency or other establishment in the place where the action is raised. The Article is thought to apply to claims of any kind, whether contractual, delictual or restitutionary, provided that they arise out of the "operations" of the establishment in question.[85]

In the *Somafer* case,[86] the European Court was asked whether the words "branch, agency or other establishment" were to be construed in accordance with the law of the State in which the proceedings were brought, in accordance with the law to be applied to the substantial issues between the parties, or in accordance with independent criteria uniformly applicable to Contracting States, and, if the latter, what these criteria were. The Court concluded that the need for legal certainty and equality in the rights and obligations of persons throughout the Member States required an independent interpretation common to all Member States and, in answer to the last question ruled that:

> "The concept of branch, agency or other establishment implies a place of business which has the appearance of permanency, such as the extension of a parent body, has a management and is materially equipped to negotiate business with third parties so that the latter, although knowing that there will if necessary be a legal link with the parent body, the head office of which is abroad, do not have to deal directly with such parent body but may transact business at the place of business constituting the extension."

Earlier, in the *De Bloos* case[87] the Court had declared that it was of the essence of the concept of establishment, as of the concepts of branch or agency, that the entity in question should be subject to the direction and control of its parent body. It ruled that:

> "When the grantee of an exclusive sales concession is not subject either to the control or to the direction of the grantor, he cannot be regarded as being at the head of a branch, agency or other establishment of the grantor within the meaning of Article 5(5) of the Convention."

In the *De Bloos* case the Court did not have occasion to identify further the factors relevant to determining whether or not an undertaking or concern is subject to the direction and control of its parent body. This question arose, however, in the *Blanckaert and Willems* case,[88] where manufacturers domiciled in Belgium were claimed to be subject to the jurisdiction of a German court on the ground that they had an agency within its territory. But the agent in question was a commercial agent (Handelsvertreter) who under German law merely negotiated business as an independent agent, being free to represent more than one firm. Such an agent was free to arrange his work as he pleased without being subject to the instructions of the principal. At the same time he lacked the power to complete transactions and merely transmitted orders to the principal. The Court held that such an agent lacked the dependence necessary to characterise his premises as an agency or establishment of the principal.[89]

---

[84] Droz, p. 69.
[85] The meaning of the term "operations" is discussed in para. 5.47 below.
[86] *Somafer* v. *Saar-Ferngas* (33/78) [1978] E.C.R. 2183.
[87] *De Bloos* v. *Bouyer* (14/76) [1976] E.C.R. 1497.
[88] *Blanckaert and Willems* v. *Trost* (139/80) [1981] E.C.R. 819.
[89] See, in particular, para. 12 of the opinion.

5.47   In the *Somafer* case the Court was also asked to give a ruling upon the meaning of the term "operations," and replied that the concept of "operations" comprises:

> "actions relating to rights and contractual or non-contractual obligations concerning the management properly so-called of the agency, branch or other establishment itself such as those concerning the situation of the building where such entity is established or the local engagement of staff to work there; actions relating to undertakings which have been entered into at the above-mentioned place of business in the name of the parent body and which must be performed in the Contracting State where the place of business is established and also actions concerning non-contractual obligations arising from the activities in which the branch, agency or other establishment within the above defined meaning, has engaged at the place in which it is established on behalf of the parent body."

In this passage the Court uses the words "and which must be performed in the Contracting State where the place of business is established." There would appear to be no warrant for this limitation in the text of Art. 5(5) and the limitation runs counter to its *raison d'être*, namely to permit a pursuer who contracts with an organisation domiciled in another Contracting State through an establishment in his own State to sue that organisation there. The dictum, however, is *obiter* since in the *Somafer* case the demolition operations in question all took place in Germany, the State of the forum, and the dictum, therefore, may not represent the law.

5.48   In the *Somafer* case the question also arose whether the defenders might be personally barred by the terms of their own letterhead from denying that they had an establishment in Germany. Though the Court did not deal with this issue, the Advocate-General suggested that in this context the principle of personal bar did not apply. If this were the law, it might, as Collins has pointed out,[91] lead to unfortunate consequences.

5.49   Article 5(5) applies only where the defender is domiciled in a Contracting State. In insurance and consumer contracts, however, an insurer or person contracting with a consumer, who is not domiciled in a Contracting State but who possesses a branch, agency or other establishment in any one of the Contracting States is deemed to be domiciled in that State in disputes arising out of the operations of the branch, agency or other establishment.[92]

G. ARTICLE 5(6)—TRUSTS

(a) Introduction

5.50   It was explained above[93] that, although it is assumed in Arts. 5(6) and 53(2) of the Convention that trusts may have a domicile, trusts are not legal persons for the purposes of Arts. 2 and 53(1) of the Convention and, consequently, trusts as such do not fall under the general jurisdiction available against persons domiciled in a Contracting State in terms of Art. 2(1) of the Convention. The Convention, however, contains no exclusive jurisdiction in matters relating to a trust otherwise than by prorogation

---

[90] *Somafer v. Saar-Ferngas* (33/78) [1978] E.C.R. 2183.
[91] *The Civil Jurisdiction and Judgments Act 1982* (1983), p. 63.
[92] See paras. 6.10 and 6.31 below.
[93] Para. 4.04.

under Art. 17(2). It follows that a trustee, unless there has been such prorogation, may be sued in the place of his domicile in terms of Art. 2(1).[94] The special jurisdictions in Sections 2 to 6 of Title II of the Convention may also be available to deal with particular issues arising between the trustees on the one hand and persons external to the trust on the other, for example the non-exclusive contract jurisdiction in Art. 5(1) and the exclusive immoveable property jurisdiction in Art. 16(1).

.51   These jurisdictions, however, standing alone, are not well suited to dealing with issues internal to the trust, such as issues between the trustees *inter se* on the one hand or between the trustees and the beneficiaries on the other. There are disadvantages—to say the least—in suing a sole trustee in the courts of his personal domicile if the institution of trusts is unknown to those courts. Nor are the special jurisdictions well suited to dealing with issues internal to the trust. Even Art. 5(1) is not of great assistance since these issues are rarely of a contractual character, but are concerned with such questions as whether a person has been properly assumed as trustee, what are the respective powers of the trustees *inter se* and the powers of the trustees as a body to affect the rights of beneficiaries. It was agreed, therefore, in the course of the discussions on the 1978 Accession Convention to add a non-exclusive jurisdiction to Art. 5 to permit a person domiciled in a Contracting State to be sued:

> "(6) in his capacity as settlor, trustee or beneficiary of a trust created by the operation of a statute, or by a written instrument, or created orally and evidenced in writing, in the courts of the Contracting State in which the trust is domiciled."

(b) Domicile of a trust

.52   The concept of the domicile of a trust was borrowed from Scots law and a reference to a Scottish analysis of the domicile of a trust is contained in the Schlosser Report.[95] As with the seat of a company, however, no definition of the term is contained in the Convention. Art. 53(2) merely states that:

> "In order to determine whether a trust is domiciled in the Contracting State whose courts are seised of the matter, the court shall apply its rules of private international law."

Section 45 of the 1982 Act, therefore, prescribes for the purposes of the 1968 Convention (and of the Act itself) where a trust is domiciled. It states:

> "(2) A trust is domiciled in the United Kingdom if and only if it is by virtue of subsection (3) domiciled in a part of the United Kingdom.
> "(3) A trust is domiciled in a part of the United Kingdom if and only if the system of law of that part is the system of law with which the trust has its closest and most real connection."

It is possible that, in ascertaining this connection, the prior Scottish case law may have some relevance.[96] Section 45, however, may envisage a rather more objective approach to the ascertainment of the "domicile" of a trust in which the truster's own choice of system is of less weight than under the common law of Scotland.

---

[94] Schlosser Report, p. 107.
[95] pp. 106–107.
[96] As to which see Anton, p. 470; *Clark's Trustees*, 1966 S.L.T. 249 at p. 251.

(c) Courts in which proceedings may be brought

5.53   Article 5(6) refers generally to "the courts of the Contracting State in which the trust is domiciled" and not to the courts of the place where the trust is domiciled. Section 10(2) of the 1982 Act, therefore, provides that:

> "Any proceedings which by virtue of Article 5(6) (trusts) are brought in the United Kingdom shall be brought in the courts of the part of the United Kingdom in which the trust is domiciled."

5.54   It should be repeated, however, that the jurisdiction in Art. 5(6) is not an exclusive jurisdiction and, subject to Art. 17(2), nothing precludes proceedings against a trustee in matters relating to a trust in a court with jurisdiction under Art. 2 of the Convention or any relevant special jurisdiction provided for in Title II, Sections 2 to 6 of the Convention. Where, however, the trust instrument has prorogated the jurisdiction of a particular court, Art. 17(2) should have a channelling effect. The prorogated court has:

> "exclusive jurisdiction in any proceedings brought against a settlor, trustee or beneficiary, if relations between these persons or their rights or obligations under the trust are involved."

The prorogation agreement, however, is itself of no effect if it runs counter to Arts. 12 or 15 or to an exclusive jurisdiction under Art. 16.[97]

(d) Nature of proceedings which may be brought

5.55   Article 5(6) clearly applies only to an action against a person "in his capacity as settlor, trustee, or beneficiary of a trust." It is suggested in the Maxwell Report [98] that the Article applies only to actions *inter se* between settlors, trustees and beneficiaries and does not apply to actions by third parties against any of those persons. This limitation, however, does not appear from the terms of the text and it would seem unfortunate if such a limitation were to be read into the provision. A third party, for example, who has a quasi-contractual claim against a trust, should be entitled to pursue it in the courts of the domicile of the trust rather than in the courts of the domicile of any trustee.

(e) Trusts to which Article 5(6) applies

5.56   Article 5(6) will apply only to trusts falling within the scope of the Convention. Reference has been made above to the effects in relation to trusts of the exclusion from the scope of the Convention of "wills and succession".[99] But some trusts, in particular marriage contract trusts, may also be excluded as concerning "rights in property arising out of a matrimonial relationship."[1] In terms, Art. 5(6) applies only to trusts "created by the operation of a statute, or by a written instrument, or created orally and evidenced in writing." This language was apparently chosen to exclude constructive or implied trusts and to deal only with express trusts.[2]

---

[97] Art. 17(3).
[98] p. 53, founding on the Schlosser Report, p. 106.
[99] See para. 3.19 above.
[1] Art. 1(2)(1).
[2] Schlosser Report, p. 107.

H. ARTICLE 5(7)—SALVAGE

.57   The 1968 Convention in its original form contained no special rules relating to jurisdiction in maritime claims. It was assumed that this could be left to the provisions of international conventions in the particular field, whose operation is preserved by Art. 57. This was so even where, as Art. 25(2) of the 1978 Accession Convention confirms, the defender is domiciled in another Contracting State which is not a party to the particular convention relied upon. There were, however, as the Schlosser Report indicates,[2a] obvious gaps in this scheme which were of concern to the United Kingdom authorities. One relates to actions for limitation of liability, which are governed by the new Art. 6A. The other relates to jurisdiction in actions to recover salvage in respect of a ship or its cargo. The Brussels Convention of 1952 on the Arrest of Sea-going Ships enables the claimant to invoke the jurisdiction of a State in which a ship has been arrested in respect of claims for salvage of the ship, but not of the cargo or freight. This gap was closed by the Accession Convention which introduced into the 1968 Convention a new Art. 5(7). This provision allows the courts of a Contracting State under the authority of which the freight or cargo in question has been arrested, or could have been arrested but for the granting of bail or other security, to assume jurisdiction in relation to claims in respect of the salvage of the cargo or its freight. This rule goes further than the Brussels Convention of 1952 in so far as it applies where the arrest has not been carried into effect because of the provision of security. Such provision, as the Schlosser Report suggests, is often made in practice, and it was thought that the mere provision of security should not deprive the court of the place of arrest of jurisdiction.

5.58   The rules in Art. 5 are intended to be an exhaustive list of the exceptions to the general rule that a defender should be sued in the courts of his domicile and, viewed in this light, Art. 5 would seem to restrict unduly the admiralty jurisdiction of United Kingdom courts, including those of Scotland. Art. 57 of the 1968 Convention, however, as modified by Art. 25(2) of the 1978 Accession Convention, makes it clear that the 1968 Convention does not preclude a Member State exercising jurisdiction in accordance with other Conventions to which Member States are parties, even as against defenders domiciled in a Member State which is not a party to those Conventions. The most important examples of such conventions are the maritime conventions to which all or nearly all of the Member States are parties.

SPECIAL JURISDICTIONS IN ARTICLES 6 AND 6A

A. GENERAL

5.59   The special jurisdictions in Art. 5 are justified by the relationship of the subject-matter of the dispute and the territory or law of the selected forum. The special jurisdictions in Arts. 6 and 6A are more directly justified by procedural convenience, the desirability of ensuring that all relevant issues may be determined at the same time by the same court.

[2a] pp. 108–111.

B. ARTICLE 6(1)—CO-DEFENDERS

5.60   Article 6(1) provides that where a person domiciled in a Contracting State is one of a number of defenders, he may be sued in the courts for the place where any one of them is domiciled. The reference to the courts of the place, rather than to the courts of the State, where any one of them is domiciled may reflect the underlying ratio of procedural convenience.

5.61   A similar rule is known in the legal systems of Belgium, France, Italy, Luxembourg and the Netherlands.[3] The nearest Scottish analogue to this provision was the rule in section 6(*a*) of the Sheriff Courts (Scotland) Act 1907, which, in proceedings against a defender on the basis of his residence within the sheriffdom, permits a co-defender to be convened if some sheriff court in Scotland has jurisdiction over him. This provision, however, does not permit the convening of a person with no jurisdictional ties with Scotland and even the Court of Session has no jurisdiction over such a person.

5.62   Article 6(1) gives an option to a pursuer, where there are several defenders domiciled in different Contracting States, to sue all in the courts of the place where at least one of them is domiciled. The rule is not generalised to allow co-defenders to be cited in any proceedings whether or not based jurisdictionally on the domicile of the defender. The draftsmen of the Convention may have reasoned that such a generalisation was superfluous in the context of Art. 16, since that provision applies "regardless of domicile." They may also have considered that it was unnecessary in the context of the special jurisdictions in Art. 5, since they are couched in terms which confer jurisdiction on all concerned, defenders and co-defenders alike. This is certainly true of Art. 5(3) where the courts of the place where the harmful event occurred have jurisdiction over all concerned with the tort, delict or quasi-delict. It is not clear, however, that in proceedings based upon Art. 5(1) a co-defender is necessarily subject to the jurisdiction of the court trying the action against the original defender. If the European Court adheres to the approach which it adopts in *De Bloos v. Bouyer*,[4] it could be argued that the relevant element is the place of performance of the co-defender's obligation which, of course, may differ from the place of performance of the obligation of the original defender.

5.63   A further problem is raised by Droz,[5] that of the operation of Art. 6(1) where there has been a prorogation agreement. Two cases may be distinguished. The first is where the prorogation agreement affects the original defender alone and the second is where it affects also a co-defender. In relation to the first, Art. 6(1) cannot be used to attract a co-defender to the prorogated forum unless (possibly) that prorogated forum happens to be the forum of the place of the original defender's domicile. Where the prorogation agreement affects a co-defender and chooses a court other than that of the domicile of one of the defenders, Droz suggests that it would effectively bar the operation of Art. 6(1). It is thought that this must be so.

5.64   There is no proviso in Art. 6(1) equivalent to that in Art. 6(2) which excludes the operation of the rule where the proceedings were instituted

---

[3] Jenard Report, p. 26; Droz, p. 74.
[4] (14/76) [1976] E.C.R. 1497. See also paras. 5.19 and 5.20 above.
[5] pp.72–73.

solely with the object of removing a defender from the court normally competent. The Jenard Report,[6] however, explains that:

> "for this rule to be applicable there must be a connection between the claims made against each of the defendants, as for example in the case of joint debtors. It follows that action cannot be brought solely with the object of ousting the jurisdiction of the courts of the State in which the defendant is domiciled."

This explanation, however, clearly depends for its force upon the validity of its premise, which is of no more than persuasive authority.

C. ARTICLE 6(2)—THIRD PARTY CLAIMS

5.65 Article 6(2) provides that a person domiciled in a Contracting State may also be sued:

> "as a third party in an action on a warranty or guarantee or in any other third party proceedings, in the court seised of the original proceedings, unless these were instituted solely with the object of removing him from the jurisdiction of the court which would be competent in his case."

The words "other third party proceedings" translate the expression "demande en intervention" in the French text which has been explained[7] as being:

> "intended either to safeguard the interests of the third party or one of the parties to the action, or to enable judgment to be entered against a party, or to allow an order to be made for the purpose of giving effect to a guarantee or warranty."

It would seem, therefore, that the concept of actions on a warranty or guarantee is embraced in the wider notion of third party proceedings of which such actions are merely typical examples. Art. 6(2), therefore, would seem to cover all the cases where a defender claims that a third party should be made a party to an action under the Court of Session Rules,[8] notably where the defender alleges that the third party owes a duty of contribution, relief or indemnity or should be made a party to the action along with the defender as the person solely or jointly or jointly and severally liable with him in respect of the subject-matter of the action.

5.66 Article 6(2), unlike Art. 6(1), does not specify the courts of the domicile of any party to the action and confers jurisdiction in relation to a third party whatever the basis of jurisdiction of the court in the original proceedings. It may be invoked when the basis of jurisdiction is a special jurisdiction in Art. 5 and even, it is thought, when the basis of jurisdiction against the original defender is a prorogation agreement under Art. 17 or the entering of appearance by the defender under Art. 18. However, as the Jenard Report[9] states in terms, jurisdiction could not be claimed under Art. 6(2) in relation to a third party who can plead a valid agreement prorogating the jurisdiction of another court.

---

[6] p. 26.
[7] Jenard Report, p. 28.
[8] R. C. 1965, R. 85.
[9] p. 27.

5.67   Article 6(2) expressly provides that the original court will not have jurisdiction in an action on a warranty or guarantee if the original proceedings were instituted solely with a view to ousting the jurisdiction of the court normally competent in proceedings against the warrantor or guarantor. Though a similar provision applies in the laws of Belgium, France, Luxembourg and the Netherlands,[10] its precise field of application is obscure. It introduces an undesirable element of uncertainty into the application of Art. 6(2).

5.68   It is necessary, finally, to refer to the special position of Germany in relation to Art. 6(2).[11] Germany had no third party procedure equivalent to that of the other Member States. Instead, a party to proceedings in Germany who claims that he may have a right to reimbursement from a third party under, say, a guarantee can notify the third party of the proceedings with a view to a common decision. No judgment is pronounced against the third party, but the latter is bound by the common decision in subsequent proceedings against him.[12] Art. V of the Annexed Protocol provides that Art. 6(2) jurisdiction may not be resorted to in Germany, though the equivalent German procedures are to be made available to persons domiciled in the Contracting States. It also provides that any effects which the judgments of German courts may have on third parties by the application of the corresponding German procedures will be recognised in all Contracting States.

D. ARTICLE 6(3)—COUNTERCLAIMS

5.69   Article 6(3) states that a person domiciled in a Contracting State may also be sued:

> "on a counterclaim arising from the same contract or facts on which the original claim was based, in the court in which the original claim is pending."

This ground of jurisdiction was common to the original Member States,[13] and is paralleled in Scotland by the reconventional jurisdiction of the Court of Session and by section 6(h) of the Sheriff Courts (Scotland) Act 1907. The rule is narrower than the Scottish principle of reconvention, since the latter applies not only to cases where the reconventional claim arises out of the same transaction as the conventional claim but where the claim is ejusdem generis so that the one claim may be fairly set against the other.[14]

E. ARTICLE 6A—LIMITATION OF LIABILITY

5.70   Article 6 of the 1978 Accession Convention adds to Title II, Section 2 of the 1968 Convention a special provision, Art. 6A, relating to jurisdiction in actions for limitation of liability arising from the use or operation of a ship. It provides:

> "Where by virtue of this Convention a court of a Contracting State has jurisdiction in actions relating to liability arising from the use or operation of a

---

[10] Jenard Report, p. 27.
[11] Jenard Report, p. 27.
[12] Arts. 68, 72, 73 and 74 of the Code of Civil Procedure.
[13] Jenard Report, p. 28.
[14] Anton, pp. 131–138.

ship, that court, or any other court substituted for this purpose by the internal law of that State, shall also have jurisdiction over claims for limitation of such liability.''

The Brussels Convention of October 10, 1957 relating to the liability of owners of sea-going ships[15] permits shipowners to limit their liability for injuries arising out of the use or operation of ships, by creating a fund of a prescribed amount for distribution among claimants. In the United Kingdom, under Part VIII of the Merchant Shipping (Liability of Shipowners and Others) Act 1958, the owner of a ship may bring a limitation action against a claimant or potential claimant by placing such a fund in the hands of court. This would not of itself create jurisdiction under the 1968 Convention. Since the 1957 Convention itself contains no rules of jurisdiction, it is not a convention on a particular matter excluded from the scope of the 1968 Convention by Art. 57 of the latter. Art. 6A, therefore, fills the gap and, in the perspective of United Kingdom law, permits a shipowner, who could be sued in the United Kingdom[16] in an action in which his liability for the operations of the ship is in issue, himself to initiate in its courts proceedings for the limitation of his liability.

---

[15] To be replaced by the London Convention of 1976 on Limitation of Liability for Maritime Claims.

[16] *e.g.* on the basis of his domicile or under jurisdictional rules allowed by other conventions, such as the Brussels Convention of May 10, 1952 referred to in para. 3.35 above.

CHAPTER 6

JURISDICTION IN INSURANCE AND CONSUMER CONTRACTS UNDER CONVENTION

INTRODUCTION

6.01   SECTIONS 3 and 4 of Title II of the 1968 Convention contain in relation to insurance and consumer contracts special rules which, as the Jenard Report[1] explains:

> "are dictated by social considerations and are aimed in particular at preventing abuses which could result from the terms of contracts in standard form."

In relation to both insurance and consumer contracts the underlying assumption is that the policy-holder or consumer lacks bargaining power and should be assisted by limits being set to the places where he may be sued and extensions to the places where he may sue.

6.02   This bias was particularly evident in the original provisions of Section 3 relating to jurisdiction in matters of insurance. These provisions presented special problems for the United Kingdom, which enjoys a substantial share of the international insurance market.[2] In cases where large risks are insured, particularly in marine and aviation insurance, there is not necessarily any disparity of bargaining power between the parties. It seems evident, too that the wide choice of jurisdictions which the Convention made available to policy-holders against insurers, coupled with its onerous restrictions on choice of court agreements, carried the risk of litigation in courts lacking experience in the specialised and complex issues likely to arise in relation to policies of insurance with an international element, especially those covering large risks.

While the 1978 Accession Convention,[3] by modifying Arts. 8 and 12 of the 1968 Convention and adding a new Art. 12A, has greatly improved the original scheme, it is doubtful whether as so revised it fully meets the needs of United Kingdom insurers. Section 3 remains a complex body of rules with several unsatisfactory features and it is significant that its provisions have been incorporated neither into the scheme in Schedule 4 to the 1982 Act for the allocation of jurisdiction within the United Kingdom nor into that in Schedule 8 stating the rules for the assumption of jurisdiction in Scotland.

6.03   Section 4 in its original form also presented problems. It dealt with jurisdiction in matters relating to the sale of goods on instalment credit terms and to loans made to finance the sale of goods which were repayable by instalments. It offered jurisdictional advantages to the buyer or borrower at the expense of the lender or seller and, in terms at least, appeared to

---

[1] p. 29.
[2] Schlosser Report, p. 112 and n. 36.
[3] Arts. 7, 8 and 9.

do so whether or not the buyer or borrower could be described as a consumer. In *Bertrand* v. *Ott*,[4] however, the European Court inferred from the social objectives of Section 4 that its provisions were not designed to protect buyers in the course of trade or professional activities but only "private final consumers."[5] The proceedings may have influenced[6] those concerned with the accession negotiations in their decision to jettison Section 4 in its original form and to transform it into a section dealing with jurisdiction in consumer contracts only.[7] The subject-matter, moreover, of the original section was widened to cover other contracts for the supply of goods and the supply of services and in terms reflecting the then current drafts of the Obligations Convention.[8] Though the new Section 4 of the 1968 Convention is likely to present fewer practical problems than Section 3, the provisions in Art. 13 which define its sphere of application are not unlikely to present difficulties.

6.04 There are certain common elements in Sections 3 and 4. The rules in those Sections supersede the special grounds of jurisdiction in Art. 5, other than Art. 5(5) whose application itself tends to favour a policy-holder or a consumer. The rules are of a mandatory character and the cases where they may be excluded by an agreement on jurisdiction are specified limitatively in Arts. 12 and 15 respectively. The Jenard Report, however, suggests,[9] and it is reasonable to suppose, that a defender may exclude the application of these provisions by entering an appearance in terms of Art. 18. "Arbitration," moreover, is excluded from the Convention by Art. 1(2)(4), so that provisions for arbitration either in a contract of insurance or in a consumer contract would appear to take the contract out of the scope of these Sections.

6.05 The rules in Sections 3 and 4 of Title II apply only where the defender is domiciled in a Contracting State.[10] Arts. 8(2) and 13(2) however, provide that insurers and persons contracting with consumers who possess a branch, agency or other establishment in a Contracting State, in disputes arising out of the operations of that branch, agency or establishment are deemed to be domiciled in that State.[11] Where the defender is not domiciled or deemed to be domiciled in a Contracting State, or the dispute is not of an international character, each Contracting State is free to apply any rules of jurisdiction whether or not in terms of the Convention.[12]

6.06 While the Convention normally provides that the court in which recognition is sought may not review the jurisdiction of the court of origin, this is permitted where the judgment conflicts with the provisions of Sections 3 or 4 of Title II.[13] This exceptional derogation from the general scheme of the

---

[4] (150/77) [1978] E.C.R. 1431.

[5] [21].

[6] See Schlosser Report, p. 117.

[7] 1978 Accession Convention, Art. 10.

[8] See Art. 5 of that Convention.

[9] p. 29. Unlike Art. 17, Art. 18 does not preserve the operation of Arts. 12 and 13.

[10] However, the operation of Art. 4 of the Convention is preserved by Arts. 7 and 13.

[11] The meaning of the expression "branch, agency or establishment" and "operation" is discussed in paras. 5.46 and 5.47 above in the context of Art. 5(5).

[12] The 1982 Act, as has been explained, applies the rules of the 1968 Convention in insurance matters neither in Sched. 4 (inter-United Kingdom rules for the allocation of jurisdiction) nor in Sched. 8 (Scottish rules of jurisdiction). The Act, however, with certain modifications, applies in both Schedules the special rules of jurisdiction provided by the Convention in consumer matters.

[13] Art. 28(1) and (2).

Convention, it may be presumed, was designed further to protect the economically weaker party.

INSURANCE CONTRACTS

A. OUTLINE OF THE SCHEME

6.07   Section 3 of Title II concerns jurisdiction in matters of insurance. The term insurance is not defined, but it is stated in the Schlosser Report[14] that the section does not apply to re-insurance contracts. No reason is given, but it is clear that in such contracts neither party requires the protection which it is the object of Section 3 to give to an economically weaker party. It is thought, moreover—despite the generality of the language of Arts. 8 and 11—that Section 3 does not apply to *any* action by or against an insurer, but only to actions in the context of a contract or asserted contract of insurance.

6.08   The scheme of Section 3 is complicated in detail, but, at the risk of over-simplification and anticipating explanations to be given later, it may be summarised as follows:

(a) Jurisdiction in matters of insurance is governed, in principle at least, by Section 3 alone.[15]

(b) Where the defender is neither domiciled in a Contracting State nor is deemed by Art. 8(2) to be so domiciled for the purposes of particular proceedings, each Contracting State is free to apply its own rules of jurisdiction.[16]

(c) Where the defender is an insurer domiciled in a Contracting State or deemed to be so domiciled for the purposes of the particular proceedings,[17] he may be sued:

(1) in the courts of the Contracting State where he is domiciled or is deemed to be domiciled for the purposes of the particular proceedings.[18]

(2) in the courts for the place in a Contracting State where the policy-holder is domiciled.[19]

(3) if he is a co-insurer, in the courts of the Contracting State in which proceedings are brought against the leading insurer.[20]

(4) in the courts for the place where he has a branch, agency or other establishment in proceedings relating to a dispute arising out of the operations of that establishment.[21]

(5) in respect of liability insurance or the insurance of immoveable property, at the option of the pursuer in the place where the damage occurred or the place where the event giving rise to the damage occurred.[22]

---

[14] p. 117.
[15] Art. 7, which preserves the operation of Arts. 4 and 5(5).
[16] Art. 4, read along with Art. 7 and 8(2).
[17] Art. 8(2).
[18] Art. 8(1)(1) and 8(2).
[19] Art. 8(1)(2).
[20] Art. 8(1)(3).
[21] Arts. 4, 5(5) and 8(2).
[22] Art. 9, read with *Bier* v. *Mines de Potasse d'Alsace* (21/76) [1976] E.C.R. 1735.

(6) in respect of liability insurance, and in proceedings in which an injured party has brought an action against an insured, as a third party, in the court entertaining those proceedings (where its law so permits).[23]

(7) in a court whose jurisdiction has been validly prorogated under Art. 12.

(d) An insurer, whatever his own domicile, must sue a defender domiciled in a Contracting State in the courts of that State alone.[24] This rule is subject to exceptions where:

(1) the insurer is presenting a counterclaim.[25]

(2) the defender, if the policy-holder or the insured, is convened as a third party in a direct action against the insurer.[26]

(3) the jurisdiction of another court has been validly prorogated under Art. 12.

(e) The above rules are mandatory, and their exclusion by a choice of court agreement is severely restricted by Art. 12.

B. The Scheme in Detail

5.09 The scheme will be considered article by article, but it is emphasised that the comments are not intended to be exhaustive.

Article 7

5.10 Art. 7 makes it clear that Section 3 is intended to provide, in principle at least, the sole source of rules of jurisdiction in matters relating to insurance. It preserves, however, the operation of Arts. 4 and 5(5). The preservation of Art. 4 means that the provisions of Section 3 in principle do not apply to a defender who is not domiciled in a Contracting State and to such a defender Contracting States may apply their own rules of jurisdiction, however exorbitant. If, however, such a defender is an insurer who possesses a branch, agency or other establishment[27]—an establishment—in a Contracting State, he is deemed by Art. 8(2) to be domiciled in that State in proceedings arising out of the operations[28] of that establishment.[29] An

---

[23] Art. 10(1).

[24] Art. 11(1).

[25] Art. 11(2).

[26] Art. 10(3), read along with Art. 11.

[27] For the meaning of the expression "branch, agency or other establishment" reference may be made to the commentary on Art. 5(5). See para. 5.46 above. It has been held by a Dutch court that the General Accident Fire and Life Insurance Company came in proceedings before it within the scope of Art. 8(2) in respect that, though the insurance contracts had been concluded through the company's Antwerp office, the Amsterdam office had conducted for a considerable period the negotiations for the settlement of the case; *Textielindustrie* v. *General Accident*, Arrondissementsrechtsbank Amsterdam, Judgment of September 13, 1977, Digest I–8–B1.

[28] See para. 5.47 above.

[29] An insurer who by virtue of Art. 8(2) is deemed to be domiciled in the United Kingdom is treated for the purposes of those proceedings as so domiciled and as domiciled in the part of the United Kingdom in which the branch, agency or establishment in question is situated—1982 Act, s. 44.

insurer with such a "deemed domicile" is not exposed in such proceedings to the exorbitant jurisdictions of the Contracting States but, on the other hand, he may *in such proceedings* be sued in those States in terms of the provisions of Section 3 applicable to the domiciliaries of the Contracting States. The justification for this approach given in the Jenard Report[30] is that foreign insurance companies which establish a branch in a Member State normally have to put up guarantees which place them very much in the same position as national companies. Moreover, the preservation by Art. 7 of the operation of Art. 5(5) permits an insurer who is domiciled in a Contracting State or who is deemed to be so domiciled by Art. 8(2) to be sued in disputes arising out of the operations of an establishment in a Contracting State in the courts of the place where the establishment is situated.

Article 8

6.11   Article 8(1) permits an insurer domiciled in a Contracting State to be sued:

> (1) in the courts of the State where he is domiciled, or
> (2) in another Contracting State, in the courts for the place where the policy-holder is domiciled, or
> (3) if he is a co-insurer in the courts of a Contracting State in which proceedings are brought against the leading insurer.

Article 8(2) is not directly a jurisdiction-creating provision. It merely provides that an insurer who is not domiciled in a Contracting State but has a branch, agency or other establishment in a Contracting State is assimilated to the domiciliaries of that State in disputes arising out of the operations of that establishment. As explained in the preceding paragraph, that provision brings such an insurer within the ambit of Art. 5(5), which in principle applies only to defenders domiciled in a Contracting State. Art. 8(2), however, fulfils a similar function in extending the application of Arts. 8(1) 9 and 10 which, but for Art. 8(2), would apply only to an insurer domiciled in a Contracting State. Art. 8(1) is expressly declared to apply only to an insurer domiciled in a Contracting State and the effect of Art. 8(2) is to extend the application of Art. 8(1) to an insurer not domiciled in a Contracting State but who possesses an establishment in any Contracting State—at least in disputes arising out of the operations of that establishment. An insurer who fulfils these conditions may be sued, for example, under Art. 8(2) "in another Contracting State, in the courts for the place where the policy-holder is domiciled."[31] Arts. 9 and 10 are more loosely drafted, but it is thought that the same principles apply. The use in those provisions of the words "in addition" and "also" indicates that these Articles are intended to be construed along with Art. 8, so that the reference in Arts. 9 and 10 to "the insurer" must be one to the classes of insurer referred to in the preceding provision. The argument is developed elegantly by Droz, to whose examination of the matter the reader is referred.[32]

---

[30] p. 31.
[31] In this context, however, Art. 8(1)(1) would tend to overlap with Art. 5(5).
[32] p. 85.

Article 9

.12 Article 9 provides additional grounds of jurisdiction in matters relating to liability insurance—that is, the insurance of legal liability to a third party—and the insurance of immoveable property, including moveables covered by the same policy. The article is thought to apply, as explained in the preceding paragraph, only to insurers domiciled in a Contracting State or deemed to be so domiciled for the purposes of the particular proceedings by Art. 8(2). Where these conditions are fulfilled the insurer may be sued in the courts for the place where the harmful event occurred. This language follows that of Art. 5(3) of the Convention and it is thought that it must be given a similar interpretation. In other words, following the *Reinwater* case,[33] the reference is not only to the place where the damage occurred but to the place here the event which gave rise to it took place.[34]

Article 10

.13 Article 10 also deals with liability insurance. Like Art. 9, it must be read in the general context of Art. 8 and, in consequence, would apply only to insurers domiciled or deemed to be domiciled in a Contracting State.[35] Art. 10(1) provides that, *if the law of the court permits it*, the insurer may also be joined in proceedings which the injured party has brought against the insured. It is understood that this was possible, notably in motor accident cases, under the laws of the original Member States other than the Federal Republic of Germany.[36] This provision is thought to have limited application within Scotland since an insured has no general right to cause his insurer to be called as a third party.[37]

.14 Article 10(2) contemplates the position where the injured party sues the insurer directly and the Article declares that Arts. 7, 8 and 9 shall apply where direct actions are permitted. Such direct actions were known to the laws of the original Member States other than Italy, and were designed to favour the victims of road accidents.[38] Art. 10(3) adds that, if the law governing such direct actions permits the policy-holder or the insured to be joined as a party to that action, the same court is to have jurisdiction over them. The Jenard Report[39] states that the phrase "where such direct actions are permitted" was chosen to include the conflict rules of the forum. Direct actions as such are not known to Scots law. Though a right to sue an insurer may arise under the Third Parties (Rights against Insurers) Act 1930, the mechanism is not that of a direct action by the injured third party. The 1930 Act operates by way of a transference to and vesting in the third party of the rights of a bankrupt or insolvent insured against the insurer.[40] Nor are the Scottish conflict rules on this point developed: it is not clear whether the appropriate law would be the *lex fori*, the law governing the delict which is at the root of the claim, or the law governing

---

[33] *Bier* v. *Mines de Potasse d'Alsace* (21/76) [1976] E.C.R. 1735.
[34] See paras. 5.37–5.39 above.
[35] Maxwell Report, p. 65.
[36] To which the application of this provision is excluded by Art. V of the Annexed Protocol. See the Jenard Report, p. 32.
[37] Maxwell Report, p. 65.
[38] Droz, p. 87
[39] p. 32.
[40] See also the Policyholders Protection Act 1975, s. 7.

the contract of insurance. There is Australian authority favouring the last alternative.[41]

Article 11

6.15 Apart from preserving the jurisdiction of a court entertaining a direct action under Art. 10(3), Art. 11(1) has the effect of channelling actions by an insurer against any defender—whether the policy-holder, the insured or a beneficiary—into the court of the defender's domicile. The term "policy-holder" in the English text and, more especially, *"preneur d'assurance"* in the French text, are not free from ambiguity, but both terms are thought to include the successors in title to the original policyholder.[42] Art. 11(2) admits of a limited exception to this rule in cases where an insurer counter-claims in proceedings brought against him under Arts. 8, 9 or 10.

Article 12

6.16 Article 12 restricts the effect of antecedent agreements relating to juris-diction with a view to maintaining the choice available to persons intending to sue insurers in Contracting States. The Maxwell Report[43] explains that the text of Art. 12 does not indicate whether the agreements referred to must comply with the formal requirements of Art. 17, but considered that this might be inferred from the observations of the Schlosser Report[44] upon the agreements to which Art. 15 applies. In other words both Arts. 12 and 15 may appropriately be regarded as importing further restrictions upon prorogation agreements under Art. 17. This view receives confirma-tion from the approach of the European Court in *Gerling* v. *Italian State*,[45] though the Court's ruling indicates at the same time that the agreement need not necessarily have been signed by a third party beneficiary under the contract of insurance.[46]

6.17 Article 12(1) makes it clear that its provisions are not intended to restrict the freedom of the parties to select a forum after a dispute between them has arisen. It is thought, moreover, that Art. 18 applies where a person otherwise protected by Art. 12 voluntarily enters appearance.[47] On the other hand, before a dispute between the parties has arisen, Art. 12 permits the choice of other jurisdictions in four cases only. The first is where the agreement allows the policy-holder, the insured or a beneficiary to bring proceedings in courts other than those indicated in Section 3 of Title II of the Convention. It would seem that this provision is intended to cover only cases where the policy-holder, the insured or a beneficiary are given the choice of additional and not merely alternative courts.

A second and somewhat specialised exception admits that the parties to a contract of insurance who at the time when the contract was concluded are centred in one State may invoke the jurisdiction of the courts of that State (if its law so permits) even where the harmful event is localised elsewhere. The words "at the time of conclusion of the contract domi-ciled . . . etc." were introduced by the 1978 Accession Convention[48] and

---

[41] Dicey and Morris, p. 960.
[42] Schlosser Report, p. 117.
[43] p. 70.
[44] p. 120.
[45] (201/82) Judgment of July 14, 1983 (unreported).
[46] See T. Hartley, 1983 E. L. Rev. 264.
[47] See para. 6.04 above.
[48] Art. 8 of that Convention.

are clearly intended to demonstrate that the application of this exception is not nullified by a subsequent change of domicile on the part of one of the contracting parties. The third exception permits insurers to enter into agreements on jurisdiction with policy-holders who are not domiciled in a Contracting State:

> "except in so far as the insurance is compulsory or relates to immoveable property in a Contracting State."

It is treated as self-evident in the Schlosser Report[49] that, where there is a statutory obligation to take out insurance (*e.g.* motor vehicle insurance), no departure from the provisions of Arts. 8 to 11 can be permitted, even if the policy-holder is domiciled outside the Community. The most important exception, however, concerns the insurance of what may be called large risks.

Article 12A

.18   Limitations on the parties' freedom to prorogate a particular forum in matters of insurance may less easily be justified where the risks are large and the parties are likely to have taken legal advice. Following representations by the United Kingdom, the 1978 Accession Convention amended Art. 12 to exclude contracts of types in which the risks are normally large, notably marine and aviation insurance, but not risks arising out of contracts for carriage on land.

.19   These excluded contracts, in relation to which the parties may prorogate the jurisdiction of any court, are set out in Art. 12A of the Convention, but in an extremely elliptical manner. The Schlosser Report[50] purports to explain the provisions of this Article, but possibly may be thought merely to explain the intentions in relation to it of the draftsmen of the Convention. That Report's comments on Art. 12A, nevertheless, are comprehensive and must be taken into account. The following notes are based on the Report, but refer merely to selected points:

20   Paragraph (1) of Art. 12A refers in the first place to loss of or damage to:

> "(*a*) sea-going ships, installations situated offshore or on the high seas, or aircraft, arising from perils which relate to their use for commercial purposes."

Although the expression "sea-going ships" is used it is apparently intended to refer to any species of apparatus which can move or be moved about on water, whether or not under its own power. The provision is designed to cover such apparatus even while under construction, so long as it is afloat. The provision applies only in respect of loss or damage due to maritime risk, and is apparently not designed to cover damage arising in the course of the construction of the apparatus or its repair from a risk incidental to such construction or repair.

21   Paragraph (1) of Art. 12A refers, in the second place, to loss of or damage to

> "(*b*) goods in transit other than passengers' baggage where the transit consists of or includes carriage by such ships or aircraft."

---

[49] p. 113.
[50] pp. 114–116.

The exclusion of passengers' baggage from this provision is justified in the Schlosser Report[51] by reference to the weaker bargaining position of such passengers. The provision applies where the transit *merely includes* carriage by ships or aircraft. This extension of Art. 12A to carriage on land is justified by the scope of the policies covering the risk of goods in transit and the problems of ascertaining where a loss (say, from a container) took place.

6.22   Paragraph (2) of Art. 12A refers to insurance against any liability, other than for bodily injury to passengers or loss of or damage to their baggage:

> "(*a*) arising out of the use or operation of ships, installations or aircraft as referred to in (1)(*a*) above in so far as the law of the Contracting State in which such aircraft are registered does not prohibit agreements on jurisdiction regarding insurance of such risks."

The Schlosser Report[52] raises, but does not answer, a number of questions relating to the scope of this provision. It seems clear, however, that while paragraph 1 of Art. 12 refers to the insurance of any loss or damage to "sea-going ships," etc., paragraph 2 refers to the insurance of loss or damage caused by ships, etc., to persons or things external to them. The precise scope of the provision, however, will depend upon whether a wide or narrow interpretation is placed upon the qualification that the liability must arise out of the "use or operation" of the ships, etc., and no guidance on this matter is given in the Report.

6.23   Paragraph (3) of Art. 12A covers the insurance of:

> "Any financial loss connected with the use or operation of ships, installations or aircraft as referred to in (1)(*a*) above, in particular loss of freight or charter-hire."

This would cover, not only loss due to the late arrival of a ship or aircraft, but the owner's loss of charter fees, and the carrier's loss of entitlement to his charge for freight.

6.24   Paragraph (4) of Art. 12A covers the insurance of:

> "Any risk or interest connected with any of those referred to in (1) to (3) above."

The "ancillary risks" referred to here need not necessarily be insured in the same policy as the primary risks.

CONSUMER CONTRACTS

A. DEFINITION OF CONSUMER CONTRACTS

6.25   Section 4 of Title II of the 1968 Convention is concerned with jurisdiction in proceedings relating to certain consumer contracts. Art. 13(1) defines a consumer contract as being one:

> "concluded by a person for a purpose which can be regarded as being outside his trade or profession."

---

[51] p. 115.
[52] *Ibid.*

Not all such contracts, however, fall within the scope of Section 4. They must, additionally, fall into one or other of the following classes;

"(1) a contract for the sale of goods on instalment credit terms, or
(2) a contract for a loan repayable by instalments, or for any other form of credit, made to finance the sale of goods, or
(3) any other contract for the supply of goods or a contract for the supply of services and
  (*a*) in the State of the consumer's domicile the conclusion of the contract was preceded by a specific invitation addressed to him or by advertising, and
  (*b*) the consumer took in that State the steps necessary for the conclusion of the contract."[53]

These classes of contracts will be considered shortly. In the meantime, it may be noted, negatively, that Art. 13(3) excludes contracts of transport of whatever kind from the scope of Section 4. Some international contracts of transport would be excluded from the operation of the Convention as a whole by Art. 57(1) and (2). Their total exclusion from the scope of Section 4 was intended to avoid complication and to allow jurisdiction in such contracts to be governed by Sections 1 and 2.[54] It would also seem that, although the definition of consumer contracts may be wide enough to cover certain contracts of insurance, these are inferentially excluded by the existence of specific provisions in Section 3 of Title II.[55]

6.26   While the general definition of a "consumer contract" in Art. 13(1) uses language not dissimilar to that of Art. 5(1) of the Obligations Convention, the interpretation of Art. 13(1) presents greater difficulties. Art. 5 of the Obligations Convention so defines the term "consumer" that it clearly applies to the recipient, but not to the supplier, of the goods or services. In Art. 13 of the 1968 Convention the same conclusion rests only on the use of the word "consumer." Neither provision makes it entirely clear whether the *supplier* of the goods, services or credit must have acted in the course of his trade or profession.[56] The Obligations Report,[57] however, states:

"The definition of consumer contracts corresponds to that contained in Article 13 of the Convention on jurisdiction and enforcement of judgments. It should be interpreted in the light of its purpose which is to protect the weaker party . . . Thus, in the opinion of the majority of the delegations, it will, normally, only apply where the person who supplies goods or services or provides credit acts in the course of his trade or profession."

The Obligations Report goes on to deal with other ambiguous points in the text of the Obligations Convention which are similarly ambiguous in the context of Art. 13 of the 1968 Convention. It suggests[58] in relation to Art. 5 of the Obligations Convention that:

"the rule does not apply to contracts made by traders, manufacturers or persons in the exercise of a profession (doctors, for example) who buy equipment or obtain services for that trade or profession. If such a person acts partly

---

[53] Art. 13(1).
[54] Schlosser Report, p. 119.
[55] Schlosser Report, p. 118.
[56] *Cf*. Unfair Contract Terms Act 1977, s. 25(1).
[57] p. 23. See, however, the Schlosser Report, p. 119.
[58] p. 23.

within, partly outside his trade or profession the situation only falls within the scope of Article 5 if he acts primarily outside his trade or profession.

Where the receiver of goods or services or credit in fact acted primarily outside his trade or profession but the other party did not know this and, taking all the circumstances into account should not reasonably have known it, the situation falls outside the scope of Article 5. Thus if the receiver of goods or services holds himself out as a professional, *e.g.* by ordering goods which might well be used in his trade or profession on his professional paper the good faith of the other party is protected and the case will not be governed by Article 5."

In the context of Art. 13 of the 1968 Convention these questions must remain speculative until the European Court has considered them.

6.27   It will be apparent that there is some overlap in the specification of the consumer contracts to which Art. 13(1) applies, since the three classes of contracts specified may all be contracts of or relating to the sale of goods. In part the explanation may lie in the desire of the draftsmen to retain as much as possible of the original text of Art. 13 in the 1968 Convention. This read:

"In matters relating to the sale of goods on instalment credit terms, or to loans expressly made to finance the sale of goods and repayable by instalments, jurisdiction shall be determined by this Section, without prejudice to the provisions of Articles 4 and 5(5)."

This provision was not confined in its application to consumer contracts, but related only to contracts involving, or collateral to, the sale of goods. In its revised form, Art. 13 narrows the provision to cases where the consumer acts outwith the course of his trade or profession but widens it by extending the provision to cover all loans (whether or not payable by instalments) made to finance the sale of goods and to cover any other contract for the supply of goods or, indeed, services where the consumer responded in his own State to "a specific invitation addressed to him or by advertising."

6.28   The first class of consumer contracts to which Art. 13 applies are contracts "for the sale of goods on instalment credit terms." In *Bertrand* v. *Ott*[59] the European Court held that, since the concept of "instalment credit" varied considerably in the Member States a uniform and independent interpretation must be given to it. A restrictive interpretation of the provisions was desirable to confine the advantages of Section 4 to those buyers who were in need of protection, namely those who were economically in a weaker position than sellers in that they were buying privately and not in the course of their trade or professional activities. The Court ruled, therefore, that:

"The concept of the sale of goods on instalment credit terms within the meaning of Article 13 of the Brussels Convention of 27 September 1968 is not to be understood to extend to the sale of a machine which one company agrees to make to another company on the basis of a price to be paid by way of bills of exchange spread over a period."

The Court, therefore, went on to declare that the concept of the sale of goods on instalment credit terms referred rather to a transaction in which the price was discharged by a series of payments or which was linked to a

---

[59] (150/77) [1978] E.C.R. 1431.

financing contract. The Schlosser Report[60] suggests that the concept of "instalment credit" covers hire-purchase contracts under the law of the United Kingdom. The matter, however, must await the determination of the European Court.

.29 The second category of consumer contract—"a contract for a loan, repayable by instalments, or for any other form of credit, made to finance the sale of goods"[61]—extends the protection of Section 4 to cases where a consumer finances the purchase of goods by credit which is not necessarily extended by the seller and not necessarily repayable by instalments.

.30 The third category of consumer contracts protected by Section 4 is wider than the two previous categories in that it is not necessarily confined in its application to contracts for the sale of goods or loan contracts to finance the sale of goods, but applies to any contract for the supply of goods or services where two conditions are fulfilled:

> "(*a*) in the State of the consumer's domicile the conclusion of the contract was preceded by a specific invitation addressed to him or by advertising, and
> (*b*) the consumer took in that State the steps necessary for the conclusion of the contract."[62]

This provision adopts language similar to that of Art. 5(2) of the Obligations Convention but still presents certain problems of interpretation. It seems clear at least that the "specific invitation" or, as the case may be, the "advertising" must have been addressed to the consumer in the State of his own domicile. The localisation of the invitation is more easily envisaged than that of the advertising. A typical illustration of the former is where a wine-merchant based in the Federal Republic of Germany calls upon a person in Denmark and invites him to purchase his wines. Art. 13(3) would appear to apply both here and where, in similar circumstances, the wine-merchant had advertised in the Danish newspapers. The question would be more controversial, however, where the advertisement appears in a paper published in Germany and happens to be read by persons in Denmark. Despite the commentary in the Obligations Report[63] on the corresponding words of the Obligations Convention the matter is not free from doubt. A further element of doubt is introduced by the subsequent requirement that the consumer should have taken in the State of his domicile "the steps necessary for the conclusion of the contract." This language was apparently designed to avoid the classic problem of determining the place where the contract was concluded, but some ambiguity remains. The question "what steps are necessary for the conclusion of the contract" may not always admit of a simple answer. It is itself a question of law rather than one of fact.

B. JURISDICTIONAL RULES

31 Article 13(1) of the 1968 Convention *inter alia* preserves the effect of Art. 4. In consequence the provisions of Section 4 of Title II in principle do not apply to a defender who is not domiciled in a Contracting

---

[60] p. 118.
[61] Art. 13(1)(2).
[62] Art. 13(1)(3).
[63] p. 24.

State. If, however, such a defender possesses a branch, agency or other establishment in a Contracting State, Art. 13(2) deems him to have a domicile in that State in proceedings arising out of the operations[64] of that branch, agency or establishment.[65] This entails that he is not exposed, at least in such proceedings, to the exorbitant jurisdictions of the Contracting States but may be sued only where a person domiciled in one of those States may be convened.

6.32   By the combined effect, therefore, of Arts. 13 and 14(1) it appears that a consumer may bring proceedings against the other party to a contract within the scope of Art. 13 notably—

> (1) in the courts of the Contracting State of that other party's domicile;
> (2) in the courts of the Contracting State of that other party's deemed domicile under Art. 13(2), but only in disputes arising out of the operations of a branch, agency or other establishment which he may possess in that State;
> (3) by virtue of the rule of direct jurisdiction in Art. 5(5)[66] in the courts *for the place* in a Contracting State where that other party has a branch, agency or other establishment, but only in dispute arising out of the operations of that establishment;
> (4) by virtue of a prorogation agreement valid under Art. 15.

A consumer, on the other hand, may be sued only in the courts of the Contracting State in which he himself is domiciled[67] unless the proceedings take the form of a counterclaim or are brought by virtue of a prorogation agreement recognised by Art. 15.

C. Agreements on Jurisdiction

6.33   With a view to maintaining the choice of courts available to consumers under Section 4, Art. 15 restricts the effects of an agreement inconsistent with the provisions of the Section. As in the case of Art. 12, it is thought that the term "agreement" is intended to refer to one which complies with the formal requirements of Art. 17.[68] Like Art. 12, Art. 15 does not invalidate a consumer's agreement to sue elsewhere made after a dispute has arisen. Nor, it is thought, does Art. 15 restrict the effect of Art. 18 in conferring jurisdiction upon a court before which the defender enters an appearance.[69] An antecedent choice of court, however, is invalidated unless it widens the courts available to the consumer or refers to the courts of a country in which at the time of the agreement both parties were either domiciled or habitually resident, and such a choice of court is not inconsistent with the law of that country.[70]

---

[64] See para. 5.47 above.
[65] See para. 5.46 above. A person who by virtue of this provision is deemed to be domiciled in the United Kingdom is treated for the purposes of those proceedings as so domiciled and as domiciled in the part of the United Kingdom in which the branch, agency or establishment in question was situated—1982 Act, s. 44.
[66] Preserved by Art. 13(1).
[67] Art. 14(2).
[68] Schlosser Report, p. 120.
[69] Unlike Art. 17, Art. 18 does not preserve the operation of Art. 15.
[70] Art. 15(3).

CHAPTER 7

OTHER RULES OF JURISDICTION
UNDER THE CONVENTION

INTRODUCTION

.01 THIS Chapter considers the remaining rules of jurisdiction in Title II of the 1968 Convention, those in Section 5 concerned with exclusive jurisdictions, those in Section 6 concerned with prorogation, those in Section 7 concerned with a court's duty to consider whether it possesses jurisdiction, the related rules in Section 8 concerned with *lis pendens* and related actions, and the single rule in Section 9 concerned with provisional and protective measures.

EXCLUSIVE JURISDICTIONS

A. GENERAL

.02 Article 16 of the Convention provides that, in certain categories of proceedings – notably proceedings having as their subject-matter rights *in rem* over immoveable property, the validity of the constitution of companies, the validity of entries on public registers, and the enforcement of judgments – the courts of a specified Contracting State are to have exclusive jurisdiction. The article applies only where the subject-matter of the action is connected with a Contracting State, and does not concede the same exclusivity to proceedings where the relevant territorial connection is with a non-Contracting State. Where the article applies, it applies regardless of the domicile of the defender,[1] and regardless of the agreement of the parties.[2] Even the fact that the defender has voluntarily entered an appearance in proceedings brought before the courts of a country other than that specified by Art. 16 does not clothe the court with jurisdiction.[3] Although the jurisdictions in Art. 16 are described as being "exclusive jurisdictions," cases may arise where more than one court may claim to have exclusive jurisdiction.[4]

.03 The European Court has declared that the courts which were given exclusive jurisdiction were those best placed to deal with the disputes in question,[5] and it is evident that the basis of the rules in Art. 16 is the close relationship between the subject-matter of the proceedings and the law and administrative apparatus of the States on whose courts the article confers jurisdiction. Where this close relationship does not exist, a restrictive interpretation is given to Art. 16. The European Court has said that:

---

[1] Art. 16(1) (introductory words) and Art. 4(1).
[2] Art. 17(3).
[3] Art. 18.
[4] See para. 7.17 below.
[5] *Sanders* v. *Van der Putte* (73/77) [1977] E.C.R. 2383 [11].

"the assignment, in the interests of the proper administration of justice, of exclusive jurisdiction to the courts of one Contracting State in accordance with Article 16 of the Convention results in depriving the parties of the choice of forum which would otherwise be theirs and, in certain cases, results in their being brought before a court which is not that of the domicile of any of them. Having regard to that consideration the provisions of Article 16 must not be given a wider interpretation than is required by their objectives."[6]

7.04 Where Art. 16 applies, the observance of its rules is regarded as being of such special importance that the prorogation of the jurisdiction of other courts is incompetent.[7] Art. 19, moreover, prescribes that when a court is:

"seized of a claim which is principally concerned with a matter over which the courts of another Contracting State have exclusive jurisdiction by virtue of Article 16, it shall declare of its own motion that it has no jurisdiction."

Exceptionally, too, Art. 28 permits of the non-recognition of a judgment emanating from a court which disregards the effect of Art. 16.

7.05 The terms of Art. 19 make it clear that the rules in Art. 16 apply only where the principal issue in the case falls within the scope of one of the jurisdictions specified in the latter. It would seem to follow that when, in a case primarily concerned with a matter outwith the scope of Art. 16, an issue which would otherwise fall within its scope arises as a subsidiary matter, the court may deal incidentally with that issue. The Convention gives no guidance on the converse question whether, when a court is dealing with a matter within the scope of an exclusive jurisdiction, it may deal incidentally with matters which are not within the scope of that exclusive jurisdiction. In cases, however, where neither the Convention nor the scheme in Schedule 4 for the allocation of jurisdiction within the United Kingdom applies, a general power is conferred upon the Scottish courts by section 22(4) of the 1982 Act to deal with preliminary questions and matters ancillary or incidental to their proceedings.

7.06 A final general point is that the rules in Art. 16 specify merely the Contracting State whose courts have jurisdiction under it. It is left to the Contracting States themselves to specify which of their courts should exercise this jurisdiction. The 1982 Act adopts the principles embodied in Art. 16 both in relation to the allocation of jurisdiction within the United Kingdom and in relation to the general scheme of jurisdiction for the Scottish courts and, to achieve this result, substitutes in Schedules 4 and 8, in place of references in the Convention to the courts of a Contracting State, references respectively to the "part of the United Kingdom" concerned and to the "place where" the property, etc., is situated.

B. The Rules in Detail

Article 16(1)—Immoveables

7.07 Article 16(1) provides that in proceedings which have as their object rights *in rem* in, or tenancies of, immoveable property, the courts of the Contracting State in which the property is situated are to have exclusive

---

[6] *Sanders* v. *Van der Putte*, above, [17] and [18].
[7] Art. 17(3).

jurisdiction. Though this provision is examined at some length in the Jenard[8] and Schlosser[9] Reports, its domain of application remains unclear. It may be said, however, that it does not create an exclusive jurisdiction in all issues relating to immoveable property but merely in respect of two types of question, questions relating to rights *in rem* in immoveable property and questions relating to the tenancies of such property.

In the French text reference is made to "*droits réels immobiliers*" and it seems evident that the reference to rights *in rem* in immoveables was designed to reflect the distinction, known to Scots law as well as to the laws of France[10] and of most European States, between real and personal rights in property. Erskine explains the nature of the distinction in a well-known passage:[11]

> "A real right, or *jus in re*, whether of property or of an inferior kind – as servitude – entitles the party vested with it to possess the subject as his own; or, if it be possessed by another, to demand it from the possessor, in consequence of the right which he hath in the subject itself; whereas the creditor in a personal right or obligation has only a *jus ad rem*, or a right of action against the debtor or his representatives, by which they may be compelled to fulfil that obligation, but without any right in the subject which the debtor is obliged to transfer to him."

This distinction has been obscured in English law because, as Lawson has explained: "Equity is normally prepared to treat a contractual right relating to property not only as a right *in personam* entitling one person to a performance from another person in respect of the property but as a right *in rem* analogous to ownership of the property."[12] The distinction, though clearly made in the legal systems of other Member States, is not necessarily drawn by them in precisely the same way. It seems likely, therefore, that the European Court will attach an independent or Community meaning to Art. 16(1): indeed, this seems implicit in its opinion in *Sanders* v. *Van der Putte*[13] that a restrictive interpretation – its own – should be given to the other element in Art. 16(1), tenancies of immoveable property.

The Jenard Report explains that Art. 16(1) was extended to tenancies of immoveable property because;

> "tenancies of immoveable property are usually governed by special legislation which, in view of its complexity, should preferably be applied only by the courts of the country in which it is in force. Moreover, several States provide for exclusive jurisdiction in such proceedings, which is usually conferred on special tribunals."[14]

These considerations apply in large measure to the law of leases in Scotland. For example, while most issues arising under the Agricultural Holdings Act 1949 are to be determined by arbitration,[15] and are thus outwith the scope of the 1968 Convention, they are otherwise to be determined by a court with a special constitution, the Scottish Land Court. While the

---

[8] pp. 34 and 35.
[9] pp. 120–122.
[10] See J. Carbonnier, *Droit Civil* (1969), Vol. 3, pp. 39–48.
[11] III.i. 2.
[12] F.H. Lawson, *Introduction to the Law of Property* (1958), p. 49.
[13] (73/77) [1977] E.C.R. 2383.
[14] p. 35.
[15] s. 68, but see the terms of s. 78.

same cannot be said of urban tenancies, the scheme of the Rent (Scotland) Act 1971, with its complex interweaving of administrative control by rent officers, by rent assessment committees and by rent tribunals whose members are appointed by the Secretary of State, suggests that its draftsmen did not envisage issues arising under the Act being determined by courts other than Scottish courts.

7.10   It would be tempting, therefore, to suppose that the exclusive jurisdiction in actions relating to the tenancies of immoveables was intended to apply to all issues relating to such tenancies. Indeed a German court, in a claim for the payment of rent, held that the courts of the situs have exclusive jurisdiction because the right to payment of rent is intimately linked with the provisions of national law relating to the obligations of lessor and lessee. It would not be easy, it explained, to draw a line between pure rent claims and other actions concerning the contract of lease.[16] In the *Van der Putte* case,[17] however, as we have seen, the European Court adopted a relatively restrictive interpretation of the words "tenancies of immoveable property." Two persons domiciled in the Netherlands had entered into an agreement, described as a "usufructuary lease," under which Sanders was to take over from Van der Putte the running of a florist's business in a shop in West Germany which the latter had leased from a third party. In proceedings by Van der Putte against Sanders in the Dutch courts to secure the implementation of the agreement the latter denied the existence of the agreement and claimed that, supposing that its existence were upheld, the Dutch courts had no jurisdiction because the agreement was a tenancy of immoveable property subject to the exclusive jurisdiction of the German courts. The Dutch Supreme Court referred these issues to the European Court. That Court declared that:

> "Tenancies of immoveable property are generally governed by special rules and it is preferable, in the light of their complexity, that they be applied only by the courts of the States in which they are in force [14]. The foregoing considerations explain the assignment of exclusive jurisdiction to the courts of the State in which the immoveable property is situated in the case of disputes relating to the tenancies of immoveable property properly so-called, that is to say, in particular, disputes between lessors and tenants as to the existence or interpretation of leases or to compensation for damage caused by the tenant and to giving up possession of the premises [15]. The same considerations do not apply where the principal aim of the agreement is of a different nature, in particular, where it concerns the operation of a business" [16].

After pointing out that to apply Art. 16 in the present case would deprive the parties of the choice of forum which would otherwise be theirs, the Court declared that "matters relating to tenancies of immoveable property" did not include an agreement to rent under a "usufructuary lease" a retail business carried on in property rented from a third person and, further, that the fact that the existence of the agreement was denied by the defender was immaterial to the jurisdictional issue.[18]

7.11   This decision does not deal with the question whether a "pure" claim for rent would fall within the exclusive jurisdiction prescribed in Art. 16(1),

---

[16] Landgericht Aachen, October 24, 1975, Digest I– 16.1—B.1.
[17] *Sanders* v. *Van der Putte* (73/77) [1977] E.C.R. 2383.
[18] This last ruling was relied upon subsequently in the case of *Effer* v. *Kantner* (38/81) [1982] E.C.R. 825.

but the tendency of the European Court to place a relatively restrictive interpretation upon the article lends credence to the view expressed in the Jenard Report that the rule was not intended to apply:

> "to proceedings concerned only with the recovery of rent, since such proceedings can be considered to relate to a subject-matter which is quite distinct from the rented property itself."[19]

Article 16(2)—Companies and associations

Article 16(2) provides that, regardless of the domicile of the parties to those proceedings, the courts of the Contracting State in which a company, legal person or association has its seat have exclusive jurisdiction in proceedings relating to the constitution, the nullity or the dissolution of those entities or the decisions of their organs. The expression "company, legal person or association" is nowhere defined, but is thought to refer in an abbreviated way to the entities specified in Art. 53 of the Convention. If so, the expression would seem to refer to any entity other than an individual, which may be a party to legal proceedings.[20] This view derives some support from the remark in the Schlosser Report[21] that it "applies to partnerships established under United Kingdom and Irish law." This remark was presumably made, not merely in the perspective of Scottish partnerships, which are endowed with a measure of legal personality,[22] but partnerships in other parts of the United Kingdom which are not so endowed.

It has been explained above[23] that the identification of the seat of a company or other legal person or association is a matter for the rules of private international law of the forum[24] and that, for the purposes of Art. 16, the relevant rules of United Kingdom law are set out in section 43 of the 1982 Act. That section applies also for the purposes of Art. 5A and 16(2) of Schedule 4 (inter-United Kingdom allocation of jurisdiction) and of Rules 2(12) and 4(1)(b) of Schedule 8 (Scottish rules of jurisdiction).

The Jenard Report[25] gives the following justification for making this jurisdiction an exclusive one:

> "It is important, in the interests of legal certainty, to avoid conflicting judgments being given as regards the existence of a company or association or as regards the validity of the decisions of its organs. For this reason, it is obviously preferable that all proceedings should take place in the courts of the State in which the company or association has its seat."

The concept of the "nullity" of a corporation or association utilised in Art. 16(2) is one unknown to Scots law. The term, however, is understood to refer to provisions of French law which enable a company to be "annulled" in circumstances in which the contract for its formation might be

---

[19] p. 35.
[20] See para. 4.24 above.
[21] p. 120.
[22] It may be noted that 6.50 of the 1982 Act defines a corporation as including "a partnership subsisting under the law of Scotland." It defines an association as meaning "an unincorporated body of persons," which would presumably cover a partnership in English law.
[23] See paras. 4.22–4.25.
[24] Art. 53(1).
[25] p. 35.

voidable on grounds of error, fraud or failure to comply with certain essential requirements. The circumstances in which such actions of nullity may now be invoked have been narrowed since 1966 and no action for annulment may be brought more than three years after the date of the event founded upon.[26] Art. 16(2) also refers to the "dissolution" of a corporation or association. This clearly does not refer to the winding-up of insolvent corporations or associations since proceedings relating to their winding-up are expressly excluded by Art. 1(2)(2). Problems relating to the winding-up of solvent companies would come within the scope of Art. 16(2) but only questions internal to the organisation of the company or association. Sections 399 and 400 of the Companies Act 1948 will now require to be read subject to Art. 16(2) in their application to solvent companies having their seat in a Contracting State.

7.16   Article 16(2) refers also to proceedings relating to the decisions of the organs of a company, legal person or association. These are channelled to the courts of the Contracting State of their seat. The English text of this provision presents some difficulty. It is not clear whether it should be read as applying to all proceedings relating to such decisions or, as other texts suggest, only to proceedings relating to the *validity* of such decisions. It is thought that the latter and narrower reading is preferable as conforming better to the justification for the existence of this provision given in the Jenard Report.[27]

7.17   It may be recalled, finally, that although Art. 16(2) is described as an "exclusive" jurisdiction, a different definition of seat may be given in the laws of other Contracting States and it is possible, therefore, for a corporation to have its seat simultaneously in more than one country, even for the purposes of Art. 16(2). At the stage of recognition, Art. 28(1) is relevant. If a court of another Contracting State were to judge to be void a decision of the organ of a company which, though having its seat in that State under its own law, has its seat in the United Kingdom in terms of the definition in section 43 of the 1982 Act, that judgment need not be recognised in the United Kingdom. Prior to the stage of recognition, Art. 23 may be relevant since it states that:

> "Where actions come within the exclusive jurisdiction of several courts, any court other than the court first seized shall decline jurisdiction in favour of that court."

In invoking this provision in the context of Art. 16(2), a party to proceedings in the United Kingdom would require to bear in mind the terms of section 43(7) of the 1982 Act, which declares that a corporation or association shall not be regarded as having its seat in a Contracting State other than the United Kingdom if it has its seat in the United Kingdom by virtue of the fact that it was incorporated or formed under the law of the United Kingdom or would not be regarded as having its seat in that other State by the law of that State.[28]

---

[26] Law No. 66–367 of July 6, 1966, especially Arts. 302, 360, 363(1), 367 and 368.
[27] p.35.
[28] The 1982 Act, it would appear, may so provide, even in relation to corporations or associations having a seat in another Contracting State under the law of that State, because of the terms of Art. 53(1) of the 1968 Convention.

Article 16(3)—Public registers

18   Article 16(3) provides that, in proceedings which have as their object the validity of entries in public registers, the courts of the Contracting State in which the register is kept are to have exclusive jurisdiction, regardless of the domicile of the defender. This rule seems a relatively simple one.[29] Droz[30] suggests that its underlying ratio is that the courts of one country should not challenge the functioning of the public service of another.

Article 16(4)—Patents, trade marks, etc.

19   Article 16(4) provides that, regardless of domicile, the courts of the Contracting State in which the deposit or registration of a patent, trade mark, design or similar right has been applied for, has taken place, or is under the terms of an international convention deemed to have taken place, shall have exclusive jurisdiction in proceedings concerned with the registration of such rights or their validity. The Jenard Report[31] explains that:

> "Since the grant of a national patent is an exercise of national sovereignty, Article 16(4) of the Judgments Convention provides for exclusive jurisdiction in proceedings concerned with the validity of patents."

The European Court has recently held [32] that the expression "proceedings concerned with the registration or validity of patents" must be given a Community interpretation and applied uniformly among the Contracting States. It does not cover proceedings between an employee, who has patented or has applied to patent an invention, and his employer concerned with their respective rights to the patent derived from their relationship.

20   The Jenard Report, however, went on to add that:

> "Other actions, including those for infringement of patents, are governed by the general rules of the Convention."

Apart from the effect of conventions on particular matters, such other actions would normally proceed, therefore, in the courts of the infringer's domicile in terms of Art. 2 or in the courts for the place where the infringement took place or the damage was sustained in terms of Art. 5(3). Art. 57, however, of the 1968 Convention , concedes priority to other conventions to which a Contracting State is a party, which, in relation to particular matters, govern jurisdiction or the recognition or enforcement of judgments. In relation to patents, two conventions contain specific provisions of this nature.[33] The first is the Munich Convention on the Grant of European Patents signed on October 5, 1973 which introduces a common patent application procedure for the Contracting States, though

---

[29] The question, however, may arise as to whether the reference to "public registers" is one to registers *open to the public* or to registers *kept under public authority*. It is thought probable that the draftsmen of the Convention intended to refer to the latter class.

[30] p. 104.

[31] p. 36.

[32] *Goderbauer* v. *Syndic in Bankruptcy of B.V. Schroefboutenfabriek* (288/82), Judgment of November 15, 1983 (unreported).

[33] For these conventions, see the Schlosser Report, p. 123. The Munich Convention is not as yet in force.

the subsequent patent is national. The second is the Luxembourg Convention signed on December 15, 1975, which provides for patents which may be valid at the outset in all Community countries and will expire uniformly throughout those countries. Both Conventions contain provisions of the kind envisaged in Art. 57, and to that extent may supersede the terms of Art. 16(4). The jurisdictions available under Art. 69 of the Luxembourg Convention are particularly wide on the assumption that that Convention contains a species of uniform law, which will be uniformly applied.

7.21   The reference, however, in Art. 16(4) to the courts of the Contracting State in which the *deposit or registration of the patent has been applied for or taken place* introduced an element of doubt as to whether the courts in Contracting States other than Germany can assume jurisdiction in relation to patents granted under the Munich Convention. This doubt has been resolved by the new Art. V D of the Annexed Protocol, which provides that:

> "Without prejudice to the jurisdiction of the European Patent Office under the Convention on the Grant of European Patents, signed at Munich on 5 October 1973, the courts of each Contracting State shall have exclusive jurisdiction, regardless of domicile, in proceedings concerned with the registration or validity of any European patent granted for that State which is not a Community patent by virtue of the provisions of Article 86 of the Convention for the European Patent for the Common Market, signed at Luxembourg on 15 December 1975."

This provision does not apply to Community patents under the Luxembourg Convention, on the view that such patents are granted on a community basis for all Member States. It may be noted, also, that in Art. 69(5) of the Luxembourg Convention the term "residence" is used and, for the meaning of that term, reference is made to Arts. 52 and 53 of the 1968 Convention – which are concerned with "domicile" rather than with residence. To avoid the risk of confusion, Article V C of the Annexed Protocol makes it clear that, in the application of Art. 69(5) of the Luxembourg Convention, the references to "residence" shall be construed as if residence in that context were the same as "domicile" in Arts. 52 and 53 of the 1968 Convention.

Article 16(5)—Enforcement of judgments.

7.22   Article 16(5) provides that, in proceedings concerned with the enforcement of judgments, the courts of the Contracting States in which the judgment has been or is to be enforced have exclusive jurisdiction. This provision hardly calls for comment, except perhaps to say that the same principle would appear to apply by analogy to the enforcement of "authentic instruments" and court settlements under Arts. 50 and 51 of the Convention. It may be noted also that, in terms of Art. 32(2), the jurisdiction of local courts is determined by reference to the place of the domicile of the party against whom enforcement is sought. If he is not domiciled in the State in which enforcement is sought, local jurisdiction is determined by reference to the place of enforcement.

PROROGATION AND SUBMISSION

A. PROROGATION—GENERAL RULES

(a) Introduction

23   Articles 12 and 15 make specific provision for prorogation agreements in insurance and consumer contracts. Art. 17 contains the general rules. These general rules may also seem relatively restrictive, but the codes of civil procedure of the original Member States adopted a more cautious approach to choice of court agreements than the common law legal systems or Scots law. Art. 2, for example, of the Italian Code of Civil Procedure declares that the jurisdiction of the Italian courts cannot be excluded by agreement. Without going quite so far, the legislation of the other Member States tended to take a restrictive approach to such agreements in the interest of the protection of the weaker party.[34] The same concern evidently persisted among the draftsmen of the 1968 Convention. The Jenard Report explains[35]:

> "Like the draftsmen of the Convention between Germany and Belgium, the report of which may usefully be quoted, the Committee's first concern was 'not to impede commercial practice, yet at the same time to cancel out the effects of clauses in contracts which might go unread. Such clauses will therefore be taken into consideration only if they are the subject of an agreement, and this implies the consent of all the parties. Thus, clauses in printed forms for business correspondence or in invoices will have no legal force if they are not agreed to by the party against whom they operate' . . . The Committee was further of the opinion that, in order to ensure legal certainty, the formal requirements applicable to agreements conferring jurisdiction should be expressly prescribed, but that 'excessive formality which is incompatible with commercial practice' should be avoided."

24   In its original form, therefore, Art. 17 required not merely the agreement of the parties, but that this agreement should be in writing or at least evidenced in writing. This requirement was clearly incompatible with commercial practice in the United Kingdom and was modified by the 1978 Accession Convention[36] to admit also the operation of agreements which:

> "in international trade or commerce, [are] in a form which accords with practices in that trade or commerce of which the parties are or ought to have been aware."

In England, the Rules of the Supreme Court allow the court to assume jurisdiction in matters relating to a contract if the contract "is by its terms, or by implication, governed by English law."[37] The United Kingdom,

---

[34] Arthur Lenhoff, "The party's choice of forum: prorogation agreements," in 1961 *Rutgers Law Review*, No. 3, pp. 414–490; Von Bülow, "Effets de la prorogation internationale de juridiction en matière patrimoniale," in *De Conflictu Legum* (1962), pp. 89 *et seq.*

[35] p. 37.

[36] Art. 11.

[37] Rules of the Supreme Court Order 11, r. 1(1)(f) – inapplicable where the defendant is domiciled or habitually resident in Scotland. The new Order 11, r.1(1)(d)(iii) is in similar terms, but it omits the qualification relating to persons domiciled or resident in Scotland.

however, did not succeed in persuading the other Member States to admit of implied agreements on choice of court otherwise than on a transitional basis. Art. 35 of the 1978 Accession Convention merely provides that:

> "If the parties to a dispute concerning a contract had agreed in writing before the entry into force of this Convention that the contract was to be governed by the law of Ireland or of a part of the United Kingdom, the courts of Ireland or of that part of the United Kingdom shall retain the right to exercise jurisdiction in the dispute."

Under Scots law a choice of law does not imply a choice of forum[38] so that a Scottish court would appear to have no "right to exercise jurisdiction" which it could retain under Art. 35.

7.25   The European Court has tended to adopt a restrictive approach to the interpretation of Art. 17. In *Estasis Salotti* v. *RÜWA*,[39] the Court, after stating that the effect of the article is to exclude both the jurisdiction determined by the general principle laid down by Art. 2 and the special jurisdictions provided for in Arts. 5 and 6 of the Convention, went on to declare that "the requirements set out in Article 17 governing the validity of clauses conferring jurisdiction must be strictly construed."[40]

(b) Article 17

7.26   Article 17 has a deceptive air of simplicity. It is in reality a complex provision and requires several comments in detail –

(1) Art. 17 does not apply where the choice of court agreement purports to exclude the jurisdiction of a court having exclusive jurisdiction under Art. 16. In the case of insurance and consumer contracts, Art. 17 is supplanted by the even more rigorous rules in Arts. 12 and 15.[41]

(2) In its original form, Art. 17 had no application to agreements on choice of court entered into between parties neither of whom was domiciled in a Contracting State. Thus Contracting States would have been free to refuse to recognise such agreements, even when they selected a court in, or the courts of, another Contracting State, and would have been free also to apply to the parties to such an agreement their own rules of jurisdiction. This would have been a serious matter from the standpoint of the English courts owing to the frequency with which the parties to international contracts confer jurisdiction upon those courts. It could also have led to concurrent assumptions of jurisdiction and conflicting decisions. The 1978 Accession Convention,[42] therefore, added to Art. 17(1) a rule which in such cases denies jurisdiction to the courts of Contracting States other than those of the chosen court or courts, unless the latter have declined jurisdiction.

(3) Apart from the preceding rule, Art. 17 applies only where one or more of the parties is domiciled in a Contracting State.[43] But, even if this

---

[38] *Blasquez (Raymond)* v. *Levy and Sons* (1893) 1 S.L.T. 14.

[39] (24/76) [1976] E.C.R. 1831 [7]. *Cf. Segoura* v. *Bonakdarian* (25/76) [1976] E.C.R. 1851 [6].

[40] The Court of Session has also tended to adopt a relatively restrictive approach to the construction of prorogation agreements. The jurisdiction of the court normally competent can be ousted only where this is "expressly specified" or "distinctly expressed". See *Scotmotors (Plant Hire) Ltd.* v. *Dundee Petrosea Ltd.*, 1980 S.C. 351; 1982 S.L.T. 181.

[41] Art. 17(3).

[42] Art. 11.

[43] Art. 17(1).

condition is fulfilled, a choice of court agreement may be outwith the scope of Art. 17 unless the transaction to which it relates is of an international character. The Jenard Report[44] has suggested that Art. 17:

> "does not apply where two parties who are domiciled in the same Contracting State have agreed that a court of that State shall have jurisdiction, since the Convention, under the general principle laid down in the preamble, determines only the international jurisdiction of courts."

This view has been challenged on the grounds that the domicile of the parties may change and that, in any event, there may be other foreign elements in the case.[45] The Jenard Report[46] goes on to suggest that Art. 17 applies where two parties domiciled in the same Contracting State agree that a particular court of another Contracting State shall have jurisdiction. Doubt, however, is thrown on this proposition by the Schlosser Report,[47] which commences its commentary upon Art. 17 with the observation that the mere fact of choosing a court in a particular State is by no means sufficient to establish the international character of the transaction in question.

(4) Art. 17(1) applies only to agreements "to settle any disputes which have arisen or which may arise in connection with *a particular legal relationship*." This language reflects that of Art. 1 of the draft Hague Convention on Choice of Court, but the precise sense of the provision is not clear. It is possibly designed to exclude a general agreement between two parties, not currently in any specific legal relationship, binding themselves to have any future disputes between them adjudicated in a particular forum. Such a choice might not be appropriate in the circumstances of a particular relationship between the parties in the future.

(5) The European Court, following the Jenard Report,[48] has placed considerable stress upon the existence of an agreement, saying that this implies that the party alleged to be bound by it "really consented to the clause waiving the normal rules of jurisdiction" and that "the purpose of the formal requirements imposed by Art. 17 is to ensure that the consensus between the parties is in fact established."[49] The Court has held, nevertheless, that, where a contract of insurance contains provisions for prorogation of jurisdiction conceived in favour not only of the person taking out the insurance but of third-party beneficiaries of the policy who were not themselves parties to the contract of insurance, those third parties may found on the prorogation provisions if otherwise there has been compliance with the formal requirements of Art. 17.[50]

(6) Apart from agreements in a form according with the practice of international trade or commerce, the agreement must be "in writing or evidenced in writing." Although it is thought that the term "writing" will be construed broadly to include, for example, printed general conditions

---

[44] pp. 37 and 38.

[45] Collins, *The Civil Jurisdiction and Judgments Act 1982* (1983), p. 84.

[46] p. 38. See also Maxwell Report, p. 85.

[47] p. 123.

[48] p. 37

[49] *Estasis Salotti* v. *RÜWA* (24/76) [1976] E.C.R. 1831 [9] and [7].

[50] *Gerling* v. *Italian State* (201/82), Judgment of July 14, 1983 (unreported). Though the point was not in issue in this case, an agreement on jurisdiction in matters of insurance must presumably also comply with the conditions of Art. 12.

and telegrams, the European Court[51] has stressed that a jurisdiction clause, however expressed, proponed by one party must be accepted in writing by the other party and has ruled that:

> "Where a clause conferring jurisdiction is included among the general conditions of sale of one of the parties, printed on the back of a contract, the requirement of a writing under the first paragraph of Article 17 of the Convention . . . is fulfilled only if the contract signed by both parties contains an express reference to those general conditions."

The European Court[52] applied the same principle to an oral agreement between the parties where the seller gave to the buyer a document described as a "confirmation of order and invoice," which contained a clause stipulating that all disputes were to be decided exclusively by the Hamburg courts. This document was not confirmed in writing by the purchaser, and it was held, in consequence, that there had been no binding prorogation of the Hamburg courts. The Court, however, conceded that this rule might suffer exception where:

> "the oral agreement comes within the framework of a continuing trading relationship between the parties which is based on the general conditions of one of them, and those conditions contain a clause conferring jurisdiction."

This exception was generalised in the 1978 Accession Convention[53] by the addition to the text of a reference to agreements:

> "in international trade or commerce, in a form which accords with practices in that trade or commerce of which the parties are or ought to have been aware."

The Schlosser Report indicates that it was thought that:

> "the requirement that the other party to a contract with anyone employing general conditions of trade has to give written confirmation of their inclusion in the contract before any jurisdiction clause in those conditions can be effective is unacceptable in international trade. International trade is heavily dependent on standard conditions which incorporate jurisdiction clauses . . . Owing to the need for calculations based on constantly fluctuating market prices, it has to be possible to conclude contracts swiftly by means of a confirmation of order incorporating sets of conditions."[54]

The new provision dealing with international trade or commerce imposes no requirements of form, even in relation to the agreement between the parties to accept the *general* conditions of the particular trade or commerce. Everything is left to the practices of that trade and, if those practices of which the parties were or ought to have been aware involve the inclusion of a choice of court agreement, it will be binding upon both parties.

(7) A provision in a contract stipulating for a place of performance which is not that which would otherwise be inferred by the law may indirectly in terms of Art. 5(1) confer jurisdiction upon the courts of the stipulated place of performance. Such provision is not regarded as a choice of court

---

[51] *Estasis Salotti* v. *RÜWA*, above, [6]–[10].
[52] *Segoura* v. *Bonakdarian* (25/76) [1976] E.C.R. 1851, 1863.
[53] Art. 11, now incorporated in the 1968 Convention, Art. 17(1), second sentence.
[54] p. 125.

agreement and compliance with the formal requirements of Art. 17 is unnecessary.[55]

(8) Art. 17 is thought to be concerned only with the express choice of a forum and not with the choice of a forum which may be implied, for example, that implied by the English courts by reason of a choice of English law to govern a contract. This point has already been discussed.[56]

(9) In *Meeth* v. *Glacetal*[57] the European Court had to consider whether Art. 17 applied to an agreement under which two parties to a contract of sale, who were domiciled in different Contracting States, undertook to initiate proceedings against the other only in that other's courts. The Court answered this question in the affirmative and stated also that the agreement could not be interpreted as prohibiting the court in which one of the parties had commenced proceedings taking account of a set-off connected with the legal relationship in dispute. The Court left open the parallel question whether under such an agreement a counterclaim might be permissible.[58]

(10) Art. 17 contains no specific rules as to the validity, other than in point of form, of the choice of court agreement. The matter has been left, presumably intentionally, to be dealt with by any forum in which the issue arises in accordance with its rules of private international law. In contrast with Art. 4 of the draft Hague Convention on the Choice of Court, Art. 17 of the 1968 Convention contains no specific provision as to the effect of agreements obtained by "an abuse of economic power or other unfair means."

(11) So far as the choice of court agreement is a valid one, it creates an exclusive jurisdiction in the sense of superseding the general rules for the assumption of jurisdiction in the Convention.[59] It would seem, too, that a court must of its own motion consider whether there is a valid agreement on jurisdiction in terms of Art. 17, and decline jurisdiction if its own assumption of jurisdiction would be inconsistent with the exclusive jurisdiction so created.[60]

(12) Art. 17(4) provides that:

> "If an agreement conferring jurisdiction was concluded for the benefit of only one of the parties, that party shall retain the right to bring proceedings in any other court which has jurisdiction by virtue of this Convention."

This provision is an obscure one and its meaning is not clarified in the Reports on the Convention. Normally, a choice of court provision will be proposed by one of the parties to a contract in his own interest, often in the context of general conditions of business. Art. 17(4), therefore, may have the effect of allowing the contracting party in the dominant position to ignore a contractual provision which he himself has proposed.[61] No analogue to this provision is included in Schedules 4 and 8 to the 1982 Act.

(13) Art. I(2) of the Annexed Protocol provides that:

---

[55] See para. 5.22 above and *Zelger* v. *Salinitri* (56/79) [1980] E.C.R. 89.
[56] See para. 7.24 above.
[57] (23/78) [1978] E.C.R. 2133.
[58] On this point see the observations of the Advocate-General at p. 2149.
[59] Art. 17(1).
[60] Schlosser Report, p. 81.
[61] See Landgericht Trier, October 30, 1975 and Landgericht Mainz, February 24, 1978, Digest I–17.3 – B.1 and B.2.

> "An agreement conferring jurisdiction, within the meaning of Article 17, shall be valid with respect to a person domiciled in Luxembourg only if that person has expressly and specifically so agreed."

This provision contains a special privilege which it is not easy to justify. Whether the courts of other Contracting States require to take account of it of their own motion is not clear. The genesis and purpose of this provision has been explained by the European Court in *Porta-Leasing* v. *Prestige International*.[62] Its ruling was as follows:

> "The second paragraph of Article I of the Protocol annexed to the Convention of 27 September 1968 . . . must be interpreted as meaning that a clause conferring jurisdiction within the meaning of that provision may not be considered to have been expressly and specifically agreed to by a person domiciled in Luxembourg unless that clause, besides being in writing as required by Article 17 of the Convention, is mentioned in a provision specially and exclusively meant for this purpose and specifically signed by the party domiciled in Luxembourg: in this respect the signing of the contract as a whole does not, in itself, suffice. It is not, however, necessary for that clause to be mentioned in a document separate from the one which constitutes the written instrument of the contract."

(14) Art. 17 must be read subject to Art. 57. It is possible that a convention on a particular matter binding States parties to the 1968 Convention may have less restrictive rules of jurisdiction than are prescribed by Art. 17 (or indeed by Arts. 12 or 15). Art. 31, for example, of the Convention on the Contract for the International Carriage of Goods by Road (CMR) allows the parties to stipulate, by an agreement with no special requirements of form, that a designated court in one of the States parties to that Convention has exclusive jurisdiction.[63] Art. 57 would secure that this agreement would not be invalidated merely because it failed to comply with the formal requirements of Art. 17.

(15) The effect of prorogation agreements entered into before the 1968 Convention enters into force is considered above.[64]

B. Prorogation—Trusts

7.27   The central principle in Art. 17 is that the choice of a court other than one possessing jurisdiction under Title II of the Convention must arise from an agreement between the parties.[65] A trust, however, is not necessarily created by an agreement, and often arises from a unilateral instrument. Yet a court upon which a trust instrument has conferred jurisdiction is likely to be the most appropriate court to resolve disputes concerning the internal relationships of those with an interest in the trust.[66] Art. 11, therefore, of the 1978 Accession Convention adds to Art. 17 a provision that:

> "The court or courts of a Contracting State on which a trust instrument has

---

[62] (784/79) [1980] E.C.R. 1517, 1525.
[63] See the Landgericht Aachen, January 16, 1976, Digest I–57 – B.2.
[64] para. 3.50.
[65] See para. 7.26(5) and (6) above.
[66] See Schlosser Report, p. 106.

conferred jurisdiction shall have exclusive jurisdiction in any proceedings brought against a settlor, trustee or beneficiary, if relations between these persons or their rights or obligations under the trust are involved."

This provision – Art. 17(2) – appears to clothe the chosen court with exclusive jurisdiction even where the trust instrument does not in terms so state and may reflect a concern that the court otherwise possessing jurisdiction might be a court of a system ignoring the institution of trusts. Though the last words of Art. 17(2) arguably permit of a wider construction, it is thought that the provision would be construed as being confined to the internal relationships of the persons concerned. Art. 17(3) declares that the provisions of a trust instrument conferring jurisdiction will be of no effect if contrary to the provisions of Arts. 12, 15 or 16. These contingencies cannot often arise if only the internal relationships of persons with an interest in the trust are in point.

C. SUBMISSION

28   Article 18 confers jurisdiction upon a court of a Contracting State entertaining proceedings in which the defender has entered appearance without submitting a plea to the jurisdiction. The Jenard Report explains its purpose and effect clearly:

> "By conferring jurisdiction on a court in circumstances where the defendant does not contest that court's jurisdiction, the Convention extends the scope of Title II and avoids any uncertainty. The main consequence of this rule is that if a defendant domiciled in a Contracting State is, notwithstanding the provisions of the second paragraph of Article 3, sued in another Contracting State on the basis of a rule of exorbitant jurisdiction, for example in France on the basis of Article 14 of the Civil Code, the court will have jurisdiction if this is not contested. The only cases in which a court must declare that it has no jurisdiction and where jurisdiction by submission will not be allowed are those in which the courts of another State have exclusive jurisdiction by virtue of Article 16."[67]

A court before which the defender enters appearance without contesting the jurisdiction is a competent one even where the parties have earlier by agreement prorogated the jurisdiction of another court.[68] It was at one time argued, from the inclusion of the word "solely" in most of the texts of the second sentence of Art. 18, that a defender impliedly submits to the jurisdiction if, simultaneously with a plea to the jurisdiction, he makes any submission on the merits. This view, however, has been rejected by the European Court:

> "In fact under the law of civil procedure of certain Contracting States a defendant who raises the issue of jurisdiction and no other might be barred from making his submissions as to the substance if the court rejects his plea that it has no jurisdiction. An interpretation of Article 18 which enabled such a result to be arrived at would be contrary to the right of the defendant to defend

---

[67] p. 38. It is not thought, however, that submission to a court of a Contracting State brings a matter within the scope of the 1968 Convention which would otherwise be outwith its scope. See the comments of the Advocate-General in *C.H.W.* v. *G.J.H.* (25/81) [1982] E.C.R. 1189, at pp. 1208–1209.

[68] *Elefanten Schuh* v. *Jacqmain* (150/80) [1981] E.C.R. 1671, 1689.

himself in the original proceedings, which is one of the aims of the Convention.

However, the challenge to jurisdiction may have the result attributed to it by Article 18 only if the plaintiff and the court seized of the matter are able to ascertain from the time of the defendant's first defence that it is intended to contest the jurisdiction of the court."[69]

Though this ruling appears reasonably clear the European Court has reiterated that Art. 18 must be interpreted in the sense that the defender who simultaneously contests jurisdiction and submits in the alternative a defence on the merits is not barred from insisting on any competent objection to the jurisdiction.[70]

VERIFICATION OF JURISDICTION AND DUE SERVICE

A. Verification of Jurisdiction

7.29   Where a court of a Contracting State is seized of a claim which is principally concerned with a matter over which the courts of another Contracting State have exclusive jurisdiction under Art. 16, Art. 19 imposes upon the court a duty to declare of its own motion that it has no jurisdiction. Unless its jurisdiction is derived from the provisions of the 1968 Convention, Art. 20 requires the court to do so in all other cases where a defender domiciled in another Contracting State does not enter an appearance.[71] These requirements derive from the aim of the draftsmen of the Convention to secure that, in proceedings for the recognition and enforcement of the judgments to which it applies, there shall – in principle at least – be no examination of the jurisdiction of the court of origin. That court, therefore, must police its own right to assume jurisdiction under the Convention.

7.30   The duty of the court under Arts. 19 and 20(1) to verify its own jurisdictional competence is a novel one—for the Scottish courts at least—in relation to personal actions.[72] While both in the Court of Session and in the sheriff court, the clerk of court, when considering a pursuer's or petitioner's application for a warrant to serve, as an act of administration verifies that, *prima facie*, the court has jurisdiction and might decline to grant warrant where it appears to lack it, the duty imposed on the court in Arts. 19 and 20 is more explicit. The European Court has emphasised in a recent case that a national court must apply Art. 19 of its own motion when no party has raised the point in his own pleadings and even when its own procedural law limits the national court to disposing of arguments presented by the parties.[73]

---

[69] *Elefanten Schuh* v. *Jacqmain*, above, [14] and [15]. See also para. 2.21 above.

[70] *Rohr* v. *Ossberger* (27/81) [1981] E.C.R. 2431; *C.H.W.* v. *G.J.H.* (25/81) [1982] E.C.R. 1189 (third ruling); *Gerling* v. *Italian State* (201/82) Judgment of July 14, 1983 (unreported). It may be assumed that this view will be reflected in any relevant Acts of Sederunt.

[71] Where he does enter an appearance without challenging the jurisdiction of the court, the defender will be held to have submitted to the jurisdiction under Art. 18 unless another court has exclusive jurisdiction by virtue of Art. 16.

[72] See *Wall's Trustees* v. *Drynan* (1888) 15 R. 359, *per* Lord President Inglis at p. 363.

[73] *Goderbauer* v. *Syndic in Bankruptcy of B.V. Schroefboutenfabriek* (288/82), Judgment of November 15, 1983, (unreported).

B. VERIFICATION OF DUE SERVICE

7.31   Article 20(2) and (3) deal with a different topic, verification by the court of origin, in cases where the defender has not entered appearance, of the fact that he was duly served with the proceedings. The corresponding rights of the court addressed to examine the sufficiency of the service is considered in Chapter 8.[74] Before considering Art. 20(2) and (3), however, it seems desirable to point out that, with one exception, the 1968 Convention is not directly concerned with the service of writs abroad. The exception is found in Art. IV of the Annexed Protocol. This allows the transmission of documents abroad for service in accordance with the procedures laid down in any conventions or agreements concluded between the Contracting States. But it also provides:

> "Unless the State in which service is to take place objects by declaration to the Secretary General of the Council of the European Communities, such documents may also be sent by the appropriate public officers of the State in which the document has been drawn up directly to the appropriate public officers of the State in which the addressee is to be found."

This provision envisages the transmission of documents by messengers-at-arms or sheriff officers directly to their analogues in other Contracting States and is designed to avoid the delays which may arise when documents are transmitted through Government agencies such as the Ministries of Foreign Affairs.[75] The Maxwell Report[76] states:

> "We consider it desirable that service by *huissiers*, or transmission by messengers-at-arms or sheriff officers, should be allowed. This is likely to be the quickest and most reliable method."

7.32   Article 20(2) and (3) were drafted against the background of the laws of the original Member States[77] which, apart from those of Germany, permitted service upon the public prosecutor (or the walls of court in Italy) in cases where the defender could be served within the territory and, although in some of those States further steps were taken to secure the onward transmission of the writ, there was no assurance that the defender would receive the initiating document or receive it in adequate time to prepare his defence. The 1968 Convention sought to improve this situation in relation to defenders domiciled in another Contracting State, and Art. 20(2) and (3) impose on the court a duty, when examining its competence, to stay proceedings against a defender domiciled in another Contracting State who has not entered appearance:

> "so long as it is not shown that the defendant has been able to receive the document instituting the proceedings or an equivalent document in sufficient time to enable him to arrange for his defence, or that all necessary steps have been taken to this end."

Among the (limited) grounds for the non-recognition or non-enforcement

---

[74] paras. 8.17–8.18.
[75] Jenard Report, p. 41.
[76] p. 97.
[77] See Droz, pp. 165–167.

of a judgment under the Convention is the fact that, in cases where a judgment has been rendered in default of appearance, "the defender was not duly served with the document which instituted the proceedings or with an equivalent document in sufficient time to enable him to arrange for his defence."[78] One of the objects, therefore, of Art. 20(2) and (3) would seem to be that of reducing to a minimum the cases where Arts. 27(2) and 34(2) may be relied upon by defenders. This is in accordance with the general policy of the Convention to assure the quasi-automatic recognition and enforcement of judgments emanating from one Contracting State in the territories of the other Contracting States.

7.33   It is thought that Art. 20(2) and (3) apply only where the defender is domiciled in another Contracting State. This appears merely from the context in the English text but, by utilising the expression "*ce défendeur*," the French text makes the matter clearer.

7.34   Article 20(2) applies only if and so long as the Hague Convention of November 15, 1965 on the Service Abroad of Judicial and Extrajudicial Documents in Civil or Commercial Matters[79] does not apply in the circumstances of the case. The Convention is printed as Appendix 3 to this book. The United Kingdom became a party to the Convention on February 10, 1969, and most other Contracting States are parties to it.[80] Art. 20(2) is in effect a species of summary of Art. 15 of the 1965 Convention and as such it is somewhat lacking in precision. When the defender has not in fact received the initiating document "in sufficient time to enable him to arrange for his defence," it will suffice that "all necessary steps" have been taken to this end. In appreciating what steps will suffice, the court will no doubt have regard to the terms of Art. 15 of the 1965 Convention.

7.35   Article 20(3) of the 1968 Convention, however, contemplates as the norm that Art. 15 of the 1965 Hague Convention applies as between Member States. This provides:

> "Where a writ or summons or an equivalent document had to be transmitted abroad for the purpose of service, under the provisions of the present Convention, and the defendant has not appeared, judgment shall not be given until it is established that –
> (a) the document was served by a method prescribed by the internal law of the State addressed for the service of documents in domestic actions upon persons who are within its territory, or
> (b) the document was actually delivered to the defendant or to his residence by another method provided for by this Convention,

---

[78] Arts. 27(2) and 34(2).
[79] Cmnd. 3986 (1969). The Hague Convention is now in force as between the United Kingdom and, *inter alia*, Belgium, Denmark, the Federal Republic of Germany, France, Greece, Italy, Luxembourg and the Netherlands.
[80] In becoming a party to the Convention the United Kingdom specified in accordance with Arts. 2 and 18 that Her Majesty's Principal Secretary of State for Foreign Affairs is designated as the central authority; and the Senior Master, Royal Courts of Justice, Strand, London W.C.2., the Crown Agent for Scotland, 9 Parliament Square, Edinburgh 1, and the Registrar of the Supreme Court, Royal Courts of Justice, Belfast 1, are designated as additional authorities for England and Wales, Scotland and Northern Ireland respectively. The United Kingdom also specified that these authorities would be competent under Art. 6 to complete the Certificate of Service specified under Arts. 2 and 18. The same authorities are nominated under Art. 9 as receivers of process through consular channels.

and that in either of these cases the service or the delivery was effected in sufficient time to enable the defendant to defend.

Each Contracting State shall be free to declare that the judge, notwithstanding the provisions of the first paragraph of this article, may give judgment even if no certificate of service or delivery has been received, if all the following conditions are fulfilled –

(a) the document was transmitted by one of the methods provided for in this Convention,

(b) a period of time of not less than six months, considered adequate by the judge in the particular case, has elapsed since the date of the transmission of the document,

(c) no certificate of any kind has been received, even though every reasonable effort has been made to obtain it through the competent authorities of the State addressed.

Notwithstanding the provisions of the preceding paragraphs the judge may order, in case of urgency, any provisional or protective measures."

7.36   It is not within the scope of this book to comment in detail on Art. 15 of the 1965 Hague Convention; but certain points may be made –

(1) Art. 15 should be read in the light of the Convention as a whole, and in that of the official report upon it by M. Taborda Ferreira.[81] There are also useful comments in the Jenard Report.[82]

(2) The United Kingdom has made the declaration referred to in Art. 15, paragraph 2.[83]

(3) The 1965 Convention in terms applies only when the address of the person to be served is known.[84] This is likely to present problems of application where the address is thought to be known but is in fact incorrectly given. In such cases, it may be presumed, Art. 20(2) of the 1968 Convention becomes applicable.

(4) It is suggested in the Maxwell Report[85] that:

"Whatever method [sc. of service under the 1965 Convention] is used Article 15 requires actual delivery to the defender or his residence and proof of it will be needed."

It is doubtful whether this proposition is strictly accurate: para. 1(a) of Art. 15 refers to it being established that:

"the document was served by a method prescribed by the internal law of the State addressed for the service of documents in domestic actions upon persons who are within its territory."

The theory underlying the Hague Convention is that a defender resident in the State where service is to be effected cannot complain if he is duly

---

[81] Hague Conference on Private International Law, *Acts and Documents of the 10th Session*, Vol.III (The Hague, 1965), pp. 363–381.

[82] pp. 39–40.

[83] T.M.C. Asser Institute, *Les Nouvelles Conventions de la Haye (Supplément 1972)* (1972), p. 105, for this and other elements of the United Kingdom's declaration.

[84] Art. 1(2).

[85] p. 95.

served in accordance with the law of that State.[86] Certainly, this is all that seems necessary under Art. 27(2) of the 1968 Convention.[87]

(5) Contrary to the general policy of the 1968 Convention, a decision of the court of origin under Art. 20(2) and (3) of that Convention—read alongside Art. 15 of the 1965 Hague Convention—that a non-appearing defender did receive the document instituting the proceedings in sufficient time to arrange for his defence does not preclude the court of the State in which enforcement is sought from reaching a different conclusion on the facts.[88]

LIS PENDENS AND RELATED ACTIONS

7.37   Where actions have been raised contemporaneously before the courts of different Contracting States, Arts. 21, 22 and 23 regulate conflicts by prescribing rules of temporal priority. The legal systems of the original Member States had no analogue to the Scottish rule of *forum non conveniens*.[89] In internal conflicts the laws of those States generally applied the principle of *lis pendens*, which permitted the courts to dismiss an action when an earlier action had been instituted in another court between the same parties, founded on the same allegations, and having the same purpose. Only the law of Germany, however, applied this principle where the court involved was a foreign court.[90]

7.38   The risk, however, of contradictory judgments each with a claim to recognition under the Convention, persuaded its draftsmen to apply the principle of *lis pendens* in relation to proceedings in other Contracting States. It is not extended to proceedings in "third" States. Art. 21(1) states the principle of *lis pendens* in terms which are classic to French law[91] and the systems which follow it –

(1) An action must be pending in the other court. Different systems have different rules for determining the date when proceedings may be said to be pending for this purpose. While it may seem evident that it is for the procedural law of each court to determine whether proceedings are pending before it,[92] it is not so clear that the choice of the date of commencement of the proceedings, almost taken for granted both in the Schlosser Report[93] and in the Maxwell Report,[94] can lead to a satisfying

---

[86] *Acts and Documents*, above, p. 95.

[87] This is implicit in the decision of the Court in *Klomps* v. *Michel* (166/80) [1981] E.C.R. 1593.

[88] *Pendy Plastic* v. *Pluspunkt* (228/81) [1982] E.C.R. 2723.

[89] For the authorities, see para. 5.09 above, n. 22.

[90] Droz, pp. 181–186.

[91] Code of Civil Procedure, Art. 100; Giverdon, *Recueil Dalloz-Sirey* (1973) Chron., p. 155; Viatte, *Gazette du Palais*, (1976) 1. Doctrine, p. 354.

[92] Jenard Report, p. 41. See now *Zelger* v. *Salinitri* (No. 2) (129/83), Judgment of June 7, 1984 (unreported).

[93] p. 125.

[94] pp. 99–100.

solution in international situations.[95] Arguably, it opens the door to abuse of judicial procedure. Though it is recognised that this door can never be wholly closed, it is hoped that the European Court, which has a locus to elucidate the meaning of Art. 21, will have an opportunity to consider the matter.

(2) The action must involve the same parties. This does not mean, however, that they should appear in the same role: in the usual case, indeed, the defender in the first forum will be pursuer in the second.

(3) The actions must involve the same "cause of action." This term is less familiar to Scots lawyers than to English lawyers but its intended meaning becomes more apparent from the French text which states that the action must have "*le même objet et la même cause.*" This language echoes that of the internal law of France and that of Art. 5(3) of the Hague Convention of February 1, 1971 on the Recognition and Enforcement of Judgments in Civil and Commercial Matters. The phrase "*la même cause*" refers to the factual basis of the pursuer's claim. The phrase "*le même objet*" refers to the nature of the claim presented on the basis of those averments of fact. There will, however, always be differences, greater or lesser, in the averments of fact and the nature of the claims presented before the courts of different legal systems and, it is reasonably clear that it must be for the *lex fori* to appreciate whether these differences are such as to render Art. 21(1) inapplicable. If it so decides, however, the two actions are likely to be "related actions" in the sense of Art. 22 where the court has a discretion whether or not to stay or sist an action before it in the face of proceedings in another Contracting State.

7.39   In cases where the jurisdiction of the court first seized is contested, Art. 21(2) allows the second court merely to stay or sist the proceedings. One of the purposes of this provision is to ensure that no lacuna arises because both courts decline jurisdiction. The provision should not lead to the existence of more than one judgment, because the second court has merely the power to dismiss the action under Art. 20(1) or to stay or sist the action under Art. 20(2) and in the latter case—it may be presumed—only until the first court has determined whether or not it has jurisdiction in the circumstances of the case.

7.40   Where the concurrent actions before the courts of different Contracting States do not have identical parties, grounds of action, or conclusions but are related to one another, Art. 22 permits, but does not require, the court in which the later proceedings are brought to stay those proceedings. The term "related actions" is defined in Art. 22(3) to mean:

> "actions . . . so closely connected that it is expedient to hear and determine them together to avoid the risk of irreconcilable judgments resulting from separate proceedings."

---

[95] In the context of a plea of *forum non conveniens* Lord Hunter preferred to adopt the date of litiscontestation: "In principle, litiscontestation takes place when issue is joined. In modern Scottish practice, litiscontestation takes place when defences are lodged. It is at this stage that a decree *in foro* first becomes a possibility. Both parties become subject to the procedure of the Court and neither can escape from its toils until the action is judicially disposed of" – *Argyllshire Weavers Ltd.* v. *A. Macaulay (Tweeds) Ltd.*, 1962 S.C. 388 at p. 394. The author's attention to this point was drawn by Mr Paul R. Beaumont.

It may be observed – (1) that the power to stay is conferred only on courts other than the first court, and that the first court has no such power; and (2) that the power to stay may be exercised only where the actions are pending at first instance.

7.41   Article 22(1) permits a court in which later proceedings are brought only to stay or to sist the proceedings before it. The court has no power to dismiss the action. A power to dismiss an action is conferred by Art. 22(2), but subject to certain conditions. Before describing these, it must be explained that the English text of Art. 22(2) is not wholly clear and that reference has been made to the other texts in construing it. It may be assumed from their language, that paras. 1 and 2 are closely interrelated and that the operation of para. 2 as of para. 1 is conditional –

(a) on there being related actions pending in the courts of different Contracting States[96] and

(b) on those actions being pending at first instance only.

The main ambiguity in the text may be summed up in the question whether it is the law of the second court or that of the first court which must permit the consolidation of related actions. A literal interpretation of the English text points, though not conclusively, to the law of the first court and a similar interpretation of the French and other texts points to the law of the second court. The Jenard Report,[97] however, favours applying the law of the first court. That approach coheres with the thrust of Art. 21 which is intended to permit the dismissal of the action by the second court in favour of a first court having jurisdiction to try the two actions and, presumably, to try them together.

7.42   Article 23 provides that:

"Where actions come within the exclusive jurisdiction of several courts, any court other than the court first seized shall decline jurisdiction in favour of that court."

This provision has been discussed above.[98]

PROVISIONAL AND PROTECTIVE MEASURES

7.43   Article 24 provides that:

"Application may be made to the courts of a Contracting State for such provisional, including protective, measures as may be available under the law of that State, even if, under this Convention, the courts of another Contracting State have jurisdiction as to the substance of the matter."

7.44   The background to this provision (and analogous provisions contained in bilateral conventions to which the original Member States were parties) is

---

[96] In *Elefanten Schuh* v. *Jacqmain* (150/80) [1981] E.C.R. 1671, 1689, the European Court in its third ruling declared: "Article 22 of the Convention of September 27, 1968 applies only where related actions are brought before courts of two or more Contracting States."

[97] p 41.

[98] para. 7.17

the fact that many legal systems admit of provisional or protective measures only in the context of proceedings before their own courts and not in the context of proceedings before the courts of other countries. This was the position in Scotland: powers to arrest assets situated in Scotland, to grant warrant of inhibition over property situated in Scotland, to grant interim interdict and to make orders under section 1 of the Administration of Justice (Scotland) Act 1972 could be exercised only in the context of proceedings before a court in Scotland. It was also the position in England.[99] It was presumably thought that this limitation upon the availability of provisional measures was inappropriate in the context of a Convention one of whose main objects was to secure the equal treatment[1] of litigants throughout the Community.

7.45 Provisional or protective measures under Art. 24 may be ordered in the context of other judicial proceedings In *De Cavel* v. *De Cavel* (No.1)[2] the United Kingdom Government in its observations argued that, if provisional or protective measures were sought in the context of proceedings (in this case divorce proceedings) which were outside the scope of the Convention, the provisional measures themselves necessarily fell outside its scope. The European Court preferred a criterion related to the object of the provisional measures. A provisional measure may be within the scope of the Convention to the extent that its object is to protect maintenance obligations[3] (which fall within the scope of the Convention) but outside its scope if its purpose is to protect claims to matrimonial property[4] (which fall outside its scope).

7.46 The terms in which Art. 24 are expressed are extremely general and do not make clear whether the article may be invoked only as an adjunct to proceedings in another Contracting State with jurisdiction over the substance of the matter or independently of such proceedings. Since the taking of the measures to which the article refers may be required as a matter of urgency even prior to the initiation of proceedings in the appropriate forum, the wider interpretation is likely to be the correct one. Sections 25(1)(*b*) and 27(2)(*a*) of the 1982 Act appear to be drafted on this assumption. Apart, moreover, from stating that applications under Art. 24 may be made even if the courts of another Contracting State have jurisdiction as to the substance of the matter, Art. 24 does not indicate its relationship with the remaining provisions of the Convention, particularly those on recognition and enforcement. In *Denilauler* v. *Couchet Frères*[5] the question arose whether a French order arresting in security the assets of a German company in a bank in Frankfurt could be enforced in Germany notwithstanding that the document instituting the proceedings had not been served on the defender. It is, of course, normally a condition of the

---

[99] See the observations of the United Kingdom Government in *Denilauler* v. *Couchet Frères* (125/79) [1980] E.C.R. 1553, 1559.

[1] This is explicit in the references of the European Court to "the need to ensure . . . equality of the rights and obligations for the parties" under the Convention. *Cf. Somafer* v. *Saar-Ferngas* (33/78) [1978] E.C.R. 2183; *LTU* v. *Eurocontrol* (29/76) [1976] E.C.R. 1541 [3]; and, in the more general context of Community law, *Bergman* v. *Grows-Farm* (114/76) [1977] E.C.R. 1211 (the skimmed-milk powder case).

[2] (143/78) [1979] E.C.R. 1055.

[3] See *De Cavel* v. *De Cavel* (No. 2) (120/79) [1980] E.C.R. 731.

[4] See also *C.H.W.* v. *G.J.H.* (25/81) [1982] E.C.R. 1189.

[5] (125/79) [1980] E.C.R. 1553.

enforcement under the Convention of a judgment given in default of appearance that the applicant for enforcement should provide proof of service of the document instituting the proceedings.[6] Although in its observations the United Kingdom Government accepted the possible need for surprise in the taking of protective measures, it stressed the serious practical consequences which might arise if such orders were enforceable throughout the Community in the absence of any opportunity to present a defence. The European Court ruled that:

> "Judicial decisions authorising provisional or protective measures, which are delivered without the party against which they are directed having been summoned to appear and which are intended to be enforced without prior service do not come within the system of recognition and enforcement [of the Convention]."

The effect, therefore, of *ex parte* orders authorising such measures is limited to the State in which the order is made.

7.47   The Jenard Report[7] states that the measures to be taken under Art. 24 are a matter for the internal law of the country concerned. The maintenance of the existing law of Scotland, however, would have given little assistance to litigants in other Contracting States and section 27 of the 1982 Act makes express provision for Scotland[8] empowering the Court of Session (and the Court of Session only), in cases where proceedings have been commenced but not concluded in another Contracting State or in England and Wales or Northern Ireland, to grant warrant for the arrestment of any assets situated in Scotland or to grant warrant of inhibition over any property situated in Scotland, where such a warrant could competently have been granted in equivalent proceedings before a Scottish court. It may also grant interim interdict where such proceedings have been commenced or are to be commenced in those places. It is in all cases a condition that the subject-matter of the proceedings is within the scope of the 1968 Convention. It is not, however, a condition that there should have been any prior service upon or notice to the defender. Section 28 of the 1982 Act extends the power of the Court of Session (and that Court only) to make in the context of such external proceedings an order under section 1 of the Administration of Justice (Scotland) Act 1972 as if the proceedings in question had been brought, or were likely to be brought, in that court.[9]

7.48   The 1982 Act, moreover, makes it clear in s. 24 that any power of a court in Scotland – and this includes any court – to grant protective measures pending the decision of any hearing shall apply to a case where:

> "(*a*) the subject of the proceedings includes a question as to the jurisdiction of the court to entertain them; or
> (*b*) the proceedings involve the reference of a matter to the European Court under the 1971 Protocol."

---

[6] Arts. 27(2), 46(2) and 47(1).

[7] p. 42.

[8] For England, see 1982 Act, s. 25.

[9] The 1982 Act, s. 27(3), empowers the making of statutory instruments conferring wide powers on the Court of Session to make orders of the kinds specified in ss. 27 and 28 in relation to proceedings which do not fall within the scope of these sections, notably proceedings commenced otherwise than in a Contracting State and arbitration proceedings.

In contrast to section 27, this provision is general in its application and applies whether or not the subject-matter of the proceedings is within the scope of the 1968 Convention.

CHAPTER 8

RECOGNITION AND ENFORCEMENT UNDER THE CONVENTION

INTRODUCTION

8.01   THE 1968 Convention is unusual in that, in Titles III and IV, it regulates the procedures in, as well as matters of substantive law governing, the recognition and enforcement of the judgments to which it applies. It does so in some detail with a view, presumably, to ensuring that a substantially uniform scheme applies throughout the Contracting States. This scheme, like the rest of the Convention, is given the force of law in the United Kingdom[1] and must be interpreted in accordance with the principles laid down by the European Court.[2] The 1982 Act, as might be expected, contains certain additional provisions relating to the procedure for recognition and enforcement of judgments to which the Convention applies, but they are merely of a supplementary character.[3] They are likely to be reinforced in relation to Scotland by certain rules of court.[4]

8.02   The Convention is also distinctive in relation to the wide scope of the judgments to which it applies. Art. 25 contemplates the enforcement of any judgment in matters within the scope of the Convention. While the United Kingdom has in the past conceded certain preclusive effects to non-money judgments, it has enforced only external money judgments, either orders for the payment of fixed sums or, in the case of maintenance orders, periodic payments.[5] The Convention requires the United Kingdom to enforce non-money judgments, such as interdicts and orders for specific implement whose sanction is not necessarily execution against the assets of the defender. While in the past, moreover, the United Kingdom enforced only judgments which were "final and conclusive as between the parties thereto,"[6] the Convention carries with it the obligation to enforce interim orders. Finally, the scheme for recognition and enforcement applies not merely (as the 1933 Act contemplates)[7] to the judgments of superior courts but to those of any court or, indeed, tribunal in a Contracting State.[8]

8.03   The Convention is unusual, too, in respect of the relative narrowness of the grounds which it admits as justifying a refusal to recognise an external judgment. Jurisdictional controls are admitted only in relation to the special jurisdictions provided in insurance and consumer matters, to the exclusive jurisdictions specified in Art. 16 and to the special case provided for in Art. 59. Otherwise, as Art. 28 enunciates, "the jurisdiction of the court of the State in which the judgment was given may not be reviewed."

---

[1] 1982 Act, s. 2(1).
[2] 1982 Act, s. 3 and Chap. 2 above.
[3] 1982 Act, ss. 4–8, 11–13, 15 and 40.
[4] Not available at the time of publication.
[5] *Cf.* 1933 Act, s. 1(2)(*b*).
[6] *Cf.* 1933 Act, s 1(2)(*a*).
[7] s. 1 (1) and (2).
[8] Art. 25, applied to Part I of the 1982 Act by s. 15(1). *Cf.* also ss. 18(2) and 50 of the 1982 Act.

Earlier bilateral treaties on the recognition and enforcement of foreign judgments, whether entered into by the United Kingdom[9] or by the original Member States of the European Community, allowed of the examination by the court where recognition or enforcement was sought of the grounds upon which jurisdiction was assumed by the court of origin. Controls on public policy and other grounds are admitted by Art. 27 of the present Convention; but the limited scope of the jurisdictional controls represents a departure from previous practice rendered practicable only by the common acceptance by the original Member States of the jurisdictional provisions of the Convention.[10]

8.04   It follows that, apart from the cases specified in the previous paragraph, any challenge to the jurisdiction may be made only in the court of origin. In relation to defenders domiciled in a Contracting State the use of exorbitant jurisdictions is controlled by that court in accordance with Art. 3. But that article does not apply to defenders not domiciled in a Contracting State and the scheme of the Convention requires Contracting States to recognise and enforce judgments emanating from other Contracting States (subject only to the controls referred to in the previous paragraph), even when rendered on a basis of jurisdiction which, in terms of Art. 3, could not be applied to a person domiciled in a Contracting State. This has important implications which are discussed below.[11]

JUDGMENTS TO WHICH THE SCHEME APPLIES

8.05   Article 25 specifies the judgments which are to be recognised and enforced under the 1968 Convention. Some aspects of that article have been mentioned above,[12] but a few points may be considered in greater detail –

(1) Art. 25 applies only to judgments coming within the scope of the Convention, that is, to judgments in civil and commercial matters not otherwise specifically excluded by Art. 1. The European Court, as explained above,[13] has given a Community interpretation to the provisions of Art. 1 and a court in which recognition and enforcement of a judgment is sought is not bound by the determination of the court of origin that the matter falls within the scope of the Convention.[14] Partial enforcement is admissible[15] and so, presumably, is partial recognition.

(2) The judgment must emanate from "a court or tribunal of a Contracting State." The words "court or tribunal" are not defined, but it is thought that they are to be read in a broad sense so as to include any body, including an administrative tribunal such as an employment tribunal, which is bound to apply rules of law and follows a procedure which is essentially judicial in its character.[16] Art. VA of the Annexed Protocol provides that

---

[9] *Cf.* 1933 Act. s. 4(1)(*a*)(ii).

[10] An analogous point in relation to the preservation of the rights of the defence is made in *Denilauler* v. *Couchet Frères* (125/79) [1980] E.C.R. 1553 [13].

[11] See paras 8.23 and 8.24.

[12] para. 8.02.

[13] paras. 2.28–2.29 and 3.03.

[14] This is a matter of inference from Art. 42. See *LTU* v. *Eurocontrol* (29/76) [1976] E.C.R. 1541; *Gourdain* v. *Nadler* (133/78) [1979] E.C.R. 733.

[15] Art. 42.

[16] Droz, p. 267. The same words are used in Art. 177 of the EEC Treaty and, for their meaning in that context, see *Vassen* v. *Beambtenfonds Mijnbedrijf* (61/65) [1966] E.C.R. 261.

in matters relating to maintenance, the expression "court" includes the Danish administrative authorities.

(3) The reference in Art. 25 to judgments emanating from "a court or tribunal of a Contracting State" would appear to exclude decisions given by international tribunals sitting in a Contracting State.[17] Whether these words exclude decisions emanating from the courts of a third country and rendered enforceable by judicial decision in a Contracting State is less clear, but the scheme of the Convention suggests that it does not extend to "laundered" external decisions.[18]

(4) Provided that the judgment emanates from "a court or tribunal of a Contracting State," the jurisdictional basis of the judgment is in principle immaterial. The words "in principle" are used because the provision is subject to important qualifications described elsewhere.[19]

(5) The judgment must be recognised whatever the level in the judicial hierarchy of the court which rendered the decision.

(6) There is no indication in Art. 25 that it is intended to exclude judgments other than final judgments and the *De Cavel* (No. 1) case[20] confirms that interlocutory orders come within the scope of the provisions in the Convention for the recognition and enforcement of judgments. A German court, indeed, has given effect under the Convention to an interim award of damages made by a French court against German defenders.[21] But the Convention was apparently not intended to apply to interlocutory orders of a procedural kind, such as orders for the taking of evidence or for the recovery of documents. The original Member States were parties to the 1954 Hague Convention on civil procedure (which governs judicial assistance and the taking of evidence abroad), to the 1965 Hague Convention on the service of judicial and extra-judicial documents abroad, and, apart from Belgium, to the 1970 Hague Convention on the taking of evidence abroad. It was envisaged, therefore, that these Conventions would continue to apply under Art. 57 of the 1968 Convention. The United Kingdom is a party only to the 1965 and 1970 Conventions, but has also bilateral judicial assistance agreements with Germany[22] and the Netherlands.[23] Denmark is a party to all three Hague Conventions, Greece only to the 1965 Convention, and Ireland, apparently, to none of them.

(7) The nature of the judgment, whether for the payment of money, to interdict the commission of an act or to require the doing of an act, is *prima facie* irrelevant. Art. 25 specifically includes among the judgments to which it applies "the determination of costs or expenses by an officer of the court." It is thought to apply to orders for the payment of interest.[24]

(8) The courts of the State of recognition, including those of the United Kingdom, must endeavour to give effect to the judgment even if it takes a form unknown to the law of that State. The fact that this may pose difficulties is recognised by a specific provision in Art. 43 relating to "*astreintes.*" The reader is referred to the discussion of this matter below.[25]

---

[17] Droz, p. 268.
[18] See Droz, p. 270, and compare also 1982 Act, s. 18(7).
[19] See paras. 8.22–8.27 below and 1968 Convention, Art. 28.
[20] *De Cavel* v. *De Cavel* (No. 1) (143/78) [1979] E.C.R. 1055.
[21] Oberlandesgericht Celle, June 2, 1977, Digest I–27.1 – B1.
[22] Agreement of March 20, 1928.
[23] Agreement of November 17, 1967.
[24] See 1982 Act, s. 7.
[25] para. 8.36.

8.06   The question whether special considerations apply to judgments dismissing an action is discussed elsewhere.[26]

RECOGNITION

A. INTRODUCTION

8.07   The provisions for the recognition of judgments under the 1968 Convention are set out in Section 1 of Title III of the Convention. There is a close relationship, however, between those provisions and the provisions of the Convention relating to the enforcement of judgments. Firstly, the class of judgments to which the enforcement procedures apply is identical with that of the judgments which attract recognition and the reader is referred to the discussion of Art. 25 above. Secondly, the grounds in Arts. 27 and 28 which justify the non-recognition of such judgments may also be adduced in terms of Art. 34 to justify their non-enforcement. Thirdly, the procedures adopted to secure or to contest the enforcement of judgments in Sections 2 and 3 of Title III of the Convention are adopted by Art. 26(2) for the adjudication of similar issues in the context of their recognition. The most evident difference between the two sets of provisions is that the provisions for enforcement apply only to a judgment which is enforceable in the Contracting State where it was given.[27]

B. CONCEPT OF RECOGNITION

8.08   Article 26(1) states quite simply that:

> "A judgment given in a Contracting State shall be recognised in the other Contracting States without any special procedure being required."

Despite the unqualified language of Art. 26(1) it must be read subject to Arts. 27 and 28 which state limited grounds for challenging recognition. The procedure is prescribed in Art. 26(2) and (3). Such a challenge will normally arise as an incident in the course of other proceedings and, in this case, Art. 26(3) provides that the court dealing with the principal question has jurisdiction to deal with the incidental question. But the duty to recognise a judgment within the scope of the Convention may arise as a separate issue, for example, when one of the parties to the original proceedings or an interested third party seeks to secure the recognition of a judgment which is not necessarily itself susceptible of enforcement. In such a case Art. 26(2) requires the application – presumably, *mutatis mutandis* – of the procedures designed for the enforcement of foreign judgments.

8.09   Article 26 stands in contrast with the general laws of the Member States which, apart from those of Germany, subordinate even the recognition of foreign judgments to certain procedures designed to demonstrate their

---

[26] para. 8.11.
[27] Art. 31(1).

authority, the procedure of *delibazione* in Italy, that of *exequatur* in France, Belgium and Luxembourg, and a form of judicial authorisation in Dutch law. Art. 26, however, had its analogues in bilateral treaties entered into by the Member States with others of their number or with non-Member States. The relevant provisions of these conventions generally state that the recognised decision should have in the other State the force of *la chose jugée* or *res judicata*. These words are omitted in Art. 26 because, as the Jenard Report explains,[28] the Convention applies to interlocutory decisions, and these do not always have the effect of *res judicata*. It is thought, however, with Droz,[29] that the omission of these words has little practical significance. The recognition of a judgment implies, to borrow the language of s. 8(1) of the 1933 Act, that it:

> "shall be recognised as conclusive between the parties thereto in all proceedings founded upon the same cause of action and may be relied on by way of defence or counterclaim in any such proceedings."

Droz[30] distinguishes between the positive and the negative effects of recognition. Positively, for example, a money judgment emanating from one Contracting State and falling to be recognised under the Convention, could be founded upon in another Contracting State to extinguish in whole or in part by way of compensation a debt due by the judgment creditor to the judgment debtor. Again, a judgment in one Contracting State concerning the ownership of a painting would confer a title on the owner to recover the painting from a dealer or other person holding a temporary title. Negatively, the recognition of a foreign decision implies that neither party to the proceedings in the court of origin may institute other proceedings on the same grounds in the courts of another Contracting State.

8.10   The latter proposition is illustrated by the decision of the European Court in *De Wolf* v. *Cox*.[31] After obtaining decree against a Netherlands company in a Belgian court the pursuer brought fresh proceedings for a similar order in the Netherlands on the ground that this course of action would be less expensive than enforcement under the Convention. On the issue being referred to it, the European Court ruled that:

> "The provisions of the Convention . . . prevent a party who has obtained a judgment in his favour in a Contracting State, being a judgment for which an order for enforcement under Article 31 of the Convention may issue in another Contracting State, from making an application to a court in that other State for a judgment against the other party in the same terms as the judgment delivered in the first State."

This decision was followed by a Belgian court in a case[32] where German proceedings had terminated in a settlement between the parties approved by the court and declared enforceable in Germany. This was held to preclude the party in whose favour the judgment had been given applying to a Belgian court for a judgment in the same terms as the German judgment.

---

[28] p. 43.
[29] p. 275.
[30] pp. 275–280.
[31] (42/76) [1976] E.C.R. 1759.
[32] *Clausen-Werft KG and Clausen* v. *Internationale Stoombootdiensten*, Vredegerecht, Antwerp, February 15, 1977. Digest I–51 – B1.

8.11   A special problem, however, arises in relation to judgments which dismiss an action without deciding upon the merits of the case, such as judgments dismissing an action on the ground of lack of jurisdiction or because it is time-barred.[33] There is no question of the *enforcement* of such a judgment, because there is no decree which has operational effect.[34] What, however, does the *recognition* of such a judgment imply? In relation to judgments dismissing an action on the ground of lack of jurisdiction, it is hardly convincing to argue that the dismissal of an action by a French court because it lacks jurisdiction under the Convention should bar a Scottish court from subsequently assuming jurisdiction to entertain the proceedings. The Scottish court, nevertheless, might require to take notice of certain aspects of the French judgment. It should recognise and give appropriate effect to the French court's grounds for dismissing the action, *e.g.* its determination that the defender was not domiciled in France. It should also, it is thought, apply the principle that the initiation of the French proceedings might itself be sufficient to interrupt the running of any prescription or period of limitation in Scotland.[35] Judgments of another Contracting State dismissing an action on the basis of a procedural limitation under the *lex fori* would seem to be *in pari casu*. The fact that an action has been dismissed as time-barred in Germany does not necessarily mean that it should not be open to the pursuer to initiate fresh proceedings in Scotland, where the action may not be time-barred. This view is taken despite the fact that clause 3 of the Foreign Limitation Periods Bill, now before Parliament, provides that a foreign decision on a limitation point is to be treated, at least for England and Wales, as a decision on the merits.[36]

C. PRINCIPAL GROUNDS OF NON-RECOGNITION

(a) Introduction

8.12   A judgment, however, though falling within the scope of Art. 25, need not be recognised if, and to the extent that, it falls within one or more of the five exceptions specified in Art. 27. The words "and to the extent that" have no express justification in the language of Art. 27. Art. 42, however, provides that:

> "Where a foreign judgment has been given in respect of several matters and enforcement cannot be authorised for all of them, the court shall authorise enforcement for one or more of them."

Since the grounds of non-enforcement – with one principal exception, the non-enforceability of the judgment in the State of origin – are identical with the grounds of non-recognition, it would seem that partial recognition only is not excluded.

---

[33] See Schlosser Report, pp. 127–128.
[34] Excluding, of course, any order for costs or expenses.
[35] *Cf.* Oberlandesgericht Düsseldorf, December 9, 1977, Digest I–26 – B1.
[36] *Cf. Black-Clawson International Ltd.* v. *Papierwerke Waldhof-Aschaffenburg* [1975] A.C. 591. The Foreign Limitation Periods Bill, which has already passed in the House of Lords, is to have its second reading in the House of Commons on March 19, 1984.

(b) Public policy

8.13   The first of the exceptions in Art. 27 is the classic exception that a judgment need not be recognised if such recognition is contrary to public policy in the State in which recognition is sought. The use of the words "such recognition" was intended, the Jenard Report states,[37] to emphasise that the *de quo* is not whether the foreign judgment is contrary to the public policy of the State where recognition is sought but rather whether *recognition* of the judgment would be contrary to such policy.[38] As a French judgment[39] explains:

> "Mere differences between the laws involved did not . . . lead to incompatibility with French public policy. That policy did not in principle prevent positions reached in private law abroad from having effect in France. Moreover, although the Brussels Convention also contained in Article 27 a public policy provision corresponding to that in French law, it only took effect in exceptional cases. It was not the task of the court to ascertain the compatibility of the foreign judgment with domestic public policy but rather to consider whether recognition of that judgment offended against public policy."

8.14   Public policy is not defined in the Convention and only one limitation upon its application is specified, that it cannot be used to challenge the assumption of jurisdiction by the court of origin.[40] It will be noticed, too, that the public policy referred to is "public policy in the State in which recognition is sought." This suggests that public policy in this context is the public policy of that State and not a Community concept of public policy. Yet it is possible that the European Court might intervene if an unreasonably wide scope were given to the concept of public policy in any Contracting State. In two cases concerned with the concept in general Community law the European Court has ruled that, in so far as public policy may be used as a justification for departing from fundamental principles of that law:

> "its scope cannot be determined unilaterally by each Member State without being subject to control by the institutions of the Community. Nevertheless, the particular circumstances justifying recourse to the concept of public policy may vary from one country to another and from one period to another and it is therefore necessary in this matter to allow the competent national authorities an area of discretion within the limits imposed by the Treaty."[41]

8.15   But there is no Scottish authority and little United Kingdom authority on the ambit of public policy in this context. The issue is confused by the existence in the 1933 Act of the further exception that the judgment was obtained by fraud. It is thought, nevertheless, that the enforcement of decisions impetrated by fraud is best regarded as excluded by the public policy exception in Art. 27(1).[42]

---

[37] p. 44.
[38] *Cf.* 1933 Act, s. 4(1)(*a*)(v), which states that a judgment may be set aside "if the enforcement of the judgment would be contrary to public policy in the country of the registering court."
[39] *Almacoa* v. *Éts. Moteurs Cérès*, Tribunal de Grande Instance, Troyes, October 4. 1978. Digest I–27. 1 – B4; 1979 *Clunet* p. 623, note Huet and Kovar.
[40] Art. 28(3).
[41] *Van Duyn* v. *Home Office* (41/74) [1974] E.C.R. 1337 [18]; *R.* v. *Bouchereau* (30/77) [1977] E.C.R. 1999 [33] and [34].
[42] Schlosser Report, p. 128; Droz, pp. 311–313.

8.16 Lord Denning has suggested,[43] obiter, that the enforcement of a judgment for exemplary or punitive damages is not contrary to public policy, but the issue cannot be regarded as being conclusively decided. The matter arises with some force in relation to judgments for multiple damages as defined in section 5(3) of the Protection of Trading Interests Act 1980. Under section 5(1) of that Act such judgments can neither be registered under Part II of the Administration of Justice Act 1920 nor under Part I of the Foreign Judgments (Reciprocal Enforcement) Act 1933 and *no court in the United Kingdom shall entertain proceedings at common law for the recovery of a sum payable under such a judgment*. These last words suggest that there is at least an arguable case for saying that the enforcement of a judgment for multiple damages may be regarded as contrary to public policy in the legal systems of the United Kingdom even when the judgment emanates from a Contracting State.

(c) Absence of service

8.17 The second of the exceptions in Art. 27 excludes the recognition of a judgment:

> "given in default of appearance, if the defendant was not duly served with the document which instituted the proceedings or with an equivalent document in sufficient time to enable him to arrange for his defence."[44]

This does not:

> "require proof that the document which instituted the proceedings was actually brought to the knowledge of the defendant . . . the court in which enforcement is sought is ordinarily justified in considering that, following due service, the defendant is able to take steps to defend his interests as soon as the document has been served on him at his habitual residence or elsewhere . . ."[45]

Although it was argued in the *Pendy Plastic* case[46] that any control by the court in which recognition was sought was excluded where the court of origin had already held that the corresponding requirements of Art. 20 had been fulfilled, the European Court stressed that the purpose of Art. 27(2) is to ensure that the defender's rights are adequately protected:

> "For that reason, jurisdiction to determine whether the document introducing the proceedings was properly served was conferred both on the court of the original State and on the court of the State in which enforcement is sought. Thus, in accordance with the objective of Article 27 of the Convention, the court of the State in which enforcement is sought must examine the question posed by paragraph (2) of that article, notwithstanding the decision given by the court of the original State on the basis of the second and third paragraphs of Article 20."

---

[43] *S.A. Consortium General Textiles* v. *Sun and Sand Agencies* [1978] Q.B. 279, 299–300.

[44] *Cf.* 1933 Act, s. 4(1)(*a*)(iii) and Hague Convention of February 1, 1971 on the Recognition and Enforcement of Foreign Judgments in Civil and Commercial Matters, Cmnd. 3986 (1969), Art. 6.

[45] *Klomps* v. *Michel* (166/80) [1981] E.C.R. 1593 [19].

[46] *Pendy Plastic* v. *Pluspunkt* (288/81) [1982] E.C.R. 2723 [13], affirming its previous decision in *Klomps* v. *Michel* (166/80) [1981] E.C.R. 1593.

This principle also applies to orders for provisional and protective measures made under Art. 24 of the Convention.[47]

8.18   The expression "document instituting the proceedings" in Art. 27(2) has been intepreted by the European Court so as to:

> ". . . cover any document, such as an order for payment (Zahlungsbefehl) in German law, service of which enables the plaintiff, under the law of the State of the court in which the judgment was given, to obtain, in default of appropriate action taken by the defendant, a decision capable of being recognised and enforced under the provisions of the Convention."[48]

(d) Conflicting judgments

8.19   Article 27(3) declares that a judgment shall not be recognised if it is "irreconcilable with a judgment given in a dispute between the same parties in the State in which recognition is sought." Although this provision is relatively wide in the sense that, unlike Art. 27(5), it does not require that the two judgments have involved the same cause of action, Art. 27(3) is narrow in the sense that it applies only to a judgment given between the same parties in the State in which recognition is sought.

8.20   To meet this problem the 1978 Accession Convention added to Art. 27 an additional paragraph – paragraph 5 – providing that:

> "A judgment shall not be recognised . . . if it is irreconcilable with an earlier judgment given in a non-Contracting State involving the same cause of action and between the same parties, provided that this latter judgment fulfils the conditions necessary for its recognition in the State addressed."

This provision, unlike Art. 5 of the Hague Convention of February 1, 1971, upon which it is said to be based,[49] applies only to a judgment given in a non-Contracting State. It does not purport to resolve a conflict with a judgment given in another Contracting State. Such conflicts should be rare having regard to the provisions for litispendence and related actions in Arts. 21 and 22, but it would be sanguine to suppose that they will not arise. Art. 27(5) adopts the classic phraseology of continental systems relating to litispendence and comes into operation only where the earlier judgment involves the same parties and the same cause of action. Cases, however, might arise where, although the causes of action in the two proceedings were different, the recognition of a judgment emanating from a Contracting State would be inconsistent with a decision, earlier recognised, emanating from a non-Contracting State on a parallel issue arising from the same facts.

(e) Misapplication of choice of law rules

8.21   Reference has already been made to the legal background against which Art. 27(4) was written.[50] Art. 29 excludes in general terms any inquiry into the merits of a foreign judgment and so excludes in principle a refusal to recognise or enforce a decision on the ground that to reach it the court of the State of origin has applied a law other than that which would have been

---

[47] *Denilauler* v. *Couchet Frères* (125/79) [1980] E.C.R. 1553.
[48] *Klomps* v. *Michel* (166/80) [1981] E.C.R. 1593 [11].
[49] Schlosser Report, p. 131.
[50] See paras. 1.13 and 1.14 above.

applicable under the rules of private international law of the State addressed. Art. 27(4) attenuates the rigour of this principle in cases where, to
reach its decision, the court of the State of origin had to decide a preliminary question on certain issues excluded from the Convention by Art. 1 and
has reached a result different from that which would have followed from
the application to that preliminary question of the rules of private
international law of the State addressed.[51] The mere fact that the different
choice of law rule was applied is not in itself a ground for non-recognition:
the court must further examine whether the practical result reached would
be different. The object of Art. 27(4) is clearly to ensure that the
recognition of a foreign decision on a matter to which the Convention
applies does not conduce to giving indirect effect to decisions on matters to
which the Convention does not apply. Its main field of operation is likely to
be in the context of maintenance orders.

D. OTHER GROUNDS OF NON-RECOGNITION

.22   Reference was made in the introduction to this Chapter to the general
principle established in Art. 28(3) that "the jurisdiction of the court of the
State in which the judgment was given may not be reviewed." This
provision is reinforced with additional words prohibiting recourse to public
policy as an indirect way of securing jurisdictional controls. The general
principle, however, is qualified by Art. 28(1) which states that:

> "a judgment shall not be recognised if it conflicts with the provisions of
> Sections 3, 4 or 5 of Title II, or in a case provided for in Article 59."

The Jenard Report[52] explains that the rules in Sections 3, 4 and 5 of Title II
were regarded as being virtually rules of public policy so that breach of
them justified the otherwise unusual sanction of non-recognition of any
subsequent judgment. Even so, Art. 28(2) requires the court or authority
of the State of recognition to accept the findings of fact on which the court
of the State in which the judgment was given based its jurisdiction.[53] In
practice, therefore, unless in relation to Art. 59 cases, Art. 28(1) will not
often be invoked with strong prospects of success.

.23   Article 59 takes as its point of departure the fact that, except for the
provisions of Art. 16 (which are of general application), the Convention
does not preclude Contracting States applying to defenders not domiciled
in other Contracting States rules of jurisdiction other than those specified
in the Convention, and judgments proceeding on those grounds of
jurisdiction must be recognised in the other Contracting States. A French
national may sue a foreigner in France on no other basis than his (the
pursuer's) nationality,[54] and a judgment in that action would in principle
fall to be recognised and enforced in the United Kingdom under the
Convention. This may present problems. If, for example, a French
company sues a New York company in the French courts on the basis of
the former's nationality and obtains decree in France, the decree may be
enforced against assets of the New York company in Scotland, such as a

---

[51] See *Onnen* v. *Nielen*, Gerechtshof Amsterdam, February 19, 1976, Digest I–27.4 – B1.
[52] p. 46.
[53] *Cf.* Hague Convention of February 1, 1971, Art. 9.
[54] French Civil Code, Art. 14.

debt owed by a Scottish company to the New York company. The French company need only register the French judgment in Scotland under the Convention and follow this up with an arrestment and forthcoming. It is not to be expected, however, that either the French decree or the Scottish forthcoming will be recognised under New York law. Under that law, therefore, the debt owed by the Scottish company to the New York company will not necessarily be discharged. To recoup the debt, the New York company could presumably attach any funds in New York belonging to the Scottish company. The latter, and not the New York company, would be the loser.

8.24   With a view to meeting problems such as these, Art. 59 enables a Contracting State to agree with a non-Contracting State in a Convention on the recognition and enforcement of judgments not to recognise and enforce such a judgment, as Art. 59(1) puts it:

> "not to recognise judgments given in other Contracting States against defendants domiciled or habitually resident in the third State where, in cases provided for in Article 4, the judgment could only be founded on a ground of jurisdiction specified in the second paragraph of Article 3."

This power, however, is limited by the second paragraph of Art. 59 which excludes from its scope the assumption of jurisdiction based on the presence or seizure of property:

> "(1) if the action is brought to assert or declare proprietary or possessory rights in that property, seeks to obtain authority to dispose of it, or arises from another issue relating to such property, or,
> (2) if the property constitutes the security for a debt which is the subject-matter of the action."

No conventions have as yet been concluded by the United Kingdom under Art. 59. Negotiations for such a convention were initiated with the United States, but were eventually broken off. It is understood, however, that negotiations are continuing with Canada and Australia.

8.25   A specialised ground of non-recognition may be noticed at this point. Paragraph 1 of Art. II of the Annexed Protocol gives a person accused of an offence not involving intent on his part the right to be defended by "persons qualified to do so, even if [he does] not appear in person." This right is immediately qualified by paragraph 2, which permits the court to order an appearance in person and, in the event of the accused's failure to appear, the courts of other Contracting States are entitled to refuse to recognise the judgment in "the civil action" if the person concerned did not have "the opportunity to arrange for his defence." If, as might have been thought, Art. II applied only to cases where a criminal court has to judge at the same time questions of civil liability, paragraph 2 of Art. II would have been readily comprehensible. In the *Rinkau* case,[55] however, the European Court widened the application of Art. II beyond cases where in the course of criminal proceedings civil liability is in question to criminal proceedings "on which such liability might subsequently be based." It may be that the Court had in view cases where a conviction in the criminal proceedings is, in subsequent civil proceedings, evidence, or even conclusive evidence, that the person concerned committed the offence with

---

[55] (157/80) [1981] E.C.R. 1391.

which he is charged.[56] It is difficult, however, to reconcile this approach with the actual terms of Art. II, paragraph 2. This text appears to envisage only a civil action which is being tried in the course of criminal proceedings, since it is only in such proceedings that the accused (or defender) might not necessarily, without personal appearance, have "the opportunity to arrange for his defence."

.26   Articles 27 and 28 do not in terms state that they are exhaustive of the cases where a judgment coming within the scope of the Convention may be refused recognition, but an inference that they are intended to be exhaustive might be drawn from Art. 34(2). It is thought that too much should not be read into this article. The Schlosser Report[57] comments:

> "The appeal [sc. against enforcement] provided for in Article 36 can be based, inter alia, on the grounds that the judgment does not come within the scope of the 1968 Convention, that it is not yet enforceable, or that the obligation imposed by the judgment has already been complied with. However, the substance of the judgment to be enforced or the procedure by which it came into existence can be reviewed only within the limits of Articles 27 and 28."

There are two key problems in this context. The first relates to the recognition or enforcement of judgments given in a Contracting State which are inconsistent with a choice of court agreement. The Maxwell Report, [58] presumably on the view that the grounds specified in Arts. 27 and 28 were intended to be exhaustive, states that:

> "A Scottish court is bound to recognise and enforce a judgment from another Contracting State even if that judgment was pronounced in ignorance or defiance of a prorogation agreement valid under Article 17 prorogating the jurisdiction of a Scottish court."

This result, however, is a strange one, and the issue merits examination by the European Court. The second problem relates to the recognition of judgments given in a Contracting State which overlook the existence of a valid agreement between the parties to resolve the dispute by arbitration or which (wrongly) hold that the arbitration agreement is invalid. This question was discussed above,[59] where it was indicated that the Council Working Party was divided on the question. It will be an open one until the European Court pronounces upon it.

.27   In one respect at least it is clear that the specified grounds of non-recognition do not exhaust the cases where competent objections may be raised to the recognition and enforcement of a Community judgment in Scotland. Art. 57 as interpreted by Art. 25(2) of the 1978 Accession Convention states inter alia that:

> "Where a convention on a particular matter to which both the State of origin and the State addressed are parties lays down conditions for the recognition or enforcement of judgments, those conditions shall apply."

---

[56] See Law Reform (Miscellaneous Provisions) (Scotland) Act 1968, ss. 10 and 12. The principle that, as a matter of public policy, criminal convictions cannot be challenged in subsequent civil proceedings is familiar to continental legal systems.

[57] p. 134.

[58] p. 123.

[59] paras. 3.23–3.26.

One such convention is the European Convention on State Immunity, which starts from the principle of the non-enforcement of judgments against states. That Convention, however, admits of the recognition of such judgments subject to a number of conditions relating not only to public policy, due notice, *lis pendens* and *res judicata*, but to the jurisdictional basis of the judgment and the application of the appropriate law. The relevance of the European Convention on State Immunity is indirectly recognised in section 31 of the 1982 Act.

E. SISTING OF RECOGNITION PROCEEDINGS

8.28   Article 30 is a puzzling provision because (like Art. 38) it uses a distinction between ordinary and other appeals which is unknown to Scots law (or indeed to the other legal systems of the United Kingdom). In French law, however, Art. 527 of the 1975 Code of Civil Procedure specifies the ordinary appeals as being appeal (*appel*) and opposition (*opposition*) and the extraordinary appeals as third party opposition (*tierce opposition*), a petition for revision (*recours en révision*) and "appeal" to the *Cour de Cassation*. The practical distinction is that execution is suspended during the period allowed for presenting an ordinary appeal and during the course of such an appeal, but not in relation to extraordinary appeals.[60] Similar distinctions are known to other systems based on French law, but they differ considerably in detail.[61] Though, therefore, it was argued in the *Industrial Diamond Supplies* case,[62] both by the Government of the United Kingdom and the Commission, that the expression "ordinary appeal" must be construed by reference to the law of the State in which the judgment was given, the European Court pointed out that:

> "If the concept of 'ordinary appeal' were interpreted by reference to a national legal system . . . it would in certain cases be impossible to classify a specific appeal with the required degree of certainty for the purposes of Articles 30 and 38 of the Convention."

It ruled, therefore, that:

> "the expression 'ordinary appeal' within the meaning of Articles 30 and 38 of the Convention must be defined solely within the framework of the system of the Convention itself and not according to the law either of the State in which the judgment was given or of the State in which recognition or enforcement of that judgment is sought."

The European Court also pointed out that a court before which recognition or enforcement is sought is not under a duty to stay the proceedings but merely has the power to do so. This fact presupposed an interpretation of the concept of "ordinary appeal" broad enough to enable the court to stay the proceedings whenever reasonable doubt arises with regard to the fate of the decision in the State in which it was given. It concluded, therefore, that:

---

[60] See Herzog, *Civil Procedure in France* (The Hague, 1967), pp. 394–405 and 450–451; Code of Civil Procedure (1975), Arts. 539 and 579.

[61] See *Industrial Diamond Supplies* v. *Riva* (43/77) [1977] E.C.R. 2175, written observations at pp. 2178–2184.

[62] Above, at [24].

"any appeal which is such that it may result in the annulment or the amendment of the judgment which is the subject-matter of the procedure for recognition or enforcement under the Convention and the lodging of which is bound, in the State in which the judgment was given, to a period which is laid down by the law and starts to run by virtue of that same judgment constitutes an 'ordinary appeal' which has been lodged or may be lodged against a foreign judgment."

Following the criteria so laid down for determining the nature of an ordinary appeal, a Belgian court has decided that an appeal to the *Cour de Cassation* in France (though not an ordinary appeal in terms of the internal law of France) is an "ordinary appeal" in the sense of the Convention.[63]

29   The absence of any formal distinction between ordinary and other appeals in the legal systems of Ireland and of the United Kingdom persuaded the draftsmen of the 1978 Accession Convention to add an additional paragraph to Art. 30. It provides that:

"A court of a Contracting State in which recognition is sought of a judgment given in Ireland or the United Kingdom may stay the proceedings if enforcement is suspended in the State in which the judgment was given by reason of an appeal."

This criterion is significantly different from that adopted by the European Court in the *Industrial Diamond Supplies* case, but at least has the merit of clarity.

ENFORCEMENT

A. INTRODUCTION

30   The 1968 Convention sets out in some detail in Section 2 of Title III, provisions for the enforcement of external judgments. Those provisions are closely related to the provisions for recognition in Section 1 of that Title. It is clear that the judgment which it is sought to enforce must be one coming within the scope of Art. 25. It is also clear from Art. 34(2) that the grounds for the refusal to recognise a judgment specified in Arts. 27 and 28 are relevant to any refusal to enforce it. More generally, it may be inferred from the structure of the Convention that the judgment must be one entitled to recognition in the State where enforcement is sought.

31   The 1968 Convention differs from comparable instruments in that it does not leave the procedure for enforcement entirely to the laws of the States concerned but attempts to regulate it in some detail. The procedure is intended to be rapid[64] and, as a corollary, the person against whom enforcement is sought is not (at least initially) given notice of the application and the judge acts *ex parte* on the basis of the averments presented to him. The protection of the judgment debtor is secured rather by the facts that the court may consider whether one of the ·grounds for non-recognition of the judgment exists and that the person against whom

---

[63] *Continental Pharma* v. *Labuz*, Brussels Court of First Instance, February 28, 1978, Digest I–38 – B3.
[64] Art. 34(1).

the judgment is directed has a right of appeal. Otherwise the procedure laid down does not differ materially from that provided for in earlier bilateral Conventions to which the United Kingdom is a party. It is convenient to note at this point that Arts. 44 and 45 of the Convention and Article III of the Annexed Protocol facilitate the task of the applicant for enforcement by generous provision for legal aid, by disallowing any requirement for security for expenses, and by excluding the levying of *ad valorem* fees.[65]

8.32   While this is not a matter of express provision in the Convention, the European Court has inferred from the terms of Arts. 21 and 26 of the Convention that a person who has obtained a judgment in his favour in a Contracting State susceptible of enforcement in another Contracting State under Art. 31 cannot initiate fresh proceedings in that other State for a judgment in similar terms.[66] The language, indeed, of Arts. 31–45 suggests that the procedure which the Convention prescribes is intended to be the sole procedure available to applicants for enforcement.[67] An action for a decree conform, therefore, would not be a competent method of securing the enforcement in Scotland of a judgment to which the Convention applies. It may be added that section 34 of the 1982 Act provides that judgments given in another part of the United Kingdom or in an overseas country, including judgments to which the Convention applies, are a bar to further proceedings in England and Wales or Northern Ireland on the same cause of action, unless that judgment is not enforceable or entitled to recognition in England and Wales and Northern Ireland.

8.33   It must finally be emphasised that this Chapter is designed to describe *the provisions of the 1968 Convention* for the enforcement of judgments under it rather than to describe the detailed procedures of any particular State or legal system. In relation to Scotland, these detailed procedures are likely to be set out in Rules of Court. In the event, however, of any inconsistency between them, the provisions of the Convention would take precedence over those of the Rules of Court.

B. JUDGMENTS WHICH MAY BE ENFORCED

8.34   To be enforceable under the Convention a judgment must –
  (1) have been given in a Contracting State,[68] relate to a matter within the scope of the Convention, and otherwise come within the class of judgments specified by Art. 25;
  (2) not be vulnerable to the objections specified in Arts. 27 and 28[69];
  (3) be enforceable in the State of origin[70];
  (4) if the judgment is one ordering a periodic payment by way of a penalty, be in respect of a finally determined amount.[71]

---

[65] See paras. 8.69–8.71 below.
[66] *De Wolf* v. *Cox* (42/76) [1976] E.C.R. 1759.
[67] Droz, pp. 264–265; Maxwell Report, p. 161.
[68] Art. 31(1).
[69] Art. 34(2). See also paras. 8.12–8.27 above.
[70] Arts. 31 and 47(1).
[71] Art. 43.

It is thought, moreover, although it is not expressly so stated in the Convention, that enforcement may be refused to the extent that the judgment has been satisfied[72] and, it seems likely, where the applicant has failed to comply with procedural requirements, notably those prescribed by Arts. 32 and 33 and Arts. 46 and 47.[73]

8.35   Proposition (1) above calls for no further comment. In relation to proposition (2) it is evident that the court, in what is at the outset an essentially administrative procedure for the registration of a foreign judgment, will not necessarily possess the information required to enable it to decide whether any of the grounds of non-recognition are relevant to the particular case. Proposition (3) emphasises the central point that the judgment must be enforceable in the State of origin. This principle, a common feature of judgments conventions, is reflected in the drafting of the 1933 Act.[74] In relation to proposition (4), however, a fuller explanation is required.

8.36   Certain Member States enforce judgments, notably judgments requiring specific performance, by a system of *astreintes*, that is to say, orders for the payment of sums of money in respect of each day or week in which the judgment has not been complied with.[75] An *astreinte* is frequently pronounced at the same time as the principal judgment, but it may be pronounced subsequently. In the Netherlands, a party who has obtained an order for an *astreinte* may enforce the amount accrued without necessarily applying for another court order. In France, on the other hand, a further application must be made to the court before execution may proceed, and the court will not necessarily allow execution for all sums accruing to the date of the application. Art. 43 restricts the enforcement of *astreintes* to cases where the amounts of the payment due have been finally determined.

C. REQUIREMENT OF AN ORDER IN STATE OF ENFORCEMENT

8.37   While under Art. 26 of the Convention a judgment given in one Contracting State is to be recognised in the other Contracting States without the need for any special procedure, under Art. 31 the enforcement of the same judgment requires a procedure designed to obtain an order for its enforcement in the Contracting State where such enforcement is desired. To cater, however, for the fact that the United Kingdom, though not a federal State, has a number of systems of law, the 1978 Accession Convention added to Art. 31 a provision making it clear that a judgment emanating from a Contracting State will be enforced in England and Wales, in Scotland, or in Northern Ireland only when it has been registered for enforcement in that part of the United Kingdom. This provision, while taking account of the independence of the legal systems concerned, does mean that, if it is desired to secure enforcement of a judgment emanating from another Contracting State in different parts of the United Kingdom, separate applications for registration are required. The courts to which application must be made are specified below.[76]

---

[72] Inference from Art. 42(2).
[73] Jenard Report, p. 50. See also pp. 54–56.
[74] s. 2(1), proviso (b).
[75] Schlosser Report, p. 132.
[76] para. 8.43.

D. PERSONS ENTITLED TO APPLY FOR ENFORCEMENT ORDER

8.38   Article 31 states that the judgments to which it refers may be enforced in another Contracting State when, "on the application of any interested party," an order for its enforcement has been issued there. This provision is less than clear. The Jenard Report[77] merely indicates that it implies that:

> "any person who is entitled to the benefit of the judgment in the State in which it was given has the right to apply for an order for its enforcement."

E. PRELIMINARIES TO APPLICATION

8.39   Article 33(1) provides that the procedure for making an application for enforcement shall be governed by the law of the State in which enforcement is sought. In Scotland this procedure is likely to be supplemented by Rules of Court. The draftsmen of the Convention, however, have imposed a measure of uniformity on applications for enforcement throughout the Contracting States by stating a number of rules which form the nucleus of a common scheme.[78] Art. 33 starts this process by requiring the applicant (in short) to provide an address for service and to supply the documents referred to in Arts. 46 and 47.[79]

8.40   The requirement in Art. 33(2) that the applicant should provide an address for service or, where the law of the State in which enforcement is sought does not provide for this, that he should furnish a representative *ad litem*, links up with the provision in Art. 45 that no security, bond or deposit may be required of the applicant on the ground that he is a foreign national, or that he is not domiciled or resident in the State in which enforcement is sought. Art. 45 is discussed below.[80]

8.41   Articles 46–49 specify what documents are to be produced in proceedings for the recognition or enforcement of a judgment under the Convention. These articles should be read along with s. 11 of the 1982 Act and any relevant Rules of Court. Under Art. 46 a party seeking recognition or applying for the enforcement of a judgment must produce –

(1) a copy of the judgment which satisfies the conditions necessary to establish its authenticity, and

(2) in the case of a judgment granted in absence (*i.e.* in default of appearance), the original or a certified copy of the document which establishes that the party against whom judgment was granted in absence was served with the document instituting the proceedings or an equivalent document.

Under Art. 47, a party applying for enforcement must also produce –

(1) documents which establish that, according to the law of the State in which it was given, the judgment is enforceable and has been served,[81] and

---

77 p. 49.
78 See Arts. 31–49.
79 See Maxwell Report, pp. 131–132.
80 See para. 8.70 below.
81 See para. 8.50 below.

(2) where appropriate, a document showing that the applicant is in receipt of legal aid in the State which issued the judgment.

.42 Under Art. 46(1) it is for each State to determine the conditions necessary to establish the authenticity of a foreign judgment. Rather than leaving the matter in Scotland to the operation of the common law rules or in England to the relevant provisions of the Evidence Act 1851[82] and the Civil Evidence Act 1968,[83] the 1982 Act provides a common code. Section 11 in substance provides that a document which appears to be a copy of a judgment given by a court in another Contracting State and purports to bear the seal of the court or a certificate from an officer of the court will be presumed, until the contrary is established, to be a true copy of the original judgment. This provision, however, relates only to judgments and does not confer the same privileges upon the other documents referred to in Arts. 46 and 47. In relation to these, section 11(1)(b) of the 1982 Act merely averts the operation of the hearsay rule by making the original or a copy of these documents by itself sufficient evidence of any matter to which they relate and, in Scotland, makes corroborative evidence unnecessary. Art. 48 deals with the submission of alternative evidence and of translations. Art. 49 dispenses in the context of Arts. 46–48 with the need for 'legalisation'. This is a formality required in some legal systems (though not those of the United Kingdom) under which the provenance of a foreign judgment or other document must be verified by a certificate on the part of a public official, often a consul, of the country concerned.

F. Courts to which Application is Directed

.43 The courts to which an application for enforcement must be submitted are specified in Art. 32. While in the other Contracting States the application is submitted to a local court, in the United Kingdom (and Ireland) it is submitted to a superior court except in the case of maintenance judgments. The relevant courts are the High Courts in England and Wales and Northern Ireland and the Court of Session in Scotland.[84] Applications for the enforcement of maintenance orders are transmitted through the Secretary of State to the magistrates' courts in England and Wales[85] and, through the Lord Chancellor, to the magistrates' courts in Northern Ireland. They are transmitted through the Secretary of State to the sheriff courts in Scotland, and the procedure is likely to be specified in the new Rules of Court.[86]

G. Nature of Proceedings

.44 Article 34 emphasises that the proceedings are designed to be expeditious and of an *ex parte* nature. There is no procedure for notifying the person

---

[82] s. 7.
[83] ss. 2 and 4.
[84] See Schlosser Report, p. 133.
[85] 1982 Act, s. 5(1).
[86] See Maxwell Report, pp. 153–4.

against whom the enforcement order is sought and, even if he becomes aware of the proceedings, he is not at this stage entitled to make any submissions. The court is barred from reviewing the substance of the judgment[87] and Art. 34(2) states that it may refuse the application only for one of the reasons specified in Arts. 27 and 28. It is thought, however, that the court may also take account of other grounds, including the applicant's failure to comply with the procedural requirements of Arts. 32 and 33 and of Arts. 46 and 47. It may be supposed that the court is not bound by the uncontested averments of an applicant but may, where it considers this necessary, require the submission of further evidence.[88]

8.45   Article 42 provides that where a judgment has been given in respect of several matters and enforcement cannot be authorised in respect of all of them, the court may authorise enforcement in respect of one or more of them only. It may also authorise partial enforcement.[89] The possibility of partial enforcement only is reflected in the language of section 4(1) of the 1982 Act. This provision also envisages that the method of registration will be prescribed.

H. EFFECTS OF REGISTRATION

8.46   The Reports[90] on the Convention do not make it clear whether a registered judgment is to be given all the effects it has in the State of origin or those which a similar judgment would have in the State in which enforcement is sought. The 1982 Act adopts the latter view and states that a judgment registered under it:

> "shall, for the purposes of its enforcement, be of the same force and effect, the registering court shall have in relation to its enforcement the same powers, and proceedings for or with respect to its enforcement may be taken, as if the judgment had been originally given by the registering court and had (where relevant) been entered."[91]

This provision is expressly stated to be subject to Art. 39 of the Convention (restrictions on enforcement during appeal), to section 7 of the Act (interest on registered judgments) and to any provision made by Rules of Court as to the manner in which and conditions subject to which a judgment registered under section 4 may be enforced. Section 48(2) of the 1982 Act declares that:

> "Rules of Court may make provision as to the manner in which and the conditions subject to which a certificate or judgment registered in any court under any provision of this Act may be enforced."[92]

---

[87] Art. 34(3).
[88] *Cf.* Schlosser Report, p. 82.
[89] See Jenard Report, p. 53.
[90] The Jenard Report, indeed, at p. 49 uses language suggesting that the question was deliberately left open.
[91] s. 4(3). Corresponding provision is made for maintenance orders in the 1982 Act, s. 5(4) and (5).
[92] See Maxwell Report, pp. 160–161.

I. RESTRICTIONS ON ENFORCEMENT PENDING APPEAL

8.47 Since the procedure for registration proceeds on *ex parte* averments which the defender is given no opportunity to challenge, in an effort to balance the rights and interests of the parties concerned, Art. 39 provides that during the period allowed by Art. 36 for appeals against enforcement, as well as during the period while such appeals are under consideration, no definitive measures of enforcement may be taken. Protective measures, however, may be taken against the property of the person against whom such measures are sought.[93] In Scotland, those measures are likely to include arrestment, inhibition, poinding and interim interdicts. Giving effect to Art. 39 in Scotland, as the Maxwell Report indicates,[94] presents a variety of problems. Some of them, however, are resolved by the provisions of sections 27 and 28 of the 1982 Act, which give the court powers to make orders for provisional and protective measures in the absence of substantive proceedings in Scotland. These powers have been discussed above in the context of Art. 24.[95]

J. RIGHTS OF APPEAL

8.48 The provisions in the Convention relating to rights of appeal are complex[96] and it may conduce to clarity to consider separately, and in a summary way, the different rights of appeal of the applicant for enforcement and of the person against whom enforcement is sought.

(a) Rights of the applicant for enforcement

8.49 The applicant must be notified without delay of the result of his application for enforcement.[97] If the application is refused he may appeal in Scotland to the Outer House of the Court of Session[98] or, in the case of a maintenance judgment, to the sheriff court.[99] Art. 40(2) requires the judgment debtor to be summoned to answer the appeal and, if he does not appear, the court cannot proceed with the appeal unless it is satisfied

---

[93] See Jenard Report. p. 52.
[94] pp. 137–139.
[95] See paras. 7.43–7.48 above.
[96] See, generally, the Jenard Report. pp. 47–53. the Schlosser Report. pp. 131–135, and the Maxwell Report. pp. 124–126.
[97] 1968 Convention. Art. 35; R.C. 249H and Form 54.
[98] 1968 Convention Art. 40(1); Maxwell Report. p. 140.
[99] No period for this appeal is specified in Art. 40 as it is in Art. 36. R.C. 249I(5)(*b*) adopts a period of one month of the date of the interlocutor refusing the application.

that the judgment debtor has received the summons or at least that all reasonable steps to this end have been taken. In contrast with the position under Art. 20, this procedure must be followed even if the debtor is domiciled in a non-Contracting State. The Convention provides for a single further right of appeal on a point of law only, which in the result means one to the Inner House of the Court of Session.[1]

(b) Rights of "appeal" of persons against whom enforcement is authorised

8.50   Article 36 assumes rather than requires that notification of the decision on the application for enforcement must be given to the person against whom enforcement is authorised.[2] The service of a judgment on the defender is a feature of the procedural laws of France and of the legal systems based on French law, and the date of such service determines the date within which the judgment may be appealed. The ascertainment of the date of such service is thought to be a matter for the internal law of the State in which the judgment was given.[3]

8.51   Although the Convention professes to leave procedure for enforcement to the law of the State in which such enforcement is sought,[4] Art. 36 prescribes the periods within which an "appeal" against (or application to set aside)[5] the order for enforcement is competent. This period is one month, except where the person against whom the enforcement measures are authorised is domiciled in another Contracting State, when the period is one of two months. These periods may seem rather protracted, but the person seeking to enforce the judgement may apply to the court to order "protective measures" to be taken in terms of Art. 39. This "appeal" or application to set aside must be directed in Scotland to the Outer House of the Court of Session[6] or, in the case of maintenance judgments, to the sheriff court.[7] The decision on this "appeal" or application to set aside may be contested in terms of Art. 37(2) only by a single further appeal on a point of law, in Scotland to the Inner House of the Court of Session.[8]

(c) Sisting of proceedings where appeal lodged in courts of State of origin

8.52   Article 38 makes provision for the sisting of proceedings in an "appeal" or application to set aside under Art. 37(1) at the instance of the person presenting this "appeal" where an "ordinary appeal"[9] has been or may be lodged against the original judgment in the courts of the State of origin. Alternatively, the court may make enforcement conditional on the

---

[1] 1968 Convention. Art. 41 and 1982 Act. s. 6(1).

[2] The manner of such service is prescribed in Art. IV of the Annexed Protocol.

[3] Jenard Report. p. 51.

[4] Art. 33(1).

[5] Although the term "appeal" is used in Art. 36. it is envisaged in Art. 37 that the court to which the application for registration was presented should deal with this "appeal." The procedure. therefore. resembles an application under s. 4 of the 1933 Act to have the registration of a judgment set aside.

[6] See Art. 37(1)(2) and Maxwell Report. p. 135.

[7] Art. 37(1)(2) and Maxwell Report. p. 153.

[8] 1982 Act s. 6(3)(b).

[9] The meaning of this expression is considered in the context of Art. 30 at para. 8.28 above. Art. 38(2) provides that. where Ireland or the United Kingdom is the State of origin. any form of appeal will be treated as an ordinary appeal in this context.

provision of security. This provision seeks to protect the interests of both parties – so far as compatible with a system for rapid enforcement – until the issues between them have been finally resolved.

SPECIALITIES IN RELATION TO MAINTENANCE ORDERS

8.53   Matters relating to maintenance fall within the scope of the 1968 Convention. So far as relevant, the normal rules of jurisdiction apply to proceedings for maintenance but Art. 5(2) contains a special rule applicable in those proceedings. Similarly, the normal rules for the recognition and enforcement of judgments apply with only minor changes in the specification of the relevant courts in Arts. 32, 37 and 40.

8.54   These provisions, however, must be read subject to Art. 57 of the 1968 Convention which allows of the continued operation of conventions on particular matters which govern jurisdiction and the recognition and enforcement of judgments. In the field of maintenance obligations these conventions bite on matters of recognition and enforcement rather than on matters of jurisdiction. In relation to the former, it would appear that both the 1968 Convention and the 1982 Act assume the continued operation, alongside the provisions of the 1982 Act, of the relevant international agreements. The most important of these is the Hague Convention of October 2, 1973 on the Recognition and Enforcement of Decisions relating to Maintenance Obligations which as at October 24, 1983 had been ratified by France, Italy, Luxembourg, the Netherlands and the United Kingdom amoung EEC Member States. It is implemented in the United Kingdom by the Reciprocal Enforcement of Maintenance Orders (Hague Convention Countries) Order 1979, made under section 40 of the Maintenance Orders (Reciprocal Enforcement) Act 1972. The Hague Convention of 1973, as its name implies, contains provisions for recognition and enforcement only. Nothing in the 1968 Convention or in the 1982 Act appears to preclude reliance upon the Hague Convention, and the converse of this proposition would also appear to be true.[10] It will, accordingly, be for the maintenance creditor to elect which procedure to follow.[11] In relation to the Republic of Ireland special arrangements were negotiated between it and the United Kingdom and are governed by Part I of the Maintenance Orders (Reciprocal Enforcement) Act 1972 as rewritten for the purposes of those arrangements in Schedule 2 to the Reciprocal Enforcement of Maintenance Orders (Republic of Ireland) Order 1974.[12] Again, nothing would seem to preclude alternative reliance upon the special arrangements with Ireland or upon those of the 1968 Convention.

8.55   In relation to procedure under Title III of the 1968 Convention, section 5 of the 1982 Act makes special provision for the recognition and enforcement of foreign maintenance orders in Scotland.

(1) The application is made to the appropriate sheriff court under Art. 32(1)(2).

---

[10] Hague Convention of 1973, Art. 23.
[11] See Maxwell Report, p. 163.
[12] S.I. 1974 No. 2140.

(2) The application is not transmitted directly to that court but indirectly, through the Secretary of State.[13]

(3) The application is examined in the first instance by a prescribed officer of court and thereafter registered in a prescribed manner in that court.[14]

(4) A registered order is enforced as if it were an order made originally by the registering court – subject to any provision made by rules of court as to the manner in which and conditions subject to which it is to be enforced.[15]

(5) The single further appeals on a point of law referred to in Arts. 37(2) and 41 lie in Scotland to the Inner House of the Court of Session. In addition, special provision is made by section 8 of the 1982 Act as to the currency of payment of maintenance orders.[16] The detailed rules are likely to be specified by Act of Sederunt.

ENFORCEMENT OF SCOTTISH JUDGMENTS UNDER THE CONVENTION

8.56   Section 12 of the 1982 Act empowers the making of rules of court to enable any interested party wishing to secure under the 1968 Convention the recognition or enforcement in another Contracting State of a judgment given by a court in the United Kingdom to obtain, subject to any conditions specified in the rules, a copy of the judgment and a certificate relating to the judgment and the proceedings in which it was given. The detailed rules, once again, are likely to be specified by Act of Sederunt.

AUTHENTIC INSTRUMENTS AND COURT SETTLEMENTS

(a) Authentic instruments

8.57   Article 50 provides that an "authentic instrument" drawn up under the law of one Contracting State may be enforced in the other Contracting States in accordance with the procedures applicable to judgments.

8.58   Droz[17] explains that the concept of an authentic instrument is known generally to the legal systems of the Community. They are instruments which are drawn up or received by notaries and possibly by other public officers or officials and which, by virtue of their signature or registration, have a special probative force. In relation at least to some of them diligence may follow without a court order and, when this is so, Art. 50 contemplates that they should be enforceable in the other Contracting States. It is a condition, however, of enforcement that the instrument satisfies "the conditions necessary to establish its authenticity in the State of origin." In Scotland a document may be registered for execution in the Books of Council and Session or in the books of a sheriff court which, when extracted, may be enforced in Scotland as if it were a decree of the

---

[13] 1968 Convention, Art. 32(1); 1982 Act, s. 5(1).
[14] 1982 Act, s. 5(2) and (3).
[15] 1982 Act, s. 5(4) and (5). S. 5(4) is also subject to s. 7 of the 1982 Act and to Art. 39 of the 1968 Convention.
[16] See para. 8.68.
[17] pp. 391–392.

court concerned. The Schlosser Report,[18] therefore, indicates that such instruments are covered by Art. 50. There appears to be no analogue to "authentic instruments" under the laws of England and Wales or Ireland.

8.59   Such instruments are to be enforced as if they were judgments under Title III of the Convention, and Rules of Court are likely to make provision for the obtaining from the Keeper of the Registers a certificate to facilitate their enforcement in other Contracting States. In relation to incoming authentic instruments it may not always be easy to apply to them the provisions relating to judgments, such as the provisions requiring or implying that a judgment should be served.[19] Section 13 of the 1982 Act, therefore, permits the Crown by Order in Council to make modifications to the Act and to statutory provisions relating to it to take account of the specialities arising from the enforcement of such documents.

8.60   Article 50 states that an application for the enforcement of an authentic instrument may be refused "only if enforcement of the instrument is contrary to public policy in the State in which enforcement is sought." The word "only" contextually excludes the other grounds for the non-recognition of judgments in Art. 27, but can hardly be thought to exclude other possible grounds of non-enforcement, such as the fact that the instrument concerns a matter excluded from the Convention or the fact that to enforce it would breach rules relating to State immunity. Nor can it exclude inquiry into the validity of the authentic instrument in the country under the law of which it was created.[20]

(b) Court settlements

8.61   Article 51 provides for the enforcement of a settlement approved by a court under the same conditions as authentic instruments. Like the latter, a settlement must be enforceable in the State of origin.

8.62   The Jenard Report[21] explains that:

> "A provision covering court settlements was considered necessary on account of the German and Netherlands legal systems. Under German and Netherlands law, settlements approved by a court in the course of proceedings are enforceable without further formality (Article 794(1) of the German Code of Civil Procedure, and Article 19 of the Netherlands Code of Civil Procedure). The Convention, like the Convention between Germany and Belgium, makes court settlements subject to the same rules as authentic instruments, since both are contractual in nature. Enforcement can therefore be refused only if it is contrary to public policy in the State in which it is sought."

The new Code of Civil Procedure in France[22] makes provision for the conciliation of the parties on their own initiative or on that of a judge. The judge may be requested to make a record of the agreement of the parties, which is signed by him and the parties. An extract of this record may be delivered by the court and is enforceable. A similar procedure obtains in Belgium.[23]

---

[18] p. 136.
[19] *Cf.* Art. 47(1).
[20] See Droz, pp. 394–397.
[21] p. 56.
[22] Code of Civil Procedure, Arts. 127–131.
[23] Droz, p. 400.

8.63   In the application of Art. 51 the main problem is likely to be whether the accord is a simple contract between the parties which is not enforceable without further authority from the court, whether it is a judicial transaction enforceable in the state of origin in the sense of Art. 51 and which may be enforced in the same manner as an authentic instrument, or whether it is simply a court decree which falls to be enforced as a judgment under the Convention.

8.64   The Maxwell Report[24] usefully explains that in Scots practice a court, when asked to interpone authority to a joint minute settling a dispute between the parties, grants decree only in respect of those matters which had an appropriate foundation in the proceedings and such a decree is a judgment like any other Scottish judgment. The minute in relation to matters not covered by the decree is merely a contract between the parties which, not being susceptible of immediate execution, does not lend itself to enforcement under Art. 51. The Maxwell Report, however, suggests that the judgment following the minute may be enforced like other judgments under Arts. 31 and the following articles of the Convention rather than under Art. 51. The matter, however, is not wholly clear. If the purpose of Art. 51 is to assimilate court settlements of a contractual nature to authentic instruments so that they may be challenged only on the ground of public policy, it is arguable that they should be enforceable not as ordinary judgments but under that article. It does not seem appropriate that they should be open to challenge under, say Art. 27(4) or indeed any of the grounds of challenge in Arts. 27(2), (3) or (5).

8.65   The fact that a settlement otherwise coming within the terms of Art. 51 deals with matters outside the scope of the Convention as well as matters within its scope will not prevent the person in whose favour it was given enforcing the settlement in relation to those matters within the scope of the Convention. Thus the Paris Court of Appeal has held that a divorced wife could enforce in France provisions relating to maintenance contained in a settlement before a German court which regulated, apart from maintenance, *inter alia* the custody of the children of the marriage.[25]

8.66   It seems likely, too, that a settlement in terms of Art. 51 may have the effect of barring further proceedings in a Contracting State in relation to the issues disposed of in the settlement.[26]

INTEREST AND CURRENCY OF PAYMENT

(a) Interest

8.67   The Convention makes no provision for interest on judgments which fall to be enforced under it. Section 7 of the 1982 Act fills the gap, though it establishes both provisions of general application and provisions applicable only to maintenance judgments registered in a magistrates' court in England and Wales or Northern Ireland. In the provisions of general application it is laid down that a registered judgment will bear interest in respect of the period after, as well as before, registration at the rate due

---

[24] p. 167.
[25] *Hallais* v. *Kunz*, November 25, 1977, Cour d'Appel, Paris, Digest I–51 – B2.
[26] *Clausen-Werft KG and Clausen* v. *Internationale Stoombootdiensten*, Vredegerecht, Antwerp, February 15, 1977. Digest I–51 – B1.

under the law of the Contracting State in which the original judgment was given. In contrast, therefore, with the provisions of the 1933 Act which, after registration, permit of interest only at the rate applicable to judgments of the registering court,[27] those of the 1982 Act appear to treat interest throughout the whole period as a matter of substance, properly referable to the law governing the original claim. When evidence relating to the rate of interest and the date or time from which it is payable are adduced to the satisfaction of the court, both may be registered with the judgment.[28] No provision is made, otherwise than such provision as may be made by rules of court under section 7(2), for the alteration of the rate of interest so registered. Provision is made for interest to be payable on the expenses of registration recoverable under section 4(2) of the Act.[29] Although interest is in principle recoverable in Scotland on arrears of maintenance, it is not recoverable on arrears of a sum payable under a maintenance order registered in the magistrates courts – as distinct from the High Courts – of England and Wales and of Northern Ireland. It was presumably thought that the calculation of such interest would overburden those concerned with the maintenance collection functions of the magistrates' courts.

(b) Currency of payment

8.68   The Convention appears to assume that any judgments to which it applies containing orders for the payment of sums of money will be registered as to those sums in the currency of the original judgment.[30] In terms of the rule in *Commerzbank A.G.* v. *Large*[31] a Scottish court may give judgment in a foreign currency, and conversion into sterling takes place at whichever is earlier of the date of payment or date of extracting the decree. The Maxwell Report suggests that this principle might appropriately be applied to Community judgments registered under the Convention.[32] The 1982 Act, however, makes express provision for maintenance orders only which, if expressed in a currency other than that of the United Kingdom, are to be converted on the date of registration of the order and shall be payable in the currency of the United Kingdom.[33] It was presumably thought that in relation to other judgments currency conversion could be left to the general law.

LEGAL AID AND SECURITY FOR COSTS

8.69   Article 44 of the 1968 Convention envisages that, in the procedures provided for in Arts. 32 to 35 of the Convention, a person who has benefited by

---

[27] s. 2(2)(c).

[28] 1982 Act, s. 7(1).

[29] 1982 Act, s. 7(3).

[30] This has been the position under the 1933 Act since the repeal of s. 2(3) by s. 4 of the Administration of Justice Act 1977.

[31] 1977 S.L.T. 219. *Cf. L/F Føroya Fiskasola* v. *Charles Mauritzen Ltd.*, 1977 S.L.T. (Sh.Ct.) 76 and 1978 S.L.T. (Sh.Ct.) 27.

[32] p. 161.

[33] 1982 Act, s. 8.

any form of legal aid or exemption from costs or expenses in the court of origin should be granted the most favourable legal aid or exemption from costs provided for in the law of the State addressed. The restriction of this provision to the procedures which it specifies means that the United Kingdom's obligations in this respect extend only to the initial procedures for the registration of the judgment, but not to subsequent appellate procedures. The 1982 Act enables the United Kingdom to give effect to the principle embodied in Art. 44 by inserting a new provision of general application (which is already in force) into section 15 of the Legal Aid (Scotland) Act 1967 empowering the Secretary of State to modify the provisions of the 1967 Act to give effect to international agreements to which the United Kingdom is a party.[34] These agreements would presumably include, apart from the 1968 Convention, the Hague Convention of October 2, 1973 on the Recognition and Enforcement of Decisions relating to Maintenance Obligations, Art. 15 of which is in terms similar to those of Art. 44 of the 1968 Convention.

8.70   Article 45 of the 1968 Convention provides that no security, bond or deposit, however described, shall be required of a person seeking to enforce a judgment under the Convention on the ground that he is a foreign national or is not domiciled or resident in the State in which enforcement is sought. In Scotland, a pursuer resident abroad may be required to sist a mandatary. It has been held in the sheriff court that a provision in the Convention on the Contract for the International Carriage of Goods by Road that "no security for costs" could be required in proceedings arising out of a carriage under the Convention did not exclude the imposition of a requirement that a mandatary should be sisted.[35] The Maxwell Report[36] on the other hand, appears to proceed upon the assumption that the sisting of a mandatary comes within the scope of Art. 45. The interpretation of Art. 45 will ultimately be a matter for the European Court. Droz points out that, since Art. 45 makes no provision for any departure from its terms, it might put at risk a successful defender in enforcement proceedings.[37] The Scottish rule, on the other hand, is a discretionary one which may be applied to defenders as well as to pursuers, though it is normally required only of the latter.[38] It has been waived in relation to residents of countries with whom reciprocal arrangements exist for the enforcement of judgments.[39] The Maxwell Committee, in consequence, did not think that the Scottish courts would seek to impose any such requirement in the context of the 1968 Convention and considered that on that account, no legislation was required to implement Art. 45 in Scotland.[40]

---

[34] 1982 Act, s. 40(2). Corresponding provision is made for England and Wales and for Northern Ireland.

[35] *General Trading Corporation* v. *James Mills (Montrose) Ltd.*, 1982 S.L.T. (Sh.Ct.) 30.

[36] pp. 143–144.

[37] p. 377.

[38] Anton, pp. 552–554.

[39] *Doohan* v. *National Coal Board*, 1959 S.L.T. 308; *Vidlocker* v. *McWilliam*, 1964 S.L.T. (Notes) 6.

[40] p. 144.

8.71   Article III of the Annexed Protocol provides that, in enforcement proceedings, no fees or charges may be levied calculated by reference to the value of the matter in issue. It is believed that no such fees or charges are levied in Scotland.

CHAPTER 9

UNITED KINGDOM SCHEME FOR JURISDICTION
AND ENFORCEMENT

JURISDICTION

A. INTRODUCTION

9.01   THE Jenard Report stresses[1] that the Convention applies only where an international element is involved and that:

> "Proceedings instituted in the courts of a Contracting State which involve only persons domiciled in that State will not normally be affected by the Convention."

The United Kingdom, therefore, was free to retain its existing rules for the allocation of jurisdiction as between the courts of England and Wales, Scotland and Northern Ireland. Yet it seemed to the Maxwell Committee[2] and, it is understood, to the Kerr Committee, that there would be advantages in extending the jurisdictional provisions of the Convention to apply to cases involving the allocation of jurisdiction as between the courts of England and Wales, Scotland and Northern Ireland.

9.02   The reasons for this conclusion were complex. The 1868 and 1882 Acts had already been examined by the Scottish Law Commission in a consultative document,[3] and the Acts had been found defective in several respects. Apart from their archaic language and references to superseded institutions, the Maxwell Committee pointed out[4] that the Acts were confined to the enforcement of judgments for "debts, damages or costs"; the judgments to which they applied had to be registered within 12 months of their date; the distinction which they made between the judgments of superior courts and those of inferior courts was difficult to justify; nor was it easy to defend either the rigid jurisdictional conditions of the 1882 Act or the fact that it limits enforcement to the "goods and chattels" of the defender. The 1968 Convention by contrast adopts a relatively simple scheme applying in principle to any kind of judgment emanating from the courts at any level of the Contracting States, with no restrictions upon the period of registration and no restrictions upon the available methods of execution. In principle at least, moreover, no review of the grounds on which the original court exercised jurisdiction is competent.[5] This was acceptable to Member States only because they adopted simultaneously, in relation to fields covered by the Convention and to the persons to whom it

---

[1]   p. 8.

[2]   Report, pp. 16–23 and 276–279.

[3]   Memorandum No. 12.

[4]   Report, pp. 285–287.

[5]   In the special cases where such review is permissible under Art. 28 – in the cases envisaged by Sections 3, 4 and 5 of Title II and by Art. 59 – the court in which recognition or enforcement of the judgement is sought is bound by the findings of fact of the court of origin.

applies, common and acceptable grounds of jurisdiction, the observance of which in the last resort would be enforced by the European Court. Similarly, it was hardly acceptable to require the Scottish courts to give effect to the judgments of the courts of England and Wales, or of Northern Ireland, proceeding upon bases of jurisdiction which are regarded as so unfair to persons whose ties are with Contracting States that they should not be enforced under the Convention. The reverse was equally true.[6]

.03 Yet, within a unitary State like the United Kingdom, it was clearly important to simplify as far as possible the provisions for the reciprocal enforcement of the judgments of its constituent parts. It seemed inevitable, therefore, that the inter-United Kingdom scheme, like that of the 1968 Convention, should tackle the problem of exorbitant jurisdictions at its roots by specifying the rules of jurisdiction to be applied by the courts of one part of the United Kingdom in cases involving (notably) a person domiciled in another part of it. It was but a short step to conclude that it would be convenient for all concerned if, by and large, the same rules of jurisdiction were applied when the defender was domiciled in another part of the United Kingdom as would have been applicable had he been domiciled in another Contracting State.

.04 These, or similar, arguments appear to have been accepted and form the theoretical basis of sections 16 to 19 of the 1982 Act and of its associated Schedules 4 and 5. These provisions deal with the allocation of jurisdiction between the courts of the United Kingdom by applying with certain modifications the rules embodied in Title II of the 1968 Convention, and by treating each part of the United Kingdom as if it were a Contracting State under those rules. In consequence, persons domiciled in a part of the United Kingdom are to be sued in principle in the courts of that part, and may be sued in the courts of another part of the United Kingdom only on the basis of rules which are generally replicas of those specified in Sections 2, 4, 5 and 6 of Title II. Section 3 is omitted since, for reasons to be explained later,[7] it was not thought appropriate to apply within the United Kingdom the jurisdictional rules specified in the Convention for insurance matters. It will, of course, remain open to the United Kingdom to modify the scheme for the allocation of jurisdiction within the United Kingdom not only to bring Schedule 4 into closer accord with the 1968 Convention as interpreted by the European Court but, where necessary, to cause the former to diverge from the latter.[8] If, for example, the European Court were to interpret Art. 16(1) of the Convention as being applicable to simple claims for rent, it might be thought desirable to modify Schedule 4 to avoid creating an exclusive jurisdiction in such claims in that part of the United Kingdom where the property is situated.

.05 It may be useful also to recall that, in contrast with the position where the rules of jurisdiction of the Convention as such are applicable,[9] a court possessing jurisdiction under the provisions of sections 16 and 17 of, and Schedules 4 and 5 to, the 1982 Act is not bound to exercise that jurisdiction

---

[6] The 1868 Act, however, did not permit the registration in the other parts of the United Kingdom of a Court of Session decree in absence based on an arrestment to found jurisdiction – s. 8.

[7] para. 9.22.

[8] See 1982 Act, s. 47. The contrast between the language of paras. (*a*) and (*b*) of s. 47(1) is significant in this context.

[9] See paras. 5.02(5) above: Schlosser Report, pp. 97–99.

but may sist or dismiss the proceedings on the ground of *forum non conveniens* or otherwise.[10]

B. INTERPRETATION OF SCHEDULE 4

9.06   Section 16(3) provides that the court, in determining questions as to the meaning or effect of the provisions in Schedule 4, shall have regard to any relevant principles laid down by the European Court in connection with Title II of the Convention and to relevant decisions of that court thereon and may consider and give appropriate weight to the Jenard and Schlosser Reports. Where terms are defined for the purposes of the Convention by the 1982 Act, these definitions apply in the construction of Schedule 4,[11] notably the definition of the domicile of individuals in s. 41, the general definition of the domicile and seat of a corporation in s. 42, the special definition in s. 43 for the purposes of Art. 16(2) and for the other purposes specified in s. 43(1), the definition of the domicile of trusts in s. 45, and the definition of the domicile of the Crown in s. 46. Account must also be taken of the definitions contained in the 1982 Act which will apply in the construction of Schedule 4, notably the definitions of "association," "corporation" and "court" in s. 50. Finally, it must be emphasised that, whatever the apparent effects of section 16 of the 1982 Act and Schedule 4, both have to be read subject to the 1968 Convention and to section 17 of the 1982 Act.[12]

C. PROCEEDINGS WITHIN SCOPE OF SCHEDULE 4

(a) Persons to whom scheme applies

9.07   The first condition for the application of Schedule 4 is that "the defendant or defender is domiciled in the United Kingdom or the proceedings are of a kind mentioned in Article 16."[13] This requirement excludes from the ambit of Schedule 4 proceedings (other than those coming within the scope of Art. 16 of the Convention) against a defender who is neither domiciled in a Contracting State nor in the United Kingdom. Against such a defender the courts in England or Scotland may apply their own rules of jurisdiction.[14] Special provision is made for Art. 16 cases (where the courts have exclusive jurisdiction apart from domicile), to ensure that Schedule 4 allocates jurisdiction in those cases to the courts of that part of the United Kingdom in which the property is situated, the company, etc., has its seat, a public register is kept, or the judgment has been or is to be enforced.

(b) Proceedings to which scheme applies

9.08   The scheme applies only to proceedings in courts of law,[15] a term which, as defined in section 50 of the 1982 Act, excludes tribunals. Proceedings

---

[10]   1982 Act, s. 49.
[11]   *Cf.* s. 41(1).
[12]   s. 16(4).
[13]   s. 16(1)(*b*).
[14]   In the case of an English court those in R.S.C., Ord. 11 (S.I. 1983 No. 1181) (L.21) and, in the case of a Scottish court, those in Sched. 8 to the 1982 Act.
[15]   s. 16(1).

in tribunals and proceedings on appeal from, or for review of, decisions of tribunals[16] are excluded, presumably on the view that the jurisdiction of such tribunals is already the subject of statutory regulation. Some of them, such as the industrial tribunals, are organised on a United Kingdom basis. They will frequently deal, moreover, with questions which by reason of their subject-matter are excluded from the operation of the scheme.

(c) Subject-matter to which scheme applies

9.09   The subject-matter exclusions are more complex. In the first place, if the subject-matter of the proceedings would be excluded from the 1968 Convention by operation of Art. 1 (whether or not the Convention otherwise would apply to those proceedings), the proceedings are excluded from Schedule 4.[17] This would exclude from the scheme *inter alia* proceedings in status actions for which the ordinary rules of jurisdiction in patrimonial actions are inappropriate. But it would also exclude jurisdiction in matters relating to wills and succession from the inter-United Kingdom scheme, and the reasons for this exclusion – unless in relation to the resealing of grants of title to administer an estate – are less easily appreciated.[18]

9.10   Certain proceedings, however, whether or not they would otherwise come within the scope of the 1968 Convention as determined by Art. 1, are excluded by the terms of section 17 of and Schedule 5 to the 1982 Act.

(1) General exclusion

9.11   Section 17(1) provides that Schedule 4 shall not apply to proceedings in Scotland under any enactment which confers jurisdiction in respect of a specific subject-matter on specific grounds. A similar provision is included in section 21(1)(*a*) in relation to Schedule 8 (rules as to jurisdiction in Scotland). It seems likely that this provision was inserted for prudential reasons. As explained in the Maxwell Report,[19] it may not be easy to identify such rules but, where they exist, they should clearly have priority. The two cases referred to in that Report[20] are covered by special exceptions referred to in the following paragraph. Another exception is to be found in the Mobile Homes Act 1975.

(2) Particular exclusions

9.12   In addition to this general exclusion, section 17 declares that Schedule 4 shall not apply to the proceedings listed in Schedule 5 and empowers the Crown both to add to and to subtract from the list in Schedule 5 any description of proceedings in any part of the United Kingdom. The following are the proceedings specifically listed in Schedule 5:

Proceedings under the Companies Acts

"1. Proceedings for the winding up of a company under the Companies Act 1948 or the Companies Act (Northern Ireland) 1960, or proceedings relating to

---

[16] s. 17 and Sched. 5, para. 4.
[17] s. 16(1)(*a*).
[18] The *general* exclusion of jurisdiction in matters of wills and succession was not recommended by the Maxwell Committee. See Report, p. 257.
[19] p. 195.
[20] Jurisdiction to wind up unregistered companies and jurisdiction in patent matters.

a company as respects which jurisdiction is conferred on the court having winding up jurisdiction under either of those Acts."

Art. 1(2)(2) of the Convention already excludes proceedings relating to the winding-up of insolvent companies or other legal persons, judicial arrangements, compositions and analogous proceedings. The fact, however, that a company is unable to pay its debts is only one of the grounds under which it may be wound up by the court under section 222 of the Companies Act 1948. This exclusion from Schedule 4, therefore, makes it clear that the existing pattern of inter-United Kingdom allocation of jurisdiction on company matters based on the place of incorporation of the company is retained.

Patents, trade marks and designs

"2. Proceedings concerned with the registration or validity of patents, trade marks, designs or other similar rights required to be deposited or registered."

In applying Art. 16 within the scheme for the inter-United Kingdom allocation of jurisdiction, paragraph 4 of that article (concerned with the registration or validity of patents, etc.) has been omitted. The validity of patents is often put in issue in the course of infringement proceedings and there are statutory provisions relating to jurisdiction in such proceedings.[21] The jurisdictions are not exclusive.

Protection of Trading Interests Act 1980

"3. Proceedings under section 6 of the Protection of Trading Interests Act 1980 (recovery of sums paid or obtained pursuant to a judgment for multiple damages)."

Subsection (5) of s. 6 of the 1980 Act provides that a court in the United Kingdom may entertain proceedings on a claim under that section despite the fact that the person against whom the proceedings are brought is not within the jurisdiction of the court.

Appeals from tribunals

"4. Proceedings on appeal from, or for review of, decisions of tribunals."

This exclusion reflects the general exclusion from the operation of the scheme for the inter-United Kingdom allocation of jurisdiction of proceedings other than proceedings in courts of law.[22] A corresponding provision appears in Schedule 9.[23]

---

[21] Patents Act 1977, s. 72; Trademarks Act 1938, ss. 32 and 66(1); Registered Designs Act 1949, ss. 20 and 45.
[22] See para. 9.08 above.
[23] para. 12.

Maintenance payments to local and other public authorities

"5. Proceedings for . . . "

The proceedings referred to in paragraph 5 – too lengthy to cite above – are proceedings for the recovery by local and other public authorities of contributions in respect of a child in care, of payments for the recovery of expenditure on supplementary benefit, and of similar payments. These proceedings may be subject to special jurisdictional rules, including rules conferring jurisdiction on courts of the area where the assistance was given. These proceedings are left outwith the scope of Schedule 4. *A contrario* of this, it would seem that other maintenance proceedings come within the scope of that Schedule.

Proceedings under certain conventions, etc.

"6. Proceedings brought in any court in pursuance of –
(*a*) any statutory provision which, in the case of any convention to which Article 57 applies (conventions relating to specific matters which override the general rules in the 1968 Convention), implements the convention or makes provision with respect to jurisdiction in any field to which the convention relates; and
(*b*) any rule of law so far as it has the effect of implementing any such convention."

Art. 57 was examined above,[24] and illustrations were given of conventions on special matters containing rules for jurisdiction or the recognition and enforcement of judgments. The proceedings referred to are similarly excluded from the operation of the general scheme of jurisdiction of the Scottish courts in Schedule 8 to the 1982 Act.[25]

Certain Admiralty proceedings in Scotland

"7. Proceedings in Scotland in an Admiralty cause where the jurisdiction of the Court of Session or, as the case may be, of the sheriff is based on arrestment *in rem* or *ad fundandam jurisdictionem* of a ship, cargo or freight."

In England and Wales and in Northern Ireland the arrestment of ships is based on statutory provisions implementing the Brussels Convention of 1952 on the Arrest of Sea-Going Ships. Proceedings, therefore, brought under these provisions would be excluded by the operation of paragraph 6 above. The corresponding Scottish jurisdiction is primarily a common law one and in some respects wider than that provided for by the Brussels Convention. The Scottish arrest jurisdiction, therefore, is the subject of a special exclusion. A corresponding provision is contained in Schedule 9.[26]

Register of aircraft mortgages

"8. Proceedings for the rectification of the register of aircraft mortgages kept by the Civil Aviation Authority."

Under Art. 16(3) of Schedule 4 these proceedings would require to be taken only in England where the register is kept. They can at present be

---

[24] paras. 3.31–3.36.
[25] See Sched. 9(14).
[26] para. 6.

brought in the Court of Session or in the High Court in Northern Ireland, as well as in the High Court in England. This exclusion preserves the jurisdiction of the Court of Session and the High Court in Northern Ireland. A corresponding provision is contained in Schedule 9.[27]

Continental Shelf Act 1964

> "9. Proceedings brought in any court in pursuance of an order under section 3 of the Continental Shelf Act 1964."

Certain jurisdictions in the 1968 Convention, notably those in Art. 5, refer to the courts of the place (within a Contracting State) where the relevant act or event took place. Paragraph 9 was presumably inserted in case the question arose whether a relevant act or event taking place on an off-shore installation was an event taking place in the United Kingdom. It preserves the jurisdiction of the court of that part of the United Kingdom to which the relevant area of the continental shelf belongs. A corresponding provision is contained in Schedule 9.[28]

D. RULES FOR THE ASSUMPTION OF JURISDICTION

(a) General

9.13   Since the rules of jurisdiction applied in Schedule 4 for the purposes of the allocation of jurisdiction within the United Kingdom are simply a modified version of Title II of the 1968 Convention, it is necessary to comment only on some general matters and on the more significant of the modifications introduced.

9.14   The primary concepts used have the same meaning for the purposes of Schedule 4 as they have for the purposes of applying the Convention.[29] The terms "domicile" and "seat" are defined in Part V of the 1982 Act in such a way as to locate that domicile or seat both in a particular part of the United Kingdom and in a particular place there.[30] The expression "part of the United Kingdom" is defined in section 50 to mean England and Wales, Scotland, or Northern Ireland.

(b) Specific articles

Article 2

9.15   The first rule in Schedule 4 derives from Art. 2(1) of the Convention and states the primary rule for the allocation of jurisdiction among the courts of the United Kingdom that:

> "Subject to the provisions of this Title, persons domiciled in a part of the United Kingdom shall . . . be sued in the courts of that part."

The words "a part of the United Kingdom" replace the original reference to "a Contracting State" and the word "part" that to "State." The same

---

[27] para. 8.
[28] para. 10.
[29] See para. 9.06 above.
[30] See paras. 4.19 and 4.28 above

substitutions are used throughout the Schedule. There was no need to incorporate Art. 2(2) of the Convention in Schedule 4 since, in the legal systems of the United Kingdom, a person's nationality does not affect the operation of the rules of jurisdiction in civil matters.

9.16   *Article 3*

Article 3 follows Art. 3(1) of the Convention with the omission of any reference to Section 3 of Title II, which contains the Convention's rules of jurisdiction in matters relating to insurance. These are not reproduced in Schedule 4 for reasons explained below.[31] Art. 3(2) of the Convention is omitted, presumably because its inventory of exorbitant jurisdictions is of no practical relevance in the context of Schedule 4.

9.17   *Article 4*

Article 4 is omitted, because the Schedule is based on the hypothesis that the defender is domiciled in a Contracting State or that the situation comes within the scope of Art. 16.

9.18   *Article 5*

The principal alterations to Art. 5 are the inclusion of an additional paragraph (8) and the insertion of a new article, Art. 5A. Words, moreover, have been added to Art. 5(3) to make it clear that interdicts or injunctions fall within its scope.[32] Paragraph (8) introduces a new non-exclusive jurisdiction in relation to proceedings (a) concerned with debts secured over immoveable property, or (b) which are brought to assert, declare or determine, proprietary or possessory rights, or rights of security in or over moveable property, or to obtain authority to dispose of moveable property, and enables such proceedings to be taken in the courts of the part of the United Kingdom in which the property is situated. These rules follow recommendations of the Maxwell Committee.[33] The proceedings do not appear to come within the terms of Art. 16 and without such special provision it would have been necessary to sue the defender in the courts of his domicile within the United Kingdom or under another of the rules in Art. 5. This would not always be appropriate. Art. 5(2) exactly reproduces Art. 5(2) of the Convention. The Maxwell Committee recommended[34] that the existing grounds for the assumption of jurisdiction in relation to maintenance claims not ancillary to proceedings relating to status and contained in Part I of the Maintenance Orders Act 1950 should be discarded in favour of the provisions of the Convention. The 1982 Act achieves this result by repealing sections 6, 8 and 9(1)(*a*) of the 1950 Act and allowing the inter-United Kingdom allocation of jurisdiction in maintenance to rest upon the provisions of Schedule 4.[34a] Various minor amendments are made to the 1950 Act in Schedules 11 and 12 to the 1982 Act.

---

[31] para. 9.22.
[32] Whether Art. 5(3) covers proceedings relating to a threatened wrong has been debated. See para. 5.35 above.
[33] pp. 206 and 248–249.
[34] pp.209–215.
[34a] For further details, see paras, 10.29–10.31 below.

Article 5A

9.19   The inclusion of this provision is explained by the deletion in Art. 16(2) of any reference to proceedings which have as their object a decision of an organ of a company or other legal person, or association of natural or legal persons. Despite the approach adopted in Art. 16(2) of the Convention, it was apparently thought inappropriate to permit of such action *only* in the courts of the part of the United Kingdom in which that company, legal person or association has its seat. Art. 5A, therefore, states a new, non-exclusive ground of jurisdiction in such proceedings.

Article 6

9.20   Article 6 is reproduced as it appears in the 1968 Convention, the only changes being the introduction of the words in bold type designed to confine its application to cases where a person domiciled in one part of the United Kingdom is sued in the courts of another part. For a commentary upon Art. 6 of the Convention the reader is referred to Chapter 5 above.[35]

Article 6A

9.21   Article 6A similarly follows the text of Art. 6A of the Convention,[36] with amendments to make it refer to a court of a part of the United Kingdom rather than to a court of a Contracting State.

Articles 7–12A (Section 3)

9.22   A series of dots follows Art. 6A, presumably to draw attention to the fact that no analogue to Section 3 of Title II of the Convention (Jurisdiction in matters of insurance) is included in Schedule 4. The omitted *régime* has some justification in the context of contracts of insurance entered into by a private individual in one State with an insurance company operating from another State. In addition to offering a choice of courts to the person taking out the policy, it protects him from the operation of clauses conferring exclusive jurisdiction upon the insurer's own courts, with the various obstacles that would present to a private individual in another State. But, as the Maxwell Committee suggested,[37] such special protection is less necessary, if it is necessary at all, for insured persons domiciled in one part of the United Kingdom who take out policies with insurers domiciled in another part. In consequence the matter is left to the ordinary rules of jurisdiction in Schedule 4. The practical results are not very different. An insured person in Scotland who wishes to sue in Scotland an insurance company with its seat in England may be able to found upon Art. 5(1) (contract jurisdiction) of Schedule 4, and will almost certainly be able to found on Art. 5(5) (establishment jurisdiction).

Article 13

9.23   Two major amendments are made to Art. 13 of the Convention. The first consists in the deletion of Art. 13(1)(3)(*a*), which imports in the residual cases specified in Art. 13(1)(3) the condition that in the State of the consumer's domicile "the conclusion of the contract was preceded by a specific invitation addressed to him or by advertising." As the Maxwell Report indicates,[38] this condition is likely to cause difficulties of interpretation. It is in any case inappropriate in rules for the inter-United Kingdom allocation of jurisdiction, since advertisements are so often on a national

---

[35] paras. 5.59–5.69.
[36] See para. 5.70.
[37] Report, pp. 221–223.
[38] pp. 72–73.

basis. The condition was presumably omitted on that account. The second consists in the omission of Art. 13(2) of the Convention, which imputes to a party not domiciled in any Contracting State who contracts with a consumer a deemed domicile in a Contracting State where that party has a branch, agency or establishment.[39] In consequence, in relation to such a party the courts in the United Kingdom may apply their normal rules of jurisdiction, including exorbitant rules. Finally, the addition in Art. 13(3) of Schedule 4 of a reference to contracts of insurance reflects a policy choice to allow jurisdiction in matters of insurance to rest upon the general law.[40]

.24 *Article 14*

Article 14, as it governs the inter-United Kingdom allocation of jurisdiction, is reinforced by section 10(3) of the 1982 Act. This provides that:

> "Any proceedings which by virtue of the first paragraph of Article 14 (consumer contracts) are brought in the United Kingdom by a consumer on the ground that he is himself domiciled there shall be brought in the courts of the part of the United Kingdom in which he is domiciled."

.25 *Article 15*

Article 15 is reproduced as it appears in the Convention with such modifications only as are required to allocate jurisdiction within the different parts of the United Kingdom.

.26 *Article 16*

Apart from the modification referred to in paragraph 9.19 above, the main modification to Art. 16 of the Convention is the deletion of paragraph 4, concerning proceedings relating to the registration or validity of patents, trade-marks, designs or similar rights required to be deposited or registered. This paragraph could not be adopted for the allocation of jurisdiction within the United Kingdom since the registers in question are situated in London. There is a specific exclusion of those proceedings in Schedule 5, para. 2.[41]

.27 *Article 17*

Article 17 of Schedule 4 differs in several respects from Art. 17 of the 1968 Convention, from which it has been derived. Reference was made above[42] to the obscurity of the fourth paragraph of the latter, and this paragraph has been deleted. Amendments have been made to Art. 17 to ensure that it refers to the relevant part of the United Kingdom and not simply to a Contracting State, but there are two other amendments of some significance. In the 1968 Convention Art. 17(1) confers an "exclusive" jurisdiction. It is not clear why Schedule 4 drops the reference to the exclusivity of the jurisdiction conferred by a prorogation agreement, particularly when a prorogated forum is stated as an exclusive jurisdiction in Rule 5 of Schedule 8. The other significant departure from the text of the Convention is the omission of any reference to the form of the agreement. It suffices that, "apart from this Schedule, the agreement would be effective to confer jurisdiction under the law of that part [*sc.* of

---

[39] See Maxwell Report, pp. 227–228.
[40] See para. 9.22 above.
[41] See para 9.12(2) above.
[42] para. 7.26(12).

the United Kingdom]." In other words, if the agreement is effective under the law of the chosen court to confer jurisdiction upon that court, it will possess jurisdiction under Schedule 4. This provision at first sight seems clear enough. There are no rules regulating the formal validity of prorogation agreements under the general law of Scotland and, while such rules are introduced by Art. 17(1) of the Convention (where it applies) and by the corresponding provision in Rule 5(2) of Schedule 8, Schedule 8 is inapplicable where Schedule 4 applies.[43] The result, however, is inconsistent with the intentions expressed in the Maxwell Report.[44] The words printed in bold type in Art. 17(1) of Schedule 4 – "apart from this Schedule, the agreement would be effective to confer jurisdiction under the law of that part" – raise a further question. Can it be inferred from them that a choice of English law to govern a contract would by implication confer jurisdiction upon the English courts in matters relating to that contract?[45] It is considered that a negative answer is appropriate. These words appear in a context similar to that of the corresponding words in Art. 17(1) of the 1968 Convention. The fact that the latter were not intended to include a reference to choice of court agreements inferred from a choice of law is demonstrated by the inclusion in Art. 35 of the 1978 Accession Convention of a transitional provision preserving the effect of any such agreement entered into before the entry into force of the 1968 Convention. The inclusion of a similar transitional provision in Schedule 13 to the 1982 Act[46] makes it clear that Art. 17(1) of Schedule 4 is similarly to be read as excluding the inference of a choice of jurisdiction agreement from a choice of law agreement. Art. 17(1) and (3) of the 1968 Convention (which relate to trusts) are also retained in Art. 17 of Schedule 4, but the jurisdiction in the latter provision is no longer an exclusive one and the reference to Art. 12 of the Convention relating to insurance contracts has been deleted.

Article 18

9.28   Article 18 of Schedule 4 provides that a court of a part of the United Kingdom before which a defender enters an appearance shall have jurisdiction. Like Art. 18 of the Convention, on which it is based, this rule is declared not to apply where appearance was entered solely to contest the jurisdiction, or where another court has exclusive jurisdiction by virtue of Art. 16. Following the decisions in *Elefanten Schuh* v. *Jacqmain*[47] and *Rohr* v. *Ossberger*,[48] considered above,[49] it is clear that there is no submission under Art. 18 when a defender contests the merits if, at the same time, he has challenged the jurisdiction of the court.

Article 19

9.29   Article 19 restates, with amendments to adapt the provision to the allocation of jurisdiction within the United Kingdom, the rule in Art. 19 of the Convention which requires the courts to take notice of their own lack of jurisdiction in cases where Art. 16 applies.

---

[43] 1982 Act, s 20(1).
[44] p.238, para. 13.132, and the general discussion of express prorogation at pp. 237–242.
[45] See para. 7.24 above.
[46] Sched. 13, Part II, para. 1(2).
[47] (150/80) [1981] E.C.R 1671.
[48] (27/81) [1981] E.C.R. 243.
[49] para. 7.28.

Article 20

.30   The only significant departure from the text of Art. 20 of the 1968 Convention is the omission of paragraph 3 with its reference to Art. 15 of the Hague Convention on the Service of Writs Abroad. The procedures of the Hague Convention are inapplicable as between the constituent parts of the United Kingdom. One practical effect of this provision is that, where a defender does not enter appearance, the court must consider whether he is domiciled not simply in another Contracting State but in another part of the United Kingdom and, if the latter, dismiss the action unless the court has jurisdiction on one of the grounds specified in Schedule 4. It must also verify whether proper steps have been taken to serve notice of the proceedings on the defender.

Articles 21–23

.31   One of the more significant departures in Schedule 4 from the jurisdictional provisions of the Convention is the omission of the rules in Articles 21–23 relating to *lis pendens* and related actions. These were thought to be too inflexible and the matter is allowed to rest on the application of the principle of *forum non conveniens* in Scotland and of related principles in the laws of the other parts of the United Kingdom.[50]

Article 24

.32   Article 24 of Schedule 4 follows Art. 24 of the Convention with appropriate modifications to ensure its application as between the different parts of the United Kingdom. Art. 24 has been fully discussed above.[51] It need only be emphasised that the provisions for provisional and other protective measures contained in ss. 25, 27 and 28 of the 1982 Act may be applied in the context of proceedings which have been commenced or are to be commenced in other parts of the United Kingdom as they may be applied in the context of proceedings which have been or are to be commenced in another Contracting State.

RECIPROCAL RECOGNITION AND ENFORCEMENT UNDER THE 1982 ACT

A. INTRODUCTION

.33   The decision to adopt a systematic scheme for the allocation of jurisdiction between the constituent parts of the United Kingdom enabled the draftsmen of the 1982 Act to adopt relatively simple provisions for the mutual recognition of judgments within those countries and for their reciprocal enforcement.

B. RECIPROCAL RECOGNITION

.34   The Maxwell Committee considered whether it would be desirable to make express statutory provision on the lines of Art. 26(2) of the 1968

---

[50] See 1982 Act, s. 49; Maxwell Report, pp. 251–252; and above, para, 5.9n. 22 and paras. 7.37–7.42.
[51] paras. 7.43–7.48.

Convention for the recognition (as opposed to the enforcement) of the judgments of the courts of one part of the United Kingdom in the other parts.[52] Though they did not press this view strongly, they were inclined to think that no such provision should be made, partly on the view that it would not have been easy to define what recognition implied in the context of a single State.[53] The 1982 Act includes no positive provision requiring the recognition in one part of the United Kingdom of a judgment given in another part of the United Kingdom. Section 19 merely provides that:

> "A judgment . . . given in one part of the United Kingdom shall not be refused recognition in another part of the United Kingdom solely on the ground that, in relation to that judgment, the court which gave it was not a court of competent jurisdiction according to the rules of private international law in force in that other part."

This provision clearly implies that judgments given in one part of the United Kingdom are to be recognised in the other parts. It applies, subject to a few specified exceptions[54] to any judgment which is enforceable under section 18 of the 1982 Act.

C. ENFORCEMENT SCHEME WITHIN THE UNITED KINGDOM

(a) General

9.35   In relation to the enforcement of judgments as between the constituent parts of the United Kingdom, the 1982 Act adopts the main features of the proposals of the Maxwell Committee without following precisely their detailed recommendations, particularly those of a procedural character. The provisions of section 18 and its associated Schedules 6 and 7 entirely replace those of the 1868 Act and the 1882 Act.[55] Enforcement is channelled to the superior courts of each part of the United Kingdom, and no facilities for the enforcement of judgments (other than maintenance orders) through inferior courts are retained. No disadvantage to Scottish pursuers arises since a certificate registered in the High Court in England and Wales can be enforced in the county court under section 139 of the County Courts Act 1959. The jurisdictional controls of section 10 of the 1882 Act are dropped, and judgments emanating from one part of the United Kingdom must be enforced in the other parts thereof whatever their jurisdictional basis.[56] In general, indeed, it may be said that if a person against whom enforcement is sought wishes to challenge the judgment of the court of origin, he must do so in that court.[57] The enforcement scheme, like that of the 1968 Convention, applies to non-money provisions of judgments and not merely to judgments for "debts, damages or costs." In relation to the money and non-money provisions of judgments,

---

[52] pp. 274–275.
[53] They referred in this context to *Black-Clawson International Ltd.* v. *Papierwerke Waldhof-Aschaffenburg AG* [1975] A.C. 591.
[54] s. 19(3).
[55] These Acts are repealed by the 1982 Act, s. 54 and Sched. 14.
[56] s. 19(1), cited in para. 9.34 above.
[57] See para. 9.40(e) below.

however, slightly different procedures are set out in Schedules 6 and 7. Finally, although the procedures of the 1868 and 1882 Acts did not formally exclude recourse to common law procedures,[58] section 18(8) of the 1982 Act, provides that a judgment to which s. 18 applies, other than an arbitration award which has become enforceable in the United Kingdom as a judgment, shall be enforced only by registration under Schedules 6 or 7.[59]

(b) Judgments which may be enforced

36   Section 18 of the 1982 Act specifies the United Kingdom judgments which may be enforced in other parts of the United Kingdom under the procedures of Schedules 6 and 7. The specification of those judgments is very clear and it would be otiose simply to repeat the content of section 18. It may be helpful, however, to summarise its provisions, noting first the *exclusions* –

(1) Judgments given in proceedings other than civil proceedings[60] are excluded.[61] This principle is reinforced by the express exclusion of the judgments of magistrates' courts in England and Wales or Northern Ireland.[62]

(2) Most status and status-related judgments are excluded.[63] Thus decrees of or relating to divorce, separation, guardianship or custody, and the management of the affairs of an incapax are excluded.[64]

(3) As under the 1968 Convention, judgments given in proceedings relating to bankruptcy and the winding-up of corporations or associations are excluded.[65] There are already statutory provisions for the enforcement of such judgments within the United Kingdom.[66]

(4) Judgments given in proceedings relating to the obtaining of title to administer the estate of a deceased person are excluded[67] but not, as in the scheme for the allocation of jurisdiction, judgments given in other proceedings in matters relating to wills and succession.

(5) A maintenance order to which section 16 of the Maintenance Orders Act 1950 applies is excluded from the operation of section 18 of the 1982 Act. In consequence, the enforcement of maintenance orders throughout the United Kingdom continues to be governed by Part II of the Maintenance Orders Act 1950.[68]

(6) Also excluded are judgments given outside the United Kingdom which would otherwise fall to be treated as judgments of United Kingdom courts by virtue of registration under Part II of the Administration of Justice Act 1920, Part I of the 1933 Act, and Part I of the Maintenance

---

[58] Recourse to them was merely discouraged by sanctions relating to expenses: 1868 Act, s. 6 and 1882 Act, s. 8.
[59] *Cf.* 1933 Act, s. 6.
[60] Here, presumably, as opposed to criminal proceedings.
[61] s. 18(3)(*b*).
[62] s. 18(3)(*a*).
[63] s. 18(5)(*b*).
[64] s. 18(5)(*c*) and (6).
[65] s. 18(3)(*c*)(i) and (ii).
[66] See Bankruptcy (Scotland) Act 1913, s. 170; Bankruptcy Act 1914, s. 121; Companies Act 1948, s.276.
[67] s. 18(3)(*c*)(iii).
[68] s. 18(5)(*a*); and see Maxwell Report, pp. 283–284 and 287.

Orders (Reciprocal Enforcement) Act 1972 or under sections 4 and 5 of the 1982 Act itself.[69]

(7) So much of any judgment as is a provisional or protective measure falls to be excluded, unless it is an order for interim payment.[70]

9.37   The above are the exclusions and the judgments, orders, awards and documents which may be enforced under section 18 and Schedules 6 and 7 to the 1982 Act are evidently, to generalise, the other judgments made in the course of civil proceedings[71] specified in s. 18 including, in addition to judgments given by a court of law in the United Kingdom, registered decreets in Scotland, the awards or orders of tribunals which are enforceable without further order of a court of law and certain arbitration awards, namely those which become enforceable in the part of the United Kingdom in which they were given in the same manner as a judgment given by a court of law in that part.[72]

(c) Procedures for enforcement

9.38   The Maxwell Committee recommended that, for the enforcement of judgments emanating from another part of the United Kingdom, rather different procedures should be adopted respectively for money judgments and for non-money judgments. In relation to the former, the administrative system of registration of certificates of the original judgment by an official of the court addressed could be retained.[73] In relation to the latter a purely administrative system would not suffice –

(a) because the original judgment might refer to legal concepts or institutions unknown to the law of the court addressed[74]: it might be necessary for the enforcing court to amend the wording of the external judgment or to direct how it may be enforced;

(b) because the risk of a conflict between an incoming judgment and a prior judgment of the enforcing court was possibly greater and certainly more serious where it occurred; and

(c) because, in the last analysis, the enforcement of an external judgment might be impracticable because it requires a person to do something within the territory of the enforcing court which it is impracticable to do, or even illegal to do, there. Moreover, in relation to non-money judgments, the issue of a certificate of the judgment was hardly practicable because of the wide differences between the terms of such judgments.

9.39   Although the 1982 Act acknowledges these problems by setting out separately in two different Schedules the rules respectively for the enforcement of the money provisions of judgments and for their non-money provisions, there are in fact few differences between them. In relation to the money provisions of judgments Schedule 6 envisages the obtaining of a *certificate* from the court of origin and its registration following an application to *an official* of the superior court in which

---

[69] s. 18(7).

[70] s. 18(5)(*d*).

[71] s. 18(3)(*b*).

[72] s. 18(2).

[73] p. 292.

[74] The Maxwell Report, at p. 304, alludes to the particular problems which might arise as a consequence of the very different orders for provisional or protective measures available in the different parts of the United Kingdom. The 1982 Act resolves this problem by making no provision for the reciprocal enforcement of such orders, other than orders for interim payments. See 1982 Act, s. 18(5)(*d*).

enforcement is sought. In relation to the non-money provisions of judgments, Schedule 7 provides for the registration of *a certified copy* of the original judgment following an application to the *superior court*[75] of that part of the United Kingdom in which recognition is sought. No allusion is made in Schedule 7 to the possible need to adapt the wording of a non-money judgment, but this will doubtless be provided for in Rules of Court. Schedule 7, however, states in paragraph 5(5) that:

> "A judgment shall not be registered under this Schedule by the superior court in any part of the United Kingdom if compliance with the non-money provisions contained in the judgment would involve a breach of the law of that part of the United Kingdom."

9.40   Otherwise it may be said that there are no substantial differences between the procedures for the enforcement of the money provisions of judgments in Schedule 6 and those for the enforcement of their non-money provisions in Schedule 7. The procedures are so clearly set out in those Schedules and in the relevant Rules of Court[77] that it seems unnecessary to describe them in detail. A few points, however, may be explained:

(a) Under paragraph 3 of both Schedules, a certificate of a judgment or a certified copy of a judgment is not to be given where, under the law of the part of the United Kingdom in which it was given, the judgment is still appealable and or not enforceable. These dual requirements may seem strange to a Scots lawyer since in Scotland an extract decree is required for enforcement and normally an extract may not be obtained until the days for appealing have elapsed. It is understood, however, that in England and Wales and in Northern Ireland judgments under appeal may be enforced, unless the court has made an order to the contrary.[76] The reference in paragraph 3(*b*) in both Schedules to the non-expiry of the time available for the enforcement of the judgment is a reference primarily to the fact that under English law an action on a judgment becomes barred after six years under s. 24(1) of the Limitation Act 1980 and that thereafter leave of the court is required to issue execution on a judgment.[77]

(b) An application for the registration of a certificate relating to the money provisions of a judgment under paragraph 5(1) of Schedule 6 must be made within six months of its date of issue and an application for the registration of a judgment containing non-money provisions under paragraph 5 of Schedule 7 must be accompanied by a certificate issued not more than six months before the date of the application *inter alia* to the effect that the judgment is enforceable. These requirements are designed to limit the cases where certificates of judgments (or, indeed, judgments themselves) may be presented for registration after the judgment has ceased to be enforceable in its country of origin. These requirements replace those of the 1868 and 1882 Acts[78] which precluded registration

---

[75] In Scotland the application is likely to be heard in the Outer House.

[76] O. 59, r. 13(1)(*a*) and r. 10(9), proviso (*b*); P.St.J. Langan and L.D.J. Henderson, *Civil Procedure* (3rd Ed., 1983), p. 373.

[77] R.S.C., Ord. 46, r. 2(1)(*a*). Contrast the Prescription and Limitation (Scotland) Act 1973, s. 6 and Sched. 1(2)(*a*).

[78] 1868 Act, s. 1; 1882 Act, s. 4.

(unless, in the cases of the 1868 Act, with leave of the court) in all cases after the lapse of 12 months from the date of the judgment.

(c) In neither Schedule is any provision made at any stage for notice to the person against whom enforcement is being sought. Under the 1933 Act notice in writing of the registration of a judgment had to be served by the petitioner on the judgment debtor. There is no analogue to this requirement in Schedules 6 or 7.

(d) Once the court of origin has issued a certificate of the judgment under Schedule 6 or a certified copy of the judgment under Schedule 7 and an application for the registration of the certificate or of the certified copy judgment has been "duly made" to the proper officer of the superior court addressed or to that superior court itself, neither the officer nor, with one qualification, the superior court itself has any discretion in the matter but is bound to register the judgment. The qualification referred to derives from the terms of paragraph 5(5) of Schedule 7, which is set out above.[79] The application, however, must have been "duly made." This may mean that the court should satisfy itself that the application meets the requirements of section 18 of, and of Schedule 7 to, the 1982 Act.

(e) The remedies of any person who is affected by the registration of the certificate of a judgment or, as the case may be, of a judgment, arise only after registration. In the first place, such a person has a right to apply for the sisting (or staying) of proceedings for the enforcement of the judgment where he satisfies the court that he intends to apply to the court of origin for the setting aside or the quashing of the original judgment.[80] In the second place, on an application made by any interested party, the registering court is required to set aside the registration when it is satisfied that such registration was "contrary to the provisions of" the relevant Schedule and may do so when it is satisfied that the matter in dispute had previously been the subject of a judgment in another court or tribunal having jurisdiction in the matter.[81] Such a court, it is thought, need not necessarily be a court of the country or, indeed, of the State of the country where the judgment was registered.

(f) The general effects of registration are substantially similar whatever the nature of the original judgment. Though the relevant provisions of Schedule 6 and of Schedule 7[82] are couched in slightly different terms, they are essentially to the same effect and provide that the registered certificate or, as the case may be, the non-money provisions of a registered judgment shall, "for the purposes of their enforcement, be of the same force and effect, [and] the registering court shall have in relation to their enforcement the same powers" as if they had originally been issued by the registering court. The language of the relevant provisions is thought to be sufficiently wide to authorise the registering court to apply any relevant rules of its law relating to the execution of decrees including, in Scotland, rules relating to the sisting or setting aside of diligence.

---

[79] para. 9.39.
[80] Sched. 6, para. 9; Sched. 7, para. 8.
[81] Sched. 6, para. 10, and Sched. 7, para. 9.
[82] Sched. 6, para. 6 and Sched. 7, para. 6.

TRANSITIONAL PROVISIONS

41   The inter-United Kingdom scheme for jurisdiction and enforcement will come into effect on a date to be appointed.[83] The transitional provisions relating to this scheme are contained in Part II of Schedule 13. Paragraph 1 deals with the jurisdictional provisions of the scheme contained in section 16 and Schedule 4. By stating that these jurisdictional provisions shall not apply to any proceedings instituted before section 16 comes into force, sub-paragraph (1) ensures that existing proceedings may be continued under the former jurisdictional rules. Sub-paragraph (2) permits of the continued operation in England and Wales and Northern Ireland of the contract jurisdiction based on a choice of the laws of those countries in any case where the choice of law agreement was made before section 16 comes into force.

42   The 1982 Act provides for the repeal of the Judgments Extension Act 1868 and of the Inferior Courts Judgments Extension Act 1882. Notwithstanding the fact of their repeal, paragraph 2 of Part II of Schedule 13 allows of the continued operation of the 1868 and 1882 Acts in relation to certificates of money judgments registered before the repeal of those Acts. Conversely, paragraph 3 of Part II of Schedule 13 states that the provisions of section 18 and Schedule 7 relating to non-money judgments do not apply to judgments given before that section enters into force. The aim, it may be presumed, is to protect a person who may not have entered defences in the original proceedings on the view that non-money judgments given in one part of the United Kingdom would be unenforceable in other parts of that country.

43   Section 19, relating to the recognition of United Kingdom judgments in other parts of the United Kingdom, does not apply to judgments given before that section comes into force.

---

[83] 1982 Act, Sched. 13, Part I, para. 3.

CHAPTER 10

JURISDICTION OF THE SCOTTISH COURTS

INTRODUCTION

10.01   FROM the standpoint of a Scottish practitioner, the most important parts of the 1982 Act are Part III and Schedules 8 and 9. Together these create a new set of rules of jurisdiction determining, in cases whether neither the 1968 Convention nor Schedule 4 to the 1982 Act applies, "in what circumstances a person may be sued in civil proceedings in the Court of Session or in a sheriff court."[1] To a large extent these rules are borrowed from those in the Convention; but other rules have been added and the rules of the Convention have been modified, notably to take account of the fact that they must allocate jurisdiction among the Scottish courts in proceedings where the defender is domiciled in Scotland. The new set of jurisdictional rules applies to the sheriff court as well as to the Court of Session and section 6 of the 1907 Act ceases to have effect to the extent that it determines jurisdiction in any matter to which Schedule 8 applies.[2] Other rules, frequently adopted from the common law, have been added to state bases of jurisdiction applicable where the defender is not domiciled in another part of the United Kingdom or is not domiciled in another Contracting State and even, in certain matters to which the Convention does not apply, to state bases of jurisdiction in relation to defenders domiciled in a Contracting State. In contrast with the position where the rules of the Convention apply directly, a court possessing jurisdiction under Schedule 8 may, in terms of section 22(1) of the 1982 Act, decline to exercise that jurisdiction on the ground of *forum non conveniens*.

10.02   The reasons for adopting as the norm the rules set out in the Convention have been considered above.[3] As with the rules in Schedule 4,[4] the Crown may by Order in Council modify the rules in Schedule 8 in the light of decisions of the European Court as to the meaning and effect of the 1968 Convention either to bring that Schedule into closer alignment with the provisions of the Convention or to cause it to diverge still further.[5]

INTERPRETATION OF SCHEDULE 8

10.03   Consistently with an approach which takes the jurisdictional rules of the Convention as the primary rules of jurisdiction in Scots law, section 20(5) of the 1982 Act requires a Scottish court in the interpretation of provisions

---

[1] 1982 Act, s. 20(1).
[2] 1982 Act, s. 20(3).
[3] para. 1.35; *cf.* paras. 9.01–9.04 above.
[4] para. 9.04 above.
[5] 1982 Act, s. 47.

in Schedule 8 derived to any extent from Title II of the 1968 Convention to have regard to any relevant principles laid down in the interpretation of that Title by the European Court and to its decisions as to the meaning and effect of its provisions.[6] It may also consider and give appropriate weight to the Jenard and Schlosser Reports.[7] The court is assisted in ascertaining these "derived provisions" by the fact that modifications to the provisions of Title II are indicated in heavy type.

Section 20(5) is an entirely novel provision for Scots law, and its justification is similar to the justification for the adoption of the jurisdictional rules of the Convention, in particular the fact that it should conduce to simplicity and coherence in the law. It would seem strange, to the layman at least, if a Scottish court were to interpret the phrase "the courts for the place of performance of the obligation in question" in one way in the context of Art. 5(1) of the 1968 Convention and in another way in the context of Rule 2(2) of Schedule 8. It will be noticed, however, that, while in the application of the Convention the court is required by section 3(1) of the 1982 Act to decide issues in accordance with the principles laid down by and any relevant decision of the European Court, in the application of Schedule 8 (as in the application of Schedule 4) it is merely required to *have regard to* those principles and those decisions. In this context, that is to say, those principles and decisions "are to be a guide and not a fetter."[8]

The acceptance by Parliament, however, of this novel provision has a further consequence. The 1971 Protocol on the interpretation of the 1968 Convention (and its Annexed Protocol) by the European Court of Justice applies only to the interpretation of that Convention, the 1978 Accession Convention, and the 1971 Protocol itself. Despite the broad language of Art. 3 of the 1971 Protocol, it is thought that the Scottish courts cannot request the European Court to give rulings upon the interpretation of the derived provisions in Schedule 8.[9] Any questions of interpretation, therefore, will require to be adjudicated by the Scottish courts of first instance or the appropriate appellate courts. This raises the possibility of conflict between the duty of a court under the normal rules of precedent to follow the decisions of hierarchically superior courts and its duty under section 20(5) to have regard to the principles of interpretation adopted by the European Court of Justice, whether formulated before or after a decision of an appellate court in Scotland. It would be presumptuous to speculate how such conflicts will be resolved, but the scheme of the Act suggests that in the end the principles adopted by the European Court should prevail.

---

[6] See para. 2.01 above.

[7] See para. 2.02 above.

[8] *Perry* v. *Wright* [1908] 1 K.B. 441, at p. 458.

[9] Maxwell Report, p. 21; the crucial words in s. 3(1) of the 1982 Act—"if not referred to the European Court in accordance with the 1971 Protocol"—are omitted in ss. 16(3)(*a*) and 20(5)(*a*) of that Act. See also para. 2.04 above and *Bavaria Fluggesellschaft and Germanair* v. *Eurocontrol* (9 & 10/77) [1977] E.C.R. 1517 [5].

SCOPE OF SCHEDULE 8

A. Introduction

10.06   The field of application of Schedule 8, though coinciding to some extent with that of the Convention, is in many respects considerably wider. It is wider even than the field of application of Schedule 4. This is presumably designed not only to avoid the problems of interpretation which would be presented by a strict adherence to the exclusions specified in Art. 1 of the Convention[10] but, more importantly, to ensure as far as practicable that a uniform set of rules should apply to most actions of a patrimonial character.[11]

B. General Exclusion

10.07   Section 21(1)(*a*) provides that Schedule 8 shall not affect the operation of any enactment which confers jurisdiction upon a Scottish court in respect of a specific subject-matter on specific grounds. A similar exclusion is contained in section 17(1) and reference may be made to the commentary on that provision.[12]

C. Particular Exclusions

10.08   In addition to this general exclusion, section 21(1)(*b*) provides that Schedule 8 does not apply to the proceedings listed in Schedule 9, and section 21(2) and (3) empowers the Crown by Order in Council both to add to and subtract from this list any description of proceedings. The following are the proceedings specifically listed in Schedule 9:

Status and capacity of natural persons

> "1. Proceedings concerning the status or legal capacity of natural persons (including proceedings for separation) other than proceedings which consist solely of proceedings for adherence and aliment or of affiliation and aliment."

The rules of jurisdiction in Schedule 8 are designed primarily for proceedings of a patrimonial nature, *i.e.* where a property interest is in issue, and could not appropriately be applied to status-related actions where different rules of jurisdiction have customarily been applied. Proceedings concerning status clearly include actions of divorce, nullity, declarators of marriage and of legitimacy, and adoption proceedings. On one view, actions of separation are not classified as actions relating to status; but it would be inappropriate to apply to them the ordinary rules of jurisdiction in patrimonial actions and, presumably for this reason, they are specifically excluded from the operation of Schedule 8. Conversely, actions of adherence and aliment and of affiliation and aliment might be regarded as

---

[10] Maxwell Report, pp. 17–20.
[11] *Cf.* Maxwell Report, p. 19, para. 2.16(*h*).
[12] para. 9.11.

status-related actions, but their real purpose is the recovery of aliment and, for this reason, it is indicated that they fall within Schedule 8.

Custody of children

"2. Proceedings for regulating the custody of children."

Whatever the classification of such proceedings in the general law, it is clear that the ordinary grounds of jurisdiction in patrimonial actions cannot be applied to custody actions.[13]

Tutory and curatory

"3. Proceedings relating to tutory and curatory and all proceedings relating to the management of the affairs of persons who are incapable of managing their own affairs."

There is a lack of authority in Scots law relating to the basis of the jurisdiction of the Scottish courts to appoint guardians to the property of an incapax. The primary ground of jurisdiction, however, is thought to be the domicile in the traditional sense of the incapax, though the court will always make an appointment which is required by the urgency of the situation or the special circumstances of the case.[14] The effect of Schedule 9, paragraph 3, is to preserve this jurisdiction.

Insolvency proceedings

"4. Proceedings in respect of sequestration in bankruptcy; or the winding up of a company or other legal person; or proceedings in respect of a judicial arrangement or judicial composition with creditors."

As Art. 1 of the 1968 Convention itself recognises, the rules of jurisdiction in ordinary actions of a patrimonial nature are not necessarily appropriate to insolvency proceedings, and special rules have usually been applied. In relation to sequestration, the Scottish Law Commission's *Report on Bankruptcy and Related Aspects of Insolvency and Liquidation*[15] contains proposals for the amendment of the present jurisdictional rules.[16] These facts may explain the present exclusion. It will be noted that, in relation to the winding-up of a company, the exclusion is wider than that in Art. 1 of the Convention, which relates only to the winding-up of insolvent companies.

Certain proceedings relating to companies

"5. Proceedings relating to a company where, by any enactment, jurisdiction in respect of those proceedings is conferred on the court having jurisdiction to wind it up."

---

[13] See Maxwell Report, p. 256. Jurisdiction in custody is at present under consideration by the Law Commission and Scottish Law Commission. See Law Commission Working Paper No. 68 and Scottish Law Commission Memorandum No. 23.

[14] Anton, p. 380.

[15] Scot. Law Com. No. 68, published on 23 February 1982.

[16] paras. 6.17–6.23 and annexed Bill, cl. 9.

This is a specialised ground of jurisdiction related to the subject-matter of the proceedings which it was evidently thought desirable to retain.

Certain admiralty causes

> "6. Admiralty causes in so far as the jurisdiction is based on arrestment *in rem* or *ad fundandam jurisdictionem* of a ship, cargo or freight."

This is an important exclusion. It follows a similar exclusion in Schedule 5, paragraph 7, and is explained in that context. It may be useful, however, to note that the exclusion is a limited one. Though the Maxwell Committee had recommended[17] that the general rules of jurisdiction in Schedule 8 should not be applied to admiralty actions in view of their special nature, this recommendation has not been followed and only the arrest jurisdictions are excluded from the scope of Schedule 8. The general rules in that Schedule will otherwise fall to be applied unless the proceedings are brought in terms of rules implementing a convention on a particular matter and so taken out of the scope of Schedule 8 by Schedule 9, paragraph 14.

Commissary proceedings

> "7. Commissary proceedings."

This exclusion follows a proposal in the Maxwell Report.[18] It may be inferred *a contrario* that the rules of jurisdiction in Schedule 8 apply to other proceedings relating to wills and succession.

Other miscellaneous proceedings

Paragraphs 8, 10, 11, 12 and 14 of Schedule 9 contain exclusions similar to exclusions contained in Schedule 5 and undoubtedly for similar reasons. Reference, therefore, may be made to their discussion in that context.[19] Paragraph 9 of Schedule 9 has no analogue in Schedule 5, and serves to preserve a rather specialised jurisdiction. Lastly, and not unimportantly, paragraph 13 of Schedule 8 excludes:

> "Proceedings which are not in substance proceedings in which a decree against any person is sought."

This provision is at first sight rather opaque, but the Scottish courts have jurisdiction, especially in petition procedure, in proceedings where there is not necessarily a contradictor and where it would be inappropriate, if not impracticable, to apply the ordinary rules of jurisdiction in patrimonial matters.

D. GENERAL FIELD OF APPLICATION OF SCHEDULE 8

10.09   The exclusions in Schedule 9 may appear to be extensive, but they are exhaustive of the matters excluded from the scope of Schedule 8. Its field

---

[17] pp. 247–248.
[18] p. 257.
[19] para. 9.12.

of application, therefore, is extremely wide. Moreover, notwithstanding those exclusions, section 22(4) of the 1982 Act declares that:

> "Where a court has jurisdiction in any proceedings by virtue of Schedule 8, that court shall also have jurisdiction to determine any matter which—
> (*a*) is ancillary or incidental to the proceedings; or
> (*b*) requires to be determined for the purposes of a decision in the proceedings."

RELATIONSHIP OF SCOTTISH RULES TO OTHER RULES

).10   The rules of jurisdiction in the Convention clearly take precedence where they apply. Section 2(1) of the 1982 Act declares that:

> "The Conventions [*i.e.* the 1968 Convention, the 1971 Protocol and the Accession Convention] shall have the force of law in the United Kingdom, and judicial notice shall be taken of them."

This is reinforced, however, by section 20 of the 1982 Act which makes it clear that Schedule 8 is subject not merely to Part I of the Act, which imports the rules of the Convention, but to Part II, which imports those for the United Kingdom allocation of jurisdiction. In theory, therefore, problems of coherence are resolved by those rules of priority. In practice, however, the users of Schedule 8 will require to give careful attention to the possible overriding effect of Parts I and II of the Act, especially in cases where the Schedule departs materially from the terms of the Convention.

).11   The problem is greatest where Schedule 8 simply omits a provision of the Convention, since this is not signalled typographically in Schedule 8. The most important of these omissions is the set of rules of jurisdiction in matters relating to insurance contained in Title II, Section 3 of the Convention. They were omitted from Schedule 8 *inter alia* because, whatever their justification in relations between Community States, they had little justification in the context of the allocation of jurisdiction within the United Kingdom and *a fortiori* in that of the allocation of jurisdiction among the courts in Scotland.[20] Their omission, however, from Schedule 8 does not mean that a Scottish insured may not have recourse to Section 3 of Title II of the Convention where he wishes to sue in Scotland an insurer domiciled in or deemed to be domiciled in a Contracting State other than the United Kingdom. In such a case the Convention applies. A similar problem, to which reference is made below,[21] arises from the omission in the provisions of Schedule 8 for jurisdiction over consumer contracts of any analogue to Art. 13(1)(3)(*a*) of the Convention.[22]

0.12   But attention must also be paid to the overriding effect of the rules contained in Parts I and II of the 1982 Act in those cases where Schedule 8 includes rules which have no counterpart in the Convention or in Schedule 4 to the 1982 Act. Jurisdiction, for example, under Rule 2, paras. 8 and 9 will not be available against a defender domiciled in another Contracting State since these provisions run counter to specific prohibitions in Art. 3 of

---

[20] Maxwell Report, pp. 194 and 222–223.
[21] See para. 10.58 below.
[22] Following a recommendation in the Maxwell Report, p. 202, Rule 6(1) and p. 227, para. 13.92.

the Convention. Rule 2, para. 8, which has no counterpart in Schedule 4, by its own terms is inapplicable where the defender is domiciled in the United Kingdom. Again, although section 22 of the 1982 Act admits of the operation of the principle of *forum non conveniens* in the context of Schedule 8, that principle is foreign to the scheme of the Convention and cannot be applied in matters within the scope of the Convention where the defender is domiciled in another Contracting State, or indeed, where Art. 16 of the Convention applies. This point is underlined by the last words of section 49 of the 1982 Act.

10.13   Another situation where the rules in Schedule 8 may be inapplicable is where the parties have chosen another method of settling their disputes. Section 22(2) of the 1982 Act states in terms that:

> "Nothing in Schedule 8 affects the operation of any enactment or rule of law under which a court may decline to exercise jurisdiction because of the prorogation by parties of the jurisdiction of another court."

It is thought, indeed, that the same principle applies where the parties have agreed that the issues between them are to be determined by arbitration. Where the arbitration agreement is "a domestic arbitration agreement" in the sense of section 1(4) of the Arbitration Act 1975 a Scottish court is normally barred from itself deciding on the merits of the dispute, but retains a residual jurisdiction to intervene when the arbitration for any reason proves abortive or to assist a successful party in the proceedings by issuing a decree conform.[23] If the agreement is not "a domestic arbitration agreement" in this sense, the powers of the Scottish court are more limited. Any party to the agreement or any party claiming through or under him may apply to the court to sist the proceedings and:

> "the court, unless satisfied that the arbitration agreement is null and void, inoperative or incapable of being performed or that there is not in fact any dispute between the parties with regard to the matter agreed to be referred, shall make an order sisting the proceedings."[24]

It is thought that these rules remain in force notwithstanding the absence of any reference to them in the provisions of the 1982 Act introducing Schedule 8.

SCOTTISH RULES OF JURISDICTION

A. GENERAL JURISDICTION: DOMICILE

10.14   Rule 1 of Schedule 8 states the principal and general rule, derived from Art. 2(1) of the 1968 Convention,[25] that persons shall be sued in the place where they are domiciled. Rule 1, somewhat unspecifically, states that it is "subject to the following Rules". It is certainly subject to Rule 3 (jurisdiction over consumer contracts), Rule 4 (exclusive jurisdiction),

---

[23] *Hamlyn & Co.* v. *Talisker Distillery* (1894) 21 R.(H.L.) 21 at p. 25. *Cf. Mauritzen Ltd.* v. *Baltic Shipping Co. and Others*, 1948 S.C. 646; 1948 S.L.T. 300.

[24] Arbitration Act 1975, s.1, implementing Art. II(3) of the New York Convention of June 10, 1958 on the Recognition and Enforcement of Arbitral Awards.

[25] See paras. 5.04–5.07 above.

Rule 5 (prorogation of jurisdiction), and Rule 6 (appearance). Rule 1 is not subject to the special jurisdictions in Rule 2, because the latter are introduced *inter alia* by the words "a person may also be sued". The latter are *alternative* jurisdictions.

10.15 Rule 1 refers to the courts for the place of the person's domicile. That will be the Court of Session whatever that place in Scotland and the sheriff courts of the particular sheriffdom in which a person has his place of domicile, assuming in either case that the court in question is competent to deal with the subject-matter of the dispute.

10.16 Domicile for the purposes of Rule 1 is defined in exactly the same way as it is for purposes of the Convention and the specific rules applicable are those in sections 41–46 of the 1982 Act.[26] The domicile of an individual as defined by section 41 is primarily a residential test, and accordingly, does not differ in essence from the residential tests hitherto adopted by the Scottish courts. Nor can it readily be said that a domicile in this sense is more or less easily acquired than a residence or "forensic domicile" for the purposes of jurisdiction under the common law. Under the common law a presumption of such "a forensic domicile" arose after a period of residence of 40 days.[27] Under the 1982 Act a presumption of domicile in the United Kingdom or in a particular part thereof arises only after a period of residence of three months or more. But once it is established that a person is domiciled in a part of the United Kingdom, he is taken to be domiciled in a particular place within it by the mere fact of his residence at that place.

10.17 While the definition of domicile for the purposes of the Convention is fully discussed in Chapter 4, it may be useful to reiterate that the fact that a person is domiciled in another Contracting State, while material to the question whether the nature and circumstances of his residence indicate that he has a substantial connection with the United Kingdom, would not necessarily exclude the attribution to him of a domicile in the United Kingdom or in a particular part of the United Kingdom. The possibility, that is to say, of a dual domicile is not excluded. The same reasoning applies *a fortiori* where a person has connections with more than one part of the United Kingdom.

B. Special Jurisdictions

(a) General

10.18 Rule 2 of Schedule 8 sets out a number of special rules of jurisdiction, some, but by no means all, of which are based on Art. 5 of the 1968 Convention. Rule 2, as explained above,[28] states rules of jurisdiction which may be adopted by a pursuer as an alternative to suing in the courts of the defender's domicile. The Rule, however, is expressly stated to be subject to Rule 3 (jurisdiction over consumer contracts), Rule 4 (exclusive jurisdictions) and Rule 5 (prorogation).

(b) The particular rules

(1) Itinerants

10.19 Under the common law the Court of Session had jurisdiction over itinerants—that is to say, persons who had no fixed residence in Scotland

---

[26] See Chap. 4 above.
[27] Anton, p. 96.
[28] para. 10.14.

or elsewhere—if they were personally cited within Scotland. No statutory jurisdiction to the same effect was conferred upon the sheriff by the 1907 Act. Rule 2(1) of Schedule 8 provides that a person may be sued "where he has no fixed residence, in a court within whose jurisdiction he is personally cited." It would seem to apply both to the Court of Session and to the sheriff courts. Since this is essentially a statutory re-enactment of a common law jurisdiction, it is likely that the earlier case law of the Court of Session remains relevant.[29]

10.20   There is no comparable head of jurisdiction in the Convention and this ground of jurisdiction could not be invoked in relation to a person domiciled in another Contracting State.[30] An individual, however, may be resident in the United Kingdom and domiciled there under section 41(2) by virtue of his substantial connection with the United Kingdom, and yet have no substantial connection with any part of the United Kingdom. In this case section 41(5) provides that he shall be treated as domiciled in the part of the United Kingdom in which he is resident. Such a person is not an itinerant in the sense of Scots law because he has a residence somewhere.

(2) Contract

10.21   Rule 2(2) of Schedule 8 provides that, in matters relating to a contract a person may be sued in "the courts for the place of performance of the obligation in question." This provision is derived from Art. 5(1) of the Convention and the same rule appears in Schedule 4, Art. 5(1).

10.22   Under the common law of Scotland the Court of Session had jurisdiction in actions relating to contract when the cause of action arose in Scotland and the defender was personally cited there. There is authority for the view that a cause of action in contract might be said to have arisen in Scotland, both when the contract was made in Scotland and when it was to take effect there.[31] This is reflected in the language of the sheriff court rule,[32] which provides that an action relating to a contract may be brought within the jurisdiction of the sheriff:

> "Where . . . the place of execution or performance of which is within the jurisdiction, and the defender is personally cited there."

10.23   The new rule applies both to the Court of Session and to the sheriff courts. It differs from the common law rule in that—
(a) no personal service is required;
(b) the place of execution of the contractual agreement is irrelevant;
(c) it embodies a reference to the place of performance of the particular obligation which it is sought to enforce.
Like Art. 5(1) from which it derives, the new rule is not free from difficulty and reference may be made to the discussion of Art. 5(1) above.[33] In particular, the following points may be emphasised—
(1) the question whether the obligation is or is not of a contractual character has been held to be a matter of Community law[34];

---

[29] As to which see Anton, p. 105.
[30] 1982 Act, s. 20(1).
[31] Anton, p. 118.
[32] 1907 Act, s. 6(f).
[33] See paras. 5.17–5.21 above.
[34] See para. 5.17.

(2) Rule 2(2) will probably apply where the existence of the contract is in dispute[35];

(3) Rule 2(2) refers in terms to the place of performance of "the obligation in question" rather than to the place of performance of the contract as a whole. This aspect of the rule has presented difficulties for the European Court and the law on the matter is probably not yet settled[36];

(4) the parties may themselves effectively stipulate what is to be the place of performance of a contract.[37]

(3) Delict and quasi-delict

10.24   Rule 2(3) of Schedule 8 provides that a person may also be sued:

> "in matters relating to delict or quasi-delict, in the courts for the place where the harmful event occurred."

This rule is derived from Art. 5(3) of the 1968 Convention and a corresponding provision appears in Art. 5(3) of Schedule 4. The latter provision, however, also contains the words "or in the case of a threatened wrong is likely to occur." These words were added, as explained above,[38] because of uncertainty whether Art. 5(3) applied to threatened wrongs. A similar addition is not made to Rule 2(3): Rule 2(10), however, concedes jurisdiction in proceedings for interdict to the courts for the place where it is alleged that a wrong is likely to be committed.

10.25   Under the Law Reform (Jurisdiction in Delict) (Scotland) Act 1971[39] the Court of Session and the sheriff courts were conceded jurisdiction where the delict or quasi-delict forming the cause of action was committed within Scotland or, as the case may be, within the sheriffdom in which the proceedings were raised. While the language of this provision appears to place more emphasis on the place where the wrong was committed than on the place where it took effect, it has been held[40] that:

> "if there is a material element of delict or quasi-delict in Scotland that is sufficient to provide a locus, and therefore give jurisdiction, in Scotland."

A similarly extensive interpretation of Art. 5(3) of the 1968 Convention was given by the European Court in the *Reinwater* case[41] where it was held that:

> "the defender may be sued, at the option of the pursuer, either in the courts for the place where the damage occurred or in the courts for the place of the event which gives rise to and is at the origin of that damage."

The reader is referred to the discussion of the *Reinwater* case above,[42] but the following points may be made summarily—

(1) This jurisdiction is an alternative one. Where the defender is domiciled

---

[35] See para. 5.18.

[36] See paras. 5.19–5.21.

[37] para. 5.22.

[38] para. 9.18.

[39] Repealed by the 1982 Act, s. 54 and Sched. 14.

[40] *Russell* v. *F.W. Woolworth & Co. Ltd.*, 1982 S.L.T. 428. See P. R. Beaumont, "Jurisdiction in Delict in Scotland: Before and after the Civil Jurisdiction and Judgments Act 1982" (1983) 28 J.L.S. 528.

[41] *Bier* v. *Mines de Potasse d'Alsace* (21/76) [1976] E.C.R. 1735.

[42] See paras. 5.37–5.39.

in Scotland, the pursuer also has the option of suing in the Court of Session or in the sheriff court for the place of his domicile, in either case irrespective of the place of acting of the pursuer or of the place where the damage occurred.

(2) The generality of its language suggests that Rule 2(3) may be invoked whether or not the person sued is the person primarily liable. It applies, for example, where the basis of the claim is the vicarious liability of the defender for a quasi-delict of an employee. It would be possible, also to convene a co-defender by virtue of Rule 2(15)(*a*).

(3) In cases, however, to which the Convention does not apply, the court may decline jurisdiction under section 22(1) of the 1982 Act on the ground of *forum non conveniens*.

(4) Civil claims in criminal proceedings

10.26 Rule 2(4) of Schedule 8 provides that, where a court trying criminal proceedings has concurrent jurisdiction in civil matters, a person may pursue before that court any claim he may have for damages or restitution based on the act which gave rise to the criminal proceedings. The rule follows Art. 5(4) of the Convention, and the reader is referred to the commentary on that provision above.[43] A similar rule appears in Schedule 4, Art. 5(4).

10.27 This ground of jurisdiction is a novel one in Scotland. Its practical effect depends upon whether compensation orders made under sections 58 to 67 of the Criminal Justice (Scotland) Act 1980 may be said to have been made in the exercise of a civil jurisdiction. This is doubtful, having regard both to the relationship between compensation orders and fines in sections 60 to 62 of that Act and to the fact that in calculating their amount the means of the convicted person are to be taken into account.[44]

10.28 Incidental reference may again be made here to Art. II of the Annexed Protocol.[45]

(5) Maintenance

10.29 Rule 2(5) of Schedule 8 initially follows Art. 5(2) of the Convention and the corresponding provision of Schedule 4. In proceedings for maintenance, therefore, a Scottish court will have jurisdiction—

(a) if it is the court for the place where the defender in the proceedings is domiciled[46];

(b) if it is the court for the place where the maintenance creditor is domiciled or habitually resident[47];

(c) if the matter is ancillary to proceedings concerning the status of a person,[48] and the court has jurisdiction to entertain those proceedings.

---

[43] See paras. 5.40–5.43 above.

[44] See para. 5.42 above.

[45] See para. 5.43 above.

[46] Sched. 8, Rule 1.

[47] 1982 Act, Sched. 8, Rule 2(5). "Domicile" will be ascertained in terms of Art. 52 of the Convention and s. 41 of the 1982 Act. "Habitual residence" is not defined. "Maintenance creditor" is given an extended meaning in the proviso to Rule 2(5).

[48] Under s. 20(5) of the 1982 Act these words must be construed "having regard" to any relevant principles laid down by the European Court in the interpretation of the Convention. It is thought that the European Court would follow its own rulings in the interpretation of Art. 1(2)(1) of the Convention. See para. 3.14 above.

Since some doubt exists as to whether actions for adherence and aliment or of affiliation and aliment would in this context be regarded as actions ancillary to proceedings concerning status, Rule 2(5) and Schedule 9, Rule 1 expressly provide that they are not. This means that, following a recommendation of the Maxwell Committee,[49] Arts. 2 and 5(2) govern jurisdiction in actions for adherence and aliment and of affiliation and aliment, and not the rules of jurisdiction appropriate to status actions. The last portion of Rule 2(5) enables a local authority or the Secretary of State claiming aliment in respect of a child to convene the maintenance debtor in any court which would be available to the mother of the child.

10.30   The term "maintenance" will require to be given the wide meaning that it bears in the Convention, and will include claims for periodic payments and lump sum payments as well as alimentary payments in the strict sense. Payments, however, in respect of the division of matrimonial property on the dissolution of a marriage by death or divorce would not be included.[50]

10.31   In relation to the assumption of jurisdiction in maintenance, the provisions of Rule 2(5) supersede the grounds of jurisdiction in sections 6, 8 and 9(1)(*a*) of the Maintenance Orders Act 1950, as well as the provision in section 16(2)(*b*)(v) of that Act relating to contribution orders under section 91 of the Children and Young Persons (Scotland) Act 1937.[51] These provisions are repealed.[52] Rule 2(5) also supersedes the special grounds of jurisdiction in section 4(1) and (2) of the Maintenance Orders (Reciprocal Enforcement) Act 1972.[53] Where the defender is resident in a "reciprocating country" under the 1972 Act, and the sheriff assumes jurisdiction under Rule 2(5), any maintenance order he makes will be a provisional order only.

(6) Establishment

10.32   Under Rule 2(6) of Schedule 8, in a dispute arising out of the operations of a branch, agency or other establishment, a person may be sued "in the courts for the place in which the branch, agency or other establishment is situated." This provision is a restatement of Art. 5(5) of the Convention with the important modification that it applies generally, and not merely as against defenders domiciled in another Contracting State. There was no identical ground of jurisdiction in Scots law, though the Court of Session had jurisdiction over companies and firms, and possibly over individuals, who had a place of business in Scotland and who carried on business there. Section 6(*b*) of the 1907 Act conferred a similar jurisdiction upon the sheriff court, but makes it clear that the defender must be cited either personally or at such place of business.

10.33   The ground of jurisdiction stated in Rule 2(6) may be useful where it is difficult to discover whether the defender, notably a defending company, is 'domiciled' in Scotland or in a particular sheriffdom in Scotland in the sense of the 1982 Act.[54]

---

[49] pp. 210–211.
[50] See paras. 5.29–5.31 above.
[51] As amended, *e.g.* by s. 17 of the Matrimonial Proceedings (Children) Act 1958.
[52] s. 54 and Sched. 14.
[53] See 1982 Act, Sched. 12, Part II, para. 3.
[54] For the interpretation of this provision reference should be made to paras. 5.46–5.49 above.

(7) Trusts

10.34   Rule 2(7) of Schedule 8 provides that a person may be sued:

> "in his capacity as settlor, trustee or beneficiary of a trust domiciled in Scotland created by the operation of a statute, or by a written instrument, or created orally and evidenced in writing, in the Court of Session, or the appropriate sheriff court within the meaning of section 24A of the Trusts (Scotland) Act 1921."

10.35   This provision replicates—with modifications to point to particular courts—the terms of Art. 5(6) of the Convention. For its explanation, therefore, the reader is referred to the discussion of that article above.[55] Certain points, however, may be emphasised—

(1) Art. 5(6) was introduced into the Convention by the 1978 Accession Convention at the request of the United Kingdom on the lines of the special common law jurisdiction of the Court of Session where a trust is domiciled in Scotland.

(2) The "domicile of a trust" is defined for the purposes both of the 1968 Convention and of the 1982 Act by section 45 of that Act, subsection (3) of which states:

> "A trust is domiciled in a part of the United Kingdom if and only if the system of law of that part is the system of law with which the trust has its closest and most real connection."

(3) Rule 2(7) will not be confined in its application to trusts falling within the scope of the Convention, but will apply also to any other trust falling within the scope of Schedule 8, notably testamentary trusts and marriage contract trusts.[56]

(4) Rule 2(7) evidently applies only to actions against a person "in his capacity as settlor, trustee or beneficiary of a trust" but, for reasons stated above,[57] it is possible that it is not limited to actions *inter se* between or among those persons.

(5) The jurisdiction conferred by Rule 2(7) is not an exclusive jurisdiction. An exclusive jurisdiction in matters relating to trusts arises only by virtue of Rule 5(3) of Schedule 8, where a trust instrument has conferred jurisdiction on a particular court. This provision is considered below,[58] but in essence it involves only questions internal to the trust. In matters external to the trust—which will normally involve proceedings by a third party against the trustee—the former may sue the latter in the court of the trustee's own domicile under Rule 1, in the court of the trust's domicile under Rule 2(7) and (where available in the circumstances of the case) any other special jurisdictions in Schedule 8.

(6) The Maxwell Report recommended[59] that jurisdiction should be allocated among the sheriff courts on the basis of the place of administration of the trust. This recommendation has not been followed and jurisdiction is related, through the application of section 24A of the Trusts (Scotland) Act 1921, to "domicile" within the sheriffdom of the

---

[55] See paras. 5.50–5.56.
[56] Inference from the narrow terms of Sched. 9, para. 7.
[57] para. 5.55.
[58] See para. 10.76 below.
[59] p. 217.

truster or, in the case of marriage contracts, to that of either spouse. In the context of the 1921 Act "domicile" is presumably used in its traditional sense in Scots law rather than in the special sense attached to this term by the 1982 Act. It may, perhaps, seem strange to use the same word in two senses in the same Act, but the risk of confusion seems remote. The device permits of coherence with the general scheme of the 1921 Act.

(8) General jurisdiction based on arrestment of moveables or situs of immoveables

(i) General

.36   Rule 2(8) of Schedule 8 provides that, where a person is not domiciled in the United Kingdom, he may be sued in the courts for any place where:

"(*a*) any moveable property belonging to him has been arrested; or
(*b*) any immoveable property in which he has any beneficial interest is situated."

There are no analogous grounds of jurisdiction in the Convention. Indeed, the Convention by Art. 3(2) specifically bans the application of these grounds of jurisdiction in relation to persons domiciled in a Contracting State. Since the rules of the Convention take priority without any express statement to this effect, the disapplication of Rule 2(8) of Schedule 8 simply to persons domiciled in the United Kingdom is somewhat misleading. Rule 2(8) applies in relation only to defenders domiciled neither in the United Kingdom nor in any Contracting State. The expression "not domiciled in the United Kingdom" was presumably advisedly chosen to exclude the application of Rule 2(8) to persons domiciled in Scotland as well as to persons domiciled in other parts of the United Kingdom.

.37   This provision restricts the power of the Court of Session to convene defenders domiciled in other parts of the United Kingdom, both in relation to the jurisdiction conferred by the arrestment of moveables within Scotland and in relation to the general jurisdiction arising from the ownership of heritage. Scottish decrees, however, based upon the arrestment of moveables could not be enforced in other parts of the United Kingdom under the Judgments Extension Act 1868.[60] The Maxwell Committee[61] saw no justification for the retention of either jurisdiction in relation to the domiciliaries of other parts of the United Kingdom and recommended that, in relation to such persons, these jurisdictions should be given up.

(ii) Arrestment of Moveables

0.38   The Court of Session has for long assumed jurisdiction in personal actions on the basis of the arrestment of moveables within Scotland. The principle was extended to the sheriff courts, and latterly embodied in section 6(*c*) of the 1907 Act. The somewhat laconic terms of Schedule 8, Rule 2(8)(*a*), appear to import a reference to the existing common law. This is described fully in the writer's *Private International Law*,[62] and it is necessary here merely to refer to its salient features—
(1) The ground of jurisdiction is a general one in all actions of a

---

[60] s. 8.
[61] Report, pp. 245–246.
[62] pp. 106–117.

patrimonial character and is not confined to actions relating to the moveables themselves.

(2) Arrestment proceeds on the principle that there is something belonging to the defender within the territory which may be taken in execution or part execution of any decree pronounced in the action to follow. The assets arrested, therefore, must be susceptible of arrestment in execution and so must be either goods belonging to the defender or debts due to the defender. Despite the fact that Rule 2(8) of Schedule 8 refers to moveable property only, and not to debts, it is thought that in this respect no change in the existing law was intended.

(3) The subjects arrested must belong to the defending common debtor, and do so in the capacity in which he is sued. Thus the arrestment of assets belonging to a person as trustee or executor would not found jurisdiction in an action against that person in a private capacity.

(4) The goods (or debts) must, it is thought, be arrested in the hands of a third party who is himself subject to the jurisdiction.

(5) The value of the goods arrested is immaterial, though the subjects arrested must have some commercial value. Even a claim to an accounting may be arrestable, provided that it is immediately verifiable that some balance is due.

(iii) Situs of Immoveables

10.39   It has again long been the rule that any person with a beneficial interest in heritage in Scotland is subject to the jurisdiction of the Court of Session. This common law jurisdiction did not extend to the sheriff court, though section 6(d) of the 1907 Act conferred jurisdiction upon the sheriff where the defender owned an interest in heritage within the sheriffdom, and the action related to the property or the defender's interest in it.

10.40   Rule 2(8)(b) of Schedule 8, like Rule 2(8)(a), is thought merely to import a reference to the existing law as developed by the Court of Session. This is described elsewhere,[63] but the following points may be made—

(1) The jurisdiction is a general one in actions of a patrimonial character. It includes, but is not confined to, actions relating to the heritage itself.

(2) The basis of this jurisdiction is effectiveness. The defender must have a real and beneficial interest in heritage situated in Scotland which admits of being available to the pursuer through a judgment of the Scottish courts.[64] This condition, a recent case[65] indicates, is not fulfilled when the defender is merely alleged to have purchased heritage in Scotland by missives of sale. Such a person has a personal claim against the sellers but no beneficial interest in the property itself.

(3) The defender must possess this interest in the character in which he is being sued. His ownership *qua* trustee of heritage in Scotland would not subject a person to the jurisdiction of the Scottish courts in actions unrelated to the trust.

(4) The value of the interest is immaterial. The possession of a mid-superiority, alleged to be of no value, has been held to suffice.[66]

---

[63] Anton, pp. 102–105.
[64] *Caledonian Fish Selling Marine Stores* v. *Allard Hewson*, 1970 S.L.T. 195, *per* Lord Hunter at p. 197.
[65] *Llewellyn* v. *Hebbert*, 1983 S.L.T. 370 (O.H.).
[66] *Kirkpatrick* v. *Irvine* (1838) 16 S. 1200. Cf. *McArthur* v. *McArthur* (1842) 4 D. 354 at p. 362; *Bowman* v. *Wright* (1877) 4 R. 322 at p. 326.

(9) Jurisdiction in proprietary and possessory actions relating to moveables

.41   Under the common law of Scotland the Court of Session had jurisdiction in proprietary and possessory actions relating to moveable property, based on its presence within the territory of the court.[67] It was of particular utility in actions of multiplepoinding. The sheriff also had jurisdiction under section 6(*g*) of the 1907 Act:

> "Where in an action of furthcoming or multiplepoinding the fund or subject *in medio* is situated within the jurisdiction . . . "

There are clearly circumstances where jurisdiction is best exercised by the courts of the place which has jurisdiction over a disputed fund or thing rather than of the place of residence of the persons who claim an interest in it, who may be scattered throughout the world. While this ground of jurisdiction is proscribed by Art. 3(2) of the Convention, its utility persuaded the Maxwell Committee to recommend[68] that it should be retained where possible and, accordingly, Rule 2(9) of Schedule 8 provides that the courts for the place where the moveable property in question is situated have jurisdiction:

> "in proceedings which are brought to assert, declare or determine proprietary or possessory rights, or rights of security in, or over moveable property, or to obtain authority to dispose of moveable property."

There is a corresponding provision in Art. 5(8)(*b*) of Schedule 4 so that, while this jurisdiction is not available against a defender domiciled in another Contracting State, it may be invoked both against a defender domiciled in a non-Contracting State and against a defender domiciled in any part of the United Kingdom.

.42   In relation to this provision the following points may be made—
(1) The reference to the "courts for the place where the property is situated" makes it clear that the provision may be founded upon in the sheriff court as well as in the Court of Session, and serves to allocate jurisdiction among the sheriff courts.
(2) Although no express reference to multiplepoindings is made in this provision, its language is wide enough to cover them. While this rule cannot by itself found jurisdiction against a person domiciled in another Contracting State, it suffices for any one of the defenders in an action of multiplepoinding to be domiciled within the United Kingdom to clothe a Scottish court with jurisdiction.[69] The Maxwell Report,[70] therefore, recommended that the Rules of Court relating to multiplepoindings should be altered so that in future such actions need not necessarily be raised in the name of the holder of the fund.[71] They should be raised either by the holder of the fund, who will call as defenders persons having an interest in the fund, or by persons having an interest in or claim upon the fund, who will call as defenders other persons having an interest in the fund,

---

[67] Anton, p. 123.
[68] Report, p. 246.
[69] 1968 Convention, Art. 6(1).
[70] pp. 246 and 269–273.
[71] Compare Act of Sederunt (Ordinary Cause Rules, Sheriff Court) 1983, Rule 113.

including the holder of the fund himself. In relation to a fund in Scotland, the chances are that the holder of the fund, or at least one of the claimants upon it, will be domiciled in Scotland (or in the United Kingdom) to the effect of rendering the action competent in relation to all defenders, including defenders domiciled in another Contracting State. There might, of course, be another available ground of jurisdiction, as where the action is concerned with rights *in rem* in immoveable property, where Art. 16(1) of the Convention would confer exclusive jurisdiction upon the Scottish court.

(10) Interdict

10.43   Rule 2(10) of Schedule 8, again following a proposal in the Maxwell Report,[72] allows a person to be sued:

> "in proceedings for interdict, in the courts for the place where it is alleged that the wrong is likely to be committed."

This recommendation was presumably made because it is at best not clear whether Art. 5(3) of the Convention and Rule 2(3) of Schedule 8 cover the case of wrongs which are merely prospective. Art. 24 possibly allows of *interim interdict* by creating a special jurisdiction in respect of provisional or protective measures, but again the matter is not wholly clear. The terms in which Rule 2(10) are couched differ from those of section 6(*e*) of the 1907 Act and are presumably designed to reflect the traditional approach of the Court of Session. It is thought, therefore, that guidance may be derived from the existing case law and reference is made to its discussion elsewhere.[73]

(11) Debts secured over immoveables

10.44   Rule 2(11) of Schedule 8, again following a proposal made in the Maxwell Report,[74] allows a person to be sued:

> "in proceedings concerning a debt secured over immoveable property, in the courts for the place where the property is situated."

The Court of Session, therefore, has jurisdiction wherever in Scotland the property is situated and a sheriff court has jurisdiction where the property is situated within its territory. This jurisdiction was thought to be a useful one. The situation is not comprehensively covered by the exclusive jurisdiction in Rule 4(1)(*a*) of Schedule 8 (based on Art. 16(1) of the 1968 Convention). While it would appear to be covered by the non-exclusive jurisdiction in Rule 2(8)(*b*) of that Schedule, the operation of that provision is excluded where the defender is domiciled in the United Kingdom. Rule 2(11) of Schedule 8 therefore, provides in effect that any party to a standard security over immoveable property in Scotland other than a party domiciled in another Contracting State may be convened in the Scottish courts in proceedings in relation to that security. Since a similar rule appears in Art. 5(8)(*a*) of Schedule 4, this jurisdiction may be

---

[72] pp. 246–247.

[73] Anton, pp. 121–122. It may be stressed that this jurisdiction is an alternative one. There is no reason why the defender should not be sued in the courts of his domicile. *Cf. Allen & Leslie (International) Ltd.* v. *Wagley*, 1976 S.L.T. (Sh.Ct.) 12.

[74] pp. 248–249.

founded upon in relation to defenders domiciled in other parts of the United Kingdom. It cannot be used, however, in relation to defenders domiciled in another Contracting State.

.45   The reference in Rule 2(11) to "the courts for the place where the property is situated" permits of a defender domiciled in another part of Scotland being sued for a debt in the sheriff court for the place of the situation of the property over which the debt is secured.

(12) Decisions of the organs of corporations and associations

46   Rule 2(12) of Schedule 8 declares that the courts for the place where a company or other legal person or of an association of natural or legal persons has its seat shall have jurisdiction in proceedings which have as their object a decision of an organ of that company or legal person. Unlike Art. 16(2) of the Convention, on which it is modelled, Rule 2(12) is not an exclusive jurisdiction. This was thought to be inappropriate in a United Kingdom context. A similar non-exclusive jurisdiction is provided in Art. 5A of Schedule 4 in relation to defenders domiciled in another part of the United Kingdom. Neither will apply in relation to persons domiciled in another Contracting State.

47   An exclusive jurisdiction in matters relating to companies and other legal persons is conferred only in what may be described as "constitutional" matters relating to those entities. This is prescribed by Rule 4(1)(b) of Schedule 8 and is discussed in paragraphs 10.66 to 10.68 below. Rule 2(12) must also be read along with paragraphs 4 and 5 of Schedule 9, which exclude from the scope of Schedule 8 proceedings relating to the winding-up of a company or other legal person and proceedings relating to a company where, by any enactment, jurisdiction in respect of those proceedings is conferred on the court having jurisdiction to wind it up.

(13) Arbitration

48   Rule 2(13) of Schedule 8 provides that the Court of Session has jurisdiction:

> "in proceedings concerning an arbitration which is conducted in Scotland or in which the procedure is governed by Scots law."

Although "arbitration" is excluded from the scope of the Convention,[75] and there is no rule in Schedule 4 corresponding to Rule 2(13) of Schedule 8, it seemed to the Maxwell Committee[76] that there was no need to exclude judicial proceedings following upon arbitration proceedings, or judicial decisions in the course of such proceedings, from the Scottish rules for the assumption of jurisdiction in Schedule 8. It seemed clear that, irrespective of the availability of any other ground of jurisdiction in Schedule 8, in a Scottish arbitration the Court of Session should have jurisdiction to appoint an arbiter or an overseer under sections 2, 3 and 4 of the Arbitration (Scotland) Act 1894 or where a case is stated by the arbiter. It should also have jurisdiction when any question of law is presented under section 3 of the Administration of Justice (Scotland) Act 1972.

---

[75] See Art. 1(2)(4) and paras. 3.23–3.26 above.
[76] Report, pp. 199 and 259.

10.49   The common law rules relating to jurisdiction in arbitration proceedings are not well developed in Scotland possibly because, as Lord Watson has put it:

> "The law of Scotland has, from the earliest times, permitted private parties to exclude the merits of any dispute between them from the consideration of the Court by simply naming their arbiter."[77]

An agreement, however, for arbitration in Scotland may on construction be held to be an implied submission to the jurisdiction of the Scottish courts in matters relating to the arbitration proceedings.[78] Rule 2(13) makes it clear that the Scottish courts have jurisdiction both where the arbitration proceedings are held in Scotland and, even when they are held elsewhere, if the "curial law" of the proceedings is Scots law. This jurisdiction is a non-exclusive one and is not inconsistent with recourse to other grounds specified in Schedule 8, notably a prorogated forum under Rule 5.

10.50   It may also be noticed that, since arbitration proceedings are excluded from the scope of the 1968 Convention, the jurisdictional rules in Schedule 8—so far as they may be invoked in arbitration proceedings—are general in their application and, with the exception of Rules 1 and 15(a), apply to defenders wherever domiciled, including defenders domiciled in another Contracting State. Rule 2(8), however, does not apply to a defender domiciled in the United Kingdom.

(14) Patents, trade marks, etc.

10.51   Rule 4(1) of Schedule 8, which sets out certain exclusive jurisdictions modelled upon Art. 16 of the 1968 Convention, does not include a provision analogous to Art. 16(4) of the Convention which gives the state of deposit or registration exclusive jurisdiction in proceedings concerned with the registration or validity of patents, trade marks, designs or other similar rights. Rule 2(14), fills the gap by conferring a non-exclusive jurisdiction in such proceedings upon the Court of Session. The reason for this departure from the principle of Art. 16(4) is stated in the Maxwell Report.[79] Since all the registers in question are situated in London, that principle could not be used to allocate jurisdiction as between the courts of the United Kingdom. The Court of Session has been accustomed to try actions concerning the validity in the United Kingdom of those rights, and that jurisdiction is retained subject, of course, to the principle of *forum non conveniens*.[80] The word "principally" is used in Rule 2(14) partly because in many cases the question of validity of a patent or similar right will arise as an incidental question in other proceedings. Where the court has jurisdiction under Schedule 8 to entertain such other proceedings, it may also entertain in terms of section 22(4) of the 1982 Act any ancillary or incidental question relating to patents, trade marks, etc.

---

[77] *Hamlyn & Co.* v. *Talisker Distillery* (1894) 21 R. (H.L.) 21 at p. 27. Though a reference to arbitration does not entirely oust the jurisdiction of the court—*Sanderson & Son* v. *Armour & Co.*, 1922 S.C. (H.L.) 117 *per* Lord Dunedin at p. 126—it has meant that judicial interventions in arbitration proceedings have been considerably reduced.

[78] *Cooper & Co.* v. *Jessop Brothers* (1906) 8 F. 714; *United Creameries Co.* v. *Boyd & Co.*, 1912 S.C. 617.

[79] p. 237.

[80] 1982 Act, s. 22(1).

(15) Co-defenders, third party proceedings and counterclaims

(i) General

.52   Rule 2(15) reproduces with one verbal amendment the terms of Art. 6 of the Convention and, in conjunction with Art. 6 of Schedule 4, in substance generalises the rule which these articles embody to apply whatever the domicile of the defender, whether in another Contracting State, in Scotland or in another part of the United Kingdom or in a non-Contracting State.

(ii) Co-Defenders

.53   Subparagraph (*a*) of Rule 2(15) states that a person may be sued:

> "where he is one of a number of defenders, in the courts for the place where any one of them is domiciled."

This reproduces Art. 6(1) of the Convention and is a novel ground of jurisdiction for the Scottish courts. So far, the Court of Session has not assumed jurisdiction over a co-defender merely on the ground that the principal defender is subject to the jurisdiction. Although jurisdiction over co-defenders was admitted in sheriff court practice, the co-defenders themselves had to be subject to the jurisdiction of some sheriff court in Scotland.[81] Rule 2(15)(*a*) follows Art. 6(1) of the Convention, and reference may be made to the commentary upon it above.[82]

(iii) Claims Against Third Parties

.54   Subparagraph (*b*) of Rule 2(15) reproduces the terms of Art. 6(2) of the Convention, conferring jurisdiction on the court seized of the original proceedings in claims against a third party in an action on a warranty or guarantee or in any other third party proceedings:

> "unless these were instituted solely with the object of removing him from the jurisdiction of the court which would be competent in his case."

This is a new ground of jurisdiction for the Scottish courts. Although the rules of the Court of Session allow a third party to be added to the proceedings where the defender has a claim against him in relation to the same facts, the third party must himself be subject to the jurisdiction of the court. In the sheriff court there has hitherto been no general provision for third parties to be added to the proceedings. For a detailed commentary, reference may be made to the discussion of Art. 6(2) above.[83]

(iv) Counterclaims

.55   Subparagraph (*c*) of Rule 2(15) permits a person to be sued:

> "on a counterclaim arising from the same contract or facts on which the original claim was based, in the court in which the original claim is pending."

---

[81] 1907 Act, s. 6(*a*).
[82] paras. 5.60–5.64.
[83] paras. 5.65–5.67.

This paragraph reproduces the terms of Art. 6(3) of the Convention, which has been considered above.[84]

10.56   Rule 2(15)(c) differs both from the common law reconventional jurisdiction of the Court of Session and the statutory reconventional jurisdiction of the sheriff court under section 6(h) of the 1907 Act. The former allows the Court of Session to assume jurisdiction in any proceedings against a person who has already instituted proceedings in any Scottish court not only where the actions arise out of the same event but where the actions are *ejusdem generis*. The sheriff court rule, if it is to be taken at its face value, contains no restrictions based on a correspondence in substance of the two claims.

C. RULES CONCERNING CONSUMER CONTRACTS

10.57   Rule 3 of Schedule 8 states the rules of jurisdiction which are to be applied by a Scottish court in proceedings concerning a contract concluded by a person for a purpose outside his trade or profession—a consumer contract. Apart from alterations designed to make Rule 3 cohere with the remaining provisions of Schedule 8, other alterations designed to secure its more convenient application, and an important omission referred to below, Rule 3 simply reproduces Arts. 13, 14 and 15 of the 1968 Convention. The reader, therefore, is referred to the discussion of these articles above.[85]

10.58   Certain observations, however, may be apposite—
(1) Where the rules depart from the rules in Arts, 13, 14 and 15 of the Convention, the latter rules must be applied in relation to a person domiciled in another Contracting State. For example, under Art. 13(1)(3), a contract for the supply of goods or services not included in Art. 13(1)(1) or (2) of the Convention falls within the scope of Arts. 13 to 15 only if:
(a) in the State of the consumer's domicile the conclusion of the contract was preceded by a specific invitation addressed to him or by advertising; *and*
(b) the consumer took in that State the steps necessary for the conclusion of the contract.[86]
The Maxwell Report[87] recommended the omission of the requirement in Art. 13(1)(3) (a) both because its meaning was uncertain and because it required proof of a difficult question of fact as a precondition of the application of the rule. That requirement, therefore, is omitted in Rule 3(1)(c) of Schedule 8, and it suffices either that:
(a) the consumer took in Scotland the steps necessary for the conclusion of the contract; *or*
(b) proceedings are brought in Scotland by virtue of section 10(3) of the 1982 Act.
The priority, nevertheless, which must be given to the rules of the Convention where the defender is domiciled in another Contracting State entails that, with regard to such a defender and in relation to contracts for the supply of goods or services where the conditions (a) and (b) in Art. 13(1)(3) are not cumulatively fulfilled, the ordinary rules of the

---

[84] para. 5.69.
[85] paras. 6.24–6.32.
[86] Art. 13(1)(3)(a) and (b).
[87] pp. 227–228.

Convention apply, notably Arts. 2, 5(1) and 5(5), and neither the special provisions in Arts. 14 and 15 of the Convention nor the provisions in Rule 3 of Schedule 8.

(2) In relation to a defender domiciled in a Contracting State other than the United Kingdom itself, a consumer, it is thought, could not rely upon Rule 3(3)(*c*) of Schedule 8 to the extent that it refers to Rule 2(9) of Schedule 8, because no such jurisdiction is admitted by the Convention. A similar observation may be made in the context of actions against a consumer under Rule 3(4) of Schedule 8.

(3) Subparagraph (ii) of Rule 3(1)(*c*) is at first sight obscure. But the provision falls into place when it is noticed that Rule 3(1)(*c*)(i) refers only to the consumer taking in *Scotland* the steps necessary for the conclusion of the contract. He may, however, be domiciled in Scotland and have taken the steps necessary for the conclusion of the contract in England. In such an event section 10(3) of the 1982 Act, read along with Art. 14 of the Convention would appear to permit him to take the proceedings in Scotland.

10.59   The Maxwell Report[88] drew attention to the lack of coherence between the rules in the Convention from which the preceding rules were derived and the jurisdictional provisions in section 4 of the Law Reform (Miscellaneous Provisions) (Scotland) Act 1940 and in section 141(3) of the Consumer Credit Act 1974. The 1940 Act declares to be void any prorogation of the jurisdiction of a particular sheriff court in contracts for the sale of goods. Part II of Schedule 12 to the 1982 Act allows of prorogation after the dispute has actually arisen and, to avoid any inconsistency with Rule 3 of Schedule 8, disapplies section 4 of the 1940 Act to any consumer contracts within the scope of Rule 3. Section 4 of the 1940 Act, therefore, will apply only to contracts for the sale of goods which are not consumer contracts for the purposes of Rule 3.

10.60   Section 141(3) of the Consumer Credit Act 1974 deals *inter alia* with actions by a creditor or owner to enforce a regulated agreement and in Scotland gives exclusive jurisdiction to the sheriff court for the district where the debtor or hirer resides or carries on business. Part II of Schedule 12 to the 1982 Act amends section 141(3) *inter alia* by disapplying it where there is an agreement for jurisdiction entered into after the dispute has arisen or where Rule 3 of Schedule 8 to the 1982 Act applies. Where section 141(3) continues to apply the basis of jurisdiction is altered to permit of the debtor or hirer being sued in the courts of his domicile (in the sense of the 1982 Act), in the courts for the place where he carries on business and, where the issue relates to proprietary or possessory rights in moveables or to obtain authority to dispose of moveables, in the court for the place where the property is situated.

D. EXCLUSIVE JURISDICTIONS

(a) General

10.61   The rules in Art. 16 of the Convention creating exclusive jurisdictions differ from the other jurisdictional rules which the Convention contains in that they apply, in principle at least, whatever the domicile of the

---

[88] pp. 230–232.

defender. Their application, however, is limited in a different way since they refer to the courts of the *Contracting State* where immoveable property is situated, where the company, legal person or association has its seat, where the public register is kept, etc., etc. They do not apply, therefore, to exclude the jurisdiction of the Scottish courts where the immoveable property is situated, the company has its seat, or the public register is kept in a State which is not a Contracting State. Nor do they apply to allocate jurisdiction internally between the courts of a Contracting State. Rule 4 of Schedule 8 abandons these internal and external limitations by referring merely to *the place* where the immoveable property is situated, *the place* where the company, legal person or association has its seat, and *the place* where the register is kept. By referring to the *place* where the immoveable property is situated, the *place* where the legal person or association has its seat, etc., Rule 4 has the incidental effect of allocating jurisdiction among the sheriff courts of Scotland.

10.62   Rule 4 is general in its application and this generality is reinforced by paragraph 3 of Rule 4 which states that:

> "No court shall exercise jurisdiction in a case where immoveable property, the seat of a body mentioned in paragraph 1(*b*) above, a public register or the place where a judgment has been or is to be enforced is situated outside Scotland and where paragraph (1) above would apply if the property, seat, register, or, as the case may be, place of enforcement were situated in Scotland."

This approach has the advantage of simplicity for litigants and for the court since it avoids the risk that the court may assume jurisdiction in cases inconsistent with Art. 16 of the Convention and proceed to a judgment which, in terms of Art. 28 of the Convention, would not fall to be recognised in other Contracting States.

10.63   The terms of Rule 4(3) are such that the Scottish courts may not assume jurisdiction even on the basis of submission where the immoveable property or other matter is situated outside Scotland, and the issue is one coming within the scope of Rule 4(1). This approach is in general consonance with the existing law. In relation to Contracting States, submission in this context is precluded by Art. 18 of the Convention. Although it would have been possible, as the Maxwell Report recommended,[89] to allow submission in relation to immoveable property, etc., situated in a non-Contracting State, this solution was not adopted in the 1982 Act, presumably in the interests of simplicity and coherence in the law.

(b) Rule 4(1)(a)

10.64   Rule 4(1)(*a*) of Schedule 8 confers upon the Court of Session or the sheriff court of the place where immoveable property is situated exclusive jurisdiction in "proceedings which have as their object rights *in rem* in, or tenancies of, immoveable property." This jurisdiction broadly corresponds with the common law jurisdiction of the Court of Session to entertain proprietary or possessory actions relating to heritage in Scotland. The jurisdiction is rather narrower than that conferred upon the sheriff courts having regard to the fact that section 6(*d*) of the 1907 Act applies not only

---

[89] p. 235.

to proprietary or possessory actions but to any action which relates to the defender's property or to his interest therein.

65   The fact that the jurisdiction in Rule 4(1)(*a*) is an exclusive one—in the sense that proceedings are channelled to a single forum—entails that the precise ambit of the provision is of crucial importance. Rule 4(1)(*a*) follows the language of Art. 16(1) of the Convention and that of Art. 16(1) of Schedule 4 to the 1982 Act. Despite the explanations in the Jenard[90] and Schlosser Reports[91] the circumstances in which Art. 16(1) falls to be applied are far from clear. All that can be said is that the European Court is disposed to construe this provision relatively narrowly as an exception to the more general provisions in Sections 1 and 2 of Title II of the Convention. Reference may be made to the discussion of Art. 16(1) above.[92]

(c) Rule 4(1)(b)

66   Rule 4(1)(*b*) of Schedule 8 follows, with one significant omission, the terms of Art. 16(2) of the Convention. It is evidently intended to confer upon the Court of Session or the sheriff court of the place where a legal person or association has its "seat" an exclusive jurisdiction in what may be broadly described as constitutional matters relating to such legal persons or associations. The "seat" of a legal person or association is defined for the purposes *inter alia* of Rule 4(1)(*b*) by section 43 of the 1982 Act. The terms of the definition are complicated,[93] but in relation to Scotland or a particular place in Scotland the definition of a legal person or association is such that it must have its registered office or some other official address in Scotland or at that particular place or, if not, that its central management and control is exercised in Scotland or at that place.

67   The exclusion from the scope of Schedule 8 of proceedings for the winding-up of a company or other legal person[94] and the fact that the concept of the "nullity"[95] of a company or other legal person is for the present unknown to Scots law, diminish somewhat the impact in Scotland of Rule 4(1)(*b*), but it has some utility in channelling actions relating to the constitution of a company to the most appropriate forum.

68   The "significant omission" alluded to above relates to the fact that Rule 4(1)(*b*)—like Art. 16(2) of Schedule 4 to the 1982 Act—omits the reference contained in Art. 16(2) of the Convention to the "decisions of the organs" of such legal persons or associations. This follows a recommendation of the Maxwell Committee.[96] The Committee explained that if a local committee in Scotland of an association which has its seat in England were to expel a member of the association in Scotland and that member wished to challenge the decision as being *ultra vires* of the association, there seemed no reason to require him necessarily to go to the courts for the place where the association has its seat.

---

[90] pp. 34 and 35.
[91] pp. 120 and 121.
[92] See paras. 7.07–7.11.
[93] See paras. 4.32–4.33 above.
[94] Sched. 9(4).
[95] See para. 7.15 above.
[96] pp. 233–234.

(d) Rule 4(1)(c) and Rule 4(2)

10.69　　Rule 4(1)(*c*) of Schedule 8 confers exclusive jurisdiction in proceedings which have as their object the validity of entries in public registers upon the courts for the place where the register is kept. The provision in general follows Art. 16(3) of the Convention which has been discussed above[97] and a similar provision is contained in Art. 16(3) of Schedule 4.

10.70　　Two differences exist between Rule 4(1)(*c*) and Art. 16(3) of the Convention. The reference to the "place" (rather than to the "State") where the register is kept means that the Court of Session and the sheriff court of that place will have concurrent jurisdiction. More importantly, Rule 4(2) makes it clear that such jurisdiction as the Court of Session may possess to entertain actions concerning the validity of entries in registers of patents, trade marks, designs or similar rights is preserved despite the fact that these registers may be kept in England. An issue of validity will usually arise incidentally in the course of an action concerning an alleged infringement of the patent, etc. In such an action, the normal rules of jurisdiction apply and the court trying the action would have jurisdiction to determine the incidental issue under section 22(4) of the 1982 Act.

(e) Rule 4(1)(d)

10.71　　Rule 4(1)(*d*) gives exclusive jurisdiction in proceedings concerned with the enforcement of judgments to "the courts for the place where the judgment has been or is to be enforced." This provision follows Art. 16(5) of the Convention with the substitution of the words "for the place where" for the words "the Contracting State in which". Art. 16(5) of Schedule 4 is in similar terms. The Maxwell Committee[98] considered that Art. 16(5) of the Convention might be:

> "widely interpreted to allow the Scottish courts all the control and discretionary powers which they at present exercise over the execution of judgments. This will apply both to Scottish judgments and to foreign judgments registered under the Convention."

At first sight this proposition may seem inconsistent with the disposition of the European Court to give a narrow interpretation to Art. 16,[99] but this narrow interpretation may go simply to the ambit of the phrase "proceedings concerned with the enforcement of judgments" and would not necessarily restrict the powers of the court in relation to proceedings falling within that class.

E. PROROGATION AND SUBMISSION

(a) Prorogation

10.72　　The provision in Schedule 8 for prorogation and submission, following a recommendation in the Maxwell Report,[1] closely follows the terms of Arts. 17 and 18 of the Convention. The Committee wished to make it unnecessary to determine the often difficult questions whether or not a

---

[97] See para. 7.18 above.
[98] Report, p. 85.
[99] para. 7.03 above.
[1] pp. 237–242.

prorogation agreement related to a subject-matter within the scope of the 1968 Convention or was concluded by persons, at least one of whom is domiciled in a Contracting State.

10.73   In relation to prorogation agreements the main departure from the present law is that an effective prorogation agreement must be:

> "either in writing or evidenced in writing or, in trade or commerce, in a form which accords with practices in that trade or commerce of which the parties are or ought to have been aware."[2]

This language is derived from Art. 17(1) of the 1968 Convention, and reference may be made to the commentary upon it above.[3]

10.74   A prorogation agreement is invalid if it purports to exclude an exclusive jurisdiction under Rule 4.[4] It would also be ineffective if, in relation to consumer contracts within the scope of Rule 3, it did not comply with the more restrictive rules in Rule 3(6).

10.75   If the parties have entered into a valid prorogation agreement, Rule 5(1) confers an exclusive jurisdiction upon the chosen court or courts, so that no court other than the chosen court may henceforth assume jurisdiction in matters to which the prorogation agreement applies.

10.76   Rule 5(3), in language similar to that of Art. 17(2)[5] confers an exclusive jurisdiction on a court upon which a trust instrument has conferred jurisdiction "in any proceedings brought against a settlor, trustee or beneficiary, if relations between these persons or their rights or obligations under the trust are involved." By deleting the reference in that article to the court of a Contracting State, Rule 5(3) makes this principle one of general application. As with the jurisdiction conferred by Art. 17(2), this provision appears to confer an exclusive jurisdiction even where the trust instrument does not so provide: but a court otherwise possessing jurisdiction under this rule would lack it if the choice of court were inconsistent with the "primary" exclusive jurisdictions in Rule 4.

10.77   Rule 5(4) is designed to deal with cases where the agreement or trust instrument prorogates generally the jurisdiction of the courts of the United Kingdom or of Scotland. In such a case proceedings may be brought in any court in Scotland, though such a court may decline jurisdiction on the ground of *forum non conveniens*.[6]

(b) Submission

10.78   Rule 6 of Schedule 8 following Art. 18 of the Convention, confers jurisdiction on any court before whom a defender enters an appearance and, like that article does not apply:

> "where appearance was entered solely to contest jurisdiction, or where another court has exclusive jurisdiction by virtue of Rule 4 or where Rule 4(3) applies."

---

   [2] Sched. 8, Rule 5(2). The 1982 Act, Sched. 12, Pt. II, makes consequential amendments to s. 4 of the Law Reform (Miscellaneous Provisions) (Scotland) Act 1940 and to s. 141 of the Consumer Credit Act 1974.
   [3] para. 7.26(6).
   [4] See R. 5(5).
   [5] para. 7.27 above.
   [6] 1982 Act, s. 22(1).

The reference to appearance being entered *solely* to contest the jurisdiction might be thought to be unnecessary, having regard to the decisions of the European Court in *Elefanten Schuh* v. *Jacqmain*[7] and *Rohr* v. *Ossberger*,[8] to the discussion of which the reader is referred.[9] It is to be expected that the Court of Session Rules will be amended to enable a defender who contests the jurisdiction of the court either to lodge defences relating only to the question of jurisdiction in the first instance or defences relating to both jurisdiction and the substantive issues of the action.

F. VERIFICATION OF JURISDICTION

(a) Rule 7

10.79   Rule 7 adopts the principle embodied in Art. 19 of the Convention[10] and requires the court to declare of its own motion that it has no jurisdiction in respect of a claim which is principally concerned with a matter in relation to which another court has an exclusive jurisdiction under Rule 4(1) or which it cannot entertain by virtue of Rule 4(3).

(b) Rule 8

10.80   Rule 8 adopts the principle embodied in Art. 20(1) of the Convention and requires the court to declare of its own motion that it has no jurisdiction in any case where the defender has not entered an appearance and the pursuer can found on no jurisdiction compatible with the 1982 Act. This is a novel principle for Scots law, and for an explanation the reader is referred to the discussion of Art. 20(1) above,[11] and to the Maxwell Report.[12] There is a comparable provision in Schedule 4, Art. 20(1).

10.81   It should be emphasised in this context that where a defender is domiciled in another Contracting State or in another part of the United Kingdom the provisions of Art. 20 of the Convention or of Art. 20 of Schedule 4 respectively apply to the effect of requiring the Scottish court to sist the proceedings until it is satisfied that the defender had adequate notice of them or that all necessary steps to that end have been taken.

---

[7] (150/80) [1981] E.C.R. 1671.
[8] (27/81) [1981] E.C.R. 2431.
[9] See above, para. 7.28.
[10] See paras. 7.29–7.30 above.
[11] *Id.*
[12] pp. 90–92.

CHAPTER 11

MISCELLANEOUS MATTERS

INTRODUCTION

.01   PART IV of the 1982 Act makes a number of changes in the law relating to the assumption of jurisdiction and to the recognition and enforcement of external judgments which go beyond the requirements of the 1968 Convention or even those of the scheme set out in the 1982 Act for the assumption of jurisdiction and the recognition and enforcement of judgments as between United Kingdom countries. Some of these changes are common to the legal systems of the United Kingdom: others directly affect only the laws of England and Wales and Northern Ireland, though they may have indirect consequences for persons within Scotland.

PROVISIONS DIRECTLY AFFECTING SCOTS LAW

A. PROTECTIVE MEASURES IN CASES OF DOUBTFUL JURISDICTION

.02   Section 24 of the 1982 Act empowers the United Kingdom courts to make orders concerning protective measures in proceedings where one of the issues relates to the jurisdiction of the court in those proceedings and in proceedings which involve a reference to the European Court. This provision is self-explanatory.

B. PROVISIONAL AND PROTECTIVE MEASURES IN THE ABSENCE OF PROCEEDINGS IN SCOTLAND

.03   The Maxwell Committee[1] were concerned by the fact that the principal provisional and protective measures at the disposal of the Scottish courts—arrestment on the dependence and inhibition on the dependence—were available only in the context of proceedings before those courts and were not available—as would seem to have been envisaged in Art. 24 of the Convention—to aid litigants in the courts of other countries. Section 27 of the 1982 Act remedies this situation. In cases where proceedings have commenced in another Contracting State or in another part of the United Kingdom, it empowers the Court of Session to grant a warrant for the arrestment of any assets situated in Scotland or a warrant of inhibition over any property situated in Scotland. Presumably for the sake of completeness, it provides also that the Court of Session may grant interim interdict not only where proceedings have commenced in the courts of other countries but are to be commenced there. Warrant for

---

[1] Report, pp. 101–108.

arrestment or inhibition may be granted only where such a warrant could have been granted in equivalent proceedings before a Scottish court. No similar restriction is imposed in relation to the granting of interim interdict: it will be a matter, presumably, for the court's own discretion. It is not a necessary condition of the making of orders under section 27 that notice of the external proceedings has been given to the defender. In relation to the nature of proceedings to which section 27 applies, the only requirement is that their subject-matter should be within the scope of the 1968 Convention as determined by Art. 1. This is true both of proceedings commenced or to be commenced in another Contracting State and of proceedings commenced or to be commenced in England and Wales or Northern Ireland. It follows that, in the latter case, warrant for provisional or protective measures may in some instances be competently granted by the Court of Session in relation to proceedings to which the inter-United Kingdom scheme for allocation of jurisdiction does not apply, *e.g.* because the defender is not domiciled in the United Kingdom. Under section 27(3) the Crown retains power by Order in Council to alter the proceedings to which section 27 (and, incidentally, section 28) of the 1982 Act apply.

C. ORDERS FOR THE RECOVERY AND PRESERVATION OF EVIDENCE OR OF PROPERTY

11.04 Section 1 of the Administration of Justice (Scotland) Act 1972 empowers the court to make orders for the inspection, photographing, preservation, custody and detention of documents and other property (including land) as to which it appears to the court that questions may arise in proceedings before the court, and also empowers the court to make orders for the production and recovery of such property, the taking of samples and the carrying out of experiments on or in relation to it. Section 28 of the 1982 Act extends these powers to cases where proceedings have been brought or are likely to be brought in another Contracting State or in England and Wales or Northern Ireland. In either case these powers may be exercised only by the Court of Session and in relation only to matters within the scope of the 1968 Convention as determined by Art. 1. However, as mentioned in the previous paragraph, section 27 enables the Crown by Order in Council to alter the proceedings to which section 28 applies.

D. OVERSEAS JUDGMENTS AGAINST STATES

11.05 Section 31 of the 1982 Act, which is already in force,[2] provides for the recognition and enforcement in the United Kingdom of judgments given by the courts of overseas countries against States in cases where the original court would have had jurisdiction if it had applied rules corresponding to those laid down for proceedings in the United Kingdom against States by the State Immunity Act 1978.

11.06 Until recently, United Kingdom law assumed that a foreign State was entitled to absolute immunity in any proceedings against the sovereign or head of State and its government or any department of its government and

---

[2] s. 53 and Sched. 13, Pt. I, para. 2. A transitional provision is contained in Sched. 13, Pt. II, para. 7, as to which see para. 11.19 below.

that this immunity extended not only to proceedings in the United Kingdom directly against the foreign State, but to proceedings for the enforcement of an external judgment against that State. Many countries, however, including the United Kingdom, have recently accepted the principle embodied in the 1972 European Convention on State Immunity[3] (the "1972 Convention") that a State should enjoy immunity only in respect of acts done in the exercise of sovereign authority. This principle, sometimes referred to as the doctrine of "relative immunity," was given effect within the United Kingdom by the State Immunity Act 1978. Though the 1978 Act requires the recognition in the United Kingdom of judgments given against the United Kingdom in other States which are parties to the 1972 Convention,[4] it does not otherwise affect the recognition or enforcement in the United Kingdom of judgments against States. It is the purpose of section 31 of the 1982 Act to do so. To avoid the risk of inconsistency with the provisions of the State Immunity Act 1978, section 31 does not apply to judgments against the United Kingdom; nor does it apply to judgments against the State to which the foreign court belongs since it can be left to that court to protect the interests of its own State. Section 31 applies to judgments given in one overseas country against another State, and its most important effect is that foreign judgments given against the State trading organisations[5] of other States will become enforceable in the United Kingdom.

.07   Subsection (3) excludes the operation of section 31 in relation to judgments enforceable under Part I of the 1933 Act in terms of specified statutory provisions. These statutory provisions are in each case a part of legislation designed to implement international conventions which, in their own fields, make rules which apply to States. Subsection (3), for example, refers to section 4 of the Carriage of Goods by Road Act 1965. That Act in turn implements the Convention on the Contract for the International Carriage of Goods by Road signed at Geneva on May 19, 1956, Art. 1(3) of which provides:

> "This Convention shall also apply where carriage coming within its scope is carried out by States or by governmental institutions or organisations."

Consistently with its international obligations, the United Kingdom could not allow section 31 of the 1982 Act to derogate from the provisions of the 1965 Act relating to the enforcement of judgments against States.

E. Overseas Judgments Given in Proceedings Inconsistent with Agreements for the Settlement of Disputes

.08   The 1982 Act in section 32, which is already in force,[6] provides that, subject to specified conditions, a judgment given by a court in an overseas

---

[3] Cmnd. 5081 (1972).

[4] 1978 Act, ss. 18, 19.

[5] No immunity is given to an entity distinct from the executive organs of government, unless the proceedings relate to anything done by that entity in the exercise of the sovereign authority of the State—s. 31(2)(a) of the 1982 Act read with para. (c) of the same subsection.

[6] It was applied in *Tracomin S.A.* v. *Sudan Oil Seeds Co. Ltd.* [1983] 1 W.L.R. 662; [1983] 1 Lloyd's Rep. 560; [1983] 2 Lloyd's Rep. 384. See para. 11.19 below.

country in any proceedings shall not be recognised or enforced in the United Kingdom if:

> "the bringing of those proceedings in that court was contrary to an agreement under which the dispute in question was to be settled otherwise than by proceedings in the courts of that country."

This provision, which (in effect) restates section 4(3)(*b*) of the 1933 Act, is extremely wide in its scope and applies both to choice of court agreements and to agreements for arbitration. The application, however, of this principle is subject to certain conditions, namely that—

(a) the agreement in question was not illegal, void or unenforceable, or was incapable of being performed for reasons not attributable to the fault of the party bringing the proceedings in which the judgment was given;

(b) the proceedings were not brought by or with the agreement of the person against whom judgment was given; and

(c) that person did not counterclaim in those proceedings or otherwise submit to the jurisdiction of that court.

In relation to these matters a United Kingdom court is not bound by a decision of an overseas court.[7] The question whether the original prorogation or arbitration agreement is valid or not is presumably to be determined in accordance with the proper law of that agreement. Section 32 provides[8] that the principle which it embodies shall not affect the recognition of a judgment which is required to be recognised or enforced in the United Kingdom under the 1968 Convention. This might include, if an observation of the Maxwell Committee referred to above is correct,[9] a judgment pronounced in a Contracting State in ignorance or defiance of an agreement valid under Art. 17 prorogating the jurisdiction of a Scottish court. It might also include, on one view of the matter, judgments given in a Contracting State which ignore the existence of a valid agreement between the parties to resolve their disputes by arbitration or which hold wrongly that the arbitration agreement is invalid.[10]

11.09   The operation of section 32 is also excluded in relation to judgments enforceable under Part I of the 1933 Act by virtue of specified statutory provisions. These provisions form part of legislation designed to give effect to international conventions which, in special fields, do not permit of choice of court agreements or agreements to arbitrate, or permit of them only subject to stringent conditions.[11] To give effect to the international obligations of the United Kingdom, the recognition and enforcement of judgments in the application of those Conventions is allowed to rest upon the existing law.

---

[7] s. 32(3).

[8] s. 32(4)(*a*).

[9] para. 8.26.

[10] See paras. 3.25–26 and 8.26 above.

[11] The Carriage of Passengers by Road Act 1974, for example, is intended to give effect to the Convention on the Contract for the International Carriage of Passengers and Luggage by Road. Art. 23 of that Convention provides for the nullity of any stipulation derogating from its provisions, including: "3. Any clause assigning to an arbitral tribunal a jurisdiction which is stipulated before the event that caused the damage."

F. Minor Amendments to the Administration of Justice Act 1920 and to the Foreign Judgments (Reciprocal Enforcement) Act 1933

10   Section 35(1) introduces Schedule 10, which contains amendments whose main purposes are to enable the 1933 Act to be applied on a reciprocal basis to the judgments of foreign courts other than superior courts and to the judgments of certain tribunals, and to extend the scope of the Act to apply to judgments for interim payments and to arbitral awards. Although the definition of judgment in the Administration of Justice Act 1920[12] was such as to include arbitral awards, no comparable provision was made in the 1933 Act. Paragraph 4 of Schedule 10 rectifies this omission by providing that the provisions of the 1933 Act, except sections 1(5)[13] and 6, shall apply, as they apply to a judgment, to an award in arbitral proceedings, if under the law of the place where the award was made, it has become enforceable in the same manner as a judgment given by a court in that place. This provision is important even in relation to States which are parties to the 1968 Convention since "arbitration" is excluded from that Convention.[14] Sections 1(5) and 6 of the 1933 Act are excluded from the scope of this provision, the former because it is merely provisional in character and the latter presumably because it bars enforcement otherwise than under the 1933 Act. This would have been inconsistent with the New York Convention of June 10, 1958 on the Recognition and Enforcement of Foreign Arbitral Awards which contains its own provisions for recognition and enforcement.[15]

11   Section 35(2) makes certain changes to the Administration of Justice Act 1920. The original version of section 10 of the 1920 Act required a person seeking a certified copy of the judgment from the court of origin to establish that the judgment debtor was resident in some part of the Dominions other than the United Kingdom. The purpose of this requirement was not clear, since such residence is not a condition of the enforcement of a judgment under the Act. This requirement, therefore, has been omitted from the new version of section 10 set out in section 35(2) of the 1982 Act.

G. Minor Amendments relating to Maintenance

12   Section 37 authorises the amendments in Schedule 11. This Schedule is in three parts. Part I contains amendments designed to extend to lump sum orders Part I of the Maintenance Orders (Reciprocal Enforcement) Act 1972 and certain other provisions. Such lump sum orders are enforceable under the 1968 Convention and their enforcement was envisaged under the Hague Convention of October 2, 1973 on the Recognition and Enforcement of Decisions relating to Maintenance Obligations. In ratifying the 1973 Convention the United Kingdom required to make under Art. 26 of that Convention a reservation excluding its application to

---

[12] s. 12(1).
[13] As inserted by the 1982 Act, Sched. 10, para. 1(3).
[14] Art. 1.
[15] Arts. III–VII.

decisions unless they provide for periodical payments. This reservation could now be withdrawn.

11.13   Part II of Schedule 11 to the 1982 Act concerns the recovery of interest on arrears of maintenance. Allusion has been made to this matter in the context of the 1968 Convention.[16] Apart from this, problems could arise relating to interest in the context of Scottish orders registered in magistrates' courts in England and Wales and Northern Ireland under the Maintenance Orders Act 1950 and in relation to foreign orders registered in magistrates' courts under Part II of the Maintenance Orders (Reciprocal Enforcement) Act 1972.[17] While the recovery of such interest in the magistrates' courts in England and Wales or Northern Ireland is not possible, Part II of Schedule 11 to the 1982 Act makes indirect provision for the recovery of such interest if the magistrates' court order is subsequently registered in the High Court.

11.14   Part III of Schedule 11 to the 1982 Act takes as its point of departure the fact that neither the 1968 Convention[18] nor the 1973 Hague Convention[19] on the Recognition and Enforcement of Decisions Relating to Maintenance Obligations precludes a maintenance creditor enforcing an order against the debtor's assets in a country other than that of his domicile or habitual residence. The Maintenance Orders (Reciprocal Enforcement) Act 1972, however, permits of enforcement only where the payer is "residing" in the country of enforcement. Part III of Schedule 11 alters this position, by permitting enforcement also where the debtor has assets within the relevant country. In relation to orders registered in a magistrates' court in England and Wales or Northern Ireland (where enforcement against assets is apparently impracticable in the absence of the payer) provision is made for the registered order to be re-registered in the High Court.

H. Protection of Trading Interests Act 1980

11.15   Section 5 of the Protection of Trading Interests Act 1980 prevents the enforcement in the United Kingdom of overseas awards for multiple damages as defined in that section, and section 6 of the 1980 Act permits the recovery in the United Kingdom of the non-compensatory element in such awards. Section 7 of the 1980 Act permits the making of Orders in Council to provide on a reciprocal basis for the enforcement in the United Kingdom of judgments given in another country under any provision of the law of that country "corresponding to" section 6 of the 1980 Act. Since section 7 could be construed as limiting the Crown to providing for the enforcement in the United Kingdom of judgments ordering the recovery of the non-compensatory element in multiple damages awards, and not the whole of such awards, section 38 of the 1982 Act widens the Crown's powers under section 7 of the 1980 Act *inter alia* to permit of the specification of any judgments countering awards of multiple damages.

---

[16] See para. 8.67.
[17] See s. 1(4) of the Maintenance Orders Act 1958, added by the 1972 Act, Sched., para. 4.
[18] See Art. 32(2).
[19] Inference from the fact that Art. 2(3) applies irrespective of the habitual residence of the parties.

I. Recognition and Enforcement in Relation to the Isle of Man, the Channel Islands and Certain other Places

16   Article 60 of the 1968 Convention empowers the United Kingdom by declaration to extend its operation to any European territory situated outside the United Kingdom for the international relations of which the United Kingdom is responsible.[20] The making of such a declaration, however, would not by itself cause the provisions of the 1968 Convention to apply as between the United Kingdom and the territory concerned, and existing arrangements would continue to apply. Since this might seem anomalous, section 39 of the 1982 Act confers a wide power on the Crown to make provision by Order in Council corresponding to the provisions made by the 1968 Convention as between the States parties thereto (with such modifications as appear to be appropriate) for regulating, as between the United Kingdom and those territories, the jurisdiction of courts and the recognition and enforcement of judgments. In addition, without prejudice to the powers conferred by section 39 of the 1982 Act, s. 52(2) of the Act empowers the Crown by Order in Council to direct that all or any of the provisions of the Act apart from s. 39 shall extend to those territories with such modifications as may be specified in the Order.

J. Provisions for Legal Aid

17   In relation to Scotland, section 40(2) of the 1982 Act empowers the Secretary of State to make regulations modifying the provisions of the Legal Aid (Scotland) Act 1967 in cases where their modification is considered necessary to fulfil obligations imposed on the United Kingdom by any international agreement or (presumably irrespectively of any such formal obligations) in relation to proceedings for securing the recognition or enforcement in Scotland of judgments given outside the United Kingdom under any international agreement. This provision, as explained above,[21] is required not only in the context of Art. 44 of the 1968 Convention but in that of Art. 17 of the 1973 Hague Convention on Maintenance Obligations.

K. Commencement of 1982 Act and Transitional Provisions

18   Section 53 of the 1982 Act introduces the unusually complicated set of commencement and transitional provisions contained in Schedule 13 to the Act. The text deserves careful examination, since considerations of space preclude more than the briefest of comments. Only the short title and the commencement provisions themselves came into force on the date of the Royal Assent, July 13, 1982. The miscellaneous provisions in Part IV of the 1982 Act which are not directly related to the 1968 Convention for the most part came into force (subject to transitional provisions) six weeks after the

---

[20] See paras. 3.43–3.44 above.
[21] para. 8.69.

Royal Assent, on August 24, 1982. The other provisions come into force on such day as the Lord Chancellor and the Lord Advocate may appoint by statutory instrument. It may be assumed, however, that they will be brought into force after the United Kingdom's ratification of the 1978 Accession Convention and in accordance with its transitional provisions, which themselves will have the force of law.[22]

11.19   Part II of Schedule 13 to the 1982 Act contains the transitional rules relevant to that Act. They are specific to the provisions to which they relate, and generalisation is almost certainly perilous. While it might have been inferred from the terms of several of those transitional rules that the underlying policy of Part II of Schedule 13 was to preserve the *status quo* in proceedings begun before the relevant commencement date, it was held in *Tracomin S.A.* v. *Sudan Oil Seeds Co. Ltd.*[23] that, in relation to section 32 of the 1982 Act, the specification in Schedule 13, paragraph 8, of the circumstances where s. 32 did not have retroactive effect raised an inference that otherwise that section applied retrospectively. In delivering the judgment of the Court of Appeal, the Master of the Rolls indicated that there were equivalent provisions in paragraph 9 of Part II of Schedule 13 applicable to section 33 (which does not apply to Scotland), to which the same argument would apply. If so, it would apply also to section 31, for which paragraph 7 of Part II of the Schedule contains analogous transitional provisions.

PROVISIONS NOT DIRECTLY AFFECTING SCOTS LAW

11.20   Allusion may be made to certain provisions of the 1982 Act which, though not directly applicable within Scotland, are important in their own right and may have implications for Scottish practitioners.

A. Trespass to Foreign Land

11.21   Section 30 provides that:

> "The jurisdiction of any court in England and Wales or Northern Ireland to entertain proceedings for trespass to, or any other tort affecting, immovable property shall extend to cases in which the property in question is situated outside that part of the United Kingdom unless the proceedings are principally concerned with a question of the title to, or the right to possession of, that property."

This provision has the effect of abolishing what was known in England as the rule in *British South Africa Co.* v. *Companhia de Moçambique.*[24] Though that case was concerned solely with damages for trespass to foreign land, the rule it embodied was said to rest upon substantial grounds and may not have been confined to actions of damages for trespass. This decision was recently followed without enthusiasm by the House of Lords

---

[22] See paras. 3.47–3.51 above.
[23] [1983] 1 W.L.R. 662; [1983] 1 Lloyd's Rep. 560; [1983] 2 Lloyd's Rep. 384.
[24] [1893] A.C. 602.

in *Hesperides Hotels Ltd.* v. *Aegean Turkish Holidays Ltd.*[25] Section 30, in eliminating this rule, is careful to exclude cases where the proceedings are principally concerned with questions of title to, or the right to possession of, foreign land. The provision is expressly stated to be subject to the 1968 Convention and to the provisions set out in Schedule 4, though it is not clear that the application of section 30 would be inconsistent with either. The Schlosser Report[26] suggests that Art. 16(1) of the Convention does not include proceedings for damages for torts to the property concerned. The liberalisation effected by the rule extends to cases where the land is situated in another part of the United Kingdom and would presumably permit the English courts, subject only to any English rules of equivalent effect to the Scottish principle of *forum non conveniens*,[27] to entertain against a person domiciled in England an action for damages for the wrongful disturbance of a grouse moor in Scotland. Section 30 is already in force.[28]

B. THE RULE IN HENRY V. GEOPROSCO INTERNATIONAL LTD.

22   In *Henry* v. *Geoprosco International Ltd.*[29] the Court of Appeal held that under the common law of England and Wales an appearance before a foreign court might be treated as a voluntary appearance even when the appearance was coupled with a protest against that court's assumption of jurisdiction. This rule is reversed by section 33 of the 1982 Act, which is now in force.[30] To put the matter beyond doubt it is expressly provided that a person is not deemed to have submitted to a court of an overseas country where he appeared for all or any of the following purposes:

"(*a*) to contest the jurisdiction of the court;
(*b*) to ask the court to dismiss or stay the proceedings on the ground that the dispute in question should be submitted to arbitration or to the determination of the courts of another country;
(*c*) to protect, or obtain the release of, property seized or threatened with seizure in the proceedings."

The reference in section 33(1) to "a court of an overseas country" indicates that the rule does not in terms apply to proceedings before a Scottish court. This is presumably on the ground that the matter is regulated within the United Kingdom by Art. 18 of Schedule 4. Section 33 is expressly made subject to the recognition and enforcement proceedings of the 1968 Convention. Here Art. 18 of the Convention is relevant, and, as explained above,[31] that provision is now to be read as if the word "solely" did not appear therein.

---

[25] [1979] A.C. 508.
[26] p. 120.
[27] Preserved by s. 49 of the 1982 Act.
[28] 1982 Act, s. 53 and Sched. 13, Pt. I, para. 2.
[29] [1976] Q.B. 726.
[30] 1982 Act, s. 53 and Sched. 13. Pt. I, para. 2. For its possible retrospective effect, see para. 11.19 above.
[31] para. 7.28.

C. ABOLITION OF THE "NON-MERGER" RULE

11.23   Section 34 of the 1982 Act abolishes the former rule of English law that a plaintiff who has obtained judgment outwith the jurisdiction is not barred, as he would have been if the judgment had been obtained within the jurisdiction, from suing in the English courts on the original cause of action.[32] This result is achieved by barring a person from bringing proceedings in a court in England and Wales or Northern Ireland on a cause of action in respect of which judgment has been given in his favour in external proceedings unless that judgment is unenforceable or not entitled to recognition in that court. Section 34 came into force on August 24, 1982, but does not apply to judgments given before that date.[33]

---

[32] See Cheshire and North, *Private International Law* (10th ed., 1979), p. 631.
[33] 1982 Act, s. 53 and Sched. 13, Pt. I, para. 2 and Pt. II, para. 10.

APPENDICES

APPENDIX 1

CIVIL JURISDICTION AND JUDGMENTS ACT 1982

(1982 c.27)

ARRANGEMENT OF SECTIONS

PART I

IMPLEMENTATION OF THE CONVENTIONS

Main implementing provisions

SECT.
1. Interpretation of references to the Conventions and Contracting States.
2. The Conventions to have the force of law.
3. Interpretation of the Conventions.

Supplementary provisions as to recognition and enforcement of judgments

4. Enforcement of judgments other than maintenance orders.
5. Recognition and enforcement of maintenance orders.
6. Appeals under Article 37, second paragraph and Article 41.
7. Interest on registered judgments.
8. Currency of payment under registered maintenance orders.

Other supplementary provisions

9. Provisions supplementary to Title VII of 1968 Convention.
10. Allocations within U.K. of jurisdiction with respect to trusts and consumer contracts.
11. Proof and admissibility of certain judgments and related documents.
12. Provision for issue of copies of, and certificates in connection with, U.K. judgments.
13. Modifications to cover authentic instruments and court settlements.
14. Modifications consequential on revision of the Conventions.
15. Interpretation of Part I and consequential Amendments.

PART II

JURISDICTION, AND RECOGNITION AND ENFORCEMENT OF JUDGMENTS, WITHIN UNITED KINGDOM

16. Allocation within U.K. of jurisdiction in certain civil proceedings.
17. Exclusion of certain proceedings from Schedule 4.
18. Enforcement of U.K. judgments in other parts of U.K.
19. Recognition of U.K. judgments in other parts of U.K.

PART III

JURISDICTION IN SCOTLAND

20. Rules as to jurisdiction in Scotland.
21. Continuance of certain existing jurisdictions.
22. Supplementary provisions.
23. Savings and consequential amendments.

PART IV

MISCELLANEOUS PROVISIONS

Provisions relating to jurisdiction

24. Interim relief and protective measures in cases of doubtful jurisdiction.
25. Interim relief in England and Wales and Northern Ireland in the absence of substantive proceedings.

26. Security in Admiralty proceedings in England and Wales or Northern Ireland in case of stay, etc.
27. Provisional and protective measures in Scotland in the absence of substantive proceedings.
28. Application of s.1 of Administration of Justice (Scotland) Act 1972.
29. Service of county court process outside Northern Ireland.
30. Proceedings in England and Wales or Northern Ireland for torts to immovable property.

Provisions relating to recognition and enforcement of judgments
31. Overseas judgments given against states, etc.
32. Overseas judgments given in proceedings brought in breach of agreement for settlement of disputes.
33. Certain steps not to amount to submission to jurisdiction of overseas court.
34. Certain judgments a bar to further proceedings on the same cause of action.
35. Minor amendments relating to overseas judgments.
36. Registration of maintenance orders in Northern Ireland.
37. Minor amendments relating to maintenance orders.
38. Overseas judgments counteracting an award of multiple damages.

Jurisdiction, and recognition and enforcement of judgments, as between United Kingdom and certain territories
39. Application of provisions corresponding to 1968 Convention in relation to certain territories.

Legal aid
40. Power to modify enactments relating to legal aid, etc.

PART V

SUPPLEMENTARY AND GENERAL PROVISIONS

Domicile
41. Domicile of individuals.
42. Domicile and seat of corporation or association
43. Seat of corporation or association for purposes of Article 16(2) and related provisions.
44. Persons deemed to be domiciled in the United Kingdom for certain purposes.
45. Domicile of trusts.
46. Domicile and seat of the Crown.

Other supplementary provisions
47. Modifications occasioned by decisions of European Court as to meaning or effect of Conventions.
48. Matters for which rules of court may provide.
49. Saving for powers to stay, sist, strike out or dismiss proceedings.

General
50. Interpretation: general.
51. Application to Crown.
52. Extent.
53. Commencement, transitional provisions and savings.
54. Repeals.
55. Short title.

SCHEDULES
    Schedule 1—Text of 1968 Convention, as amended.
    Schedule 2—Text of 1971 Protocol, as amended.
    Schedule 3—Text of Titles V and VI of Accession Convention.
    Schedule 4—Title II of 1968 Convention as modified for allocation of jurisdiction within U.K.
    Schedule 5—Proceedings excluded from Schedule 4.
    Schedule 6—Enforcement of U.K. judgments (money provisions),
    Schedule 7—Enforcement of U.K. judgments (non–money provisions).
    Schedule 8—Rules as to jurisdiction in Scotland.
    Schedule 9—Proceedings excluded from Schedule 8.
    Schedule 10—Amendments of Foreign Judgments (Reciprocal Enforcement) Act 1933.
    Schedule 11—Minor amendments relating to maintenance orders.

Schedule 12—Consequential amendments.
Schedule 13—Commencement, transitional provisions and savings.
Schedule 14—Repeals.

An Act to make further provision about the jurisdiction of courts and tribunals in the United Kingdom and certain other territories and about the recognition and enforcement of judgments given in the United Kingdom or elsewhere; to provide for the modification of certain provisions relating to legal aid; and for connected purposes.

[13th July 1982]

PART I

IMPLEMENTATION OF THE CONVENTIONS

Main implementing provisions

Interpretation of references to the Conventions and Contracting States

1.—(1) In this Act—

"the 1968 Convention" means the Convention on jurisdiction and the enforcement of judgments in civil and commercial matters (including the Protocol annexed to that Convention), signed at Brussels on 27th September 1968;

"the 1971 Protocol" means the Protocol on the interpretation of the 1968 Convention by the European Court, signed at Luxembourg on 3rd June 1971;

"the Accession Convention" means the Convention on the accession to the 1968 Convention and the 1971 Protocol of Denmark, the Republic of Ireland and the United Kingdom, signed at Luxembourg on 9th October 1978;

"the Conventions" means the 1968 Convention, the 1971 Protocol and the Accession Convention.

(2) In this Act, unless the context otherwise requires—

(*a*) references to, or to any provision of, the 1968 Convention or the 1971 Protocol are references to that Convention, Protocol or provision as amended by the Accession Convention; and

(*b*) any reference to a numbered Article is a reference to the Article so numbered of the 1968 Convention, and any reference to a sub-division of a numbered Article shall be construed accordingly.

(3) In this Act "Contracting State" means—

(*a*) one of the original parties to the 1968 Convention (Belgium, the Federal Republic of Germany, France, Italy, Luxembourg and the Netherlands); or

(*b*) one of the parties acceding to that Convention under the Accession Convention (Denmark, the Republic of Ireland and the United Kingdom),

being a state in respect of which the Accession Convention has entered into force in accordance with Article 39 of that Convention.

The Conventions to have the force of law

2.—(1) The Conventions shall have the force of law in the United Kingdom, and judicial notice shall be taken of them.

(2) For convenience of reference there are set out in Schedules 1, 2 and 3 respectively the English texts of—

(*a*) the 1968 Convention as amended by Titles II and III of the Accession Convention;

(*b*) the 1971 Protocol as amended by Title IV of the Accession Convention; and

(*c*) Titles V and VI of the Accession Convention (transitional and final provisions),

being texts prepared from the authentic English texts referred to in Articles 37 and 41 of the Accession Convention.

Interpretation of the Conventions

3.—(1) Any question as to the meaning or effect of any provision of the Conventions shall, if not referred to the European Court in accordance with the 1971 Protocol, be determined in accordance with the principles laid down by and any relevant decision of the European Court.

(2) Judicial notice shall be taken of any decision of, or expression of opinion by, the European Court on any such question.

(3) Without prejudice to the generality of subsection (1), the following reports (which are reproduced in the Official Journal of the Communities), namely—

(*a*) the reports by Mr. P. Jenard on the 1968 Convention and the 1971 Protocol; and

(*b*) the report by Professor Peter Schlosser on the Accession Convention,

may be considered in ascertaining the meaning or effect of any provision of the Conventions and shall be given such weight as is appropriate in the circumstances.

Supplementary provisions as to recognition and enforcement of judgments

Enforcement of judgments other than maintenance orders

4.—(1) A judgment, other than a maintenance order, which is the subject of an application under Article 31 for its enforcement in any part of the United Kingdom shall, to the extent that its enforcement is authorised by the appropriate court, be registered in the prescribed manner in that court.

In this subsection "the appropriate court" means the court to which the application is made in pursuance of Article 32 (that is to say, the High Court or the Court of Session).

(2) Where a judgment is registered under this section, the reasonable costs or expenses of and incidental to its registration shall be recoverable as if they were sums recoverable under the judgment.

(3) A judgment registered under this section shall, for the purposes of its enforcement, be of the same force and effect, the registering court shall have in relation to its enforcement the same powers, and proceedings for or with respect to its enforcement may be taken, as if the judgment had been originally given by the registering court and had (where relevant) been entered.

(4) Subsection (3) is subject to Article 39 (restriction on enforcement where appeal pending or time for appeal unexpired), to section 7 and to any provision made by rules of court as to the manner in which and conditions subject to which a judgment registered under this section may be enforced.

Recognition and enforcement of maintenance orders

5.—(1) The function of transmitting to the appropriate court an application under Article 31 for the recognition or enforcement in the United Kingdom of a maintenance order shall be discharged—

(a) as respects England and Wales and Scotland, by the Secretary of State;

(b) as respects Northern Ireland, by the Lord Chancellor.

In this subsection "the appropriate court" means the magistrates' court or sheriff court having jurisdiction in the matter in accordance with the second paragraph of Article 32.

(2) Such an application shall be determined in the first instance by the prescribed officer of that court.

(3) Where on such an application the enforcement of the order is authorised to any extent, the order shall to that extent be registered in the prescribed manner in that court.

(4) A maintenance order registered under this section shall for the purposes of its enforcement, be of the same force and effect, the registering court shall have in relation to its enforcement the same powers, and proceedings for or with respect to its enforcement may be taken, as if the order had been originally made by the registering court.

(5) Subsection (4) is subject to Article 39 (restriction on enforcement where appeal pending or time for appeal unexpired), to section 7 and to any provision made by rules of court as to the manner in which and condition subject to which an order registered under this section may be enforced.

(6) A maintenance order which by virtue of this section is enforceable by a magistrates' court in England and Wales or Northern Ireland shall be enforceable in the same manner as an affiliation order made by that court.

(7) The payer under a maintenance order registered under this section in a magistrates' court in England and Wales or Northern Ireland shall give notice of any change of address to the clerk of that court.

A person who without reasonable excuse fails to comply with this subsection shall be guilty of an offence and liable on summary conviction to a fine not exceeding £50.

Appeals under Article 37, second paragraph and Article 41

6.—(1) The single further appeal on a point of law referred to in Article 37, second paragraph and Article 41 in relation to the recognition or enforcement of a judgment other than a maintenance order lies—

(a) in England and Wales or Northern Ireland, to the Court of Appeal or to the House of Lords in accordance with Part II of the Administration of Justice Act 1969 (appeals direct from the High Court to the House of Lords);

(b) in Scotland, to the Inner House of the Court of Session.

(2) Paragraph (a) of subsection (1) has effect notwithstanding section 15(2) of the Administration of Justice Act 1969 (exclusion of direct appeal to the House of Lords in cases where no appeal to that House lies from a decision of the Court of Appeal).

(3) The single further appeal on a point of law referred to in Article 37, second paragraph and Article 41 in relation to the recognition or enforcement of a maintenance order lies—

(a) in England and Wales, to the High Court by way of case stated in accordance with section 111 of the Magistrates' Courts Act 1980;

(b) in Scotland, to the Inner House of the Court of Session;

(*c*) in Northern Ireland, to the Court of Appeal.

Interest on registered judgments

7.—(1) Subject to subsection (4), where in connection with an application for registration of a judgment under section 4 or 5 the applicant shows—

(*a*) that the judgment provides for the payment of a sum of money; and

(*b*) that in accordance with the law of the Contracting State in which the judgment was given interest on that sum is recoverable under the judgment from a particular date or time,

the rate of interest and the date or time from which it is so recoverable shall be registered with the judgment and, subject to any provision made under subsection (2), the debt resulting, apart from section 4(2), from the registration of the judgment shall carry interest in accordance with the registered particulars.

(2) Provision may be made by rules of court as to the manner in which and the periods by reference to which any interest payable by virtue of subsection (1) is to be calculated and paid, including provision for such interest to cease to accrue as from a prescribed date.

(3) Costs or expenses recoverable by virtue of section 4(2) shall carry interest as if they were the subject of an order for the payment of costs or expenses made by the registering court on the date of registration.

(4) Interest on arrears of sums payable under a maintenance order registered under section 5 in a magistrates' court in England and Wales or Northern Ireland shall not be recoverable in that court, but without prejudice to the operation in relation to any such order of section 2A of the Maintenance Orders Act 1958 or section 11A of the Maintenance and Affiliation Orders Act (Northern Ireland) 1966 (which enable interest to be recovered if the order is re–registered for enforcement in the High Court).

(5) Except as mentioned in subsection (4), debts under judgments registered under section 4 or 5 shall carry interest only as provided by this section.

Currency of payment under registered maintenance orders

8.—(1) Sums payable in the United Kingdom under a maintenance order by virtue of its registration under section 5, including any arrears so payable, shall be paid in the currency of the United Kingdom.

(2) Where the order is expressed in any other currency, the amounts shall be converted on the basis of the exchange rate prevailing on the date of registration of the order.

(3) For the purposes of this section, a written certificate purporting to be signed by an officer of any bank in the United Kingdom and stating the exchange rate prevailing on a specified date shall be evidence, and in Scotland sufficient evidence, of the facts stated.

Other supplementary provisions

Provisions supplementary to Title VII of 1968 Convention

9.—(1) The provisions of Title VII of the 1968 Convention (relationship between that convention and other conventions to which Contracting States are or may become parties) shall have effect in relation to—

(*a*) any statutory provision, whenever passed or made, implementing any such other convention in the United Kingdom; and (*b*) any rule of law so far as it has the effect of so implementing any such other convention,

as they have effect in relation to that other convention itself.

(2) Her Majesty may by Order in Council declare a provision of a convention entered into by the United Kingdom to be a provision whereby the United Kingdom assumed an obligation of a kind provided for in Article 59 (which allows a Contracting State to agree with a third State to withhold recognition in certain cases from a judgment given by a court in another Contracting State which took jurisdiction on one of the grounds mentioned in the second paragraph of Article 3).

Allocation within U.K. of jurisdiction with respect to trusts and consumer contracts

10.—(1) The provisions of this section have effect for the purpose of allocating within the United Kingdom jurisdiction in certain proceedings in respect of which the 1968 Convention confers jurisdiction on the courts of the United Kingdom generally and to which section 16 does not apply.

(2) Any proceedings which by virtue of Article 5(6) (trusts) are brought in the United Kingdom shall be brought in the courts of the part of the United Kingdom in which the trust is domiciled.

(3) Any proceedings which by virtue of the first paragraph of Article 14 (consumer contracts) are brought in the United Kingdom by a consumer on the ground that he is himself domiciled there shall be brought in the courts of the part of the United Kingdom in which he is domiciled.

Proof and admissibility of certain judgments and related documents

11.—(1) For the purposes of the 1968 Convention—
(*a*) a document, duly authenticated, which purports to be a copy of a judgment given by a court of a Contracting State other than the United Kingdom shall without further proof be deemed to be a true copy, unless the contrary is shown; and
(*b*) the original or a copy of any such document as is mentioned in Article 46(2) or 47 (supporting documents to be produced by a party seeking recognition or enforcement of a judgment) shall be evidence, and in Scotland sufficient evidence, of any matter to which it relates.

(2) A document purporting to be a copy of a judgment given by any such court as is mentioned in subsection (1)(*a*) is duly authenticated for the purposes of this section if it purports—
(*a*) to bear the seal of that court; or
(*b*) to be certified by any person in his capacity as a judge or officer of that court to be a true copy of a judgment given by that court.

(3) Nothing in this section shall prejudice the admission in evidence of any document which is admissible apart from this section.

Provision for issue of copies of, and certificates in connection with, U.K. judgments

12. Rules of court may make provision for enabling any interested party wishing to secure under the 1968 Convention the recognition or enforcement in another Contracting State of a judgment given by a court in the United Kingdom to obtain, subject to any conditions specified in the rules—
(*a*) a copy of the judgment; and

(*b*) a certificate giving particulars relating to the judgment and the proceedings in which it was given.

Modifications to cover authentic instruments and court settlements

13.—(1) Her Majesty may by Order in Council provide that—
(*a*) any provision of this Act relating to the recognition or enforcement in the United Kingdom or elsewhere of judgments to which the 1968 Convention applies; and
(*b*) any other statutory provision, whenever passed or made, so relating, shall apply, with such modifications as may be specified in the Order, in relation to documents and settlements within Title IV of the 1968 Convention (authentic instruments and court settlements enforceable in the same manner as judgments) as if they were judgments to which that Convention applies.

(2) An Order in Council under this section may make different provision in relation to different descriptions of documents and settlements.

(3) Any Order in Council under this section shall be subject to annulment in pursuance of a resolution of either House of Parliament.

Modifications consequential on revision of the Conventions

14.—(1) If at any time it appears to Her Majesty in Council that Her Majesty's Government in the United Kingdom have agreed to a revision of any of the Conventions, including in particular any revision connected with the accession to the 1968 Convention of one or more further states, Her Majesty may by Order in Council make such modifications of this Act or any other statutory provision, whenever passed or made, as Her Majesty considers appropriate in consequence of the revision.

(2) An Order in Council under this section shall not be made unless a draft of the Order has been laid before Parliament and approved by a resolution of each House of Parliament.

(3) In this section "revision" means an omission from, addition to or alteration of any of the Conventions and includes replacement of any of the Conventions to any extent by another convention, protocol or other description of international agreement.

Interpretation of Part I and consequential amendments

15.—(1) In this Part, unless the context otherwise requires—
"judgment" has the meaning given by Article 25;
"maintenance order" means a maintenance judgment within the meaning of the 1968 Convention;
"payer", in relation to a maintenance order, means the person liable to make the payments for which the order provides;
"prescribed" means prescribed by rules of court.

(2) References in this Part to a judgment registered under section 4 or 5 include, to the extent of its registration, references to a judgment so registered to a limited extent only.

(3) Anything authorised or required by the 1968 Convention or this Part to be done by, to or before a particular magistrates' court may be done by, to or before any magistrates' court acting for the same petty sessions area (or, in Northern Ireland, petty sessions district) as that court.

(4) The enactments specified in Part I of Schedule 12 shall have effect with the amendments specified there, being amendments consequential on this Part.

PART II

JURISDICTION, AND RECOGNITION AND ENFORCEMENTS OF JUDGMENTS, WITHIN UNITED KINGDOM

Allocation within U.K. of jurisdiction in certain civil proceedings

16.—(1) The provisions set out in Schedule 4 (which contains a modified version of Title II of the 1968 Convention) shall have effect for determining, for each part of the United Kingdom, whether the courts of law of that part, or any particular court of law in that part, have or has jurisdiction in proceedings where—
  (a) the subject–matter of the proceedings is within the scope of the 1968 Convention as determined by Article 1 (whether or not the Convention has effect in relation to the proceedings); and
  (b) the defendant or defender is domiciled in the United Kingdom or the proceedings are of a kind mentioned in Article 16 (exclusive jurisdiction regardless of domicile).

(2) In Schedule 4 modifications of Title II of the 1968 Convention are indicated as follows—
  (a) modifications by way of omission are indicated by dots; and
  (b) within each Article words resulting from modifications by way of addition or substitution are printed in heavy type.

(3) In determining any question as to the meaning or effect of any provision contained in Schedule 4—
  (a) regard shall be had to any relevant principles laid down by the European Court in connection with Title II of the 1968 Convention and to any relevant decision of that court as to the meaning or effect of any provision of that Title; and
  (b) without prejudice to the generality of paragraph (a), the reports mentioned in section 3(3) may be considered and shall, so far as relevant, be given such weight as is appropriate in the circumstances.

(4) The provisions of this section and Schedule 4 shall have effect subject to the 1968 Convention and to the provisions of section 17.

(5) In section 15(1)(a) of the Maintenance Orders Act 1950 (domestic proceedings in which initial process may be served in another part of the United Kingdom), after sub-paragraph (v) there shall be added—
  "(vi) Article 5(2) of Schedule 4 to the Civil Jurisdiction and Judgments Act 1982; or".

Exclusion of certain proceedings from Schedule 4

17.—(1) Schedule 4 shall not apply to proceedings of any description listed in Schedule 5 or to proceedings in Scotland under any enactment which confers jurisdiction on a Scottish court in respect of a specific subject–matter on specific grounds.

(2) Her Majesty may by Order in Council—
  (a) add to the list in Schedule 5 any description of proceedings in any part of the United Kingdom; and

[219]

(*b*) remove from that list any description of proceedings in any part of the United Kingdom (whether included in the list as originally enacted or added by virtue of this subsection).

(3) An Order in Council under subsection (2)—

    (*a*) may make different provisions for different descriptions of proceedings, for the same description of proceedings in different courts or for different parts of the United Kingdom; and

    (*b*) may contain such transitional and other incidental provisions as appear to Her Majesty to be appropriate.

(4) An Order in Council under subsection (2) shall not be made unless a draft of the Order has been laid before Parliament and approved by a resolution of each House of Parliament.

Enforcement of U.K. judgments in other parts of U.K.

18.—(1) In relation to any judgment to which this section applies—

    (*a*) Schedule 6 shall have effect for the purpose of enabling any money provisions contained in the judgment to be enforced in a part of the United Kingdom other than the part in which the judgment was given; and

    (*b*) Schedule 7 shall have effect for the purpose of enabling any non–money provisions so contained to be so enforced.

(2) In this section "judgment" means any of the following (references to the giving of a judgment being construed accordingly)—

    (*a*) any judgment or order (by whatever name called) given or made by a court of law in the United Kingdom;

    (*b*) any judgment or order not within paragraph (*a*) which has been entered in England and Wales or Northern Ireland in the High Court or a county court;

    (*c*) any document which in Scotland has been registered for execution in the Books of Council and Session or in the sheriff court books kept for any sheriffdom;

    (*d*) any award or order made by a tribunal in any part of the United Kingdom which is enforceable in that part without an order of a court of law;

    (*e*) an arbitration award which has become enforceable in the part of the United Kingdom in which it was given in the same manner as a judgment given by a court of law in that part;

and, subject to the following provisions of this section, this section applies to all such judgments.

(3) Subject to subsection (4), this section does not apply to—

    (*a*) a judgment given in proceedings in a magistrates' court in England and Wales or Northern Ireland;

    (*b*) a judgment given in proceedings other than civil proceedings;

    (*c*) a judgment given in proceedings relating to—

        (i) bankruptcy; or

        (ii) the winding up of a corporation or association; or

        (iii) the obtaining of title to administer the estate of a deceased person.

(4) This section applies, whatever the nature of the proceedings in which it is made, to—

    (*a*) a decree issued under section 13 of the Court of Exchequer

(Scotland) Act 1856 (recovery of certain rent–charges and penalties by process of the Court of Session);

(*b*) an order which is enforceable in the same manner as a judgment of the High Court in England and Wales by virtue of section 16 of the Contempt of Court Act 1981 or section 140 of the Supreme Court Act 1981 (which relate to fines for contempt of court and forfeiture of recognisances).

(5) This section does not apply to so much of any judgment as—

(*a*) is an order to which section 16 of the Maintenance Orders Act 1950 applies (and is therefore an order for whose enforcement in another part of the United Kingdom provision is made by Part II of that Act);

(*b*) concerns the status or legal capacity of an individual;

(*c*) relates to the management of the affairs of a person not capable of managing his own affairs;

(*d*) is a provisional (including protective) measure other than an order for the making of an interim payment;

and except where otherwise stated references to a judgment to which this section applies are to such a judgment exclusive of any such provisions.

(6) The following are within subsection (5)(*b*), but without prejudice to the generality of that provision—

(*a*) a decree of judicial separation or of separation;

(*b*) any provision relating to guardianship or custody.

(7) This section does not apply to a judgment of a court outside the United Kingdom which falls to be treated for the purposes of its enforcement as a judgment of a court of law in the United Kingdom by virtue of registration under Part II of the Administration of Justice Act 1920, Part I of the Foreign Judgments (Reciprocal Enforcement) Act 1933, Part I of the Maintenance Orders (Reciprocal Enforcement) Act 1972 or section 4 or 5 of this Act.

(8) A judgment to which this section applies, other than a judgment within paragraph (*e*) of subsection (2), shall not be enforced in another part of the United Kingdom except by way of registration under Schedule 6 or 7.

Recognition of U.K. judgments in other parts of U.K.

19.—(1) A judgment to which this section applies given in one part of the United Kingdom shall not be refused recognition in another part of the United Kingdom solely on the ground that, in relation to that judgment, the court which gave it was not a court of competent jurisdiction according to the rules of private international law in force in that other part.

(2) Subject to subsection (3), this section applies to any judgment to which section 18 applies.

(3) This section does not apply to—

(*a*) the documents mentioned in paragraph (*c*) of the definition of "judgment" in section 18(2);

(*b*) the awards and orders mentioned in paragraphs (*d*) and (*e*) of that definition;

(*c*) the decrees and orders referred to in section 18(4).

Appendix 1

PART III

JURISDICTION IN SCOTLAND

Rules as to jurisdiction in Scotland

20.—(1) Subject to Parts I and II and to the following provisions of this Part, Schedule 8 has effect to determine in what circumstances a person may be sued in civil proceedings in the Court of Session or in a sheriff court.

(2) Nothing in Schedule 8 affects the competence as respects subject–matter or value of the Court of Session or of the sheriff court.

(3) Section 6 of the Sheriff Courts (Scotland) Act 1907 shall cease to have effect to the extent that it determines jurisdiction in relation to any matter to which Schedule 8 applies.

(4) In Schedule 8—

    (*a*) words resulting from modifications of Title II of the 1968 Convention, by way of addition or substitution, and provisions not derived from that Title are printed in heavy type; and

    (*b*) the marginal notes show, where appropriate, of which provision of Title II a provision of Schedule 8 is a modified version.

(5) In determining any question as to the meaning or effect of any provision contained in Schedule 8 and derived to any extent from Title II of the 1968 Convention—

    (*a*) regard shall be had to any relevant principles laid down by the European Court in connection with Title II of the 1968 Convention and to any relevant decision of that court as to the meaning or effect of any provision of that Title; and

    (*b*) without prejudice to the generality of paragraph (*a*), the reports mentioned in section 3(3) may be considered and shall, so far as relevant, be given such weight as is appropriate in the circumstances.

Continuance of certain existing jurisdictions

21.—(1) Schedule 8 does not affect—

    (*a*) the operation of any enactment which confers jurisdiction on a Scottish court in respect of a specific subject-matter on specific grounds;

    (*b*) without prejudice to the foregoing generality, the jurisdiction of any court in respect of any matter mentioned in Schedule 9.

(2) Her Majesty may by Order in Council—

    (*a*) add to the list in Schedule 9 any description of proceedings; and

    (*b*) remove from that list any description of proceedings (whether included in the list as originally enacted or added by virtue of this subsection).

(3) An Order in Council under subsection (2) may—

    (*a*) make different provision for different descriptions of proceedings or for the same description of proceedings in different courts; and

    (*b*) contain such transitional and other incidental provisions as appear to Her Majesty to be appropriate.

(4) An Order in Council under subsection (2) shall not be made unless a draft of the Order has been laid before Parliament and approved by a resolution of each House of Parliament.

Supplementary provisions

22.—(1) Nothing in Schedule 8 shall prevent a court from declining jurisdiction on the ground of *forum non conveniens*.

(2) Nothing in Schedule 8 affects the operation of any enactment or rule of law under which a court may decline to exercise jurisdiction because of the prorogation by parties of the jurisdiction of another court.

(3) For the avoidance of doubt, it is declared that nothing in Schedule 8 affects the *nobile officium* of the Court of Session.

(4) Where a court has jurisdiction in any proceedings by virtue of Schedule 8, that court shall also have jurisdiction to determine any matter which—

(*a*) is ancillary or incidental to the proceedings; or

(*b*) requires to be determined for the purposes of a decision in the proceedings.

Savings and consequential amendments

23.—(1) Nothing in Schedule 8 shall affect—

(*a*) the power of any court to vary or recall a maintenance order granted by that court;

(*b*) the power of a sheriff court under section 22 of the Maintenance Orders Act 1950 (discharge and variation of maintenance orders registered in sheriff courts) to vary or discharge a maintenance order registered in that court under Part II of that Act; or

(*c*) the power of a sheriff court under section 9 of the Maintenance Orders (Reciprocal Enforcement) Act 1972 (variation and revocation of maintenance orders registered in United Kingdom courts) to vary or revoke a registered order within the meaning of Part I of that Act.

(2) The enactments specified in Part II of Schedule 12 shall have effect with the amendments specified there, being amendments consequential on Schedule 8.

PART IV

MISCELLANEOUS PROVISIONS

Provisions relating to jurisdiction

Interim relief and protective measures in cases of doubtful jurisdiction

24.—(1) Any power of a court in England and Wales or Northern Ireland to grant interim relief pending trial or pending the determination of an appeal shall extend to a case where—

(*a*) the issue to be tried, or which is the subject of the appeal, relates to the jurisdiction of the court to entertain the proceedings; or

(*b*) the proceedings involve the reference of any matter to the European Court under the 1971 Protocol.

(2) Any power of a court in Scotland to grant protective measures pending the decision of any hearing shall apply to a case where—

(*a*) the subject of the proceedings includes a question as to the jurisdiction of the court to entertain them; or

(*b*) the proceedings involve the reference of a matter to the European Court under the 1971 Protocol.

(3) Subsections (1) and (2) shall not be construed as restricting any power to grant interim relief or protective measures which a court may have apart from this section.

Interim relief in England and Wales and Northern Ireland in the absence of substantive proceedings

25.—(1) The High Court in England and Wales or Northern Ireland shall have power to grant interim relief where—

(*a*) proceedings have been or are to be commenced in a Contracting State other than the United Kingdom or in a part of the United Kingdom other than that in which the High Court in question exercises jurisdiction; and

(*b*) they are or will be proceedings whose subject-matter is within the scope of the 1968 Convention as determined by Article 1 (whether or not the Convention has effect in relation to the proceedings).

(2) On an application for any interim relief under subsection (1) the court may refuse to grant that relief if, in the opinion of the court, the fact that the court has no jurisdiction apart from this section in relation to the subject-matter of the proceedings in question makes it inexpedient for the court to grant it.

(3) Her Majesty may by Order in Council extend the power to grant interim relief conferred by subsection (1) so as to make it exercisable in relation to proceedings of any of the following descriptions, namely—

(*a*) proceedings commenced or to be commenced otherwise than in a Contracting State;

(*b*) proceedings whose subject-matter is not within the scope of the 1968 Convention as determined by Article 1;

(*c*) arbitration proceedings.

(4) An Order in Council under subsection (3)—

(*a*) may confer power to grant only specified descriptions of interim relief;

(*b*) may make different provision for different classes of proceedings, for proceedings pending in different countries or courts outside the United Kingdom or in different parts of the United Kingdom, and for other different circumstances; and

(*c*) may impose conditions or restrictions on the exercise of any power conferred by the Order.

(5) An Order in Council under subsection (3) which confers power to grant interim relief in relation to arbitration proceedings may provide for the repeal of any provisions of section 12(6) of the Arbitration Act 1950 or section 21(1) of the Arbitration Act (Northern Ireland) 1937 to the extent that it is superseded by the provisions of the Order.

(6) Any Order in Council under subsection (3) shall be subject to annulment in pursuance of a resolution of either House of Parliament.

(7) In this section "interim relief", in relation to the High Court in England and Wales or Northern Ireland, means interim relief of any kind which that court has power to grant in proceedings relating to matters within its jurisdiction, other than—

(*a*) a warrant for the arrest of property; or

(*b*) provision for obtaining evidence.

Security in Admiralty proceedings in England and Wales or Northern Ireland in case of stay, etc.

26.—(1) Where in England and Wales or Northern Ireland a court stays or dismisses Admiralty proceedings on the ground that the dispute in question should be submitted to arbitration or to the determination of the courts of another part of the United Kingdom or of an overseas country, the court may, if in those proceedings property has been arrested or bail or other security has been given to prevent or obtain release from arrest—

    (*a*) order that the property arrested be retained as security for the satisfaction of any award or judgment which—

        (i) is given in respect of the dispute in the arbitration or legal proceedings in favour of which those proceedings are stayed or dismissed; and

        (ii) is enforceable in England and Wales or, as the case may be, in Northern Ireland; or

    (*b*) order that the stay or dismissal of those proceedings be conditional on the provision of equivalent security for the satisfaction of any such award or judgment.

(2) Where a court makes an order under subsection (1), it may attach such conditions to the order as it thinks fit, in particular conditions with respect to the institution or prosecution of the relevant arbitration or legal proceedings.

(3) Subject to any provision made by rules of court and to any necessary modifications, the same law and practice shall apply in relation to property retained in pursuance of an order made by a court under subsection (1) as would apply if it were held for the purposes of proceedings in that court.

Provisional and protective measures in Scotland in the absence of substantive proceedings

27.—(1) The Court of Session may, in any case to which this subsection applies—

    (*a*) subject to subsection (2)(*c*), grant a warrant for the arrestment of any assets situated in Scotland;

    (*b*) subject to subsection (2)(*c*), grant a warrant of inhibition over any property situated in Scotland; and

    (*c*) grant interim interdict.

(2) Subsection (1) applies to any case in which—

    (*a*) proceedings have been commenced but not concluded, or, in relation to paragraph (*c*) of that subsection, are to be commenced, in another Contracting State or in England and Wales or Northern Ireland;

    (*b*) the subject-matter of the proceedings is within the scope of the 1968 Convention as determined by Article 1; and

    (*c*) in relation to paragraphs (*a*) and (*b*) of subsection (1), such a warrant could competently have been granted in equivalent proceedings before a Scottish court;

but it shall not be necessary, in determining whether proceedings have been commenced for the purpose of paragraph (*a*) of this subsection, to show that any document has been served on or notice given to the defender.

(3) Her Majesty may by Order in Council confer on the Court of Session power to do anything mentioned in subsection (1) or in section 28 in relation to proceedings of any of the following descriptions, namely—

    (*a*) proceedings commenced otherwise than in a Contracting State;

(*b*) proceedings whose subject-matter is not within the scope of the 1968 Convention as determined by Article 1;

(*c*) arbitration proceedings;

(*d*) in relation to subsection (1)(*c*) or section 28, proceedings which are to be commenced otherwise than in a Contracting State.

(4) An Order in Council under subsection (3)—

    (*a*) may confer power to do only certain of the things mentioned in subsection (1) or in section 28;

    (*b*) may make different provision for different classes of proceedings, for proceedings pending in different countries or courts outside the United Kingdom or in different parts of the United Kingdom, and for other different circumstances; and

    (*c*) may impose conditions or restrictions on the exercise of any power conferred by the Order.

(5) Any Order in Council under subsection (3) shall be subject to annulment in pursuance of a resolution of either House of Parliament.

Application of s.1 of Administration of Justice (Scotland) Act 1972

28. When any proceedings have been brought, or are likely to be brought, in another Contracting State or in England and Wales or Northern Ireland in respect of any matter which is within the scope of the 1968 Convention as determined in Article 1, the Court of Session shall have the like power to make an order under section 1 of the Administration of Justice (Scotland) Act 1972 as if the proceedings in question had been brought, or were likely to be brought, in that court.

Service of county court process outside Northern Ireland

29. The County Court Rules Committee established by Article 46 of the County Courts (Northern Ireland) Order 1980 may make county court rules with respect to the service of process outside Northern Ireland and the conditions subject to which process may be so served; and accordingly in Article 48 of that Order (powers of Rules Committee), after paragraph (*e*) there shall be added—

    "(*f*) the service of process outside Northern Ireland, and the conditions subject to which process may be so served.".

Proceedings in England and Wales or Northern Ireland for torts to immovable property

30.—(1) The jurisdiction of any court in England and Wales or Northern Ireland to entertain proceedings for trespass to, or any other tort affecting, immovable property shall extend to cases in which the property in question is situated outside that part of the United Kingdom unless the proceedings are principally concerned with a question of the title to, or the right to possession of, that property.

(2) Subsection (1) has effect subject to the 1968 Convention and to the provisions set out in Schedule 4.

Provisions relating to recognition and enforcement of judgments

Overseas judgments given against states, etc.

31.—(1) A judgment given by a court of an overseas country against a state other than the United Kingdom or the state to which that court belongs shall be recognised and enforced in the United Kingdom if, and only if—

(*a*) it would be so recognised and enforced if it had not been given against a state; and

(*b*) that court would have had jurisdiction in the matter if it had applied rules corresponding to those applicable to such matters in the United Kingdom in accordance with sections 2 to 11 of the State Immunity Act 1978.

(2) References in subsection (1) to a judgment given against a state include references to judgments of any of the following descriptions given in relation to a state—

(*a*) judgments against the government, or a department of the government, of the state but not (except as mentioned in paragraph (*c*)) judgments against an entity which is distinct from the executive organs of government;

(*b*) judgments against the sovereign or head of state in his public capacity;

(*c*) judgments against any such separate entity as is mentioned in paragraph (*a*) given in proceedings relating to anything done by it in the exercise of the sovereign authority of the state.

(3) Nothing in subsection (1) shall affect the recognition or enforcement in the United Kingdom of a judgment to which Part I of the Foreign Judgments (Reciprocal Enforcement) Act 1933 applies by virtue of section 4 of the Carriage of Goods by Road Act 1965, section 17(4) of the Nuclear Installations Act 1965, section 13(3) of the Merchant Shipping (Oil Pollution) Act 1971, section 5 of the Carriage by Railway Act 1972 or section 5 of the Carriage of Passengers by Road Act 1974.

(4) Sections 12, 13 and 14(3) and (4) of the State Immunity Act 1978 (service of process and procedural privileges) shall apply to proceedings for the recognition or enforcement in the United Kingdom of a judgment given by a court of an overseas country (whether or not that judgment is within subsection (1) of this section) as they apply to other proceedings.

(5) In this section "state", in the case of a federal state, includes any of its constituent territories.

Overseas judgments given in proceedings brought in breach of agreement for settlement of disputes

32.—(1) Subject to the following provisions of this section, a judgment given by a court of an overseas country in any proceedings shall not be recognised or enforced in the United Kingdom if—

(*a*) the bringing of those proceedings in that court was contrary to an agreement under which the dispute in question was to be settled otherwise than by proceedings in the courts of that country; and

(*b*) those proceedings were not brought in that court by, or with the agreement of, the person against whom the judgment was given; and

(*c*) that person did not counterclaim in the proceedings or otherwise submit to the jurisdiction of that court.

(2) Subsection (1) does not apply where the agreement referred to in paragraph (*a*) of that subsection was illegal, void or unenforceable or was incapable of being performed for reasons not attributable to the fault of the party bringing the proceedings in which the judgment was given.

(3) In determining whether a judgment given by a court of an overseas country should be recognised or enforced in the United Kingdom, a court

in the United Kingdom shall not be bound by any decision of the overseas court relating to any of the matters mentioned in subsection (1) or (2).

(4) Nothing in subsection (1) shall affect the recognition or enforcement in the United Kingdom of—

(*a*) a judgment which is required to be recognised or enforced there under the 1968 Convention;

(*b*) a judgment to which Part I of the Foreign Judgments (Reciprocal Enforcement) Act 1933 applies by virtue of section 4 of the Carriage of Goods by Road Act 1965, section 17(4) of the Nuclear Installations Act 1965, section 13(3) of the Merchant Shipping (Oil Pollution) Act 1971, section 5 of the Carriage by Railway Act 1972, section 5 of the Carriage of Passengers by Road Act 1974 or section 6(4) of the Merchant Shipping Act 1974.

Certain steps not to amount to submission to jurisdiction of overseas court

33.—(1) For the purposes of determining whether a judgment given by a court of an overseas country should be recognised or enforced in England and Wales or Northern Ireland, the person against whom the judgment was given shall not be regarded as having submitted to the jurisdiction of the court by reason only of the fact that he appeared (conditionally or otherwise) in the proceedings for all or any one or more of the following purposes, namely—

(*a*) to contest the jurisdiction of the court;

(*b*) to ask the court to dismiss or stay the proceedings on the ground that the dispute in question should be submitted to arbitration or to the determination of the courts of another country;

(*c*) to protect, or obtain the release of, property seized or threatened with seizure in the proceedings.

(2) Nothing in this section shall affect the recognition or enforcement in England and Wales or Northern Ireland of a judgment which is required to be recognised or enforced there under the 1968 Convention.

Certain judgments a bar to further proceedings on the same cause of action

34. No proceedings may be brought by a person in England and Wales or Northern Ireland on a cause of action in respect of which a judgment has been given in his favour in proceedings between the same parties, or their privies, in a court in another part of the United Kingdom or in a court of an overseas country, unless that judgment is not enforceable or entitled to recognition in England and Wales or, as the case may be, in Northern Ireland.

Minor amendments relating to overseas judgments

35.—(1) The Foreign Judgments (Reciprocal Enforcement) Act 1933 shall have effect with the amendments specified in Schedule 10, being amendments whose main purpose is to enable Part I of that Act to be applied to judgments of courts other than superior courts, to judgments providing for interim payments and to certain arbitration awards.

(2) For Section 10 of the Administration of Justice Act 1920 (issue of certificates of judgments obtained in the United Kingdom) there shall be substituted—

"10.—(1) Where—

(*a*) a judgment has been obtained in the High Court in

England or Northern Ireland, or in the Court of Session in
Scotland, against any person; and
- (*b*) the judgment creditor wishes to secure the enforcement of
the judgment in a part of Her Majesty's dominions outside
the United Kingdom to which this Part of this Act
extends,

the court shall, on an application made by the judgment creditor, issue to
him a certified copy of the judgment.

(2) The reference in the preceding subsection to Her Majesty's
dominions shall be construed as if that subsection had come into force in its
present form at the commencement of this Act.".

(3) In section 14 of the Administration of Justice Act 1920 (extent of
Part II of that Act), after subsection (2) there shall be inserted—

"(3) Her Majesty may by Order in Council under this section
consolidate any Orders in Council under this section which are in force
when the consolidating Order is made.".

Registration of maintenance orders in Northern Ireland

36.—(1) Where—
- (*a*) a High Court order or a Court of Session order has been
registered in the High Court of Justice in Northern Ireland
("the Northern Ireland High Court") under Part II of the
Maintenance Orders Act 1950; or
- (*b*) a county court order, a magistrates' court order or a sheriff
court order has been registered in a court of summary
jurisdiction in Northern Ireland under that Part,

an application may be made to the original court for the registration of the
order in, respectively, a court of summary jurisdiction in Northern Ireland
or the Northern Ireland High Court.

(2) In subsection (1) "the original court", in relation to an order, means
the court by which the order was made.

(3) Section 2 (except subsection (6A)) and section 2A of the
Maintenance Orders Act 1958 shall have effect for the purposes of an
application under subsection (1), and subsections (2), (3), (4) and (4A) of
section 5 of that Act shall have effect for the purposes of the cancellation of
a registration made on such an application, as if—
- (*a*) "registration" in those provisions included registration in the
appropriate Northern Ireland court ("registered" being construed
accordingly);
- (*b*) any reference in those provisions to a High Court order or a
magistrates' court order included, respectively, a Court of Session
order or a sheriff court order; and
- (*c*) any other reference in those provisions to the High Court or a
magistrates' court included the Northern Ireland High Court or a
court of summary jurisdiction in Northern Ireland.

(4) Where an order is registered in Northern Ireland under this section,
Part II of the Maintenance and Affiliation Orders Act (Northern Ireland)
1966, except sections 11, 11A and 14(2) and (3), shall apply as if the order
had been registered in accordance with the provisions of that Part.

(5) A court of summary jurisdiction in Northern Ireland shall have
jurisdiction to hear a complaint by or against a person residing outside
Northern Ireland for the discharge or variation of an order registered in
Northern Ireland under this section; and where such a complaint is made

against a person residing outside Northern Ireland, then, if he resides in England and Wales or Scotland, section 15 of the Maintenance Orders Act 1950 (which relates to the service of process on persons residing in those countries) shall have effect in relation to the complaint as it has effect in relation to the proceedings therein mentioned.

(6) The enactments specified in Part III of Schedule 12 shall have effect with the amendments specified there, being amendments consequential on this section.

Minor amendments relating to maintenance orders

37.—(1) The enactments specified in Schedule 11 shall have effect with the amendments specified there, being amendments whose main purpose is as follows—

> Part I—to extend certain enforcement provisions to lump sum maintenance orders;
>
> Part II—to provide for the recovery of interest according to the law of the country of origin in the case of maintenance orders made in other jurisdictions and registered in the High Court;
>
> Part III—to extend the Maintenance Orders (Reciprocal Enforcement) Act 1972 to cases where the payer under a maintenance order is not resident within the jurisdiction but has assets there.

(2) In section 27(1) of the Maintenance Orders (Reciprocal Enforcement) Act 1972 (application by person in convention country for recovery of maintenance in England and Wales or Northern Ireland to be treated as a complaint), after "as if it were a complaint" there shall be inserted "made at the time when the application was received by the Secretary of State or the Lord Chancellor".

Overseas judgments counteracting an award of multiple damages

38.—(1) Section 7 of the Protection of Trading Interests Act 1980 (which enables provision to be made by Order in Council for the enforcement in the United Kingdom on a reciprocal basis of overseas judgments directed to counteracting a judgment for multiple damages given in a third country) shall be amended as follows.

(2) In subsection (1) for "judgments given under any provision of the law of that country corresponding to that section" there shall be substituted "judgments of any description specified in the Order which are given under any provision of the law of that country relating to the recovery of sums paid or obtained pursuant to a judgment for multiple damages within the meaning of section 5(3) above, whether or not that provision corresponds to section 6 above".

(3) After subsection (1) there shall be inserted—

"(1A) Such an Order in Council may, as respects judgments to which it relates—

> (a) make different provisions for different descriptions of judgment; and
>
> (b) impose conditions or restrictions on the enforcement of judgments of any description.".

*Jurisdiction, and recognition and enforcement of judgments, as between
United Kingdom and certain territories*

Application of provisions corresponding to 1968 Convention in relation to certain territories

39.—(1) Her Majesty may by Order in Council make provision
corresponding to the provision made by the 1968 Convention as between
the Contracting States to that Convention, with such modifications as
appear to Her Majesty to be appropriate, for regulating, as between the
United Kingdom and any of the territories mentioned in subsection (2), the
jurisdiction of courts and the recognition and enforcement of judgments.

(2) The territories referred to in subsection (1) are—
  (*a*) the Isle of Man;
  (*b*) any of the Channel Islands;
  (*c*) Gibraltar;
  (*d*) the Sovereign Base Areas of Akrotiri and Dhekelia (that is to
        say the areas mentioned in section 2(1) of the Cyprus Act 1960).

(3) An Order in Council under this section may contain such
supplementary and incidental provisions as appear to Her Majesty to be
necessary or expedient, including in particular provisions corresponding to
or applying any of the provisions of Part I with such modifications as may
be specified in the Order.

(4) Any Order in Council under this section shall be subject to
annulment in pursuance of a resolution of either House of Parliament.

Legal aid

Power to modify enactments relating to legal aid etc.

40.—(1) In section 20 of the Legal Aid Act 1974 (power of Lord
Chancellor to make regulations), after subsection (4) there shall be
inserted as subsection (4A)—

"(4A) Without prejudice to the preceding provisions of this section or
any other provision of this Part of this Act authorising the making of
regulations, regulations may also modify the provisions of, or of any
instrument having effect under, this Part of this Act (including so much of
any of those provisions as specifies a sum of money) for the purposes of the
application of those provisions—

  (*a*) in cases where their modification appears to the Lord Chancellor
        necessary for the purpose of fulfilling any obligation imposed on the
        United Kingdom or Her Majesty's government therein by any
        international agreement; or

  (*b*) in relation to proceedings for securing the recognition or
        enforcement in England and Wales of judgments given outside the
        United Kingdom for whose recognition or enforcement in the
        United Kingdom provision is made by any international
        agreement.".

(2) In section 15 of the Legal Aid (Scotland) Act 1967 (power of
Secretary of State to make regulations), after subsection (4) there shall be
inserted as subsection (4A)—

"(4A) Without prejudice to the preceding provisions of this section or any
other provision of this Act authorising the making of regulations, regulations may also modify the provisions of, or of any instrument having effect
under, this Act (including so much of any of those provisions as specifies
a sum of money) for the purposes of the application of those provisions—

(*a*) in cases where their modification appears to the Secretary of State necessary for the purpose of fulfilling any obligation imposed on the United Kingdom or Her Majesty's government therein by any international agreement; or

(*b*) in relation to proceedings for securing the recognition or enforcement in Scotland of judgments given outside the United Kingdom for whose recognition or enforcement in the United Kingdom provision is made by any international agreement.".

(3) In Article 22 of the Legal Aid, Advice and Assistance (Northern Ireland) Order 1981 (power of Lord Chancellor to make regulations), after paragraph (4) there shall be inserted as paragraph (4A)—

"(4A) Without prejudice to the preceding provisions of this Article or any other provision of this Part authorising the making of regulations, regulations may also modify the provisions of, or of any instrument having effect under, this Part (including so much of any of those provisions as specifies a sum of money) for the purposes of the application of those provisions—

(*a*) in cases where their modification appears to the Lord Chancellor necessary for the purpose of fulfilling any obligation imposed on the United Kingdom or Her Majesty's government therein by any international agreement; or

(*b*) in relation to proceedings for securing the recognition or enforcement in Northern Ireland of judgments given outside the United Kingdom for whose recognition or enforcement in the United Kingdom provision is made by any international agreement.".

PART V

SUPPLEMENTARY AND GENERAL PROVISIONS

Domicile

Domicile of individuals

41.—(1) Subject to Article 52 (which contains provisions for determining whether a party is domiciled in a Contracting State), the following provisions of this section determine, for the purposes of the 1968 Convention and this Act, whether an individual is domiciled in the United Kingdom or in a particular part of, or place in, the United Kingdom or in a state other than a Contracting State.

(2) An individual is domiciled in the United Kingdom if and only if—

(*a*) he is resident in the United Kingdom; and

(*b*) the nature and circumstances of his residence indicate that he has a substantial connection with the United Kingdom.

(3) Subject to subsection (5), an individual is domiciled in a particular part of the United Kingdom if and only if—

(*a*) he is resident in that part; and

(*b*) the nature and circumstances of his residence indicate that he has a substantial connection with that part.

(4) An individual is domiciled in a particular place in the United Kingdom if and only if he—

(*a*) is domiciled in the part of the United Kingdom in which that place is situated; and

(*b*) is resident in that place.

(5) An individual who is domiciled in the United Kingdom but in whose case the requirement of subsection (3)(*b*) are not satisfied in relation to any particular part of the United Kingdom shall be treated as domiciled in the part of the United Kingdom in which he is resident.

(6) In the case of an individual who—

(*a*) is resident in the United Kingdom, or in a particular part of the United Kingdom; and

(*b*) has been so resident for the last three months or more,

the requirements of subsection (2)(*b*) or, as the case may be, subsection (3)(*b*) shall be presumed to be fulfilled unless the contrary is proved.

(7) An individual is domiciled in a state other than a Contracting State if and only if—

(*a*) he is resident in that state; and

(*b*) the nature and circumstances of his residence indicate that he has a substantial connection with that state.

Domicile and seat of corporation or association

42.—(1) For the purposes of this Act the seat of a corporation or association (as determined by this section) shall be treated as its domicile.

(2) The following provisions of this section determine where a corporation or association has its seat—

(*a*) for the purpose of Article 53 (which for the purposes of the 1968 Convention equates the domicile of such a body with its seat); and

(*b*) for the purposes of this Act other than the provisions mentioned in section 43(1) (*b*) and (*c*).

(3) A corporation or association has its seat in the United Kingdom if and only if—

(*a*) it was incorporated or formed under the law of a part of the United Kingdom and has its registered office or some other official address in the United Kingdom; or

(*b*) its central management and control is exercised in the United Kingdom.

(4) A corporation or association has its seat in a particular part of the United Kingdom if and only if it has its seat in the United Kingdom and—

(*a*) it has its registered office or some other official address in that part; or

(*b*) its central management and control is exercised in that part; or

(*c*) it has a place of business in that part.

(5) A corporation or association has its seat in a particular place in the United Kingdom if and only if it has its seat in the part of the United Kingdom in which that place is situated and—

(*a*) it has its registered office or some other official address in that place; or

(*b*) its central management and control is exercised in that place; or

(*c*) it has a place of business in that place.

(6) Subject to subsection (7), a corporation or association has its seat in a state other than the United Kingdom if and only if—

(*a*) it was incorporated or formed under the law of that state and has its registered office or some other official address there; or

(*b*) its central management and control is exercised in that state.

(7) A corporation or association shall not be regarded as having its seat in a Contracting State other than the United Kingdom if it is shown that the courts of that state would not regard it as having its seat there.

(8) In this section—

"business" includes any activity carried on by a corporation or association, and "place of business" shall be construed accordingly;

"official address", in relation to a corporation or association, means an address which it is required by law to register, notify or maintain for the purpose of receiving notices or other communications.

Seat of corporation or association for purposes of Article 16(2) and related provisions

43.—(1) The following provisions of this section determine where a corporation or association has its seat for the purposes of—

(a) Article 16(2) (which confers exclusive jurisdiction over proceedings relating to the formation or dissolution of such bodies, or to the decisions of their organs);

(b) Articles 5A and 16(2) in Schedule 4; and

(c) Rules 2(12) and 4(1)(b) in Schedule 8.

(2) A corporation or association has its seat in the United Kingdom if and only if—

(a) it was incorporated or formed under the law of a part of the United Kingdom; or

(b) its central management and control is exercised in the United Kingdom.

(3) A corporation or association has its seat in a particular part of the United Kingdom if and only if it has its seat in the United Kingdom and—

(a) subject to subsection (5), it was incorporated or formed under the law of that part; or

(b) being incorporated or formed under the law of a state other than the United Kingdom, its central management and control is exercised in that part.

(4) A corporation or association has its seat in a particular place in Scotland if and only if it has its seat in Scotland and—

(a) it has its registered office or some other official address in that place; or

(b) it has no registered office or other official address in Scotland, but its central management and control is exercised in that place.

(5) A corporation or association incorporated or formed under—

(a) an enactment forming part of the law of more than one part of the United Kingdom; or

(b) an instrument having effect in the domestic law of more than one part of the United Kingdom,

shall, if it has a registered office, be taken to have its seat in the part of the United Kingdom in which that office is situated, and not in any other part of the United Kingdom.

(6) Subject to subsection (7), a corporation or association has its seat in a Contracting State other than the United Kingdom if and only if—

(a) it was incorporated or formed under the law of that State; or

(b) its central management and control is exercised in that state.

(7) A corporation or association shall not be regarded as having its seat in a Contracting State other than the United Kingdom if—

(*a*) it has its seat in the United Kingdom by virtue of subsection (2)(*a*); or

(*b*) it is shown that the courts of that other state would not regard it for the purposes of Article 16(2) as having its seat there.

(8) In this section "official address" has the same meaning as in section 42.

Persons deemed to be domiciled in the United Kingdom for certain purposes

44.—(1) This section applies to—

(*a*) proceedings within Section 3 of Title II of the 1968 Convention (insurance contracts), and

(*b*) proceedings within Section 4 of that Title (consumer contracts).

(2) A person who, for the purposes of proceedings to which this section applies arising out of the operations of a branch, agency or other establishment in the United Kingdom, is deemed for the purposes of the 1968 Convention to be domiciled in the United Kingdom by virtue of—

(*a*) Article 8, second paragraph (insurers); or

(*b*) Article 13, second paragraph (supplies of goods, services or credit to consumers),

shall, for the purposes of those proceedings, be treated for the purposes of this Act as so domiciled and as domiciled in the part of the United Kingdom in which the branch, agency or establishment in question is situated.

Domicile of trusts

45.—(1) The following provisions of this section determine, for the purposes of the 1968 Convention and this Act, where a trust is domiciled.

(2) A trust is domiciled in the United Kingdom if and only if it is by virtue of subsection (3) domiciled in a part of the United Kingdom.

(3) A trust is domiciled in a part of the United Kingdom if and only if the system of law of that part is the system of law with which the trust has its closest and most real connection.

Domicile and seat of the Crown

46.—(1) For the purposes of this Act the seat of the Crown (as determined by this section) shall be treated as its domicile.

(2) The following provisions of this section determine where the Crown has its seat—

(*a*) for the purposes of the 1968 Convention (in which Article 53 equates the domicile of a legal person with its seat); and

(*b*) for the purposes of this Act.

(3) Subject to the provisions of any Order in Council for the time being in force under subsection (4)—

(*a*) the Crown in right of Her Majesty's government in the United Kingdom has its seat in every part of, and every place in, the United Kingdom; and

(*b*) the Crown in right of Her Majesty's government in Northern Ireland has its seat in, and in every place in, Northern Ireland.

(4) Her Majesty may by Order in Council provide that, in the case of proceedings of any specified description against the Crown in right of Her Majesty's government in the United Kingdom, the Crown shall be treated

for the purposes of the 1968 Convention and this Act as having its seat in, and in every place in, a specified part of the United Kingdom and not in any other part of the United Kingdom.

(5) An Order in Council under subsection (4) may frame a description of proceedings in any way, and in particular may do so by reference to the government department or officer of the Crown against which or against whom they fall to be instituted.

(6) Any Order in Council made under this section shall be subject to annulment in pursuance of a resolution of either House of Parliament.

(7) Nothing in this section applies to the Crown otherwise than in right of Her Majesty's government in the United Kingdom or Her Majesty's government in Northern Ireland.

Other supplementary provisions

Modifications occasioned by decisions of European Court as to meaning or effect of Conventions

47.—(1) Her Majesty may by Order in Council—

    (*a*) make such provision as Her Majesty considers appropriate for the purpose of bringing the law of any part of the United Kingdom into accord with the Conventions as affected by any principle laid down by the European Court in connection with the Conventions or by any decision of that court as to the meaning or effect of any provision of the Conventions; or

    (*b*) make such modifications of Schedule 4 or Schedule 8, or by any other statutory provision affected by any provision of either of those Schedules, as Her Majesty considers appropriate in view of any principle laid down by the European Court in connection with Title II of the 1968 Convention or of any decision of that court as to the meaning or effect of any provision of that Title.

(2) The provision which may be made by virtue of paragraph (*a*) of subsection (1) includes such modifications of this Act or any other statutory provision, whenever passed or made, as Her Majesty considers appropriate for the purpose mentioned in that paragraph.

(3) The modifications which may be made by virtue of paragraph (*b*) of subsection (1) include modifications designed to produce divergence between any provision of Schedule 4 or Schedule 8 and a corresponding provision of Title II of the 1968 Convention as affected by any such principle or decision as is mentioned in that paragraph.

(4) An Order in Council under this section shall not be made unless a draft of the Order has been laid before Parliament and approved by a resolution of each House of Parliament.

Matters for which rules of court may provide

48.—(1) Rules of court may make provision for regulating the procedure to be followed in any court in connection with any provision of this Act or the Conventions.

(2) Rules of court may make provision as to the manner in which and the conditions subject to which a certificate or judgment registered in any court under any provision of this Act may be enforced, including provision for enabling the court or, in Northern Ireland the Enforcement of Judgments Office, subject to any conditions specified in the rules, to give directions about such matters.

(3) Without prejudice to the generality of subsections (1) and (2), the

power to make rules of court for magistrates' courts, and in Northern Ireland the power to make Judgment Enforcement Rules, shall include power to make such provision as the rule-making authority considers necessary or expedient for the purposes of the provisions of the Conventions and this Act relating to maintenance proceedings and the recognition and enforcement of maintenance orders, and shall in particular include power to make provision as to any of the following matters—

(a) authorising the service in another Contracting State of process issued by or for the purposes of a magistrates' court and the service and execution in England and Wales or Northern Ireland of process issued in another Contracting State;

(b) requesting courts in other parts of the United Kingdom or in other Contracting States to take evidence there for the purposes of proceedings in England and Wales or Northern Ireland;

(c) the taking of evidence in England and Wales or Northern Ireland in response to similar requests received from such courts;

(d) the circumstances in which and the conditions subject to which any powers conferred under paragraphs (a) to (c) are to be exercised;

(e) the admission in evidence, subject to such conditions as may be prescribed in the rules, of statements contained in documents purporting to be made or authenticated by a court in another part of the United Kingdom or in another Contracting State, or by a judge or official of such a court, which purport—

   (i) to set out or summarise evidence given in proceedings in that court or to be documents received in evidence in such proceedings or copies of such documents; or

   (ii) to set out or summarise evidence taken for the purposes of proceedings in England and Wales or Northern Ireland, whether or not in response to any such request as is mentioned in paragraph (b); or

   (iii) to record information relating to the payments made under an order of that court;

(f) the circumstances and manner in which a magistrates' court may or must vary or revoke a maintenance order registered in that court, cancel the registration of, or refrain from enforcing, such an order or transmit such an order for enforcement in another part of the United Kingdom;

(g) the cases and manner in which courts in other parts of the United Kingdom or in other Contracting States are to be informed of orders made, or other things done, by or for the purposes of a magistrates' court;

(h) the circumstances and manner in which a magistrates' court may communicate for other purposes with such courts;

(i) the giving of notice of such matters as may be prescribed in the rules to such persons as may be so prescribed and the manner in which such notice is to be given.

(4) Nothing in this section shall be taken as derogating from the generality of any power to make rules of court conferred by any other enactment.

Saving for powers to stay, sist, strike out or dismiss proceedings

49. Nothing in this Act shall prevent any court in the United Kingdom from staying, sisting, striking out or dismissing any proceedings before it, on the ground of *forum non conveniens* or otherwise, where to do so is not inconsistent with the 1968 Convention.

General

Interpretation: general

50. In this Act, unless the context otherwise requires—
"the Accession Convention" has the meaning given by section 1(1);
"Article" and references to sub-divisions of numbered Articles are to be construed in accordance with section 1(2)(*b*);
"association" means an unincorporated body of persons;
"Contracting State" has the meaning given by section 1(3);
"the 1968 Convention" has the meaning given by section 1(1), and references to that Convention and to provisions of it are to be construed in accordance with section 1(2)(*a*);
"the Conventions" has the meaning given by section 1(1);
"corporation" means a body corporate, and includes a partnership subsisting under the law of Scotland;
"court", without more, includes a tribunal;
"court of law", in relation to the United Kingdom, means any of the following courts, namely—
    (*a*) the House of Lords,
    (*b*) in England and Wales or Northern Ireland, the Court of Appeal, the High Court, the Crown Court, a county court and a magistrates' court,
    (*c*) in Scotland, the Court of Session and a sheriff court;
"the Crown" is to be construed in accordance with section 51(2);
"enactment" includes an enactment comprised in Northern Ireland legislation;
"judgment", subject to sections 15(1) and 18(2) and to paragraph 1 of Schedules 6 and 7, means any judgment or order (by whatever name called) given or made by a court in any civil proceedings;
"magistrates' court", in relation to Northern Ireland, means a court of summary jurisdiction;
"modifications" includes additions, omissions and alterations;
"overseas country" means any country or territory outside the United Kingdom;
"part of the United Kingdom" means England and Wales, Scotland or Northern Ireland;
"the 1971 Protocol" has the meaning given by section 1(1), and references to that Protocol and to provisions of it are to be construed in accordance with section 1(2)(*a*);
"rules of court", in relation to any court, means rules, orders or regulations made by the authority having power to make rules, orders or regulations regulating the procedure of that court, and includes—
    (*a*) in Scotland, Acts of Sederunt;
    (*b*) in Northern Ireland, Judgment Enforcement Rules;
"statutory provision" means any provision contained in an Act, or in any Northern Ireland legislation, or in—
    (*a*) subordinate legislation (as defined in section 21(1) of the Interpretation Act 1978); or

(b) any instrument of a legislative character made under any Northern Ireland legislation;

"tribunal"—

(a) means a tribunal of any description other than a court of law;

(b) in relation to an overseas country, includes, as regards matters relating to maintenance within the meaning of the 1968 Convention, any authority having power to give, enforce, vary or revoke a maintenance order.

Application to Crown

51.—(1) This Act binds the Crown.

(2) In this section and elsewhere in this Act references to the Crown do not include references to Her Majesty in Her private capacity or to Her Majesty in right of Her Duchy of Lancaster or to the Duke of Cornwall.

Extent

52.—(1) This Act extends to Northern Ireland.

(2) Without prejudice to the power conferred by section 39, Her Majesty may by Order in Council direct that all or any of the provisions of this Act apart from that section shall extend, subject to such modifications as may be specified in the Order, to any of the following territories, that is to say—

(a) the Isle of Man;

(b) any of the Channel Islands;

(c) Gibraltar;

(d) the Sovereign Base Areas of Akrotiri and Dhekelia (that is to say the areas mentioned in section 2(1) of the Cyprus Act 1960).

Commencement, transitional provisions and savings

53.—(1) This Act shall come into force in accordance with the provisions of Part I of Schedule 13.

(2) The transitional provisions and savings contained in Part II of that Schedule shall have effect in relation to the commencement of the provisions of this Act mentioned in that Part.

Repeals

54. The enactments mentioned in Schedule 14 are hereby repealed to the extent specified in the third column of that Schedule.

Short title

55. This Act may be cited as the Civil Jurisdiction and Judgments Act 1982.

SCHEDULES

Section 2(2)   SCHEDULE 1

TEXT OF 1968 CONVENTION, AS AMENDED

ARRANGEMENT OF PROVISIONS

TITLE I.   SCOPE (Article 1).

TITLE II.   JURISDICTION
Section 1.   General provisions (Articles 2–4).
Section 2.   Special jurisdiction (Articles 5–6A).

Section 3. Jurisdiction in matters relating to insurance (Articles 7–12A).
Section 4. Jurisdiction over consumer contracts (Articles 13–15).
Section 5. Exclusive jurisdiction (Article 16).
Section 6. Prorogation of jurisdiction (Articles 17 and 18).
Section 7. Examination as to jurisdiction and admissibility (Articles 19–20).
Section 8. Lis pendens—Related actions (Articles 21–23).
Section 9. Provisional, including protective, measures (Article 24).

TITLE III. RECOGNITION AND ENFORCEMENT
Definition of "judgment" (Article 25).
Section 1. Recognition (Articles 26–30).
Section 2. Enforcement (Articles 31–45).
Section 3. Common provisions (Articles 46–49).

TITLE IV. AUTHENTIC INSTRUMENTS AND COURT SETTLEMENTS (Articles 50–51).

TITLE V. GENERAL PROVISIONS (Articles 52–53).

TITLE VI. TRANSITIONAL PROVISIONS (Article 54).

TITLE VII. RELATIONSHIP TO OTHER CONVENTIONS (Articles 55–59).

TITLE VIII. FINAL PROVISIONS (Articles 60–68).

Convention on Jurisdiction and the Enforcement of Judgments in Civil and Commercial Matters

Preamble

The High Contracting Parties to the Treaty establishing the European Economic Community,

Desiring to implement the provisions of Article 220 of that Treaty by virtue of which they undertook to secure the simplification of formalities governing the reciprocal recognition and enforcement of judgments of courts or tribunals;

Anxious to strengthen in the Community the legal protection of persons therein established;

Considering that it is necessary for this purpose to determine the international jurisdiction of their courts, to facilitate recognition and to introduce an expeditious procedure for securing the enforcement of judgments, authentic instruments and court settlements;

Have decided to conclude this Convention and to this end have designated as their Plenipotentiaries:

(*Designations of Plenipotentiaries of the original six Contracting States*) Who, meeting within the Council, having exchanged their Full Powers, found in good and due form,

Have agreed as follows:

TITLE I

SCOPE

ARTICLE 1

This Convention shall apply in civil and commercial matters whatever the nature of the court or tribunal. It shall not extend, in particular, to revenue, customs or administrative matters.

The Convention shall not apply to:

(1) the status or legal capacity of natural persons, rights in property arising out of a matrimonial relationship, wills and succession;

(2) bankruptcy, proceedings relating to the winding-up of insolvent companies or other legal persons, judicial arrangements, compositions and analogous proceedings;

(3) social security;

(4) arbitration.

TITLE II

JURISDICTION

Section 1

General provisions

ARTICLE 2

Subject to the provisions of this Convention, persons domiciled in a Contracting State shall, whatever their nationality, be sued in the courts of that State.

Persons who are not nationals of the State in which they are domiciled shall be governed by the rules of jurisdiction applicable to nationals of that State.

ARTICLE 3

Persons domiciled in a Contracting State may be sued in the courts of another Contracting State only by virtue of the rules set out in Sections 2 to 6 of this Title.

In particular the following provisions shall not be applicable as against them:

—in Belgium:	Article 15 of the civil code (*Code civil—Burgerlijk Wetboek*) and article 638 of the Judicial code (*Code judiciaire—Gerechtelijk Wetboek*);
—in Denmark:	Article 248(2) of the law on civil prodedure (*Lov om rettens pleje*) and Chapter 3, Article 3 of the Greenland law on civil procedure (*Lov for Grønland om rettens pleje*);
—in the Federal Republic of Germany:	Article 23 of the code of civil procedure (*Zivilprozessordnung*);
—in France:	Articles 14 and 15 of the civil code (*Code civil*);
—in Ireland:	the rules which enable jurisdiction to be founded on the document instituting the proceedings having been served on the defendant during his temporary presence in Ireland;
—in Italy:	Article 2 and Article 4, Nos. 1 and 2 of the code of civil procedure (*Codice di procedura civile*);
—in Luxembourg:	Articles 14 and 15 of the civil code (*Code civil*);
—in the Netherlands:	Article 126(3) and Article 127 of the code of civil procedure (*Wetboek van Burgerlijke Rechtsvordering*);
—in the United Kingdom:	the rules which enable jurisdiction to be founded on: (*a*) the document instituting the proceedings having been served on the defendant during his temporary presence in the United Kingdom; or (*b*) the presence within the United Kingdom of property belonging to the defendant; or (*c*) the seizure by the plaintiff of property situated in the United Kingdom.

ARTICLE 4

If the defendant is not domiciled in a Contracting State, the jurisdiction of the courts of each Contracting State shall, subject to the provisions of Article 16, be determined by the law of that State.

As against such a defendant, any person domiciled in a Contracting State may, whatever his nationality, avail himself in that State of the rules of jurisdiction there in force, and in particular those specified in the second paragraph of Article 3, in the same way as the nationals of that State.

Section 2

Special jurisdiction

ARTICLE 5

A person domiciled in a Contracting State may, in another Contracting State, be sued:

(1) in matters relating to a contract, in the courts for the place of performance of the obligation in question;

(2) in matters relating to maintenance, in the courts for the place where the maintenance creditor is domiciled or habitually resident or, if the matter is ancillary to proceedings concerning the status of a person, in the court which, according to its own law, has

jurisdiction to entertain those proceedings, unless that jurisdiction is based solely on the nationality of one of the parties;

(3) in matters relating to tort, delict or quasi-delict, in the courts for the place where the harmful event occurred;

(4) as regards a civil claim for damages or restitution which is based on an act giving rise to criminal proceedings, in the court seised of those proceedings, to the extent that that court has jurisdiction under its own law to entertain civil proceedings;

(5) as regards a dispute arising out of the operations of a branch, agency or other establishment, in the courts for the place in which the branch, agency or other establishment is situated;

(6) in his capacity as settlor, trustee or beneficiary of a trust created by the operation of a statute, or by a written instrument, or created orally and evidenced in writing, in the courts of the Contracting State in which the trust is domiciled;

(7) as regards a dispute concerning the payment of remuneration claimed in respect of the salvage of a cargo or freight, in the court under the authority of which the cargo or freight in question:

(*a*) has been arrested to secure such payment, or

(*b*) could have been so arrested, but bail or other security has been given;

provided that this provision shall apply only if it is claimed that the defendant has an interest in the cargo or freight or had such an interest at the time of salvage.

ARTICLE 6

A person domiciled in a Contracting State may also be sued:

(1) where he is one of a number of defendants, in the courts for the place where any one of them is domiciled;

(2) as a third party in an action on a warranty or guarantee or in any other third party proceedings, in the court seised of the original proceedings, unless these were instituted solely with the object of removing him from the jurisdiction of the court which would be competent in his case;

(3) on a counterclaim arising from the same contract or facts on which the original claim was based, in the court in which the original claim is pending.

ARTICLE 6A

Where by virtue of this convention a court of a Contracting State has jurisdiction in actions relating to liability arising from the use or operation of a ship, that court, or any other court substituted for this purpose by the internal law of that State, shall also have jurisdiction over claims for limitation of such liability.

Section 3

Jurisdiction in matters relating to insurance

ARTICLE 7

In matters relating to insurance, jurisdiction shall be determined by this Section, without prejudice to the provisions of Articles 4 and 5(5).

ARTICLE 8

An insurer domiciled in a Contracting State may be sued:

(1) in the courts of the State where he is domiciled, or

(2) in another Contracting State, in the courts for the place where the policy-holder is domiciled, or

(3) if he is a co-insurer, in the courts of a Contracting State in which proceedings are brought against the leading insurer.

An insurer who is not domiciled in a Contracting State but has a branch, agency or other establishment in one of the Contracting States shall, in disputes arising out of the operations of the branch, agency or establishment, be deemed to be domiciled in that State.

ARTICLE 9

In respect of liability insurance or insurance of immovable property, the insurer may in addition be sued in the courts for the place where the harmful event occurred. The same applies if movable and immovable property are covered by the same insurance policy and both are adversely affected by the same contingency.

ARTICLE 10

In respect of liability insurance, the insurer may also, if the law of the court permits it, be joined in proceedings which the injured party has brought against the insured.

The provisions of Articles 7, 8 and 9 shall apply to actions brought by the injured party directly against the insurer, where such direct actions are permitted.

If the law governing such direct actions provides that the policy-holder or the insured may be joined as a party to the action, the same court shall have jurisdiction over them.

ARTICLE 11

Without prejudice to the provisions of the third paragraph of Article 10, an insurer may bring proceedings only in the courts of the Contracting State in which the defendant is domiciled, irrespective of whether he is the policy-holder, the insured or a beneficiary.

The provisions of this Section shall not affect the right to bring a counterclaim in the court in which, in accordance with this Section, the original claim is pending.

ARTICLE 12

The provisions of this Section may be departed from only by an agreement on jurisdiction:
(1) which is entered into after the dispute has arisen, or
(2) which allows the policy-holder, the insured or a beneficiary to bring proceedings in courts other than those indicated in this Section, or
(3) which is concluded between a policy-holder and an insurer, both of whom are at the time of conclusion of the contract domiciled or habitually resident in the same Contracting State, and which has the effect of conferring jurisdiction on the courts of that State even if the harmful event were to occur abroad, provided that such an agreement is not contrary to the law of that State, or
(4) which is concluded with a policy-holder who is not domiciled in a Contracting State, except in so far as the insurance is compulsory or relates to immovable property in a Contracting State, or
(5) which relates to a contract of insurance in so far as it covers one or more of the risks set out in Article 12A.

ARTICLE 12A

The following are the risks referred to in Article 12(5):
(1) Any loss of or damage to
  (a) sea-going ships, installations situated offshore or on the high seas, or aircraft, arising from perils which relate to their use for commercial purposes,
  (b) goods in transit other than passengers' baggage where the transit consists of or includes carriage by such ships or aircraft;
(2) Any liability, other than for bodily injury to passengers or loss of or damage to their baggage,
  (a) arising out of the use or operation of ships, installations or aircraft as referred to in (1)(a) above in so far as the law of the Contracting State in which such aircraft are registered does not prohibit agreements on jurisdiction regarding insurance of such risks,
  (b) for loss or damage caused by goods in transit as described in (1)(b) above;
(3) Any financial loss connected with the use or operation of ships, installations or aircraft as referred to in (1)(a) above, in particular loss of freight or charter-hire;
(4) Any risk or interest connected with any of those referred to in (1) to (3) above.

Section 4

Jurisdiction over consumer contracts

ARTICLE 13

In proceedings concerning a contract concluded by a person for a purpose which can be regarded as being outside his trade or profession, hereinafter called the "consumer", jurisdiction shall be determined by this Section, without prejudice to the provisions of Articles 4 and 5(5), if it is:
(1) a contract for the sale of goods on instalment credit terms, or
(2) a contract for a loan repayable by instalments, or for any other form of credit, made to finance the sale of goods, or
(3) any other contract for the supply of goods or a contract for the supply of services and
  (a) in the State of the consumer's domicile the conclusion of the contract was preceded by a specific invitation addressed to him or by advertising, and
  (b) the consumer took in that State the steps necessary for the conclusion of the contract.

Where a consumer enters into a contract with a party who is not domiciled in a Contracting State but has a branch, agency or other establishment in one of the Contracting States, that party shall, in disputes arising out of the operations of the branch, agency or establishment, be deemed to be domiciled in that State.

This Section shall not apply to contracts of transport.

ARTICLE 14

A consumer may bring proceedings against the other party to a contract either in the courts of the Contracting State in which that party is domiciled or in the courts of the Contracting State in which he is himself domiciled.

Proceedings may be brought against a consumer by the other party to the contract only in the courts of the Contracting State in which the consumer is domiciled.

These provisions shall not affect the right to bring a counter-claim in the court in which, in accordance with this Section, the original claim is pending.

ARTICLE 15

The provisions of this Section may be departed from only by an agreement:
(1) which is entered into after the dispute has arisen, or
(2) which allows the consumer to bring proceedings in courts other than those indicated in this Section, or
(3) which is entered into by the consumer and the other party to the contract, both of whom are at the time of conclusion of the contract domiciled or habitually resident in the same Contracting State, and which confers jurisdiction on the courts of that State, provided that such an agreement is not contrary to the law of that State.

Section 5

Exclusive jurisdiction

ARTICLE 16

The following courts shall have exclusive jurisdiction, regardless of domicile:
(1) in proceedings which have as their object rights *in rem* in, or tenancies of, immovable property, the courts of the Contracting State in which the property is situated;
(2) in proceedings which have as their object the validity of the constitution, the nullity or the dissolution of companies or other legal persons or associations of natural or legal persons, or the decisions of their organs, the courts of the Contracting State in which the company, legal person or association has its seat;
(3) in proceedings which have as their object the validity of entries in public registers, the courts of the Contracting State in which the register is kept;
(4) in proceedings concerned with the registration or validity of patents, trade marks, designs, or other similar rights required to be deposited or registered, the courts of the Contracting State in which the deposit or registration has been applied for, has taken place or is under the terms of an international convention deemed to have taken place;
(5) in proceedings concerned with the enforcement of judgments, the courts of the Contracting State in which the judgment has been or is to be enforced.

Section 6

Prorogation of jurisdiction

ARTICLE 17

If the parties, one or more of whom is domiciled in a Contracting State, have agreed that a court or the courts of a Contracting State are to have jurisdiction to settle any disputes which have arisen or which may arise in connection with a particular legal relationship, that court or those courts shall have exclusive jurisdiction. Such an agreement conferring jurisdiction shall be either in writing or evidenced in writing or, in international trade or commerce, in a form which accords with practices in that trade or commerce of which the parties are or ought to have been aware. Where such an agreement is concluded by parties, none of whom is domiciled in a Contracting State, the courts of other Contracting States shall have no jurisdiction over their disputes unless the court or courts chosen have declined jurisdiction.

The court or courts of a Contracting State on which a trust instrument has conferred jurisdiction shall have exclusive jurisdiction in any proceedings brought against a settlor, trustee or beneficiary, if relations between these persons or their rights or obligations under the trust are involved.

Agreements or provisions of a trust instrument conferring jurisdiction shall have no legal force if they are contrary to the provisions of Articles 12 or 15, or if the courts whose jurisdiction they purport to exclude have exclusive jurisdiction by virtue of Article 16.

If an agreement conferring jurisdiction was concluded for the benefit of only one of the parties, that party shall retain the right to bring proceedings in any other court which has jurisdiction by virtue of this Convention.

ARTICLE 18

Apart from jurisdiction derived from other provisions of this Convention, a court of a Contracting State before whom a defendant enters an appearance shall have jurisdiction. This rule shall not apply where appearance was entered solely to contest the jurisdiction, or where another court has exclusive jurisdiction by virtue of Article 16.

Section 7

Examination as to jurisdiction and admissibility

ARTICLE 19

Where a court of a Contracting State is seised of a claim which is principally concerned with a matter over which the courts of another Contracting State have exclusive jurisdiction by virtue of Article 16, it shall declare of its own motion that it has no jurisdiction.

ARTICLE 20

Where a defendant domiciled in one Contracting State is sued in a court of another Contracting State and does not enter an appearance, the court shall declare of its own motion that it has no jurisdiction unless its jurisdiction is derived from the provisions of this Convention.

The court shall stay the proceedings so long as it is not shown that the defendant has been able to receive the document instituting the proceedings or an equivalent document in sufficient time to enable him to arrange for his defence, or that all necessary steps have been taken to this end.

The provisions of the foregoing paragraph shall be replaced by those of Article 15 of the Hague Convention of 15 November 1965 on the Service Abroad of Judicial and Extrajudicial Documents in Civil or Commercial Matters, if the document instituting the proceedings or notice thereof had to be transmitted abroad in accordance with that Convention.

Section 8

Lis pendens—Related actions

ARTICLE 21

Where proceedings involving the same cause of action and between the same parties are brought in the courts of different Contracting States, any court other than the court first seised shall of its own motion decline jurisdiction in favour of that court.

A court which would be required to decline jurisdiction may stay its proceedings if the jurisdiction of the other court is contested.

ARTICLE 22

Where related actions are brought in the courts of different Contracting States, any court other than the court first seised may, while the actions are pending at first instance, stay its proceedings.

A court other than the court first seised may also, on the application of one of the parties, decline jurisdiction if the law of that court permits the consolidation of related actions and the court first seised has jurisdiction over both actions.

For the purposes of this Article, actions are deemed to be related where they are so closely connected that it is expedient to hear and determine them together to avoid the risk of irreconcilable judgments resulting from separate proceedings.

ARTICLE 23

Where actions come within the exclusive jurisdiction of several courts, any court other than the court first seised shall decline jurisdiction in favour of that court.

Section 9

Provisional, including protective, measures

ARTICLE 24

Application may be made to the courts of a Contracting State for such provisional, including protective, measures as may be available under the law of that State, even if, under this Convention, the courts of another Contracting State have jurisdiction as to the substance of the matter.

TITLE III

RECOGNITION AND ENFORCEMENT

ARTICLE 25

For the purposes of this Convention, "judgment" means any judgment given by a court or tribunal of a Contracting State, whatever the judgment may be called, including a decree, order, decision or writ of execution, as well as the determination of costs or expenses by an officer of the court.

Section 1

Recognition

ARTICLE 26

A judgment given in a Contracting State shall be recognised in the other Contracting States without any special procedure being required.

Any interested party who raises the recognition of a judgment as the principal issue in a dispute may, in accordance with the procedures provided for in Sections 2 and 3 of this Title, apply for a decision that the judgment be recognised.

If the outcome of proceedings in a court of a Contracting State depends on the determination of an incidental question of recognition that court shall have jurisdiction over that question.

ARTICLE 27

A judgment shall not be recognised:

    (1) if such recognition is contrary to public policy in the State in which recognition is sought;

    (2) where it was given in default of appearance, if the defendant was not duly served with the document which instituted the proceedings or with an equivalent document in sufficient time to enable him to arrange for his defence;

    (3) if the judgment is irreconcilable with a judgment given in a dispute between the same parties in the State in which recognition is sought;

    (4) if the court of the State in which the judgment was given, in order to arrive at its judgment, has decided a preliminary question concerning the status or legal capacity of natural persons, rights in property arising out of a matrimonial relátionship, wills or succession in a way that conflicts with a rule of the private international law of the State in which the recognition is sought, unless the same result would have been reached by the application of the rules of private international law of that State;

    (5) if the judgment is irreconcilable with an earlier judgment given in a non-Contracting State involving the same cause of action and between the same parties, provided that this latter judgment fulfils the conditions necessary for its recognition in the State addressed.

ARTICLE 28

Moreover, a judgment shall not be recognised if it conflicts with the provisions of Sections 3, 4 or 5 of Title II, or in a case provided for in Article 59.

In its examination of the grounds of jurisdiction referred to in the foregoing paragraph, the court or authority applied to shall be bound by the findings of fact on which the court of the State in which the judgment was given based its jurisdiction.

Subject to the provisions of the first paragraph, the jurisdiction of the court of the State in which the judgment was given may not be reviewed; the test of public policy referred to in Article 27(1) may not be applied to the rules relating to jurisdiction.

ARTICLE 29

Under no circumstances may a foreign judgment be reviewed as to its substance.

ARTICLE 30

A court of a Contracting State in which recognition is sought of a judgment given in another Contracting State may stay the proceedings if an ordinary appeal against the judgment has been lodged.

A court of a Contracting State in which recognition is sought of a judgment given in Ireland or the United Kingdom may stay the proceedings if enforcement is suspended in the State in which the judgment was given by reason of an appeal.

Section 2

Enforcement

ARTICLE 31

A judgment given in a Contracting State and enforceable in that State shall be enforced in another Contracting State when, on the application of any interested party, the order for its enforcement has been issued there.

However, in the United Kingdom, such a judgment shall be enforced in England and Wales, in Scotland, or in Northern Ireland when, on the application of any interested party, it has been registered for enforcement in that part of the United Kingdom.

ARTICLE 32

The application shall be submitted:

—in Belgium, to the *tribunal de première instance* or *rechtbank van eerste aanleg*;
—in Denmark, to the *underret*;
—in the Federal Republic of Germany, to the presiding judge of a chamber of the *Landgericht*;
—in France, to the presiding judge of the *tribunal de grande instance*;
—in Ireland, to the High Court;
—in Italy, to the *corte d'appello*;
—in Luxembourg, to the presiding judge of the *tribunal d'arrondissement*;
—in the Netherlands, to the presiding judge of the *arrondissementsrechtbank*;
—in the United Kingdom:
   (1) in England and Wales, to the High Court of Justice, or in the case of a maintenance judgment to the Magistrates' Court on transmission by the Secretary of State;
   (2) in Scotland, to the Court of Session, or in the case of a maintenance judgment to the Sheriff Court on transmission by the Secretary of State;
   (3) in Northern Ireland, to the High Court of Justice, or in the case of a maintenance judgment to the Magistrates' Court on transmission by the Secretary of State.

The jurisdiction of local courts shall be determined by reference to the place of domicile of the party against whom enforcement is sought. If he is not domiciled in the State in which enforcement is sought, it shall be determined by reference to the place of enforcement.

ARTICLE 33

The procedure for making the application shall be governed by the law of the State in which enforcement is sought.

The applicant must give an address for service of process within the area of jurisdiction of the court applied to. However, if the law of the State in which enforcement is sought does not provide for the furnishing of such an address, the applicant shall appoint a representative *ad litem*.

The documents referred to in Articles 46 and 47 shall be attached to the application.

ARTICLE 34

The court applied to shall give its decision without delay; the party against whom enforcement is sought shall not at this stage of the proceedings be entitled to make any submissions on the application.

The application may be refused only for one of the reasons specified in Articles 27 and 28.

Under no circumstances may the foreign judgment be reviewed as to its substance.

ARTICLE 35

The appropriate officer of the court shall without delay bring the decision given on the application to the notice of the applicant in accordance with the procedure laid down by the law of the State in which enforcement is sought.

ARTICLE 36

If enforcement is authorised, the party against whom enforcement is sought may appeal against the decision within one month of service thereof.

If that party is domiciled in a Contracting State other than that in which the decision authorising enforcement was given, the time for appealing shall be two months and shall run from the date of service, either on him in person or at his residence. No extension of time may be granted on account of distance.

ARTICLE 37

An appeal against the decision authorising enforcement shall be lodged in accordance with the rules governing procedure in contentious matters:

—in Belgium, with the *tribunal de première instance* or *rechtbank van eerste aanleg*;
—in Denmark, with the *landsret*;
—in the Federal Republic of Germany, with the *Oberlandesgericht*;
—in France, with the *cour d'appel*;
—in Ireland, with the High Court;
—in Italy, with the *corte d'appello*;
—in Luxembourg, with the *Cour supérieure de Justice* sitting as a court of civil appeal;
—in the Netherlands, with the *arrondissementsrechtbank*;
—in the United Kingdom:
  (1) in England and Wales, with the High Court of Justice, or in the case of a maintenance judgment with the Magistrates' Court;
  (2) in Scotland, with the Court of Session, or in the case of a maintenance judgment with the Sheriff Court;
  (3) in Northern Ireland, with the High Court of Justice, or in the case of a maintenance judgment with the Magistrates' Court.

The judgment given on the appeal may be contested only:
—in Belgium, France, Italy, Luxembourg and the Netherlands, by an appeal in cassation;
—in Denmark, by an appeal to the *højesteret*, with the leave of the Minister of Justice;
—in the Federal Republic of Germany, by a *Rechtsbeschwerde*;
—in Ireland, by an appeal on a point of law to the Supreme Court;
—in the United Kingdom, by a single further appeal on a point of law.

ARTICLE 38

The court with which the appeal under the first paragraph of Article 37 is lodged may, on the application of the appellant, stay the proceedings if an ordinary appeal has been lodged against the judgment in the State in which that judgment was given or if the time for such an appeal has not yet expired; in the latter case, the court may specify the time within which such an appeal is to be lodged.

Where the judgment was given in Ireland or the United Kingdom, any form of appeal available in the State in which it was given shall be treated as an ordinary appeal for the purposes of the first paragraph.

The court may also make enforcement conditional on the provision of such security as it shall determine.

ARTICLE 39

During the time specified for an appeal pursuant to Article 36 and until any such appeal has been determined, no measures of enforcement may be taken other than protective measures taken against the property of the party against whom enforcement is sought.

The decision authorising enforcement shall carry with it the power to proceed to any such protective measures.

ARTICLE 40

If the application for enforcement is refused, the applicant may appeal:
—in Belgium to the *cour d'appel* or *hof van beroep*;
—in Denmark, to the *landsret*;
—in the Federal Republic of Germany, to the *Oberlandesgericht*;
—in France, to the *cour d'appel*;
—in Ireland, to the High Court;
—in Italy, to the *corte d'appello*;
—in Luxembourg, to the *Cour supérieure de Justice* sitting as a court of civil appeal;
—in the Netherlands, to the *gerechtshof*;
—in the United Kingdom:
  (1) in England and Wales, to the High Court of Justice, or in the case of a maintenance judgment to the Magistrates' Court;

    (2)   in Scotland, to the Court of Session, or in the case of a maintenance judgment to the Sheriff Court;

    (3)   in Northern Ireland, to the High Court of Justice, or in the case of a maintenance judgment to the Magistrates' Court.

The party against whom enforcement is sought shall be summoned to appear before the appellate court. If he fails to appear, the provisions of the second and third paragraphs of Article 20 shall apply even where he is not domiciled in any of the Contracting States.

ARTICLE 41

A judgment given on an appeal provided for in Article 40 may be contested only:

—in Belgium, France, Italy, Luxembourg and the Netherlands, by an appeal in cassation;

—in Denmark, by an appeal to the *højesteret*, with the leave of the Minister of Justice;

—in the Federal Republic of Germany, by a *Rechtsbeschwerde*;

—in Ireland, by an appeal on a point of law to the Supreme Court;

—in the United Kingdom, by a single further appeal on a point of law.

ARTICLE 42

Where a foreign judgment has been given in respect of several matters and enforcement cannot be authorised for all of them, the court shall authorise enforcement for one or more of them.

An applicant may request partial enforcement of a judgment.

ARTICLE 43

A foreign judgment which orders a periodic payment by way of a penalty shall be enforceable in the State in which enforcement is sought only if the amount of the payment has been finally determined by the courts of the State in which the judgment was given.

ARTICLE 44

An applicant who, in the State in which the judgment was given, has benefited from complete or partial legal aid or exemption from costs or expenses, shall be entitled, in the procedures provided for in Articles 32 to 35, to benefit from the most favourable legal aid or the most extensive exemption from costs or expenses provided for by the law of the State addressed.

An applicant who requests the enforcement of a decision given by an administrative authority in Denmark in respect of a maintenance order may, in the State addressed, claim the benefits referred to in the first paragraph if he presents a statement from the Danish Ministry of Justice to the effect that he fulfils the economic requirements to qualify for the grant of complete or partial legal aid or exemption from costs or expenses.

ARTICLE 45

No security, bond or deposit, however described, shall be required of a party who in one Contracting State applies for enforcement of a judgment given in another Contracting State on the ground that he is a foreign national or that he is not domiciled or resident in the State in which enforcement is sought.

Section 3

Common provisions

ARTICLE 46

A party seeking recognition or applying for enforcement of a judgment shall produce:

    (1)   a copy of the judgment which satisfies the conditions necessary to establish its authenticity;

    (2)   in the case of a judgment given in default, the original or a certified true copy of the document which establishes that the party in default was served with the document instituting the proceedings or with an equivalent document.

ARTICLE 47

A party applying for enforcement shall also produce:

    (1)   documents which establish that, according to the law of the State in which it has been given, the judgment is enforceable and has been served;

    (2)   where appropriate, a document showing that the applicant is in receipt of legal aid in the State in which the judgment was given.

ARTICLE 48

If the documents specified in Article 46(2) and Article 47(2) are not produced, the court may specify a time for their production, accept equivalent documents or, if it considers that it has sufficient information before it, dispense with their production.

If the court so requires, a translation of the documents shall be produced; the translation shall be certified by a person qualified to do so in one of the Contracting States.

ARTICLE 49

No legalisation or other similar formality shall be required in respect of the documents referred to in Articles 46 or 47 or the second paragraph of Article 48, or in respect of a document appointing a representative *ad litem*.

TITLE IV

AUTHENTIC INSTRUMENTS AND COURT SETTLEMENTS

ARTICLE 50

A document which has been formally drawn up or registered as an authentic instrument and is enforceable in one Contracting State shall, in another Contracting State, have an order for its enforcement issued there, an application made in accordance with the procedures provided for in Article 31 *et seq*. The application may be refused only if enforcement of the instrument is contrary to public policy in the State in which enforcement is sought.

The instrument produced must satisfy the conditions necessary to establish its authenticity in the State of origin.

The provisions of Section 3 of Title III shall apply as appropriate.

ARTICLE 51

A settlement which has been approved by a court in the course of proceedings and is enforceable in the State in which it was concluded shall be enforceable in the State in which enforcement is sought under the same conditions as authentic instruments.

TITLE V

GENERAL PROVISIONS

ARTICLE 52

In order to determine whether a party is domiciled in the Contracting State whose courts are seised of the matter, the court shall apply its internal law.

If a party is not domiciled in the State whose courts are seised of the matter, then, in order to determine whether the party is domiciled in another Contracting State, the court shall apply the law of that State.

The domicile of a party shall, however, be determined in accordance with his national law if, by that law, his domicile depends on that of another person or on the seat of an authority.

ARTICLE 53

For the purposes of this Convention, the seat of a company or other legal person or association of natural or legal persons shall be treated as its domicile. However, in order to determine that seat, the court shall apply its rules of private international law.

In order to determine whether a trust is domiciled in the Contracting State whose courts are seised of the matter, the court shall apply its rules of private international law.

TITLE VI

TRANSITIONAL PROVISIONS

ARTICLE 54

The provisions of this Convention shall apply only to legal proceedings instituted and to documents formally drawn up or registered as authentic instruments after its entry into force.

However, judgments given after that the date of entry into force of this Convention in proceedings instituted before that date shall be recognised and enforced in accordance with the provisions of Title III if jurisdiction was founded upon rules which accorded with those provided for either in Title II of this Convention or in a convention concluded between the State of origin and the State addressed which was in force when the proceedings were instituted.

TITLE VII

RELATIONSHIP TO OTHER CONVENTIONS

ARTICLE 55

Subject to the provisions of the second paragraph of Article 54, and of Article 56, this convention shall, for the States which are parties to it, supersede the following conventions concluded between two or more of them:
  —the Convention between Belgium and France on Jurisdiction and the Validity and Enforcement of Judgments, Arbitration Awards and the Authentic Instruments, signed at Paris on 8 July 1899;
  —the Convention between Belgium and the Netherlands on Jurisdiction, Bankruptcy, and the Validity and Enforcement of Judgments, Arbitration Awards and Authentic Instruments, signed at Brussels on 28 March 1925;
  —the Convention between France and Italy on the Enforcement of Judgments in Civil and Commercial Matters, signed at Rome on 3 June 1930;
  —the Convention between the United Kingdom and the French Republic providing for the Reciprocal Enforcement of Judgments in Civil and Commercial Matters, with Protocol, signed at Paris on 18 January 1934;
  —the Convention between the United Kingdom and the Kingdom of Belgium providing for the Reciprocal Enforcement of Judgments in Civil and Commercial Matters, with Protocol, signed at Brussels on 2 May 1934;
  —the Convention between Germany and Italy on the Recognition and Enforcement of Judgments in Civil and Commercial Matters, signed at Rome on 9 March 1936;
  —the Convention between the Federal Republic of Germany and the Kingdom of Belgium on the Mutual Recognition and Enforcement of Judgments, Arbitration Awards and Authentic Instruments in Civil and Commercial Matters, signed at Bonn on 30 June 1958;
  —the Convention between the Kingdom of the Netherlands and the Italian Republic on the Recognition and Enforcement of Judgments in Civil and Commercial Matters, signed at Rome on 17 April 1959;
  —the Convention between the United Kingdom and the Federal Republic of Germany for the Reciprocal Recognition and Enforcement of Judgments in Civil and Commercial Matters, signed at Bonn on 14 July 1960;
  —the Convention between the Kingdom of Belgium and the Italian Republic on the Recognition and Enforcement of Judgments and other Enforceable Instruments in Civil and Commercial Matters, signed at Rome on 6 April 1962;
  —the Convention between the Kingdom of the Netherlands and the Federal Republic of Germany on the Mutual Recognition and Enforcement of Judgments and other Enforceable Instruments in Civil and Commercial Matters, signed at The Hague on 30 August 1962;
  —the Convention between the United Kingdom and the Republic of Italy for the Reciprocal Recognition and Enforcement of Judgments in Civil and Commercial Matters, signed at Rome on 7 February 1964, with amending Protocol signed at Rome on 14 July 1970;
  —the Convention between the United Kingdom and the Kingdom of the Netherlands providing for the Reciprocal Recognition and Enforcement of Judgments in Civil Matters, signed at The Hague on 17 November 1967,
and, in so far as it is in force:
  —the Treaty between Belgium, the Netherlands and Luxembourg on Jurisdiction, Bankruptcy, and the Validity and Enforcement of Judgments, Arbitration Awards and Authentic Instruments, signed at Brussels on 24 November 1961.

ARTICLE 56

The Treaty and the conventions referred to in Article 55 shall continue to have effect in relation to matters to which this Convention does not apply.

They shall continue to have effect in respect of judgments given and documents formally drawn up or registered as authentic instruments before the entry into force of this Convention.

ARTICLE 57

This Convention shall not affect any conventions to which the Contracting States are or will be parties and which, in relation to particular matters, govern jurisdiction or the recognition or enforcement of judgments.

This convention shall not affect the application of provisions which, in relation to particular matters, govern jurisdiction or the recognition or enforcement of judgments and which are or will be contained in acts of the Institutions of the European Communities or in national laws harmonised in implementation of such acts.

(Article 25(2) of the Accession Convention provides:
"With a view to its uniform interpretation, paragraph 1 of Article 57 shall be applied in the following manner:
  (*a*) The 1968 convention as amended shall not prevent a court of a Contracting State which is a party to a convention on a particular matter from assuming jurisdiction in accordance with that convention, even where the defendant is domiciled in another Contracting State which is not a party to that convention. The court shall, in any event, apply Article 20 of the 1968 Convention as amended.
  (*b*) A judgment given in a Contracting State in the exercise of jurisdiction provided for in a convention on a particular matter shall be recognised and enforced in the other Contracting States in accordance with the 1968 Convention as amended.
  Where a convention on a particular matter to which both the State of origin and the State addressed are parties lays down conditions for the recognition or enforcement of judgments, those conditions shall apply. In any event, the provisions of the 1968 convention as amended which concern the procedures for recognition and enforcement of judgments may be applied.")

ARTICLE 58
This convention shall not affect the rights granted to Swiss nationals by the Convention concluded on 15 June 1869 between France and the Swiss Confederation on Jurisdiction and the Enforcement of Judgments in Civil Matters.

ARTICLE 59
This Convention shall not prevent a Contracting State from assuming, in a convention on the recognition and enforcement of judgments, an obligation towards a third State not to recognise judgments given in other Contracting States against defendants domiciled or habitually resident in the third State where, in cases provided for in Article 4, the judgment could only be founded on a ground of jurisdiction specified in the second paragraph of Article 3.

However, a Contracting State may not assume an obligation towards a third State not to recognise a judgment given in another Contracting State by a court basing its jurisdiction on the presence within that State of property belonging to the defendant, or the seizure by the plaintiff of property situated there:
  (1) if the action is brought to assert or declare proprietary or possessory rights in that property, seeks to obtain authority to dispose of it, or arises from another issue relating to such property, or,
  (2) if the property constitutes the security for a debt which is the subject-matter of the action.

TITLE VIII

FINAL PROVISIONS

ARTICLE 60
This Convention shall apply to the European territories of the Contracting States, including Greenland, to the French overseas departments and territories, and to Mayotte.

The Kingdom of the Netherlands may declare at the time of signing or ratifying this Convention or at any later time, by notifying the Secretary-General of the Council of the European Communities, that this Convention shall be applicable to the Netherlands Antilles. In the absence of such declaration, proceedings taking place in the European territory of the Kingdom as a result of an appeal in cassation from the judgment of a court in the Netherlands Antilles shall be deemed to be proceedings taking place in the latter court.

Notwithstanding the first paragraph, this convention shall not apply to:
  (1) the Faroe Islands, unless the Kingdom of Denmark makes a declaration to the contrary,
  (2) any European territory situated outside the United Kingdom for the international relations of which the United Kingdom is responsible, unless the United Kingdom makes a declaration to the contrary in respect of any such territory.

Such declarations may be made at any time by notifying the Secretary-General of the Council of the European Communities.

Proceedings brought in the United Kingdom on appeal from courts in one of the territories referred to in subparagraph (2) of the third paragraph shall be deemed to be proceedings taking place in those courts.

Proceedings which in the Kingdom of Denmark are dealt with under the law on civil procedure for the Faroe Islands (*lov for Faerøerne om rettens pleje*) shall be deemed to be proceedings taking place in the courts of the Faroe Islands.

ARTICLE 61

This Convention shall be ratified by the signatory States. The instruments of ratification shall be deposited with the Secretary-General of the Council of the European Communities.

ARTICLE 62

This convention shall enter into force on the first day of the third month following the deposit of the instrument of ratification by the last signatory State to take this step.

ARTICLE 63

The Contracting States recognise that any State which becomes a member of the European Economic Community shall be required to accept this Convention as a basis for the negotiations between the Contracting States and that State necessary to ensure the implementation of the last paragraph of Article 220 of the Treaty establishing the European Economic Community.

The necessary adjustments may be the subject of a special convention between the Contracting States of the one part and the new Member State of the other part.

ARTICLE 64

The Secretary-General of the Council of the European Communities shall notify the signatory States of:

(*a*)   the deposit of each instrument of ratification;
(*b*)   the date of entry into force of this Convention;
(*c*)   any declaration received pursuant to Article 60;
(*d*)   any declaration received pursuant to Article IV of the Protocol;
(*e*)   any communication made pursuant to Article VI of the Protocol.

ARTICLE 65

The Protocol annexed to this Convention by common accord of the Contracting States shall form an integral part thereof.

ARTICLE 66

This convention is concluded for an unlimited period.

ARTICLE 67

Any Contracting State may request the revision of this Convention. In this event, a revision conference shall be convened by the President of the Council of the European Communities.

ARTICLE 68

This convention, drawn up in a single original in the Dutch, French, German and Italian languages, all four texts being equally authentic, shall be deposited in the archives of the Secretariat of the Council of the European Communities. The Secretary-General shall transmit a certified copy to the Government of each signatory State.

(*Signatures of Plenipotentiaries of the original six Contracting States*)

ANNEXED PROTOCOL

ARTICLE I

Any person domiciled in Luxembourg who is sued in a court of another Contracting State pursuant to Article 5(1) may refuse to submit to the jurisdiction of that court. If the defendant does not enter an appearance the court shall declare of its own motion that it has no jurisdiction.

An agreement conferring jurisdiction, within the meaning of Article 17, shall be valid with respect to a person domiciled in Luxembourg only if that person has expressly and specifically so agreed.

ARTICLE II

Without prejudice to any more favourable provisions of national laws, persons domiciled in a Contracting State who are being prosecuted in the criminal courts of another Contracting

State of which they are not nationals for an offence which was not intentionally committed may be defended by persons qualified to do so, even if they do not appear in person.

However, the court seised of the matter may order appearance in person; in the case of failure to appear, a judgment given in the civil action without the person concerned having had the opportunity to arrange for his defence need not be recognised or enforced in the other Contracting States.

ARTICLE III

In proceedings for the issue of an order for enforcement, no charge, duty or fee calculated by reference to the value of the matter in issue may be levied in the State in which enforcement is sought.

ARTICLE IV

Judicial and extrajudicial documents drawn up in one Contracting State which have to be served on persons in another Contracting State shall be transmitted in accordance with the procedures laid down in the conventions and agreements concluded between the Contracting States.

Unless the State in which service is to take place objects by declaration to the Secretary-General of the Council of the European Communities, such document may also be sent by the appropriate public officers of the State in which the document has been drawn up directly to the appropriate public officers of the State in which the addressee is to be found. In this case the officer of the State of origin shall send a copy of the document to the officer of the State addressed who is competent to forward it to the addressee. The document shall be forwarded in the manner specified by the law of the State addressed. The forwarding shall be recorded by a certificate sent directly to the officer of the State of origin.

ARTICLE V

The jurisdiction specified in Article 6(2) and Article 10 in actions on a warranty or guarantee or in any other third party proceedings may not be resorted to in the Federal Republic of Germany. In that State, any person domiciled in another Contracting State may be sued in the courts in pursuance of Articles 68, 72, 73 and 74 of the code of civil procedure (*Zivilprozessordnung*) concerning third-party notices.

Judgments given in the other Contracting States by virtue of Article 6(2) or Article 10 shall be recognised and enforced in the Federal Republic of Germany in accordance with Title III. Any effects which judgments given in that State may have on third parties by application of Articles 68, 72, 73 and 74 of the code of civil procedure (*Zivilprozessordnung*) shall also be recognised in the other Contracting States.

ARTICLE VA

In matters relating to maintenance, the expression "court" includes the Danish administrative authorities.

ARTICLE VB

In proceedings involving a dispute between the master and a member of the crew of a sea-going ship registered in Denmark or in Ireland, concerning remuneration or other conditions of service, a court in a Contracting State shall establish whether the diplomatic or consular officer responsible for the ship has been notified of the dispute. It shall stay the proceedings so long as he has not been notified. It shall of its own motion decline jurisdiction if the officer, having been duly notified, has exercised the powers accorded to him in the matter by a consular convention, or in the absence of such a convention, has, within the time allowed, raised any objection to the exercise of such jurisdiction.

ARTICLE VC

Articles 52 and 53 of this Convention shall, when applied by Article 69(5) of the Convention for the European Patent for the Common market, signed at Luxembourg on 15 December 1975, to the provisions relating to "residence" in the English text of that Convention, operate as if "residence" in that text were the same as "domicile" in Articles 52 and 53.

ARTICLE VD

Without prejudice to the jurisdiction of the European Patent Office under the Convention on the Grant of European patents, signed at Munich on 5 October 1973, the courts of each Contracting State shall have exclusive jurisdiction, regardless of domicile, in proceedings concerned with the registration of validity of any European patent granted for that State which is not a Community patent by virtue of the provisions of Article 86 of the Convention for the European Patent for the Common market, signed at Luxembourg on 15 December 1975.

ARTICLE VI

The Contracting States shall communicate to the Secretary-General of the Council of the European Communities the text of any provisions of their laws which amend either those articles of their laws mentioned in the Convention or the lists of courts specified in Section 2 of Title III of the Convention.

Section 2(2) SCHEDULE 2

TEXT OF 1971 PROTOCOL, AS AMENDED

ARTICLE 1

The Court of Justice of the European Communities shall have jurisdiction to give rulings on the interpretation of the Convention on Jurisdiction and the Enforcement of Judgments in Civil and Commercial Matters and of the Protocol annexed to that Convention signed at Brussels on 27 September 1968, and also on the interpretation of the present Protocol.

The Court of Justice of the European Communities shall also have jurisdiction to give rulings on the interpretation of the Convention on the Accession of the Kingdom of Denmark, Ireland and the United Kingdom of Great Britain and Northern Ireland to the Convention of 27 September 1968 and to this Protocol.

ARTICLE 2

The following courts may request the Court of Justice to give preliminary rulings on questions of interpretation:

(1) —in Belgium: *la Cour de Cassation—het Hoof van Cassatie* and *le Conseil d'Etat—de Raad van State,*

   —in Denmark: *højesteret,*

   —in the Federal Republic of Germany: *die oberrsten Gerichtshöfe des Bundes,*

   —in France: *la Cour de Cassation* and *le Conseil d'Etat,*

   —in Ireland: the Supreme Court,

   —in Italy: *la Corte Suprema di Cassazione,*

   —in Luxembourg: *la Cour supérieure de Justice* when sitting as *Cour de Cassation,*

   —in the Netherlands: *de Hoge Raad,*

   —in the United Kingdom: the House of Lords and courts to which application has been made under the second paragraph of Article 37 or under Article 41 of the Convention;

(2) the courts of the contracting States when they are sitting in an appellate capacity;

(3) in the cases provided for in Article 37 of the Convention, the courts referred to in that Article.

ARTICLE 3

(1) Where a question of interpretation of the Convention or of one of the other instruments referred to in Article 1 is raised in a case pending before one of the courts listed in Article 2(1) that court shall, if it considers that a decision on the question is necessary to enable it to give judgment, request the Court of Justice to give a ruling thereon.

(2) Where such a question is raised before any court referred to in Article 2(2) or (3), that court may, under the conditions laid down in paragraph (1), request the Court of Justice to give a ruling thereon.

ARTICLE 4

(1) The competent authority of a Contracting State may request the Court of Justice to give a ruling on a question of interpretation of the Convention or of one of the other instruments referred to in Article 1 if judgments given by courts of that State conflict with the interpretation given either by the Court of Justice or in a judgment of one of the courts of another Contracting State referred to in article 2(1) or (2). The provisions of this paragraph shall apply only to judgments which have become *res judicata.*

(2) The interpretation given by the Court of Justice in response to such a request shall not affect the judgments which gave rise to the request for interpretation.

(3) The Procurators-General of the Courts of Cassation of the Contracting States, or any other authority designated by a Contracting State, shall be entitled to request the Court of Justice for a ruling on interpretation in accordance with paragraph (1).

(4) The Registrar of the Court of Justice shall give notice of the request to the Contracting States, to the Commission and to the Council of the European Communities; they shall then

be entitled within two months of the notification to submit statements of case or written observations to the Court.

(5) No fees shall be levied or any costs or expenses awarded in respect of the proceedings provided for in this Article.

ARTICLE 5

(1) Except where this Protocol otherwise provides, the provisions of the Treaty establishing the European Economic Community and those of the Protocol on the Statute of the Court of Justice annexed thereto, which are applicable when the Court is requested to give a preliminary ruling, shall also apply to any proceedings for the interpretation of the Convention and the other instruments referred to in Article 1.

(2) The Rules of Procedure of the Court of Justice shall, if necessary, be adjusted and supplemented in accordance with Article 188 of the Treaty establishing the European Economic Community.

ARTICLE 6

This Protocol shall apply to the European territories of the Contracting States, including Greenland, to the French overseas departments and territories, and to Mayotte.

The Kingdom of the Netherlands may declare at the time of signing or ratifying this Protocol or at any later time, by notifying to the Secretary-General of the Council of the European Communities, that this Protocol shall be applicable to the Netherlands Antilles.

Notwithstanding the first paragraph, this Protocol shall not apply to:

(1)   the Faroe Islands, unless the Kingdom of Denmark makes a declaration to the contrary,

(2)   any European territory situated outside the United Kingdom for the international relations of which the United Kingdom is responsible, unless the United Kingdom makes a declaration to the contrary in respect of any such territory.

Such declarations may be made at any time by notifying the Secretary-General of the Council of the European Communities.

ARTICLE 7

This Protocol shall be ratified by the signatory States. The instruments of ratification shall be deposited with the Secretary-General of the Council of the European Communities.

ARTICLE 8

This Protocol shall enter into force on the first day of the third month following the deposit of the instrument of ratification by the last signatory State to take this step; provided that it shall at the earliest enter into force at the same time as the Convention of 27 September 1968 on Jurisdiction and the Enforcement of Judgments in Civil and Commercial Matters.

ARTICLE 9

The Contracting States recognise that any State which becomes a member of the European Economic Community, and to which Article 63 of the Convention on Jurisdiction and the Enforcement of Judgments in Civil and Commercial Matters applies, must accept the provisions of this Protocol, subject to such adjustments as may be required.

ARTICLE 10

The Secretary-General of the Council of the European Communities shall notify the signatory States of:

(a)   the deposit of each instrument of ratification;

(b)   the date of entry into force of this Protocol;

(c)   any designation received pursuant to Article 4(3);

(d)   any declaration received pursuant to Article 6.

ARTICLE 11

The Contracting States shall communicate to the Secretary-General of the Council of the European Communities the texts of any provisions of their laws which necessitate an amendment to the list of courts in Article 2(1).

ARTICLE 12

This Protocol is concluded for an unlimited period.

ARTICLE 13

Any Contracting State may request the revision of this Protocol. In this event, a revision conference shall be convened by the President of the Council of the European Communities.

ARTICLE 14

This Protocol, drawn up in a single original in the Dutch, French, German and Italian languages, all four texts being equally authentic, shall be deposited in the archives of the Secretariat of the Council of the European Communities. The Secretary-General shall transmit a certified copy to the Government of each signatory State.

Section 2(2) SCHEDULE 3

TEXT OF TITLES V AND VI OF ACCESSION CONVENTION

TITLE V

TRANSITIONAL PROVISIONS

ARTICLE 34

(1) The 1968 convention and the 1971 Protocol, with the amendments made by this Convention, shall apply only to legal proceedings instituted and to authentic instruments formally drawn up or registered after the entry into force of this Convention in the State of origin and, where recognition or enforcement of a judgment or authentic instrument is sought, in the State addressed.

(2) However, as between the six Contracting States to the 1968 Convention, judgments given after the date of entry into force of this Convention in proceedings instituted before that date shall be recognised and enforced in accordance with the provisions of Title III of the 1968 Convention as amended.

(3) Moreover, as between the six Contracting States to the 1968 Convention and the three States mentioned in Article 1 of this Convention, and as between those three States, judgments given after the date of entry into force of this Convention between the State of origin and the State addressed in proceedings instituted before that date shall also be recognised and enforced in accordance with the provisions of Title III of the 1968 Convention as amended if jurisdiction was founded upon rules which accorded with the provisions of Title II, as amended, or with provisions of a convention concluded between the State of origin and the State addressed which was in force when the proceedings were instituted.

ARTICLE 35

If the parties to a dispute concerning a contract had agreed in writing before the entry into force of this Convention that the contract was to be governed by the law of Ireland or of a part of the United Kingdom, the courts of Ireland or of that part of the United Kingdom shall retain the right to exercise jurisdiction in the dispute.

ARTICLE 36

For a period of three years from the entry into force of the 1968 Convention for the Kingdom of Denmark and Ireland respectively, jurisdiction in maritime matters shall be determined in these States not only in accordance with the provisions of that Convention but also in accordance with the provisions of paragraphs (1) to (6) following. However, upon the entry into force of the International Convention relating to the Arrest of Sea-going Ships, signed at Brussels on 10 May 1952, for one of these States, these provisions shall cease to have effect for that State.

(1) A person who is domiciled in a Contracting State may be sued in the courts of one of the States mentioned above in respect of a maritime claim if the ship to which the claim relates or any other ship owned by him has been arrested by judicial process within the territory of the latter State to secure the claim, or could have been so arrested there but bail or other security has been given, and either:

(*a*) the claimant is domiciled in the latter State; or
(*b*) the claim arose in the latter State; or
(*c*) the claim concerns the voyage during which the arrest was made or could have been made; or
(*d*) the claim arises out of a collision or out of damage caused by a ship to another ship or to goods or persons on board either ship, either by the execution or non-execution of a manoeuvre or by the non-observance of regulations; or
(*e*) the claim is for salvage; or
(*f*) the claim is in respect of a mortgage or hypothecation of the ship arrested.

(2) A claimant may arrest either the particular ship to which the maritime claim relates, or any other ship which is owned by the person who was, at the time when the maritime claim

arose, the owner of the particular ship. However, only the particular ship to which the maritime claim relates may be arrested in respect of the maritime claims set out in subparagraphs (*o*), (*p*), or (*q*) of paragraph (5) of this Article.

(3) Ships shall be deemed to be in the same ownership when all the shares therein are owned by the same person or persons.

(4) When in the case of a charter by demise of a ship the charterer alone is liable in respect of a maritime claim relating to that ship, the claimant may arrest that ship or any other ship owned by the charterer, but no other ship owned by the owner may be arrested in respect of such claim. The same shall apply to any case in which a person other than the owner of a ship is liable in respect of a maritime claim relating to that ship.

(5) The expression "maritime claim" means a claim arising out of one or more of the following:

(*a*) damage caused by any ship either in collision or otherwise;
(*b*) loss of life or personal injury caused by any ship or occurring in connection with the operation of any ship;
(*c*) salvage;
(*d*) agreement relating to the use or hire of any ship whether by charterparty or otherwise;
(*e*) agreement relating to the carriage of goods in any ship whether by charterparty or otherwise;
(*f*) loss of or damage to goods including baggage carried in any ship;
(*g*) general average;
(*h*) bottomry;
(*i*) towage;
(*j*) pilotage;
(*k*) goods or materials wherever supplied to a ship for her operation or maintenance;
(*l*) construction, repair or equipment of any ship or dock charges and dues;
(*m*) wages of masters, officers or crew;
(*n*) master's disbursements, including disbursements made by shippers, charterers or agents on behalf of a ship or her owner;
(*o*) dispute as to the title to or ownership of any ship;
(*p*) disputes between co-owners of any ship as to the ownership, possession, employment or earnings of that ship;
(*q*) the mortgage or hypothecation of any ship.

(6) In Denmark, the expression "arrest" shall be deemed as regards the maritime claims referred to in subparagraphs (*o*) and (*p*) of paragraph (5) of this Article, to include a *forbud*, where that is the only procedure allowed in respect of such a claim under Articles 646 to 653 of the law on civil procedure (*lov om rettens pleje*).

TITLE VI

FINAL PROVISIONS

ARTICLE 37

The Secretary-General of the Council of the European Communities shall transmit a certified copy of the 1968 Convention and of the 1971 Protocol in the Dutch, French, German and Italian languages to the Governments of the Kingdom of Denmark, Ireland and the United Kingdom of Great Britain and Northern Ireland.

The texts of the 1968 Convention and the 1971 Protocol, drawn up in the Danish, English and Irish languages, shall be annexed to this Convention. The texts drawn up in the Danish, English and Irish languages shall be authentic under the same conditions as the original texts of the 1968 Convention and the 1971 Protocol.

ARTICLE 38

This Convention shall be ratified by the signatory States. The instruments of ratification shall be deposited with the Secretary-General of the Council of the European Communities.

ARTICLE 39

This Convention shall enter into force, as between the States which shall have ratified it, on the first day of the third month following the deposit of the last instrument of ratification by the original Member States of the Community and one new Member State.

It shall enter into force for each new Member State which subsequently ratifies it on the first day of the third month following the deposit of its instrument of ratification.

ARTICLE 40

The Secretary-General of the Council of the European Communities shall notify the

signatory States of:
- (*a*) the deposit of each instrument of ratification,
- (*b*) the dates of entry into force of this Convention for the Contracting States.

ARTICLE 41
This Convention, drawn up in a single original in the Danish, Dutch, English, French, German, Irish and Italian languages, all seven texts being equally authentic, shall be deposited in the archives of the Secretariat of the Council of the European Communities. The Secretary-General shall transmit a certified copy to the Government of each signatory State.

Section 16   SCHEDULE 4

TITLE II OF 1968 CONVENTION AS MODIFIED FOR ALLOCATION
OF JURISDICTION WITHIN U.K.

TITLE II

JURISDICTION

Section 1

General Provisions

ARTICLE 2
Subject to the provisions of this **Title,** persons domiciled in a **part of the United Kingdom** shall . . . be sued in the courts of that **part.**

*   *   *   *

ARTICLE 3
Persons domiciled in a **part of the United Kingdom** may be sued in the courts of another **part of the United Kingdom** only by virtue of the rules set out in Sections **2, 4, 5 and 6** of this Title.

*   *   *   *

Section 2

Special jurisdiction

ARTICLE 5
A person domiciled in a **part of the United Kingdom** may, in another **part of the United Kingdom,** be sued:
- (1) in matters relating to a contract, in the courts for the place of performance of the obligation in question;
- (2) in matters relating to maintenance, in the courts for the place where the maintenance creditor is domiciled or habitually resident or, if the matter is ancillary to proceedings concerning the status of a person, in the court which, according to its own law, has jurisdiction to entertain those proceedings, unless that jurisdiction is based solely on the nationality of one of the parties;
- (3) in matters relating to tort, delict or quasi-delict, in the courts for the place where the harmful event occurred **or in the case of a threatened wrong is likely to occur**;
- (4) as regards a civil claim for damages or restitution which is based on an act giving rise to criminal proceedings, in the court seised of those proceedings, to the extent that that court has jurisdiction under its own law to entertain civil proceedings;
- (5) as regards a dispute arising out of the operations of a branch, agency or other establishment, in the courts for the place in which the branch, agency or other establishment is situated;
- (6) in his capacity as a settlor, trustee or beneficiary of a trust created by the operation of a statute, or by a written instrument, or created orally and evidenced in writing, in the courts of the **part of the United Kingdom** in which the trust is domiciled;
- (7) as regards a dispute concerning the payment of remuneration claimed in respect of the salvage of a cargo or freight, in the court under the authority of which the cargo or freight in question

(*a*) has been arrested to secure such payment, or

(*b*) could have been so arrested, but bail or other security has been given;
provided that this provision shall apply only if it is claimed that the defendant has an interest in the cargo or freight or had such an interest at the time of salvage;

(8) in proceedings—

(a) concerning a debt secured on immovable property; or

(b) which are brought to assert, declare or determine proprietary or possessory rights, or rights of security, in or over movable property, or to obtain authority to dispose of movable property,

in the courts of the part of the United Kingdom in which the property is situated.

ARTICLE 5A

Proceedings which have as their object a decision of an organ of a company or other legal person or of an association of natural or legal persons may, without prejudice to the other provisions of this Title, be brought in the courts of the part of the United Kingdom in which that company, legal person or association has its seat.

ARTICLE 6

A person domiciled in a **part of the United Kingdom** may, **in another part of the United Kingdom,** also be sued:

(1) where he is one of a number of defendants, in the courts for the place where any one of them is domiciled;

(2) as a third party in an action on a warranty or guarantee or in any other third party proceedings, in the court seised of the original proceedings, unless these were instituted solely with the object of removing him from the jurisdiction of the court which would be competent in his case;

(3) on a counterclaim arising from the same contract or facts on which the original claim was based, in the court in which the original claim is pending.

ARTICLE 6A

Where by virtue of this **Title** a court of a **part of the United Kingdom** has jurisdiction in actions relating to liability arising from the use or operation of a ship, that court, or any other court substituted for this purpose by the internal law of that **part,** shall also have jurisdiction over claims for limitation of such liability.

*   *   *   *

Section 4

Jurisdiction over consumer contracts

ARTICLE 13

In proceedings concerning a contract concluded by a person for a purpose which can be regarded as being outside his trade or profession, hereinafter called "the consumer", jurisdiction shall be determined by this Section, without prejudice to the provisions of Articles . . . 5(5) **and (8)(b),** if it is:

(1) a contract for the sale of goods on instalment credit terms, or

(2) a contract for a loan repayable by instalments, or for any other form of credit, made to finance the sale of goods, or

(3) any other contract for the supply of goods or a contract for the supply of services and . . . the consumer took in **the part of the United Kingdom in which he is domiciled** the steps necessary for the conclusion of the contract.

*   *   *   *

This Section shall not apply to contracts of transport **or insurance.**

ARTICLE 14

A consumer may bring proceedings against the other party to a contract either in the courts of the **part of the United Kingdom** in which that party is domiciled or in the courts of the **part of the United Kingdom** in which he is himself domiciled.

Proceedings may be brought against a consumer by the other party to the contract only in the courts of the **part of the United Kingdom** in which the consumer is domiciled.

These provisions shall not affect the right to bring a counterclaim in the court in which, in accordance with this Section, the original claim is pending.

ARTICLE 15

The provisions of this Section may be departed from only by an agreement:
(1) which is entered into after the dispute has arisen,
    or
(2) which allows the consumer to bring proceedings in courts other than those indicated in this Section,
    or
(3) which is entered into by the consumer and the other party to the contract, both of whom are at the time of conclusion of the contract domiciled or habitually resident in the same **part of the United Kingdom**, and which confers jurisdiction on the courts of that **part**, provided that such an agreement is not contrary to the law of that **part**.

Section 5

Exclusive jurisdiction

ARTICLE 16

The following courts shall have exclusive jurisdiction, regardless of domicile:
(1) in proceedings which have as their object rights *in rem* in, or tenancies of, immovable property, the courts of the **part of the United Kingdom** in which the property is situated;
(2) in proceedings which have as their object the validity of the constitution, the nullity or the dissolution of companies or other legal persons or associations of natural or legal persons . . . the courts of the **part of the United Kingdom** in which the company, legal person or association has its seat;
(3) in proceedings which have as their object the validity of entries in public registers, the courts of the **part of the United Kingdom** in which the register is kept;

*   *   *   *

(5) in proceedings concerned with the enforcement of judgments, the courts of the **part of the United Kingdom** in which the judgment has been or is to be enforced.

Section 6

Prorogation of jurisdiction

ARTICLE 17

If the parties . . . have agreed that a court or the courts of a **part of the United Kingdom** are to have jurisdiction to settle any disputes which have arisen or which may arise in connection with a particular legal relationship, **and, apart from this Schedule, the agreement would be effective to confer jurisdiction under the law of that part**, that court or those courts shall have . . . jurisdiction . . .

The court or courts of a **part of the United Kingdom** on which a trust instrument has conferred jurisdiction shall have . . . jurisdiction in any proceedings brought against a settlor, trustee or beneficiary, if relations between these persons or their rights or obligations under the trust are involved.

Agreements or provisions of a trust instrument conferring jurisdiction shall have no legal force if they are contrary to the provisions of Article . . . 15, or if the courts whose jurisdiction they purport to exclude have exclusive jurisdiction by virtue of Article 16.

*   *   *   *

ARTICLE 18

Apart from jurisdiction derived from other provisions of this **Title**, a court of a **part of the United Kingdom** before whom a defendant enters an appearance shall have jurisdiction. This rule shall not apply where appearance was entered solely to contest the jurisdiction, or where another court has exclusive jurisdiction by virtue of Article 16.

Section 7

Examination as to jurisdiction and admissibility

ARTICLE 19

Where a court of a **part of the United Kingdom** is seised of a claim which is principally concerned with a matter over which the courts of another **part of the United Kingdom** have exclusive jurisdiction by virtue of Article 16, it shall declare of its own motion that it has no jurisdiction.

ARTICLE 20

Where a defendant domiciled in one **part of the United Kingdom** is sued in a court of another **part of the United Kingdom** and does not enter an appearance, the court shall declare of its own motion that it has no jurisdiction unless its jurisdiction is derived from the provisions of this **Title**.

The court shall stay the proceedings so long as it is not shown that the defendant has been able to receive the document instituting the proceedings or an equivalent document in sufficient time to enable him to arrange for his defence, or that all necessary steps have been taken to this end.

*   *   *   *

Section 9

Provisional, including protective, measures

ARTICLE 24

Application may be made to the courts of a **part of the United Kingdom** for such provisional, including protective, measures as may be available under the law of that **part,** even if, under this **Title,** the courts of another **part of the United Kingdom** have jurisdiction as to the substance of the matter.

Section 17   SCHEDULE 5

PROCEEDINGS EXCLUDED FROM SCHEDULE 4

Proceedings under the Companies Acts

1. Proceedings for the winding up of a company under the Companies Act 1948 or the Companies Act (Northern Ireland) 1960, or proceedings relating to a company as respects which jurisdiction is conferred on the court having winding up jurisdiction under either of those Acts.

Patents, trade marks, designs and similar rights

2. Proceedings concerned with the registration or validity of patents, trade marks, designs or other similar rights required to be deposited or registered.

Protection of Trading Interests Act 1980

3. Proceedings under section 6 of the Protection of Trading Interests Act 1980 (recovery of sums paid or obtained pursuant to a judgment for multiple damages).

Appeals etc. from tribunals

4. Proceedings on appeal from, or for review of, decisions of tribunals.

Maintenance and similar payments to local and other public authorities

5. Proceedings for, or otherwise relating to, an order under any of the following provisions—

(*a*) section 47 or 51 of the Child Care Act 1980, section 80 of the Social Work (Scotland) Act 1968 or section 156 of the Children and Young Persons Act (Northern Ireland) 1968 (contributions in respect of children in care, etc.);

(*b*) section 49 or 50 of the Child Care Act 1980, section 81 of the Social Work (Scotland) Act 1968 or section 159 of the Children and Young Persons Act (Northern Ireland) 1968 (applications for, or for variation of, affiliation orders in respect of children in care, etc.);

(*c*) section 43 of the National Assistance Act 1948, section 18 of the Supplementary Benefits Act 1976, Article 101 of the Health and Personal Social Services (Northern Ireland) Order 1972 or Article 23 of the Supplementary Benefits (Northern Ireland) Order 1977 (recovery of cost of assistance or benefit from person liable to maintain the assisted person);

(*d*) section 44 of the National Assistance Act 1948, section 19 of the Supplementary Benefits Act 1976, Article 102 of the Health and Personal Social Services (Northern Ireland) Order 1972 or Article 24 of the Supplementary Benefits (Northern Ireland) Order 1977 (applications for, or for variation of, affiliation orders in respect of children for whom assistance or benefit provided).

Proceedings under certain conventions, etc.

6. Proceedings brought in any court in pursuance of—
   (*a*) any statutory provision which, in the case of any convention to which Article 57 applies (conventions relating to specific matters which override the general rules in the 1968 Convention), implements the convention or makes provision with respect to jurisdiction in any field to which the convention relates; and
   (*b*) any rule of law so far as it has the effect of implementing any such convention.

Certain Admiralty proceedings in Scotland

7. Proceedings in Scotland in an Admiralty cause where the jurisdiction of the Court of Session or, as the case may be, of the sheriff is based on arrestment *in rem* or *ad fundandam jurisdictionem* of a ship, cargo or freight.

Register of aircraft mortgages

8. Proceedings for the rectification of the register of aircraft mortgages kept by the Civil Aviation Authority.

Continental Shelf Act 1964

9. Proceedings brought in any court in pursuance of an order under section 3 of the Continental Shelf Act 1964.

———

Section 18   SCHEDULE 6

ENFORCEMENT OF U.K. JUDGMENTS (MONEY PROVISIONS)

Preliminary

1. In this Schedule—
   "judgment" means any judgment to which section 18 applies and references to the giving of a judgment shall be construed accordingly;
   "money provision" means a provision for the payment of one or more sums of money;
   "prescribed" means prescribed by rules of court.

Certificates in respect of judgments

2.—(1) Any interested party who wishes to secure the enforcement in another part of the United Kingdom of any money provisions contained in a judgment may apply for a certificate under this Schedule.

(2) The application shall be made in the prescribed manner to the proper officer of the original court, that is to say—
   (*a*) in relation to a judgment within paragraph (*a*) of the definition of "judgment" in section 18(2), the court by which the judgment or order was given or made;
   (*b*) in relation to a judgment within paragraph (*b*) of that definition, the court in which the judgment or order is entered;
   (*c*) in relation to a judgment within paragraph (*c*) of that definition, the court in whose books the document is registered;
   (*d*) in relation to a judgment within paragraph (*d*) of that definition, the tribunal by which the award or order was made;
   (*e*) in relation to a judgment within paragraph (*e*) of that definition, the court which gave the judgment or made the order by virtue of which the award has become enforceable as mentioned in that paragraph.

3. A certificate shall not be issued under this Schedule in respect of a judgment unless under the law of the part of the United Kingdom in which the judgment was given—
   (*a*) either—
      (i) the time for bringing an appeal against the judgment has expired, no such appeal having been brought within that time; or
      (ii) such an appeal having been brought within that time, that appeal has been finally disposed of; and

(*b*) enforcement of the judgment is not for the time being stayed or suspended, and the time available for its enforcement has not expired.

4.—(1) Subject to paragraph 3, on an application under paragraph 2 the proper officer shall issue to the applicant a certificate in the prescribed form—

(*a*) stating the sum or aggregate of the sums (including any costs or expenses) payable under the money provisions contained in the judgment, the rate of interest, if any, payable thereon and the date or time from which any such interest began to accrue;

(*b*) stating that the conditions specified in paragraph 3(*a*) and (*b*) are satisfied in relation to the judgment; and

(*c*) containing such other particulars as may be prescribed.

(2) More than one certificate may be issued under this Schedule (simultaneously or at different times) in respect of the same judgment.

Registration of certificates

5.—(1) Where a certificate has been issued under this Schedule in any part of the United Kingdom, any interested party may, within six months from the date of its issue, apply in the prescribed manner to the proper officer of the superior court in any other part of the United Kingdom for the certificate to be registered in that court.

(2) In this paragraph "superior court" means, in relation to England and Wales or Northern Ireland, the High Court and, in relation to Scotland, the Court of Session.

(3) Where an application is duly made under this paragraph to the proper officer of a superior court, he shall register the certificate in that court in the prescribed manner.

General effect of registration

6.—(1) A certificate registered under this Schedule shall, for the purposes of its enforcement, be of the same force and effect, the registering court shall have in respect to its enforcement the same powers, and proceedings for or with respect to its enforcement may be taken, as if the certificate had been a judgment originally given in the registering court and had (where relevant) been entered.

(2) Sub-paragraph (1) is subject to the following provisions of this Schedule and to any provision made by rules of court as to the manner in which and the conditions subject to which a certificate registered under this Schedule may be enforced.

Costs or expenses

7. Where a certificate is registered under this Schedule, the reasonable costs or expenses of and incidental to the obtaining of the certificate and its registration shall be recoverable as if they were costs or expenses stated in the certificate to be payable under a money provision contained in the original judgment.

Interest

8.—(1) Subject to any provision made under sub-paragraph (2), the debt resulting, apart from paragraph 7, from the registration of the certificate shall carry interest at the rate, if any, stated in the certificate from the date or time so stated.

(2) Provision may be made by rules of court as to the manner in which and the periods by reference to which any interest payable by virtue of sub-paragraph (1) is to be calculated and paid, including provision for such interest to cease to accrue as from a prescribed date.

(3) All such sums as are recoverable by virtue of paragraph 7 carry interest as if they were the subject of an order for costs or expenses made by the registering court on the date of registration of the certificate.

(4) Except as provided by this paragraph sums payable by virtue of the registration of a certificate under this Schedule shall not carry interest.

Stay or sisting of enforcement in certain cases

9. Where a certificate in respect of a judgment has been registered under this Schedule, the registering court may, if it is satisfied that any person against whom it is sought to enforce the certificate is entitled and intends to apply under the law of the part of the United Kingdom in which the judgment was given for any remedy which would result in the setting aside or quashing of the judgment, stay (or, in Scotland, sist) proceedings for the enforcement of the certificate, on such terms as it thinks fit, for such period as appears to the court to be reasonably sufficient to enable the application to be disposed of.

Cases in which registration of a certificate must or may be set aside

10. Where a certificate has been registered under this Schedule, the registering court—

(*a*) shall set aside the registration if, on an application made by any interested party, it is satisfied that the registration was contrary to the provisions of this Schedule;

(*b*) may set aside the registration if, on an application so made, it is satisfied that the matter in dispute in the proceedings in which the judgment in question was given had previously been the subject of a judgment by another court or tribunal having jurisdiction in the matter.

Section 18   SCHEDULE 7

ENFORCEMENT OF U.K. JUDGMENTS (NON-MONEY PROVISIONS)

Preliminary

1. In this Schedule—
   "judgment" means any judgment to which section 18 applies and references to the giving of a judgment shall be construed accordingly;
   "non-money provision" means a provision for any relief or remedy not requiring payment of a sum of money;
   "prescribed" means prescribed by rules of court.

Certified copies of judgments

2.—(1) Any interested party who wishes to secure the enforcement in another part of the United Kingdom of any non-money provisions contained in a judgment may apply for a certified copy of the judgment.

(2) The application shall be made in the prescribed manner to the proper officer of the original court, that is to say—
   (*a*) in relation to a judgment within paragraph (*a*) of the definition of "judgment" in section 18(2), the court by which the judgment or order was given or made;
   (*b*) in relation to a judgment within paragraph (*b*) of that definition, the court in which the judgment or order is entered;
   (*c*) in relation to a judgment within paragraph (*c*) of that definition, the court in whose books the document is registered;
   (*d*) in relation to a judgment within paragraph (*d*) of that definition, the tribunal by which the award or order was made;
   (*e*) in relation to a judgment within paragraph (*e*) of that definition, the court which gave the judgment or made the order by virtue of which the award has become enforceable as mentioned in that paragraph.

3. A certified copy of a judgment shall not be issued under this Schedule unless under the law of that part of the United Kingdom in which the judgment was given—
   (*a*) either—
      (i) the time for bringing an appeal against the judgment has expired, no such appeal having been brought within that time; or
      (ii) such an appeal having been brought within that time, that appeal has been finally disposed of; and
   (*b*) enforcement of the judgment is not for the time being stayed or suspended, and the time available for its enforcement has not expired.

4.—(1) Subject to paragraph 3, on an application under paragraph 2 the proper officer shall issue to the applicant—
   (*a*) a certified copy of the judgment (including any money provisions or excepted provisions which it may contain); and
   (*b*) a certificate stating that the conditions specified in paragraph 3(*a*) and (*b*) are satisfied in relation to the judgment.

(2) In sub-paragraph 1(*a*) "excepted provision" means any provision of a judgment which is excepted from the application of section 18 by subsection (5) of that section.

(3) There may be issued under this Schedule (simultaneously or at different times)—
   (*a*) more than one certified copy of the same judgment; and
   (*b*) more than one certificate in respect of the same judgment.

Registration of judgments

5.—(1) Where a certified copy of a judgment has been issued under this Schedule in any part of the United Kingdom, any interested party may apply in the prescribed manner to the superior court in any other part of the United Kingdom for the judgment to be registered in that court.

(2) In this paragraph "superior court" means, in relation to England and Wales or Northern Ireland, the High Court and, in relation to Scotland, the Court of Session.

(3) An application made under this paragraph for the registration of a judgment must be accompanied by—

(*a*) a certified copy of the judgment issued under this Schedule; and

(*b*) a certificate issued under paragraph 4(1)(*b*) in respect of the judgment not more than six months before the date of the application.

(4) Subject to sub-paragraph (5), where an application under this paragraph is duly made to a superior court, the court shall order the whole of the judgment as set out in the certified copy to be registered in that court in the prescribed manner.

(5) A judgment shall not be registered under this Schedule by the superior court in any part of the United Kingdom if compliance with the non-money provisions contained in the judgment would involve a breach of the law of that part of the United Kingdom.

General effect of registration

6.—(1) The non-money provisions contained in a judgment registered under this Schedule shall, for the purposes of their enforcement, be of the same force and effect, the registering court shall have in relation to their enforcement the same powers, and proceedings for or with respect to their enforcement may be taken, as if the judgment containing them had been originally given in the registering court and had (where relevant) been entered.

(2) Sub-paragraph (1) is subject to the following provisions of this Schedule and to any provision made by rules of court as to the manner in which and conditions subject to which the non-money provisions contained in a judgment registered under this Schedule may be enforced.

Costs or expenses

7.—(1) Where a judgment is registered under this Schedule, the reasonable costs or expenses of and incidental to—

(*a*) the obtaining of the certified copy of the judgment and of the necessary certificate under paragraph 4(1)(*b*) in respect of it; and

(*b*) the registration of the judgment,

shall be recoverable as if on the date of registration there had also been registered in the registering court a certificate under Schedule 6 in respect of the judgment and as if those costs or expenses were costs or expenses stated in that certificate to be payable under a money provision contained in the judgment.

(2) All such sums as are recoverable by virtue of sub-paragraph (1) shall carry interest as if they were the subject of an order for costs or expenses made by the registering court on the date of registration of the judgment.

Stay or sisting of enforcement in certain cases

8. Where a judgment has been registered under this Schedule, the registering court may, if it is satisfied that any person against whom it is sought to enforce the judgment is entitled and intends to apply under the law of the part of the United Kingdom in which the judgment was given for any remedy which would result in the setting aside or quashing of the judgment, stay (or, in Scotland, sist) proceedings for the enforcement of the judgment, on such terms as it thinks fit, for such period as appears to the court to be reasonably sufficient to enable the application to be disposed of.

Cases in which registered judgment must or may be set aside

9. Where a judgment has been registered under this Schedule, the registering court—

(*a*) shall set aside the registration if, on an application made by any interested party, it is satisfied that the registration was contrary to the provisions of this Schedule;

(*b*) may set aside the registration if, on an application so made, it is satisfied that the matter in dispute in the proceedings in which the judgment was given had previously been the subject of a judgment by another court or tribunal having jurisdiction in the matter.

Section 20   SCHEDULE 8

RULES AS TO JURISDICTION IN SCOTLAND

General

1. Subject to the **following Rules,** persons shall be sued in the courts **for the place where they are domiciled.**

Special jurisdiction

2. Subject to Rules 3 (jurisdiction over consumer contracts), 4 (exclusive jurisdiction) and 5 (prorogation) a person may **also** be sued—

(1) **where he has no fixed residence, in a court within whose jurisdiction he is personally cited;**

(2) in matters relating to a contract, in the courts for the place of performance of the obligation in question;

(3) in matters relating to delict or quasi-delict, in the courts for the place where the harmful event occurred;

(4) as regards a civil claim for damages or restitution which is based on an act giving rise to criminal proceedings, in the court seised of those proceedings to the extent that that court has jurisdiction to entertain civil proceedings;

(5) in matters relating to maintenance, in the courts for the place where the maintenance creditor is domiciled or habitually resident or, if the matter is ancillary to proceedings concerning the status of a person, in the court which has jurisdiction to entertain those proceedings, **provided that an action for adherence and aliment or of affiliation and aliment shall be treated as a matter relating to maintenance which is not ancillary to proceedings concerning the status of a person, and provided also that—**

    (a) **where a local authority exercises its power to raise an action under section 44(7)(a) of the National Assistance Act 1948 or under section 81(1) of the Social Work (Scotland) Act 1968; and**

    (b) **where the Secretary of State exercises his power to raise an action under section 19(8)(a) of the Supplementary Benefits Act 1976;**

    this Rule shall apply as if the reference to the maintenance creditor were a reference to the mother of the child;

(6) as regards a dispute arising out of the operations of a branch, agency or other establishment, in the courts for the place in which the branch, agency or other establishment is situated;

(7) in his capacity as settlor, trustee or beneficiary of a trust **domiciled in Scotland** created by the operation of a statute, or by a written instrument, or created orally and evidenced in writing, in the **Court of Session, or the appropriate sheriff court within the meaning of section 24A of the Trusts (Scotland) Act 1921;**

(8) where he is not domiciled in the United Kingdom, in the courts for any place where—

    (a) **any moveable property belonging to him has been arrested; or**

    (b) any immoveable property in which he has any beneficial interest is situated;

(9) **in proceedings which are brought to assert, declare or determine proprietary or possessory rights, or rights of security, in or over moveable property, or to obtain authority to dispose of moveable property, in the courts for the place where the property is situated;**

(10) **in proceedings for interdict, in the courts for the place where it is alleged that the wrong is likely to be committed;**

(11) **in proceedings concerning a debt secured over immoveable property, in the courts for the place where the property is situated;**

(12) **in proceedings which have as their object a decision of an organ of a company or other legal person or of an association of natural or legal persons, in the courts for the place where that company, legal person or association has its seat;**

(13) **in proceedings concerning an arbitration which is conducted in Scotland or in which the procedure is governed by Scots law, in the Court of Session;**

(14) **in proceedings principally concerned with the registration in the United Kingdom or the validity in the United Kingdom of patents, trade marks, designs or other similar rights required to be deposited or registered, in the Court of Session;**

(15)   (*a*) where he is one of a number of **defenders**, in the courts for the place where any one of them is domiciled;

    (*b*) as a third party in an action on a warranty or guarantee or in any other third party proceedings, in the court seised of the original proceedings, unless these were instituted solely with the object of removing him from the jurisdiction of the court which would be competent in his case;

    (*c*) on a counterclaim arising from the same contract or facts on which the original claim was based, in the court in which the original claim is pending.

Jurisdiction over consumer contracts

3.—(1) In proceedings concerning a contract concluded by a person for a purpose which can be regarded as being outside his trade or profession, hereinafter called the "consumer",

subject to Rule 4 (exclusive jurisdiction), jurisdiction shall be determined by this **Rule** if it is—

    (*a*) a contract for the sale of goods on instalment credit terms; or

    (*b*) a contract for a loan repayable by instalments, or for any other form of credit, made to finance the sale of goods; or

    (*c*) any other contract for the supply of goods or a contract for the supply of services, **if—**

        (i) the consumer took in **Scotland** the steps necessary for the conclusion of the contract; **or**

        (ii) **proceedings are brought in Scotland by virtue of section 10(3).**

(2) This **Rule** shall not apply to contracts of transport **or contracts of insurance.**

(3) A consumer may bring proceedings against the other party to a contract **only** in—

    (*a*) the courts **for the place** in which that party is domiciled;

    (*b*) the courts **for the place** in which he is himself domiciled; **or**

    (*c*) **any court having jurisdiction by virtue of Rule 2(6) or (9).**

(4) Proceedings may be brought against a consumer by the other party to the contract only in the courts **for the place where** the consumer is domiciled **or any court having jurisdiction under Rule 2(9).**

(5) **Nothing in this Rule** shall affect the right to bring a counterclaim in the court in which, **in accordance with this Rule,** the original claim is pending.

(6) The provisions of this **Rule** may be departed from only by an agreement—

    (*a*) which is entered into after the dispute has arisen; or

    (*b*) which allows the consumer to bring proceedings in **a court** other than **a court** indicated in this **Rule.**

Exclusive jurisdiction

4.—(1) **Notwithstanding anything contained in any of Rules 1 to 3 above or 5 to 8 below,** the following courts shall have exclusive jurisdiction—

    (*a*) in proceedings which have as their object rights *in rem* in, or tenancies of, immoveable property, the courts **for the place where** the property is situated;

    (*b*) in proceedings which have as their object the validity of the constitution, the nullity or the dissolution of companies or other legal persons or associations of natural or legal persons, the courts **for the place where** the company, legal person or association has its seat;

    (*c*) in proceedings which have as their object the validity of entries in public registers, the courts **for the place where** the register is kept;

    (*d*) in proceedings concerned with the enforcement of judgments, the courts **for the place where** the judgment has been or is to be enforced.

(2) **Nothing in paragraph (1)(c) above affects jurisdiction in any proceedings concerning the validity of entries in registers of patents, trade marks, designs, or other similar rights required to be deposited or registered.**

(3) **No court shall exercise jurisdiction in a case where immoveable property, the seat of a body mentioned in paragraph (1)(b) above, a public register or the place where a judgment has been or is to be enforced is situated outside Scotland and where paragraph (1) above would apply if the property, seat, register or, as the case may be, place of enforcement were situated in Scotland.**

Prorogation of jurisdiction

5.—(1) If the parties have agreed that a court is to have jurisdiction to settle any disputes which have arisen or which may arise in connection with a particular legal relationship, that court shall have exclusive jurisdiction.

(2) Such an agreement conferring jurisdiction shall be either in writing or evidenced in writing or, in trade or commerce, in a form which accords with practices in that trade or commerce of which the parties are or ought to have been aware.

(3) The court on which a trust instrument has conferred jurisdiction shall have exclusive jurisdiction in any proceedings brought against a settlor, trustee or beneficiary, if relations between these person or their rights or obligations under the trust are involved.

(4) **Where an agreement or a trust instrument confers jurisdiction on the courts of the United Kingdom or of Scotland, proceedings to which paragraph (1) or, as the case may be, (3) above applies may be brought in any court in Scotland.**

(5) Agreements or provisions of a trust instrument conferring jurisdiction shall have no legal force if the courts whose jurisdiction they purport to exclude have exclusive jurisdiction by virtue of **Rule 4 or where Rule 4(3) applies.**

6.—(1) Apart from jurisdiction derived from other provisions of this **Schedule,** a court before whom a defender enters an appearance shall have jurisdiction.

(2) This Rule shall not apply where appearance was entered solely to contest jurisdiction,

or where another court has exclusive jurisdiction by virtue of **Rule 4 or where Rule 4(3) applies.**

Examination as to jurisdiction and admissibility

7. Where a court is seised of a claim which is principally concerned with a matter over which **another court has** exclusive jurisdiction by virtue of **Rule 4, or where it is precluded from exercising jurisdiction by Rule 4(3),** it shall declare of its own motion that it has no jurisdiction.

8. Where **in any case a court has no jurisdiction which is compatible with this Act, and the defender** does not enter an appearance, the court shall declare of its own motion that it has no jurisdiction.

Section 21   SCHEDULE 9

PROCEEDINGS EXCLUDED FROM SCHEDULE 8

1. Proceedings concerning the status or legal capacity of natural persons (including proceedings for separation) other than proceedings which consist solely of proceedings for adherence and aliment or of affiliation and aliment.

2. Proceedings for regulating the custody of children.

3. Proceedings relating to tutory and curatory and all proceedings relating to the management of the affairs of persons who are incapable of managing their own affairs.

4. Proceedings in respect of sequestration in bankruptcy; or the winding up of a company or other legal person; or proceedings in respect of a judicial arrangement or judicial composition with creditors.

5. Proceedings relating to a company where, by any enactment, jurisdiction in respect of those proceedings is conferred on the court having jurisdiction to wind it up.

6. Admiralty causes in so far as the jurisdiction is based on arrestment *in rem* or *ad fundandam jurisdictionem* of a ship, cargo or freight.

7. Commissary proceedings.

8. Proceedings for the rectification of the register of aircraft mortgages kept by the Civil Aviation Authority.

9. Proceedings under section 7(3) of the Civil Aviation (Eurocontrol) Act 1962 (recovery of charges for air navigation services and proceedings for damages against Eurocontrol).

10. Proceedings brought in pursuance of an order under section 3 of the Continental Shelf Act 1964.

11. Proceedings under section 6 of the Protection of Trading Interests Act 1980 (recovery of sums paid or obtained pursuant to a judgment for multiple damages).

12. Appeals from or review of decisions of tribunals.

13. Proceedings which are not in substance proceedings in which a decree against any person is sought.

14. Proceedings brought in any court in pursuance of—
    (*a*) any statutory provision which, in the case of any convention to which Article 57 applies (conventions relating to specific matters which override the general rules in the 1968 Convention), implements the convention; and
    (*b*) any rule of law so far as it has the effect of implementing any such convention.

Section 35(1)   SCHEDULE 10

AMENDMENTS OF FOREIGN JUDGMENTS (RECIPROCAL ENFORCEMENT) ACT 1933

1.—(1) Section 1 (power to extend Part I to foreign countries giving reciprocal treatment) is amended as follows.

(2) For subsections (1) and (2) substitute—
    "(1) If, in the case of any foreign country, Her Majesty is satisfied that, in the event of

the benefits conferred by this Part of this Act being extended to, or to any particular class of, judgments given in the courts of that country or in any particular class of those courts, substantial reciprocity of treatment will be assured as regards the enforcement in that country of similar judgments given in similar courts of the United Kingdom, She may by Order in Council direct—

    (*a*)   that this Part of this Act shall extend to that country;

    (*b*)   that such courts of that country as are specified in the Order shall be recognised courts of that country for the purposes of this Part of this Act; and

    (*c*)   that judgments of any such recognised court, or such judgments of any class so specified, shall, if within subsection (2) of this section, be judgments to which this Part of this Act applies.

(2) Subject to subsection (2A) of this section, a judgment of a recognised court is within this subsection if it satisfies the following conditions, namely—

    (*a*)   it is either final and conclusive as between the judgment debtor and the judgment creditor or requires the former to make an interim payment to the latter; and

    (*b*)   there is payable under it a sum of money, not being a sum payable in respect of taxes or other charges of a like nature or in respect of a fine or other penalty; and

    (*c*)   it is given after the coming into force of the Order in Council which made that court a recognised court.

(2A) The following judgments of a recognised court are not within subsection (2) of this section—

    (*a*)   a judgment given by that court on appeal from a court which is not a recognised court;

    (*b*)   a judgment or other instrument which is regarded for the purposes of its enforcement as a judgment of that court but which was given or made in another country;

    (*c*)   a judgment given by that court in proceedings founded on a judgment of a court in another country and having as their object the enforcement of that judgment.".

(3) After subsection (4) add—

    "(5) Any Order in Council made under this section before its amendment by the Civil Jurisdiction and Judgments Act 1982 which deems any court of a foreign country to be a superior court of that country for the purposes of this Part of this Act shall (without prejudice to subsection (4) of this section) have effect from the time of that amendment as if it provided for that court to be a recognised court of that country for those purposes, and for any final and conclusive judgment of that court, if within subsection (2) of this section, to be a judgment to which this Part of this Act applies.".

2..In section 9 (power to make foreign judgments unenforceable in United Kingdom if no reciprocity), in subsection (1) omit "superior" in both places where it occurs.

3. For section 10 (issue of certificates of judgments obtained in the United Kingdom) substitute—

    "Provision for issue of copies of, and certificates in connection with, U.K. judgments

    10.—(1) Rules may make provision for enabling any judgment creditor wishing to secure the enforcement in a foreign country to which Part I of this Act extends of a judgment to which this subsection applies, to obtain, subject to any conditions specified in the rules—

        (*a*)   a copy of the judgment; and

        (*b*)   a certificate giving particulars relating to the judgment and the proceedings in which it was given.

    (2) Subsection (1) applies to any judgment given by a court or tribunal in the United Kingdom under which a sum of money is payable, not being a sum payable in respect of taxes or other charges of a like nature or in respect of a fine or other penalty.

    (3) In this section "rules"—

        (*a*)   in relation to judgments given by a court, means rules of court;

        (*b*)   in relation to judgments given by any other tribunal, means rules or regulations made by the authority having power to make rules or regulations regulating the procedure of that tribunal.".

4. After section 10 insert—

    "Arbitration awards

    10A. The provisions of this Act, except sections 1(5) and 6, shall apply, as they apply to a judgment, in relation to an award in proceedings on an arbitration which has, in pursuance of the law in force in the place where it was made, become enforceable in the same manner as a judgment given by a court in that place.".

5.—(1) Section 11(1) (interpretation) is amended as follows.

(2) After the definition of "Country of the original court" insert—

    " "Court", except in section 10 of this Act, includes a tribunal;"

(3) Omit the definition of "Judgments given in the superior courts of the United Kingdom".

Section 37(1)

SCHEDULE 11

MINOR AMENDMENTS RELATING TO MAINTENANCE ORDERS

PART I

ENFORCEMENT OF LUMP SUM ORDERS

Maintenance Orders Act 1950 (c. 37)

1. In section 18(3A) of the Maintenance Orders Act 1950 (order not to be enforced by registering court under that Act if re-registered for enforcement in another court), for "whilst it is registered" substitute "to the extent that it is for the time being registered".

Maintenance Orders Act 1958 (c.39)

2.—(1) Section 2 of the Maintenance Orders Act 1958 (registration of orders) is amended as follows.

(2) In subsection (3) (registration of magistrates' court order for enforcement in the High Court), for the words from "shall" onwards (which require the court to be satisfied that not less than a certain number of periodical payments are in arrears) substitute "may, if it thinks fit, grant the application".

(3) After subsection (3) insert—

"(3A) Without prejudice to subsection (3) of this section, where a magistrates' court order provides both for the payment of a lump sum and for the making of periodical payments, a person entitled to receive a lump sum under the order who considers that, so far as it relates to that sum, the order could be more effectively enforced if it were registered may apply to the original court for the registration of the order so far as it so relates, and the court may, if it thinks fit, grant the application.

(3B) Where an application under subsection (3A) of this section is granted in the case of a magistrates' court order, the provisions of this Part of this Act shall have effect in relation to that order as if so far as it relates to the payment of a lump sum it were a separate order.".

Maintenance and Affiliation Orders Act (Northern Ireland) 1966
(c.35) (N.I.)

3.—(1) Section 11 of the Maintenance and Affiliation Orders Act (Northern Ireland) 1966 (registration of orders) is amended as follows.

(2) In subsection (3) (registration of order made by court of summary jurisdiction for enforcement in the High Court), for the words from "shall" onwards (which require the court to be satisfied that not less than a certain number of periodical payments are in arrears) substitute "may, if it thinks fit, grant the application".

(3) After subsection (3) insert—

"(3A) Without prejudice to subsection (3), where an order made by a court of summary jurisdiction provides both for the payment of a lump sum and for the making of periodical payments, a person entitled to receive a lump sum under the order who considers that, so far as it relates to that sum the order could be more effectively enforced if it were registered may apply to the original court for the registration of the order so far as it so relates, and the court may, if it thinks fit, grant the application.

(3B) Where an application under subsection (3A) is granted in the case of an order made by a court of summary jurisdiction, the provisions of this Part shall have effect in relation to that order as if so far as it relates to the payment of a lump sum it were a separate order.".

Maintenance Orders (Reciprocal Enforcement) Act 1972 (c.18)

4.—(1) In section 9 of the Maintenance Orders (Reciprocal Enforcement) Act 1972 (variation and revocation of orders), after subsection (1) insert—

"(1A) The powers conferred by subsection (1) above are not exercisable in relation to so much of a registered order as provides for the payment of a lump sum.".

(2) In section 21 of that Act (interpretation of Part I)—

(*a*) in paragraph (*a*) of the definition of "maintenance order" in subsection (1); and

(*b*) in subsection (2),

for "periodical payment of sums of money" substitute "payment of a lump sum or the making of periodical payments".

Appendix 1

Part II

Recovery of Interest on Arrears

Maintenance Orders Act 1950 (c.37)

5. In section 18 of the Maintenance Orders Act 1950 (enforcement of registered orders), after subsection (1) (orders to be enforced in the same manner as orders made by the court of registration), insert—

"(1A) A maintenance order registered under this Part of this Act in a court of summary jurisdiction in England or Northern Ireland shall not carry interest; but where a maintenance order so registered is registered in the High Court under Part I of the Maintenance Orders Act 1958 or section 36 of the Civil Jurisdiction and Judgments Act 1982, this subsection shall not prevent any sum for whose payment the order provides from carrying interest in accordance with section 2A of the said Act of 1958 or section 11A of the Maintenance and Affiliation Orders Act (Northern Ireland) 1966.

(1B) A maintenance order made in Scotland which is registered under this Part of this Act in the Supreme Court in England or Northern Ireland shall, if interest is by the law of Scotland recoverable under the order, carry the like interest in accordance with subsection (1) of this section.".

Maintenance Orders Act 1958 (c.39)

6.—(1) The Maintenance Orders Act 1958 is amended as follows.

(2) After section 2 insert—

"Interest on sums recoverable under certain orders registered in the High Court

2A.—(1) Where, in connection with an application under section 2(3) of this Act for the registration of a magistrates' court order, the applicant shows in accordance with rules of court—

        (*a*) that the order, though deemed for the purposes of section 1 of this Act to have been made by a magistrates' court in England, was in fact made in another part of the United Kingdom or in a country or territory outside the United Kingdom; and

        (*b*) that, as regards any sum for whose payment the order provides, interest on that sum at a particular rate is, by the law of that part or of that country or territory, recoverable under the order from a particular date or time,

then, if the original court grants the application and causes a certified copy of the order to be sent to the prescribed officer of the High Court under section 2(4)(*c*) of this Act, it shall also cause to be sent to him a certificate in the prescribed form showing, as regards that sum, the rate of interest so recoverable and the date or time from which it is so recoverable.

(2) The officer of the court who receives a certificate sent to him under the preceding subsection shall cause the certificate to be registered in that court together with the order to which it relates.

(3) Where an order is registered together with a certificate under this section, then, subject to any provision made under the next following subsection, sums payable under the order shall carry interest at the rate specified in the certificate from the date or time so specified.

(4) Provision may be made by rules of court as to the manner in which and the periods by reference to which any interest payable by virtue of subsection (3) is to be calculated and paid, including provision for such interest to cease to accrue as from a prescribed date.

(5) Except as provided by this section sums payable under registered orders shall not carry interest.".

(3) In section 3(1) of that Act (enforcement of registered orders), after "Subject to the provisions of" insert "section 2A of this Act and".

Maintenance and Affiliation Orders Act (Northern Ireland) 1966
(c.35) (N.I.)

7.—(1) The Maintenance and Affiliation Orders Act (Northern Ireland) 1966 is amended as follows.

(2) After section 11 insert—

"Interest on sums recoverable under certain orders registered in the High Court

11A.—(1) Where, in connection with an application under section 11(3) for the registration of an order made by a court of summary jurisdiction, the applicant shows in accordance with rules of court—

(*a*) that the order, though deemed for the purposes of this Part to have been made by a court of summary jurisdiction in Northern Ireland, was in fact made in a country or territory outside the United Kingdom; and

(*b*) that, as regards any sum for whose payment the order provides, interest on that sum at a particular rate is, by the law of that country or territory, recoverable under the order from a particular date or time,

then, if the original court grants the application and causes a certified copy of the order to be sent to the prescribed officer of the High Court under section 11(4)(*c*) it shall also cause to be sent to him a certificate in the prescribed form showing, as regards that sum, the rate of interest so recoverable and the date or time from which it is so recoverable.

(2) The officer of a court who receives a certificate sent to him under subsection (1) shall cause the certificate to be registered in that court together with the order to which it relates.

(3) Where an order is registered together with a certificate under this section, then subject to any provision made under subsection (4), sums payable under the order shall carry interest at the rate specified in the certificate from the date or time so specified.

(4) Provision may be made by rules of court as to the manner in which and the periods by reference to which any interest payable by virtue of subsection (3) is to be calculated and paid, including provision for such interest to cease to accrue as from a prescribed date.

(5) Except as provided by this section sums payable under registered orders shall not carry interest.".

(3) In section 12(1) (enforcement of registered orders), after "Subject to the provisions of" insert "section 11A and".

(4) In section 16(2) of that Act (construction of "rules of court") at the end add "and in section 11A(4) shall be construed as including a reference to Judgment Enforcement Rules made under Article 141 of the Judgments Enforcement (Northern Ireland) Order 1981".

PART III

RECIPROCAL ENFORCEMENT FOUNDED ON PRESENCE OF ASSETS

Maintenance Orders (Reciprocal Enforcement) Act 1972 (c. 18)

8. The Maintenance Orders (Reciprocal Enforcement) Act 1972 is amended as follows.

9. In section 2 (transmission of United Kingdom order for enforcement in reciprocating country)—

(*a*) in subsections (1) and (4), after "residing" insert "or has assets"; and

(*b*) in subsection (4), after "whereabouts of the payer", in both places where it occurs, insert "and the nature and location of his assets in that country".

10. In section 6 (registration in United Kingdom of order made in reciprocating country)—

(*a*) in subsection (2), after "residing" insert "or has assets"; and

(*b*) in subsection (4)—

(i) after "is residing" insert "or has assets"; and

(ii) for "so residing" substitute "residing and has no assets within the jurisdiction of the court"; and

(iii) at the end insert "and the nature and location of his assets".

11. In section 8(5) (duty of magistrates' court and its officers to take prescribed steps for enforcing registered orders), after "enforcing" insert "or facilitating the enforcement of".

12. In section 9 (variation and revocation of orders), after the subsection (1A) inserted by paragraph 4(1) of this Schedule, insert—

"(1B) The registering court shall not vary or revoke a registered order if neither the payer nor the payee under the order is resident in the United Kingdom.".

13.—(1) Section 10 (cancellation of registration and transfer or orders) is amended as follows.

(2) In subsection (2), for "has ceased to reside within the jurisdiction of that court," substitute "is not residing within the jurisdiction of that court and has no assets within that jurisdiction against which the order can be effectively enforced,".

(3) In subsection (3), after "residing" insert "or has assets".

(4) In subsection (5), for "still residing" substitute "residing or has assets".

(5) In subsection (6)—

(*a*) after "is residing" insert "or has assets"; and

(*b*) for "so residing" insert "residing and has no assets within the jurisdiction of the court".

(6) In subsection (7)(*b*), after "payer" insert "and the nature and location of his assets".

14. In section 11(1) (steps to be taken where payer is not residing in the United Kingdom)—

(*a*) before "it appears" insert "at any time";

(*b*) for the words from "in the United Kingdom" to "therein", substitute "and has no assets in the United Kingdom,"; and

(*c*) after "payer" in paragraph (*c*) insert "and the nature and location of his assets".

15. In section 21(1) (interpretation of Part I), in the definition of "the appropriate court"—
    (i) after "residing", in the first and second places where it occurs, insert "or having assets";
    (ii) for "the sheriff court" substitute "a sheriff court"; and
    (iii) after "residing", where it last occurs, insert "or has assets".

16. In section 24 (application of Part I to certain orders and proceedings under Maintenance Orders (Facilities for Enforcement) Act 1920), in paragraph (*a*)(i) and (ii), after "residing" insert "or having assets".

17. In section 40 (power to apply Act with modifications by Order in Council)—
    (*a*) in paragraph (*a*), omit "against persons in that country or territory"; and
    (*b*) in paragraph (*b*), "against persons in the United Kingdom".

18. In section 47 (interpretation), in subsection (3) (construction of references to a court's jurisdiction), after "the reference is" insert "to assets being located or" and omit the words "or having ceased to reside".

Sections 15(4), 23(2) and 36(6)
      SCHEDULE 12

CONSEQUENTIAL AMENDMENTS

PART I

AMENDMENTS CONSEQUENTIAL ON PART I OF THIS ACT

Army Act 1955 (c. 18) and Air Force Act 1955 (c. 19)
1. In section 150 of the Army Act 1955 and in section 150 of the Air Force Act 1955 (enforcement of maintenance and other orders by deduction from pay), in subsection (5), after "Part I of the Maintenance Orders (Reciprocal Enforcement) Act 1972" insert "or Part I of the Civil Jurisdiction and Judgments Act 1982".

Naval Discipline Act 1957 (c. 53)
2. In section 101 of the Naval Discipline Act 1957 (service of process in maintenance and other proceedings), in subsection (5), after "Part I of the Maintenance Orders (Reciprocal Enforcement) Act 1972" insert "or Part I of the Civil Jurisdiction and Judgments Act 1982".

Maintenance Orders Act 1958 (c. 39)
3. In section 1 of the Maintenance Orders Act 1958 (scope of application of Part I), in subsection (4), for the words from "within the meaning" to "the said Part I" substitute "which is registered in a magistrates' court under Part I of the Maintenance Orders (Reciprocal Enforcement) Act 1972 or Part I of the Civil Jurisdiction and Judgments Act 1982".

Maintenance and Affiliation Orders Act (Northern Ireland) 1966 (c. 35) (N.I.)
4. In section 10 of the Maintenance and Affiliation Orders Act (Northern Ireland) 1966 (orders to which Part II of that Act applies), in subsections (2) and (5), after "Part I of the Maintenance Orders (Reciprocal Enforcement) Act 1972" insert "or Part I of the Civil Jurisdiction and Judgments Act 1982."

Administration of Justice Act 1970 (c. 31)
5. In Schedule 8 to the Administration of Justice Act 1970 (orders which are "maintenance orders" for the purposes of Part II of that Act and Part II of the Maintenance Orders Act 1958), after paragraph 12 insert—
    "13. A maintenance order within the meaning of Part I of the Civil Jurisdiction and Judgments Act 1982 which is registered in a magistrates' court under that Part.".

Attachment of Earnings Act 1971 (c. 32)
6. In Schedule 1 to the Attachment of Earnings Act 1971 (orders which are "maintenance orders" for the purposes of that Act), after paragraph 12 insert—

"13. A maintenance order within the meaning of Part I of the Civil Jurisdiction and Judgments Act 1982 which is registered in a magistrates' court under that Part.".

Magistrates' Courts Act 1980 (c. 43)

7. In section 65 of the Magistrates' Courts Act 1980 (definition of "domestic proceedings" for the purposes of that Act)—

(a) in subsection (1), after paragraph (l) insert—

"(m) Part I of the Civil Jurisdiction and Judgments Act 1982, so far as that Part relates to the recognition or enforcement of maintenance orders;";

(b) in subsection (2)(a), after "(k)" insert "and (m)."

Magistrates' Courts (Northern Ireland) Order 1981 (S.I. 1981/1675 (N.I.26))

8.—(1) In Article 88 of the Magistrates' Courts (Northern Ireland) Order 1981 (definition of "domestic proceedings" for the purposes of that Order), in paragraph (a), after "Part I of the Maintenance Orders (Reciprocal Enforcement) Act 1972" insert "or under Part I of the Civil Jurisdiction and Judgments Act 1982 so far as that Part relates to the recognition and enforcement of maintenance orders."

(2) In Article 98 of that Order (enforcement of orders for periodical payment of money), in sub-paragraph (b) of paragraph (11), after "Part I of the Maintenance Orders (Reciprocal Enforcement) Act 1972" insert "or Part I of the Civil Jurisdiction and Judgments Act 1982."

PART II

AMENDMENTS CONSEQUENTIAL ON SCHEDULE 8

Law Reform (Miscellaneous Provisions) (Scotland) Act 1940 (c. 42)

1. In the Law Reform (Miscellaneous Provisions) (Scotland) Act 1940 after section 4(2) there shall be inserted the following subsection—

"(3) This section does not apply—

(a) in the case of an agreement entered into after the dispute in respect of which the agreement is intended to have effect has arisen; or

(b) where the contract is one referred to in Rule 3 of Schedule 8 to the Civil Jurisdiction and Judgments Act 1982.".

Maintenance Orders Act 1950 (c. 37)

2. In section 15(1)(b) of the Maintenance Orders Act 1950 for the words "for separation and aliment" there shall be substituted the words "which contains a conclusion for aliment not falling within the scope of paragraph (a)(i) above".

Maintenance Orders (Reciprocal Enforcement) Act 1972 (c. 18)

3.—(1) In section 4 of the Maintenance Orders (Reciprocal Enforcement) Act 1972 (power of the sheriff to make a provisional maintenance order against a person residing in a reciprocating country) the following subsection shall be substituted for subsections (1) and (2)—

"(1) In any action where the sheriff has jurisdiction by virtue of Rule 2(5) of Schedule 8 to the Civil Jurisdiction and Judgments Act 1982 and the defender resides in a reciprocating country, any maintenance order granted by the sheriff shall be a provisional order.".

(2) In subsections (3), (4) and (5) of that section for the words "in which the sheriff has jurisdiction by virtue of" there shall be substituted in each place where they occur the words "referred to in."

Consumer Credit Act 1974 (c. 39)

4. In section 141 of the Consumer Credit Act 1974 the following subsections shall be substituted for subsection (3)—

"(3) In Scotland the sheriff court shall have jurisdiction to hear and determine any action referred to in subsection (1) and such an action shall not be brought in any other court.

(3A) Subject to subsection (3B) an action which is brought in the sheriff court by virtue of subsection (3) shall be brought only in one of the following courts, namely—

(a) the court for the place where the debtor or hirer is domiciled (within the meaning of section 41 or 42 of the Civil Jurisdiction and Judgments Act 1982);

(b) the court for the place where the debtor or hirer carries on business; and

Appendix 1

(c) where the purpose of the action is to assert, declare or determine proprietary or possessory right, or rights of security, in or over moveable property, or to obtain authority to dispose of moveable property, the court for the place where the property is situated.

(3B) Subsection (3A) shall not apply—

(a) where Rule 3 of Schedule 8 to the said Act of 1982 applies; or

(b) where the jurisdiction of another court has been prorogated by an agreement entered into after the dispute has arisen.".

PART III

AMENDMENTS CONSEQUENTIAL ON SECTION 36

Maintenance Orders Act 1950 (c. 37)

1.—(1) The Maintenance Orders Act 1950 is amended as follows.

(2) In section 18 (enforcement of registered orders), after subsection (3A) insert—

"(3B) Notwithstanding subsection (1) above, no court in Northern Ireland in which a maintenance order is registered under this Part of this Act shall enforce that order to the extent that it is for the time being registered in another court in Northern Ireland under section 36 of the Civil Jurisdiction and Judgments Act 1982.".

(3) In section 21(2) (evidence admissible before court where order registered)—

(a) in paragraph (a) after "1958" insert "or under section 36 of the Civil Jurisdiction and Judgments Act 1982";

(b) after "that Act" (twice) insert "of 1958";

(c) after paragraph (b) insert—

"(c) registered in a court in Northern Ireland under section 36 of the Civil Jurisdiction and Judgments Act 1982."

(4) In section 24(3) (notice of cancellation of order to be given to other courts interested), after "Part I of the Maintenance Orders Act 1958" insert "or section 36 of the Civil Jurisdiction and Judgments Act 1982."

Maintenance Orders Act 1958 (c. 39)

2. In section 23(2) of the Maintenance Orders Act 1958 (provisions which extend to Scotland and Northern Ireland) after "section 2" insert "section 2A."

Maintenance and Affiliation Orders Act (Northern Ireland) 1966 (c. 35) (N.I.)

3.—(1) The Maintenance and Affiliation Orders Act (Northern Ireland) 1966 is amended as follows.

(2) At the beginning of section 9 (introductory provisions relating to registration in one court of maintenance order made by another) insert "Without prejudice to section 36 of the Civil Jurisdiction and Judgments Act 1982,".

(3) In section 10 (orders to which Part II applies), after subsection (1) insert—

"(1A) This Part, except sections 11, 11A and 14(2) and (3), also applies in accordance with section 36 of the Civil Jurisdiction and Judgments Act 1982 to maintenance orders made by a court in England and Wales or Scotland and registered in Northern Ireland under Part II of the Maintenance Orders Act 1950.".

(4) In section 13 (variation of orders registered in courts of summary jurisdiction), after subsection (7) insert—

"(7A) No application for any variation in respect of a registered order shall be made to any court in respect of an order made by the High Court of Justice in England or the Court of Session and registered in that court under section 36 of the Civil Jurisdiction and Judgments Act 1982.".

Judgments Enforcement (Northern Ireland)
Order 1981 (S.I. 1981/266 (N.I. 6))

4. In Article 98 of the Judgments Enforcement (Northern Ireland) Order 1981, (powers of court to make attachment of earnings orders), in sub-paragraph (iv) of paragraph (a) at the end add "but not subsequently registered in a court of summary jurisdiction under section 36 of the Civil Jurisdiction and Judgments Act 1982."

Magistrates' Courts (Northern Ireland) Order 1981 (S.I. 1981/1675 (N.I.26))

5.—(1) In Article 88 of the Magistrates' Courts (Northern Ireland) Order 1981 (definition of "domestic proceedings" for the purposes of that Order)—

(a) in paragraph (a), delete the words "or the Maintenance Orders Act 1950";

(b) after paragraph (a) insert—

"(*aa*) in relation to maintenance orders registered in a court of summary jurisdiction under the Maintenance Orders Act 1950 or Part II of the Maintenance and Affiliation Orders Act (Northern Ireland) 1966 or section 36 of the Civil Jurisdiction and Judgments Act 1982, under that Act of 1950 or Part II of that Act of 1966."

(2) In Article 98 of that Order (enforcement of orders for periodical payment of money), in sub-paragraph (*d*) of paragraph (11), at the end add—

"or under section 36 of the Civil Jurisdiction and Judgments Act 1982."

Section 53

SCHEDULE 13

COMMENCEMENT, TRANSITIONAL PROVISIONS AND SAVINGS

PART I

COMMENCEMENT

Provisions coming into force on Royal Assent

1. The following provisions come into force on Royal Assent:

Provision	Subject-matter
section 53(1) and Part 1 of this Schedule.	Commencement.
section 55	Short title.

Provisions coming into force six weeks after Royal Assent

2. The following provisions come into force at the end of the period of six weeks beginning with the day on which this Act is passed:

Provision	Subject-matter
section 24(1)(*a*), (2)(*a*) and (3).	Interim relief and protective measures in cases of doubtful jurisdiction.
section 29	Service of county court process outside Northern Ireland.
section 30	Proceedings in England and Wales or Northern Ireland for torts to immovable property.
section 31	Overseas judgments given against states.
section 32	Overseas judgments given in breach of agreement for settlement of disputes.
section 33	Certain steps not to amount to submission to jurisdiction of overseas court.
section 34	Certain judgments a bar to further proceedings on the same cause of action.
section 35(3)	Consolidation of Orders in Council under section 14 of the Administration of Justice Act 1920.
section 38	Overseas judgments counteracting an award of multiple damages.
section 40	Power to modify enactments relating to legal aid, etc.
section 49	Saving for powers to stay, sist, strike out or dismiss proceedings.
section 50	Interpretation: general.
section 51	Application to Crown.
section 52	Extent.
paragraphs 7 to 10 of Part II of this Schedule and section 53(2) so far as relates to those paragraphs.	Transitional provisions and savings.
section 54 and Schedule 14 so far as relating to the repeal of provisions in section 4 of the Foreign Judgments (Reciprocal Enforcement) Act 1933.	Repeals consequential on sections 32 and 33.

Provisions coming into force on a day to be appointed

3.—(1) The other provisions of this Act come into force on such day as the Lord Chancellor and the Lord Advocate may appoint by order made by statutory instrument.

(2) Different days may be appointed under this paragraph for different purposes.

PART II

TRANSITIONAL PROVISIONS AND SAVINGS

Section 16 and Schedule 4

1.—(1) Section 16 and Schedule 4 shall not apply to any proceedings begun before the commencement of that section.

(2) Nothing in section 16 or Schedule 4 shall preclude the bringing of proceedings in any part of the United Kingdom in connection with a dispute concerning a contract if the parties to the dispute had agreed before the commencement of that section that the contract was to be governed by the law of that part of the United Kingdom.

Section 18 and Schedule 6 and associated repeals

2.—(1) In relation to a judgment a certificate whereof has been registered under the 1868 Act or the 1882 Act before the repeal of that Act by this Act, the 1868 Act or, as the case may be, the 1882 Act shall continue to have effect notwithstanding its repeal.

(2) Where by virtue of sub-paragraph (1) the 1882 Act continues to have effect in relation to an order to which section 47 of the Fair Employment (Northern Ireland) Act 1976 (damages etc. for unfair discrimination) applies, that section shall continue to have effect in relation to that order notwithstanding the repeal of that section by this Act.

(3) A certificate issued under Schedule 6 shall not be registered under that Schedule in a part of the United Kingdom if the judgment to which that certificate relates is the subject of a certificate registered in that part under the 1868 Act or the 1882 Act.

(4) In this paragraph—

"the 1868 Act" means the Judgments Extension Act 1868;

"the 1882 Act" means the Inferior Courts Judgments Extension Act 1882;

"judgment" has the same meaning as in section 18.

Section 18 and Schedule 7

3. Schedule 7 and, so far as it relates to that Schedule, section 18 shall not apply to judgments given before the coming into force of that section.

Section 19

4. Section 19 shall not apply to judgments given before the commencement of that section.

Section 20 and Schedule 8

5. Section 20 and Schedule 8 shall not apply to any proceedings begun before the commencement of that section.

Section 26

6. The power conferred by section 26 shall not be exercisable in relation to property arrested before the commencement of that section or in relation to bail or other security given—

(a) before the commencement of that section to prevent the arrest of property; or

(b) to obtain the release of property arrested before the commencement of that section; or

(c) in substitution (whether directly or indirectly), for security given as mentioned in sub-paragraph (a) or (b).

Section 31

7. Section 31 shall not apply to any judgment—

(a) which has been registered under Part II of the Administration of Justice Act 1920 or Part I of the Foreign Judgments (Reciprocal Enforcement) Act 1933 before the time when that section comes into force; or

(b) in respect of which proceedings at common law for its enforcement have been finally determined before that time.

Section 32 and associated repeal

8.—(1) Section 32 shall not apply to any judgment—

(a) which has been registered under Part II of the Administration of Justice Act 1920, Part I of the Foreign Judgments (Reciprocal Enforcement) Act 1933 or Part I of the Maintenance Orders (Reciprocal Enforcement) Act 1972 before the time when that section comes into force; or

(b) in respect of which proceedings at common law for its enforcement have been finally determined before that time.

(2) Section 4(3)(b) of the Foreign Judgments (Reciprocal Enforcement) Act 1933 shall continue to have effect, notwithstanding its repeal by this Act, in relation to a judgment registered under Part I of that Act before the commencement of section 32.

Section 33 and associated repeal

9.—(1) Section 33 shall not apply to any judgment—

(a) which has been registered under Part II of the Administration of Justice Act 1920 or Part I of the Foreign Judgments (Reciprocal Enforcement) Act 1933 before the time when that section comes into force; or

(b) in respect of which proceedings at common law for its enforcement have been finally determined before that time.

(2) The repeal by this Act of words in section 4(2)(a)(i) of the Foreign Judgments (Reciprocal Enforcement) Act 1933 shall not affect the operation of that provision in relation to a judgment registered under Part I of that Act before the commencement of section 33.

Section 34

10. Section 34 shall not apply to judgments given before the commencement of that section.

Section 54   SCHEDULE 14

REPEALS

Chapter	Short title	Extent of repeal
41 Geo. 3.c. 90.	Crown Debts Act 1801.	The preamble. Sections 1 to 8.
5 Geo. 4. c. 111.	Crown Debts Act 1824.	The whole Act.
22 & 23 Vict. c. 21.	Queen's Remembrancer Act 1859.	Section 24.
31 & 32 Vict. c. 54.	Judgments Extension Act 1868.	The whole Act.
31 & 32 Vict. c. 96.	Ecclesiastical Buildings and Glebes (Scotland) Act 1868.	In section 4, the words "of the county in which the parish concerned is situated" and the words from "provided" to the end.
45 & 46 Vict. c. 31.	Inferior Courts Judgments Extension Act 1882.	The whole Act.
7 Edw. 7. c. 51.	Sheriff Courts (Scotland) Act 1907.	In section 5, the words from the first "Provided" to "that jurisdiction."
14 & 15 Geo. 5. c. 27.	Conveyancing (Scotland) Act 1924.	In section 23(6) the words from "of the county" to "is situated."
23 & 24 Geo. 5. c. 13.	Foreign Judgments (Reciprocal Enforcement) Act 1933.	In section 4(2)(a)(i), the words from "otherwise" to "that court". Section 4(3)(b). In section 9(1), the word "superior" in both places where it occurs. In section 11(1), the definition of "Judgments given in the superior courts of the United Kingdom." In section 12, in paragraph (a) the words from "(except" to "this Act)", and paragraph(d). In section 13(b), the words "and section two hundred and thirteen," "respectively" and "and 116."

Appendix 1

Chapter	Short title	Extent of repeal
14 Geo. 6. c. 37.	Maintenance Orders Act 1950.	Section 6. Section 8. Section 9(1)(*a*). In section 16(2)(*b*)(v), the words from the begining to "or."
4 & 5 Eliz. 2. c. 46.	Administration of Justice Act 1956.	Section 51(*a*).
1963 c. 22.	Sheriff Courts (Civil Jurisdiction and Procedure) (Scotland) Act 1963.	Section 3(2).
1965 c. 2.	Administration of Justice Act 1965.	In Schedule 1, the entry relating to the Crown Debts Act 1801.
1971 c. 55.	Law Reform (Jurisdiction in Delict) (Scotland) Act 1971.	The whole Act.
1972 c. 18.	Maintenance Orders (Reciprocal Enforcement) Act 1972.	In section 40— (*a*) in paragraph (*a*), the words "against persons in that country or territory"; and (*b*) in paragraph (*b*), the words "against persons in the United Kingdom." In section 47(3), the words "or having ceased to reside." In the Schedule, paragraph 4.
1976 c. 25.	Fair Employment (Northern Ireland) Act 1976.	Section 47.
1978 c. 23.	Judicature (Northern Ireland) Act 1978.	In Part II of Schedule 5— (*a*) the entry relating to the Crown Debts Act 1801; and (*b*) in the entry relating to the Foreign Judgments (Reciprocal Enforcement) Act 1933, the word "respectively," where last occurring, and the words "and 116."
1981 c. 54	Supreme Court Act 1981.	In Schedule 5, paragraph 2 of the entry relating to the Foreign Judgments (Reciprocal Enforcement) Act 1933.

APPENDIX 2

ACCESSION CONVENTION
WITH GREECE

CONVENTION

on the accession of the Hellenic Republic to the Convention on jurisdiction
and enforcement of judgments in civil and commercial matters and to the
Protocol on its interpretation by the Court of Justice with the adjustments
made to them by the Convention on the accession of the Kingdom of
Denmark, of Ireland and of the United Kingdom of Great Britain and
Northern Ireland signed on October 25, 1982.*

TITLE I

General provisions

Article 1

1.   The Hellenic Republic hereby accedes to the Convention on jurisdiction and enforcement of judgments in civil and commercial matters,
signed at Brussels on 27 September 1968 (hereinafter called "the 1968
Convention"), and to the Protocol on its interpretation by the Court of
Justice, signed at Luxembourg on 3 June 1971 (hereinafter called "the 1971
Protocol"), with the adjustments made to them by the Convention on the
accession of the Kingdom of Denmark, of Ireland and of the United
Kingdom of Great Britain and Northern Ireland to the Convention on
jurisdiction and enforcement of judgments in civil and commercial matters
and to the Protocol on its interpretation by the Court of Justice, signed at
Luxembourg on 9 October 1978 (hereinafter called "the 1978 Convention").

2.   The accession of the Hellenic Republic extends, in particular, to
Articles 25(2), 35 and 36 of the 1978 Convention.

Article 2

The adjustments made by this Convention to the 1968 Convention and the
1971 Protocol, as adjusted by the 1978 Convention, are set out in Titles II
to IV.

---

*See O.J. L 388, December 31, 1982, pp. 1–5.

Appendix 2

TITLE II

Adjustments to the 1968 Convention

Article 3

The following shall be inserted between the third and fourth indents in the second subparagraph of Article 3 of the 1968 Convention, as amended by Article 4 of the 1978 Convention:

"— in Greece, Article 40 of the code of civil procedure (Κώδικας Πολιτικῆς Δικονομίας),".

Article 4

The following shall be inserted between the third and fourth indents in the first subparagraph of Article 32 of the 1968 Convention, as amended by Article 16 of the 1978 Convention:

"— in Greece, to the μονομελές πρωτοδικεῖο,".

Article 5

1. The following shall be inserted between the third and fourth indents of the first subparagraph of Article 37 of the 1968 Convention, as amended by Article 17 of the 1978 Convention:

"— in Greece, with the ἐφετεῖο,".

2. The following shall be substituted for the first indent of the second subparagraph of Article 37 of the 1968 Convention, as amended by Article 17 of the 1978 Convention:

"— in Belgium, Greece, France, Italy, Luxembourg and in the Netherlands, by an appeal in cassation,".

Article 6

The following shall be inserted between the third and fourth indents of the first subparagraph of Article 40 of the 1968 Convention, as amended by Article 19 of the 1978 Convention:

"— in Greece, to the ἐφετεῖο,".

Article 7

The following shall be substituted for the first indent of Article 41 of the 1968 Convention, as amended by Article 20 of the 1978 Convention:

"— in Belgium, Greece, France, Italy, Luxembourg and in the Netherlands, by an appeal in cassation,".

Article 8

The following shall be inserted at the appropriate place in chronological order in the list of Conventions set out in Article 55 of the 1968 Convention, as amended by Article 24 of the 1978 Convention:
"— the Convention between the Kingdom of Greece and the Federal Republic of Germany for the reciprocal recognition and enforcement of judgments, settlements and authentic instruments in civil and commercial matters, signed in Athens on 4 November 1961,".

TITLE III

Adjustment to the Protocol annexed to the 1968 Convention

Article 9

In the first sentence of the Article Vb added to the Protocol annexed to the 1968 Convention by Article 29 of the 1978 Convention there shall be added after the word "Denmark" a comma and the words "in Greece".

TITLE IV

Adjustments to the 1971 Protocol

Article 10

The following subparagraph shall be added to Article 1 of the 1971 Protocol, as amended by Article 30 of the 1978 Convention:
"The Court of Justice of the European Communities shall also have jurisdiction to give rulings on the interpretation of the Convention on the accession of the Hellenic Republic to the Convention of 27 September 1968 and to this Protocol, as adjusted by the 1978 Convention."

Article 11

The following shall be inserted between the third and fourth indents of point 1 of Article 2 of the 1971 Protocol, as amended by Article 31 of the 1978 Convention:
"— in Greece: the ἀνώτατα δικαστήρια,".

TITLE V

Transitional provisions

Article 12

1.   The 1968 Convention and the 1971 Protocol, as amended by the 1978 Convention and this Convention, shall apply only to legal proceedings instituted and to authentic instruments formally drawn up or registered after the entry into force of this Convention in the State of origin and, where recognition or enforcement of a judgment or authentic instrument is sought, in the State addressed.

2.   However, judgments given after the date of entry into force of this Convention between the State of origin and the State addressed in proceedings instituted before that date shall be recognized and enforced in accordance with the provisions of Title III of the 1968 Convention, as amended by the 1978 Convention and this Convention, if jurisdiction was founded upon rules which accorded with the provisions of Title II of the 1968 Convention, as amended, or with the provisions of a convention which was in force between the State of origin and the State addressed when the proceedings were instituted.

TITLE VI

Final provisions

Article 13

The Secretary-General of the Council of the European Communities shall transmit a certified copy of the 1968 Convention, of the 1971 Protocol and of the 1978 Convention in the Danish, Dutch, English, French, German, Irish and Italian languages to the Government of the Hellenic Republic.

The texts of the 1968 Convention, of the 1971 Protocol and of the 1978 Convention, drawn up in the Greek language, shall be annexed to this Convention. The texts drawn up in the Greek language shall be authentic under the same conditions as the other texts of the 1968 Convention, the 1971 Protocol and the 1978 Convention.

Article 14

This Convention shall be ratified by the signatory States. The instruments of ratification shall be deposited with the Secretary-General of the Council of the European Communities.

Article 15

This Convention shall enter into force, as between the States which have ratified it, on the first day of the third month following the deposit of the last instrument of ratification by the Hellenic Republic and those States which have put into force the 1978 Convention in accordance with Article 39 of that Convention.

It shall enter into force for each Member State which subsequently ratifies it on the first day of the third month following the deposit of its instrument of ratification.

Article 16

The Secretary-General of the Council of the European Communities shall notify the signatory States of:
  (a) the deposit of each instrument of ratification;
  (b) the dates of entry into force of this Convention for the Contracting States.

Article 17

This Convention, drawn up in a single original in the Danish, Dutch, English, French, German, Greek, Irish and Italian languages, all eight texts being equally authentic, shall be deposited in the archives of the General Secretariat of the Council of the European Communities. The Secretary-General shall transmit a certified copy to the Government of each signatory State.

CONVENTION ON THE SERVICE ABROAD OF JUDICIAL AND EXTRAJUDICIAL DOCUMENTS IN CIVIL OR COMMERCIAL MATTERS

(Concluded November 15, 1965)

The States signatory to the present Convention,

Desiring to create appropriate means to ensure that judicial and extrajudicial documents to be served abroad shall be brought to the notice of the addressee in sufficient time,

Desiring to improve the organisation of mutual judicial assistance for that purpose by simplifying and expediting the procedure,

Have resolved to conclude a Convention to this effect and have agreed upon the following provisions:

Article 1

The present Convention shall apply in all cases, in civil or commercial matters, where there is occasion to transmit a judicial or extrajudicial document for service abroad.

This Convention shall not apply where the address of the person to be served with the document is not known.

CHAPTER I—JUDICIAL DOCUMENTS

Article 2

Each contracting State shall designate a Central Authority which will undertake to receive requests for service coming from other contracting States and to proceed in conformity with the provisions of articles 3 to 6.

Each State shall organise the Central Authority in conformity with its own law.

Article 3

The authority or judicial officer competent under the law of the State in which the documents originate shall forward to the Central Authority of the State addressed a request conforming to the model annexed to the present Convention, without any requirement of legalisation or other equivalent formality.

The document to be served or a copy thereof shall be annexed to the request. The request and the document shall both be furnished in duplicate.

Article 4

If the Central Authority considers that the request does not comply with the provisions of the present Convention it shall promptly inform the applicant and specify its objections to the request.

Article 5

The Central Authority of the State addressed shall itself serve the document or shall arrange to have it served by an appropriate agency, either—

(a) by a method prescribed by its internal law for the service of documents in domestic actions upon persons who are within its territory, or

(b) by a particular method requested by the applicant, unless such a method is incompatible with the law of the State addressed.

Subject to sub-paragraph (b) of the first paragraph of this article, the document may always be served by delivery to an addressee who accepts it voluntarily.

If the document is to be served under the first paragraph above, the Central Authority may require the document to be written in, or translated into, the official language or one of the official languages of the State addressed.

That part of the request, in the form attached to the present Convention, which contains a summary of the document to be served, shall be served with the document.

Article 6

The Central Authority of the State addressed or any authority which it may have designated for that purpose, shall complete a certificate in the form of the model annexed to the present Convention.

The certificate shall state that the document has been served and shall include the method, the place and the date of service and the person to whom the document was delivered. If the document has not been served, the certificate shall set out the reasons which have prevented service.

The applicant may require that a certificate not completed by a Central Authority or by a judicial authority shall be countersigned by one of these authorities.

The certificate shall be forwarded directly to the applicant.

Article 7

The standard terms in the model annexed to the present Convention shall in all cases be written either in French or in English. They may also be written in the official language, or in one of the official languages, of the State in which the documents originate.

The corresponding blanks shall be completed either in the language of the State addressed or in French or in English.

Article 8

Each contracting State shall be free to effect service of judicial documents upon persons abroad, without application of any compulsion, directly through its diplomatic or consular agents.

Any State may declare that it is opposed to such service within its territory, unless the document is to be served upon a national of the State in which the documents originate.

Article 9

Each contracting State shall be free, in addition, to use consular channels to forward documents, for the purpose of service, to those authorities of another contracting State which are designated by the latter for this purpose.

Each contracting State may, if exceptional circumstances so require, use diplomatic channels for the same purpose.

Article 10

Provided the State of destination does not object, the present Convention shall not interfere with—

(a) the freedom to send judicial documents, by postal channels, directly to persons abroad, (*b*) the freedom of judicial officers, officials or other competent persons of the State of origin to effect service of judicial documents directly through the judicial officers, officials or other competent persons of the State of destination,

(*c*) the freedom of any person interested in a judicial proceeding to effect service of judicial documents directly through the judicial officers, officials or other competent persons of the State of destination.

Article 11

The present Convention shall not prevent two or more contracting States from agreeing to permit, for the purpose of service of judicial documents, channels of transmission other than those provided for in the preceding articles and, in particular, direct communication between their respective authorities.

Article 12

The service of judicial documents coming from a contracting State shall not give rise to any payment or reimbursement of taxes or costs for the services rendered by the State addressed.

The applicant shall pay or reimburse the costs occasioned by—

(*a*) the employment of a judicial officer or of a person competent under the law of the State of destination,

(*b*) the use of a particular method of service.

Article 13

Where a request for service complies with the terms of the present Convention, the State addressed may refuse to comply therewith only if it deems that compliance would infringe its sovereignty or security.

It may not refuse to comply solely on the ground that, under its internal law, it claims exclusive jurisdiction over the subject-matter of the action or that its internal law would not permit the action upon which the application is based.

The Central Authority shall, in case of refusal, promptly inform the applicant and state the reasons for the refusal.

Article 14

Difficulties which may arise in connection with the transmission of judicial documents for service shall be settled through diplomatic channels.

Article 15

Where a writ of summons or an equivalent document had to be transmitted abroad for the purpose of service, under the provisions of the present Convention, and the defendant has not appeared, judgment shall not be given until it is established that—

(*a*) the document was served by a method prescribed by the internal law of the State addressed for the service of documents in domestic actions upon persons who are within its territory, or

(*b*) the document was actually delivered to the defendant or to his residence by another method provided for by this Convention,

and that in either of these cases the service or the delivery was effected in sufficient time to enable the defendant to defend.

Each contracting State shall be free to declare that the judge, notwithstanding the provisions of the first paragraph of this article, may give judgment even if no certificate of service or delivery has been received, if all the following conditions are fulfilled—

(*a*) the document was transmitted by one of the methods provided for in this Convention,

(*b*) a period of time of not less than six months, considered adequate by the judge in the particular case, has elapsed since the date of the transmission of the document,

(*c*) no certificate of any kind has been received, even though every reasonable effort has been made to obtain it through the competent authorities of the State addressed.

Notwithstanding the provisions of the preceding paragraphs the judge may order, in case of urgency, any provisional or protective measures.

Article 16

When a writ of summons or an equivalent document had to be transmitted abroad for the purpose of service, under the provisions of the present Convention, and a judgment has been entered against a defendant who had not appeared, the judge shall have the power to relieve the defendant from the effects of the expiration of the time for appeal from the judgment if the following conditions are fulfilled—

(*a*) the defendant, without any fault on his part, did not have knowledge of the document in sufficient time to defend, or knowledge of the judgment in sufficient time to appeal, and

(*b*) the defendant has disclosed a *prima facie* defence to the action on the merits.

An application for relief may be filed only within a reasonable time after the defendant has knowledge of the judgment.

Each contracting State may declare that the application will not be entertained if it is filed after the expiration of a time to be stated in the declaration, but which shall in no case be less than one year following the date of the judgment.

This article shall not apply to judgments concerning status or capacity of persons.

Article 17

Extrajudicial documents emanating from authorities and judicial officers of a contracting State may be transmitted for the purpose of service in another contracting State by the methods and under the provisions of the present Convention.

CHAPTER III—GENERAL CLAUSES

Article 18

Each contracting State may designate other authorities in addition to the Central Authority and shall determine the extent of their competence.

The applicant shall, however, in all cases, have the right to address a request directly to the Central Authority.

Federal States shall be free to designate more than one Central Authority.

Article 19

To the extent that the internal law of a contracting State permits methods of transmission, other than those provided for in the preceding articles, of documents coming from abroad, for service within its territory, the present Convention shall not affect such provisions.

Article 20

The present Convention shall not prevent an agreement between any two or more contracting States to dispense with—

(a) the necessity for duplicate copies of transmitted documents as required by the second paragraph of article 3,
(b) the language requirements of the third paragraph of article 5 and article 7,
(c) the provisions of the fourth paragraph of article 5,
(d) the provisions of the second paragraph of article 12.

Article 21

Each contracting State shall, at the time of the deposit of its instrument of ratification or accession, or at a later date, inform the Ministry of Foreign Affairs of the Netherlands of the following—

(*a*) the designation of authorities, pursuant to articles 2 and 18,

(*b*) the designation of the authority competent to complete the certificate pursuant to article 6,

(*c*) the designation of the authority competent to receive documents transmitted by consular channels, pursuant to article 9.

Each contracting State shall similarly inform the Ministry, where appropriate, of—

(*a*) opposition to the use of methods of transmission pursuant to articles 8 and 10,

(*b*) declarations pursuant to the second paragraph of article 15 and the third paragraph of article 16,

(*c*) all modifications of the above designations, oppositions and declarations.

Article 22

Where Parties to the present Convention are also Parties to one or both of the Conventions on civil procedure signed at The Hague on 17th July 1905, and on 1st March 1954, this Convention shall replace as between them articles 1 to 7 of the earlier Conventions.

Article 23

The present Convention shall not affect the application of article 23 of the Convention on civil procedure signed at The Hague on 17th July 1905, or of article 24 of the Convention on civil procedure signed at The Hague on 1st March 1954.

These articles shall, however, apply only if methods of communication, identical to those provided for in these Conventions, are used.

Article 24

Supplementary agreements between parties to the Conventions of 1905 and 1954 shall be considered as equally applicable to the present Convention, unless the parties have otherwise agreed.

Article 25

Without prejudice to the provisions of articles 22 and 24, the present Convention shall not derogate from Conventions containing provisions on the matters governed by this Convention to which the contracting States are, or shall become, Parties.

Article 26

The present Convention shall be open for signature by the States represented at the Tenth Session of the Hague Conference on Private International Law.

It shall be ratified, and the instruments of ratification shall be deposited with the Ministry of Foreign Affairs of the Netherlands.

Article 27

The present Convention shall enter into force on the sixtieth day after the deposit of the third instrument of ratification referred to in the second paragraph of article 26.

The Convention shall enter into force for each signatory State which ratifies subsequently on the sixtieth day after the deposit of its instrument of ratification.

Article 28

Any State not represented at the Tenth Session of the Hague Conference on Private International Law may accede to the present Convention after it has entered into force in accordance with the first paragraph of article 27. The instrument of accession shall be deposited with the Ministry of Foreign Affairs of the Netherlands.

The Convention shall enter into force for such a State in the absence of any objection from a State, which has ratified the Convention before such deposit, notified to the Ministry of Foreign Affairs of the Netherlands within a period of six months after the date on which the said Ministry has notified it of such accession.

In the absence of any such objection, the Convention shall enter into force for the acceding State on the first day of the month following the expiration of the last of the periods referred to in the preceding paragraph.

Article 29

Any State may, at the time of signature, ratification or accession, declare that the present Convention shall extend to all the territories for the international relations of which it is responsible, or to one or more of them. Such a declaration shall take effect on the date of entry into force of the Convention for the State concerned.

At any time thereafter, such extensions shall be notified to the Ministry of Foreign Affairs of the Netherlands.

The Convention shall enter into force for the territories mentioned in such an extension on the sixtieth day after the notification referred to in the preceding paragraph.

Article 30

The present Convention shall remain in force for five years from the date of its entry into force in accordance with the first paragraph of article 27, even for States which have ratified it or acceded to it subsequently.

If there has been no denunciation, it shall be renewed tacitly every five years.

Any denunciation shall be notified to the Ministry of Foreign Affairs of the Netherlands at least six months before the end of the five year period.

It may be limited to certain of the territories to which the Convention applies.

The denunciation shall have effect only as regards the State which has notified it. The Convention shall remain in force for the other contracting States.

Article 31

The Ministry of Foreign Affairs of the Netherlands shall give notice to the States referred to in article 26, and to the States which have acceded in accordance with article 28, of the following—

(*a*) the signatures and ratifications referred to in article 26;

(*b*) the date on which the present Convention enters into force in accordance with the first paragraph of article 27;

(*c*) the accessions referred to in article 28 and the dates on which they take effect;

(*d*) the extensions referred to in article 29 and the dates on which they take effect;

(*e*) the designations, oppositions and declarations referred to in article 21;

(*f*) the denunciations referred to in the third paragraph of article 30.

In witness whereof the undersigned, being duly authorised thereto, have signed the present Convention.

Done at The Hague, on the 15th day of November, 1965, in the English and French languages, both texts being equally authentic, in a single copy which shall be deposited in the archives of the Government of the Netherlands, and of which a certified copy shall be sent, through the diplomatic channel, to each of the States represented at the Tenth Session of the Hague Conference on Private International Law.

FORMS (REQUEST AND CERTIFICATE)
SUMMARY OF THE DOCUMENT TO BE SERVED

(annexes provided for articles 3, 5, 6 and 7)

Appendix 3

SUMMARY OF THE DOCUMENT TO BE SERVED

Convention on the Service Abroad of Judicial and Extrajudicial Documents in
Civil or Commercial Matters,
signed at The Hague, the 15th of November 1965.

(article 5, fourth paragraph)

Name and address of the requesting authority: ....
....
....

Particulars of the parties*: ....
....
....

JUDICIAL DOCUMENT**

Nature and purpose of the document: ....
....

Nature and purpose of the proceedings and, where appropriate, the amount in
dispute:...
....

Date and place for entering appearance**: ....

Court which has given judgment**: ....

Date of judgment**: ....
Time-limits stated in the document**: ....
....

EXTRAJUDICIAL DOCUMENT**

Nature and purpose of the document: ....
....

Time-limits stated in the document**: ....
....
....

---

* If appropriate, identity and address of the person interested in the transmission of the
document.
** Delete if inappropriate.

Reverse of the request

CERTIFICATE

———————

The undersigned authority has the honour to certify, in conformity with article 6 of the Convention,

1) that the document has been served* —
         the (date) ....
     — at (place, street, number) ....
         ....
     — in one of the following methods authorised by article 5:
          (*a*) in accordance with the provisions of sub-paragraph (*a*) of the first paragraph of article 5 of the Convention*.
          (*b*) in accordance with the following particular method*: ....
          ....
          (*c*) by delivery to the addressee, who accepted it voluntarily*.
The documents referred to in the request have been delivered to:
     — (identity and description of person) ....
        ....
     — relationship to the addressee (family, business or other): ....
        ....
        ....

2) that the document has not been served, by reason of the following facts*:
        ....
        ....
        ....

In conformity with the second paragraph of article 12 of the Convention, the applicant is requested to pay or reimburse the expenses detailed in the attached statement*.

Annexes

Documents returned: ....
....
....

In appropriate cases, documents establishing the service:....................................
....
....
....

                             Done at ...., the........

                             Signature and/or stamp.

———————

*Delete if inappropriate.

Appendix 3

ANNEX TO THE CONVENTION

Forms

REQUEST
FOR SERVICE ABROAD OF JUDICIAL OR EXTRAJUDICIAL
DOCUMENTS

Convention on the Service Abroad of Judicial and Extrajudicial Documents in
Civil or Commercial Matters,
signed at The Hague, the 15th of November 1965.

Identity and address of the applicant	Address of receiving authority

The undersigned applicant has the honour to transmit – in duplicate – the documents listed below and, in conformity with article 5 of the above-mentioned Convention, requests prompt service of one copy thereof on the addressee, *i.e.*,
(identity and address)..
....

a) in accordance with the provisions of sub-paragraph (*a*) of the first paragraph of article 5 of the Convention*.
b) in accordance with the following particular method (sub-paragraph (*b*) of the first paragraph of article 5)*:..
....
....
c) by delivery to the addressee, if he accepts it voluntarily (second paragraph of article 5)*.

The authority is requested to return or to have returned to the applicant a copy of the documents – and of the annexes* – with a certificate as provided on the reverse side.

List of documents

....
....
....
....
....
....
....
....

Done at..........., the........

Signature and/or stamp.

---

*Delete if inappropriate.

INDEX

[References are to paragraph numbers]

ACCESSION CONVENTIONS
general, 1.07
Report on 1978 Convention, 2.02, 2.18
ACTOR SEQUITUR FORUM REI,
principle of, 5.04
ADHERENCE AND ALIMENT,
whether action relating to status, 3.14
included in Sched. 8, 10.08 (1), 10.29
ADMINISTRATIVE MATTERS,
excluded from Convention, 3.10–3.11
ADMIRALTY PROCEEDINGS. *See* MARITIME
MATTERS.
AGENCY. *See* BRANCH, AGENCY OR ESTAB-
LISHMENT.
AGREEMENTS ON JURISDICTION. *See* PROROGA-
TION AGREEMENTS.
AIRCRAFT MORTGAGES,
proceedings for rectification of the register
of,
excluded from inter-U.K. scheme, 9.12
excluded from Scottish scheme, 10.08
AKROTIRI AND DHEKELIA,
application of Convention and extension
of 1982 Act to, 3.43
ANCILLARY AND INCIDENTAL MATTERS,
jurisdiction under inter-United Kingdom
scheme, 10.09
ANNEXED PROTOCOL, 1.07
APPEALS,
under Convention,
meaning of "ordinary appeal", 8.28
right of appeal of applicant for enforcement, 8.49
rights of appeal of persons against whom
enforcement is authorised, 8.50
restrictions on enforcement during
period for, 8.28–8.29, 8.46–8.47
sisting of proceedings where appeal
lodged in courts of State of origin,
8.52
under inter-U.K. scheme,
appeals from tribunals excluded from,
9.12
APPEARANCE,
as justification for assumption of jurisdiction,
under Convention, 7.28
under inter-U.K. scheme, 9.28
under Scottish scheme, 10.78
coupled with protest to jurisdiction, 11.22
APPLICATION OF CONVENTION. *See* SCOPE;
COMMENCEMENT AND TRANSITIONAL PROVI-
SIONS; TERRITORIAL APPLICATION.
ARBITRATION,
declinature of jurisdiction by U.K. courts
where arbitration agreement operative,
3.26, 10.13
enforcement of arbitral awards,
generally, 11.10
under inter-U.K. scheme, 9.37
exclusion from scope of Convention,
3.23–3.26
effect of exclusion in relation to consumer and insurance contracts, 6.04

jurisdiction in proceedings concerning
arbitration under Scottish scheme,
10.48–10.50
ARRESTMENT OF MOVEABLES,
as ground of jurisdiction under Scottish
scheme, 10.36–10.38
excluded by Convention as exorbitant
ground of jurisdiction, 5.09
ARRESTMENT OF SHIP, 5.09, 5.57
ASSOCIATION,
domicile or seat of,
meaning of term, 4.23
under Convention, 4.22–4.25
under 1982 Act, 4.26–4.33
exclusive jurisdiction in relation to,
7.12–7.17
ASTREINTES, 8.05 (8), 8.36
AUSTRALIA, 3.40
AUTHENTIC INSTRUMENTS,
enforcement of, 7.22, 8.57–8.60
AUTHENTIC TEXTS,
of 1968 Convention, 2.15
AVIATION INSURANCE, 6.18–6.24

BANKRUPTCY AND INSOLVENCY,
excluded from scope of Convention, 3.20,
3.21
excluded from scope of Sched. 4, 9.09,
9.36 (3)
excluded from scope of Sched. 8, 10.08 (4)
BEAUMONT, P. R., 5.35, 10.25
BELLET, P., 1.05, 1.13, 1.14
BRANCH, AGENCY OR ESTABLISHMENT,
jurisdictional provisions of Convention,
generally, 5.44–5.49
in relation to consumers, 6.31
in relation to insurers, 6.10
jurisdictional provisions of inter-U.K.
scheme, 9.23
jurisdictional provisions of Scottish
scheme, 10.32

CANADA, 3.40
CAPACITY. *See* STATUS AND CAPACITY.
CAPPELLETTI, M., 1.10, 1.12
CHANNEL ISLANDS,
application of Convention to, 3.43
extension of 1982 Act to, 3.43, 11.16
CHOICE OF COURT,
inference from choice of English law,
under Convention, 7.24
under inter-U.K. scheme, 9.27, 9.41
See also PROROGATION AGREEMENTS.
CHOICE OF LAW RULES,
misapplication of, as a ground of non-
recognition, 8.21
CIVIL AND COMMERCIAL MATTERS,
Convention applies to, 3.07–3.13
CIVIL CLAIMS IN CRIMINAL PROCEEDINGS,
rules of jurisdiction,
under Convention, 5.40–5.42
under Scottish scheme, 10.26–10.28

[299]

COLLINS, L., 2.01, 5.48
CO-DEFENDERS,
jurisdiction over,
under Convention, 5.60–5.64
under Scottish scheme, 10.53
COMMENCEMENT AND TRANSITIONAL PROVISIONS,
of Convention, 3.47–3.51
of inter-U.K. scheme, 9.41–9.43
of 1982 Act, 11.18–11.19
COMMERCIAL AGENTS, 5.46
COMMISSARY PROCEEDINGS,
excluded from Scottish scheme, 10.08 (7)

COMMUNITY LEGISLATION,
in particular matters, primacy of, 3.41,
5.16
COMPANY, LEGAL PERSONA OR ASSOCIATION,
domicile or seat,
under Convention, 4.22–4.24
under 1982 Act, 4.25–4.34
insolvency of, 3.20
jurisdiction over,
under Convention, 7.12–7.17
under inter-U.K. scheme, 9.12, 9.19
under Scottish scheme, 10.08,
10.61–10.68
meaning of phrase, 7.12
nationality of, 4.22

COMPENSATION ORDERS. *See* CIVIL CLAIMS IN
CRIMINAL PROCEEDINGS.
CONCURRENT PROCEEDINGS. *See* FORUM NON
CONVENIENS *and* LIS PENDENS.
CONFLICTING JUDGMENTS,
as a ground of non-recognition under
Convention, 8.19–8.20

CONSUMER CONTRACTS,
definitions, 6.24–6.29
jurisdiction under Convention, 5.49,
6.31–6.32
jurisdiction under inter-U.K. scheme, 9.23
jurisdiction under Scottish scheme,
10.57–10.60
review of jurisdiction of court of origin,
8.03, 8.22
CONTINENTAL SHELF ACT 1964,
proceedings under s.3 excluded from,
Sched. 4, 9.12
Sched. 8, 10.08
CONTRACT,
characterisation of obligation as contractual, 5.17
jurisdiction,
under Convention, 5.17–5.25
under inter-U.K. scheme, 9.18
under Scottish scheme, 10.21–10.23
when existence of contract denied, 5.18
place of performance, 5.19–5.22
stipulations as to, 5.22

CONTRACTING STATES,
application of Convention to, 3.42
CONTRACTS OF EMPLOYMENT,
jurisdiction in, 5.20
CONVENTIONS,
For 1968 Convention, *see* JUDGMENTS CONVENTION. For Treaty of Rome, *see* EEC
CONVENTION.
Berne Convention of 1952 concerning the
Carriage of Goods by railway (CIM),
3.35
Berne Convention of 1961 concerning the
carriage of passengers and luggage by
rail, 3.35

Brussels Convention of 1952 on Certain
Rules Concerning Civil Jurisdiction in
Matters of Collision, 3.35
Brussels Convention of 1952 on the Arrest
of Sea-Going Ships, 3.35, 5.57, 9.12 (7)
Brussels Convention of 1957 on the Limitation of Liability of Owners of Sea-going
ships, 5.70
Brussels Convention of 1969 on Civil
Liability for Oil Pollution Damage, 3.36
European Convention of 1972 on State
Immunity, 11.06
Geneva Convention of 1956 on the Contract for the International Carriage of
Goods by Road (CMR), 3.35, 7.26 (14),
11.07
Hague Convention of 1965 on Agreements
for Choice of Court, 7.26 (4), 7.26 (10)
Hague Convention of 1965 on the Service
Abroad of Judicial and Extra-judicial
documents, 7.34, 7.36, 8.05 (6), 9.30
Hague Convention of 1970 on the Taking
of Evidence Abroad in Civil and Commercial Matters, 8.05 (6)
Hague Convention of 1971 on the Recognition and Enforcement of Judgments in
Civil and Commercial Matters, 1.10,
8.20
Hague Convention of 1973 on the Recognition and Enforcement of Decisions
relating to Maintenance Obligations,
5.34, 11.12, 11.17
London Convention of 1976 on the Limitation of Liability for Maritime Claims,
5.70
Luxembourg Convention of 1975 on the
European Patent for the Common Market, 7.20, 7.21
Munich Convention of 1973 on the Grant
of European Patents, 7.20, 7.21
New York Convention of 1958 on the
Recognition and Enforcement of Foreign Arbitral Awards, 3.23–3.26, 10.13,
11.10
Paris Convention of 1960 on Third-party
Liability in the Field of Nuclear Energy,
3.36
Proposed Conventions under Art. 59, 3.40
Rome Convention of 1980 on the law
applicable to Contractual Obligations,
6.26, 6.30
U.N. Convention of 1956 on the Recovery
of Maintenance Abroad, 5.34
Warsaw Convention of 1929 on International Carriage by Air, 3.35
CORPORATION. *See* COMPANY, LEGAL PERSONA
OR ASSOCIATION.
COUNTERCLAIMS.
jurisdiction over,
under Convention, 5.69
under Scottish scheme, 10.55–10.56
COURT OF JUSTICE OF EUROPEAN COMMUNITIES. *See* EUROPEAN COURT.
COURT OR TRIBUNAL,
meaning in Art. 25, 8.05 (2)–(5)
COURTS OF LAW,
definition under 1982 Act, 9.08
COURT SETTLEMENTS,
enforcement of, 8.61–8.66
CRIMINAL PROCEEDINGS,
civil claims made in the course of,
rule in Convention, 5.40–5.43
rule in inter-U.K. scheme, 10.26–10.27
right to be defended in, 8.25, 10.28

CROWN,
  domicile of, 4.35
CURRENCY OF PAYMENT, 8.68
CUSTODY OF CHILDREN,
  excluded from scope of Scottish scheme,
    10.08 (2)
CUSTOMS AND EXCISE, 3.10

DAMAGES,
  enforcement of overseas awards for multi-
    ple damages, 11.15
DEATH, DECLARATION OF, 3.14
DEBTS SECURED OVER IMMOVEABLES,
  jurisdiction in proceedings concerning,
    10.44–10.45
DECISIONS OF ORGANS OF CORPORATIONS AND
    ASSOCIATIONS,
  jurisdiction under Convention, 7.12, 7.16
  jurisdiction under inter-U.K. scheme, 9.19
  jurisdiction under Scottish scheme, 10.46,
    10.68
DELICT AND QUASI-DELICT,
  rules of jurisdiction,
    under Convention, 5.35–5.39
    under inter-U.K. scheme, 9.18
    under Scottish scheme, 10.24–10.25
DENMARK,
  maritime jurisdiction, 5.24
DESIGNS. *See* PATENTS, TRADE MARKS AND
    DESIGNS.
DISMISSAL, JUDGMENTS OF,
  effect upon running of periods of prescrip-
    tion and limitation, 8.11
  recognition of, 8.11
DOMICILE AS A GROUND OF JURISDICTION,
  under Convention,
    deemed domicile under Arts. 8 (2) and
      13 (2), 6.10, 6.35
    generally, 4.01–4.05, 5.04–5.07
    trusts, 5.50–5.52
  under 1982 Act,
    in Sched. 4, 9.15, 9.23
    in Sched. 8, 10.14–10.17
DOMICILE, ASCERTAINMENT OF,
  under Convention,
    companies, legal persons and associa-
      tions,
      for purposes of Art. 16, 4.33–4.34
      generally, 4.22–4.25
    individuals, 1.23, 4.06–4.11
    trusts, 4.04, 5.52, 10.35 (2)
  under 1982 Act,
    companies, legal persons and associa-
      tions,
      for purposes of Art. 16, 4.33–4.34
      generally, 4.26–4.32
    Crown, 4.35
    individuals,
      in another Contracting State, 4.15
      in particular place within United
        Kingdom, 4.20
      in State other than Contracting State,
        4.07, 4.21
      in United Kingdom, 4.16–4.19
    trusts, 5.52

EEC COMMISSION,
  Note of October 22, 1959, 1.05, 1.15
EEC TREATY,
  Art. 177, 2.05, 2.06, 2.08
  Art. 220, 1.05, 1.22, 1.28, 2.10, 2.13, 2.16,
    2.27
  other Articles, 1.23, 2.16–17

EMPLOYMENT, CONTRACTS OF, 3.12
ENFORCEMENT OF JUDGMENTS,
  general,
    earlier obstacles to enforcement,
      1.11–1.15
  under 1968 Convention,
    conditions,
      absence of grounds of non-
        recognition, 8.30
      enforceability in State of origin, 8.34
      other conditions, 8.34–8.38
    general matters, 8.30–8.33
    jurisdiction, 7.22
    legal aid, 8.41
    partial enforcement admissible, 8.12,
      8.45
    procedure,
      applicant's address for service,
        8.39–8.40
      courts to which application must be
        made, 8.43
      documents to be produced, 8.41
      ex parte proceedings, 8.44
      expeditious nature of, 8.44
  under inter-U.K. scheme,
    effects of registration, 9.40(f)
    general, 9.35
    judgments which may be enforced,
      9.36–9.37
    periods after which enforcement may be
      barred, 9.40(b)
    procedures for enforcement, 9.38–9.40
    remedies of person against whom en-
      forcement is sought, 9.40(e)
  under Scottish scheme,
    jurisdiction in matters of, 10.71
ENGLAND,
  special rules in relation to contracts gov-
    erned by English law, 5.25
ESTABLISHMENT. *See* BRANCH, AGENCY OR
    ESTABLISHMENT.
EUROPEAN COURT,
  concern with internal laws of Contracting
    States, 2.03
  interpretative jurisdiction under 1971 Pro-
    tocol, 2.04–2.08
EUROPEAN COURT JUDGMENTS,
  authority as precedents in that court, 2.09
  authority in national legal systems, 2.10
  authority in United Kingdom, 2.11
  judicial notice of, 2.01
  meaning and effect of, a question of law,
    2.01
EVIDENCE, PROPERTY, ETC.,
  orders for preservation, inspection, etc.,
    11.04
EXCLUSIVE JURISDICTIONS,
  under Convention, 5.02, 7.02–7.27, 7.42
    companies, legal persons or associa-
      tions, 7.12–7.17
    enforcement of judgments, 7.22
    immoveable property, 7.07–7.11
    patents, trade marks and designs,
      7.19–7.21
    prorogation agreements, 7.23–7.26
    public registers, 7.18
    trusts, 7.27
  under inter-U.K. scheme, 7.06, 9.26–9.27
  under Scottish scheme, 10.51, 10.61–10.79
    companies, legal persons or associa-
      tions, 10.61–10.68
    enforcement of judgments, 10.71
    immoveable property, 10.64–10.65
    patents, trade marks and designs, 10.70

prorogation agreements, 10.75
public registers, 10.69–10.70
trusts, 10.77
EXEQUATUR, 1.11–1.15, 8.09
EXORBITANT BASES OF JURISDICTION, 1.09,
1.10, 4.21, 5.08, 5.09, 8.04, 8.23–8.24,
9.02–9.03

FAMILY LAW, 3.14–3.18
FOREIGN JUDGMENTS. *See* RECOGNITION AND
ENFORCEMENT.
FORUM CONVENIENS, 10.12, 11.21
FORUM NON CONVENIENS, 4.32, 5.02, 5.05,
5.09, 9.05, 9.31, 10.12, 10.51, 11.21
FRAUD,
non-recognition of judgment on ground
of, 8.15

GERMANY, FEDERAL REPUBLIC OF,
special rules in relation to, 5.68
GIBRALTAR,
application of Convention to, 3.43
application of 1982 Act to, 3.43
GREECE,
Accession Treaty with, 1.07
special rules in relation to, 5.24

HABITUAL RESIDENCE,
as alternative to domicile, 4.13
in maintenance claims under Scottish
scheme, 10.29
HAGUE CONFERENCE ON PRIVATE INTERNA-
TIONAL LAW.
extraordinary session of April 1966, 1.06
HAGUE CONVENTIONS. *See under* CONVEN-
TIONS.

IMMOVEABLE PROPERTY,
jurisdiction under Convention,
insurance of immoveables, 6.08, 6.12
rights *in rem* in immoveables, 7.07–7.08
tenancies of immoveables, 7.09–7.11
jurisdiction under inter-U.K. scheme, 9.26
jurisdiction under Scottish scheme,
in proprietary and possessory actions
relating to the property, 10.41–10.42
as a general ground in personal actions,
10.39–10.40
debts secured over immoveables,
10.44–10.45
rights *in rem* in, or tenancies of, immoveable property, 10.64–10.65
IMMUNITIES,
general, 3.04
overseas judgments against States, 11.05,
11.06
INSOLVENCY,
matters relating to, excluded from,
Convention, 3.20–3.21
inter-U.K. scheme, 9.12 (1), 9.36 (3)
Scottish scheme, 10.08 (4)
INSURANCE MATTERS,
jurisdiction under Convention,
actions against insurer, 5.49, 6.09–6.13
direct actions, 6.14
general approach, 6.01–6.06
large risks, 6.18–6.24
outline of scheme, 6.07–6.08
prorogation, 6.16–6.17
jurisdiction under inter-U.K. scheme,
9.04, 9.22
jurisdiction under Scottish scheme, 10.11

INSURERS,
direct actions against, 6.14
INTERDICTS AND INJUNCTIONS, JURISDICTION
IN,
under Convention, 5.35
under inter-U.K. scheme, 9.18
under Scottish scheme, 10.43
INTEREST ON REGISTERED JUDGMENTS, 8.46,
8.67, 11.13
INTERIM ORDERS,
enforceability under Convention, 8.02
enforceability under inter-U.K. scheme,
9.36 (7)
INTERNATIONALITY, CRITERION OF, 3.05
INTERPRETATION OF CONVENTION,
adoption by European Court of previously
adopted policies, 2.19
contextual approach, 2.23–2.25
literal approach, 2.20–2.22
purposive approach, 2.26–2.27
materials available to court,
general, 2.15–2.18
Jenard and Schlosser Reports, 2.18
other language texts, 2.15
preambles, etc., 2.16–2.17, 3.05
travaux préparatoires, 2.17
policies specific to Convention,
'Community' interpretation, 2.28–2.29
broader interpretation of general provisions than of exceptions, 2.31
INTERPRETATION OF 1982 ACT,
inter-U.K. scheme, 9.06
Scottish scheme, 10.03–10.05
INTER-UNITED KINGDOM SCHEME FOR JURIS-
DICTION AND ENFORCEMENT,
application to persons, 9.07
application to subjects, 9.09–9.12
application to proceedings, 9.08
interpretation of, 9.06
justification, 9.01–9.04
preliminary outline, 1.32
rules for assumption of jurisdiction,
9.13–9.32
general, 9.13–9.14
specific rules, *See under* Sched. 4.
IRELAND,
New York Convention on Arbitration,
3.26
Civil procedure conventions, 8.05 (6)
special provisions relating to, 5.24, 5.25,
8.29
ISLE OF MAN,
application of Convention to, 3.43
extension of 1982 Act to, 3.43, 11.16
ITINERANTS,
jurisdiction over, under Scottish scheme,
10.19
Scottish jurisdiction over, contrasted with
personal presence, 5.09

JENARD REPORT,
authority of,
in relation to Convention, 2.18
under 1982 Act, 2.02
judicial notice of, 2.02
JUDGMENTS,
against States, 11.05
authenticity of external judgments, 8.42
enforceable under Convention, 8.02–8.05,
8.12, 8.34–8.36
exclusive jurisdiction in relation to enforcement of, 7.22, 10.71

inconsistent with agreements for settlement of disputes, 11.08
irreconcilable with another judgment, 8.19–8.20
recognition of. *See* RECOGNITION OF JUDGMENTS.
transmission of Scottish judgments abroad, 8.56
JUDGMENTS CONVENTION,
authentic texts, 2.15
background, 1.05, 1.09–1.15
basic features, 1.19–1.30
entry into force, 3.47–3.51
force in law in United Kingdom, 1.31, 5.01
interpretation, 2.01–2.32
scope, 3.01–3.42
supremacy of, 2.03
territorial application, 3.42–3.46
JURISDICTION UNDER CONVENTION,
appearance, 7.28
branch, agency or establishment, 5.44–5.49
civil claims in criminal proceedings, 5.40–5.43
co-defenders, 5.60–5.64
consumer contracts, 6.25–6.32
contract, 5.17–5.22
counterclaims, 5.69
delict and quasi-delict, 5.35–5.38
domicile, 4.01, 5.04–5.07
exorbitant rules. *See* EXORBITANT BASES OF JURISDICTION.
exclusive jurisdictions. *See* EXCLUSIVE JURISDICTIONS.
general scheme, 5.02
immoveables, 5.02, 7.07–7.11
limitation actions in shipping matters, 5.70
maintenance, 5.26–5.34
persons not domiciled in a Contracting State, 5.02, 5.10–5.11
review of jurisdiction of court of origin, 6.06
salvage, 5.57–5.58
special jurisdictions in Art. 5, justification of, 5.12–5.15
submission, 7.28
third party claims, 5.65–5.68
trusts, 5.50–5.56
where precluded. *See* SCOPE OF CONVENTION.
JURISDICTION UNDER INTER-UNITED KINGDOM SCHEME. *See* INTER-UNITED KINGDOM SCHEME FOR JURISDICTION AND ENFORCEMENT.
JURISDICTION UNDER SCOTTISH SCHEME. *See* SCOTTISH RULES OF JURISDICTION.

LEGAL AID AND SECURITY FOR COSTS,
empowering provisions in relation to international agreements and proceedings, 11.17
in enforcement proceedings under Convention, 8.31, 8.41, 8.69–8.71
LIABILITY INSURANCE, 6.12–6.13
LIMITATION OF LIABILITY,
jurisdiction under Convention in actions of, 5.70
LIS PENDENS, 7.37–7.39, 9.31
LITISCONTESTATION,
time of, 7.38, fn. 97
LUXEMBOURG,
choice of court agreements in relation to, 7.26 (13)

nationals sued in contract, 5.23
New York Convention on Arbitration, 3.26

MACKENZIE STUART, LORD, 2.26
MAINTENANCE, GENERAL RULES,
enforcement of maintenance orders against assets in country other than residence of debtor, 11.14
interest on arrears, 11.13
lump sum orders, 11.12
MAINTENANCE UNDER CONVENTION,
jurisdiction in maintenance claims, 5.26–5.28
meaning of "maintenance", 5.29–5.32
procedure for enforcing maintenance orders, 8.43, 8.53–8.55
provisional maintenance orders, 5.34
variation of maintenance orders, 5.33
MAINTENANCE UNDER INTER-UNITED KINGDOM SCHEME,
jurisdiction in maintenance claims, 9.12, 9.18
procedures for enforcement of maintenance orders, 9.36 (5)
MAINTENANCE UNDER SCOTTISH SCHEME,
assumption of jurisdiction, 10.29–10.31
MARITIME MATTERS,
disputes between master and crew of ship, 5.24
limitation of liability claims, 5.70
marine insurance, 6.18–6.24
proceedings excluded from inter-U.K. scheme of jurisdiction, 9.12 (7)
proceedings excluded from Scottish scheme of jurisdiction, 10.08
salvage claims, 5.57–5.58
MATRIMONIAL PROPERTY RIGHTS,
excluded from scope of Convention, 3.15, 3.18, 5.31
MERCIER, P., 1.05, 1.06, 1.11
MINOR,
domicile of, 4.07–4.08
MONEY AND NON-MONEY JUDGMENTS,
different procedures for enforcement under inter-U.K. scheme, 9.35, 9.38–9.40
non-money judgments enforced under Convention, 8.02
MOVEABLES, PRESENCE OF,
exorbitant ground of jurisdiction under Convention, 5.09
as a ground of jurisdiction in proprietary and possessory actions,
under inter-U.K. scheme, 9.18
under Scottish scheme, 10.41–10.42
MULTIPLEPOINDINGS,
jurisdiction under Scottish scheme, 10.42 (2)
MUNZER CASE, 1.13–1.14

NADELMANN, K. H., 1.06, 1.10
NATIONALITY,
as a ground of jurisdiction among Member States, 1.10
discarded as a ground of jurisdiction under Convention, 1.22
discrimination against non-nationals excluded, 5.07
relevance in ascertaining a domicile of dependence, 4.07
irrelevant in inter-U.K. scheme, 9.15

NON-MEMBER STATES,
conventions with, 3.37–3.40
"NON-MERGER",
abolition of English rule, 11.23
NULLITY OF CORPORATION OR ASSOCIATION,
7.15

OBLIGATIONS CONVENTION. *See* CONVEN-
TIONS—Rome Convention of June 19,
1980.
OBLIGATIONS REPORT, 6.26, 6.30
ORDRE PUBLIC, 1.12

PARTIAL ENFORCEMENT, 8.12, 8.45
PARTNERSHIPS,
jurisdiction in matters relating to their
constitution, etc., 7.12
seat of, 7.13
PATENTS, TRADE MARKS AND DESIGNS,
jurisdiction under Convention, 7.19–7.21
jurisdiction under inter-U.K. scheme, 9.12
(2), 9.26
jurisdiction under Scottish scheme, 10.51
PERILLO, J. M., 1.10, 1.12
PRECEDENT,
approach of European Court, 2.09
PROROGATION AGREEMENTS,
under Convention, 7.23–7.26
consensus,
denial of, by one party, 7.26 (5)
formal requirements, 7.26 (6)–(7)
consumer matters, 6.32, 6.33
implied agreement, 7.24
insurance matters, 6.16, 6.18–6.21
recognition of judgments inconsistent
with, 8.26
special privileges of persons domiciled
in Luxembourg, 7.26 (13)
under inter-U.K. scheme, 9.27
under Scottish scheme, 10.72–10.77
PROTECTION OF TRADING INTERESTS ACT 1980,
multiple-damages awards, 8.16, 11.15
proceedings under s.6,
excluded from inter-U.K. scheme, 9.12
excluded from Scottish scheme, 10.08
PROTOCOL ON INTERPRETATION,
applicable only where Convention directly
applies, 10.05
description, 1.07, 2.04–2.06
references to European Court under, 1.02,
2.06–2.08
PROVISIONAL AND PROTECTIVE MEASURES,
under Convention, 3.02, 7.43–7.48, 8.47,
8.51, 9.32
under 1982 Act, 9.32, 9.36 (7), 11.02,
11.03
PUBLIC POLICY, 1.12, 8.13–8.16
PUBLIC REGISTERS,
jurisdiction relating to validity of entries
in,
under 1968 Convention, 7.18
under inter-U.K. scheme, 9.26
under Scottish scheme, 10.69–10.70

RECOGNITION OF JUDGMENTS UNDER CONVEN-
TION,
concept of recognition and its effects,
8.08–8.11
effects of registration, 8.46

grounds of non-recognition,
absence of service, 8.17–8.18
conflicting judgments, 8.19–8.20
failure to comply with mandatory jurisdictional rules, 8.22
incompatibility with prorogation agreement, 8.26
judgment outside scope of Convention,
8.05 (1)–(3), 8.26
misapplication of choice of law rules,
8.21
public policy, 8.13–8.16
relevance of Conventions under Art. 59,
8.23–8.24
judgments susceptible of recognition,
8.02–8.05, 8.11
sisting of recognition proceedings,
8.28–8.29
RECOGNITION OF JUDGMENTS UNDER INTER-
UNITED KINGDOM SCHEME, 9.34
RECONVENTIONAL CLAIMS,
jurisdiction in, 5.69
REGISTERS. *See* PUBLIC REGISTERS.
REGISTRATION OF EXTERNAL JUDGMENT,
effect of registration under inter-U.K.
scheme, 9.40(f)
RE-INSURANCE,
jurisdiction in contracts of, 6.07
RELATED ACTIONS,
defined, 7.40–7.41
REVENUE MATTERS,
excluded from 1968 Convention, 3.10
REVISION AU FOND, 1.13

SALE OF GOODS. *See* CONSUMER CONTRACTS.
SALVAGE CLAIMS, 5.57–5.58
SCHLOSSER REPORT,
authority of,
in relation to Convention, 2.18
under 1982 Act, 2.02
judicial notice of, 2.02
SCOPE OF CONVENTION,
exclusions,
arbitration, 3.23–3.26
bankruptcy and similar proceedings,
3.20–3.21
EEC law, matters governed by, 3.41
obligations arising under international
conventions on particular matters,
3.28, 3.31–3.36
obligations arising under international
conventions within scope of Art. 59,
3.37–3.41
provisional and protective measures,
3.02
public authority acting in exercise of its
powers, 3.11
revenue, customs or administrative matters, 3.10
rights in property arising out of matrimonial relationship, 3.15–3.18
social security, 3.22
status or legal capacity of natural persons, 3.14
wills and succession, 3.19
inclusions,
civil and commercial matters, 3.07
contracts of employment, 3.12
maintenance, 3.14
interpretation of provisions relating to
scope, 2.28–2.31, 3.03
SCOPE OF INTER-UNITED KINGDOM SCHEME,
3.01, 9.07–9.12

SCOPE OF SCOTTISH SCHEME,
general application, 10.09
general exclusions, 10.07
particular exclusions, 10.08

SCOTTISH LAW COMMISSION,
Memorandum No. 12, 9.02

SCOTTISH RULES OF JURISDICTION,
application, field of, 10.06–10.09
arbitration, 10.48–10.50
arrestment of moveables, 10.36–10.38
branch, agency or establishment, 10.32–10.33
civil claims in criminal proceedings, 10.26–10.28
claims against third parties, 10.54
co-defenders, 10.53
companies, legal persons and associations, decisions of their organs, 10.46–10.47
matters relating to their constitution, 10.46, 10.66–10.68
consumer contracts, 10.57–10.60
contract, 10.21–10.23
counterclaims, matters relating to, 10.55–10.56
debts secured over immoveables, 10.44–10.45
delict and quasi-delict, 10.24–10.25
domicile, 10.14–10.17
enforcement of judgments, 10.71
exclusive jurisdictions, 10.61–10.78
forum non conveniens, 10.12
immoveables, tenancies of, 10.64–10.65
immoveables, *in personam* jurisdiction based on ownership, 10.39–10.40
immoveables, proprietary and possessory actions, 10.41–10.42
interdict, 10.43
interpretation, 10.03–10.05
itinerants, 10.19–10.20
justification, 1.35, 10.02
maintenance, 10.29–10.31
patents, trade marks, etc., 10.51
prorogation, 10.59, 10.72–10.77
public registers, 10.69–10.70
submission, 10.78–10.79
trusts, 10.34–10.35
verification of jurisdiction, 10.79–10.81
where assumption of jurisdiction precluded, 11.08

SEAT OF CORPORATIONS AND ASSOCIATIONS,
under Convention, 4.22–4.25
under 1982 Act, 4.26–4.34
See also DOMICILE, ASCERTAINMENT OF *and* DOMICILE AS A GROUND OF JURISDICTION.

SECURITY FOR COSTS
may be imposed on person challenging order for enforcement, 8.52
not to be imposed upon person seeking enforcement under Convention, 8.40, 8.70

SERVICE,
absence of, as ground of non-recognition of judgments,
under Convention, 7.31–7.36, 8.17–8.18
under inter-U.K. scheme, 9.30
methods of, 7.31
service of judgment on defender, 8.50

SETTLEMENTS,
enforcement of court, 8.61–8.66

SHIPPING. *See* MARITIME MATTERS.

SISTING OF PROCEEDINGS, 8.28–8.29, 8.52

SITUS OF IMMOVEABLES,
as ground of jurisdiction under Scottish scheme, 10.36, 10.39–10.40

SOCIAL SECURITY, 3.22

STATE IMMUNITY,
overseas judgments against States, 11.05, 11.06

STATUS AND CAPACITY, ACTIONS RELATING TO,
excluded from Convention, 3.13–3.14, 5.32
excluded under inter-U.K. scheme, 9.09, 9.36
excluded under Scottish scheme, 10.08

STATUS PROCEEDINGS,
maintenance orders made in course of, 5.28
characterisation of, 3.14, 5.32

STAY OF PROCEEDINGS. *See* SISTING OF PROCEEDINGS.

SUBMISSION TO JURISDICTION. *See* APPEARANCE.

SUCCESSION. *See* WILLS AND SUCCESSION.

TENANCIES, 7.09–7.11

TERRITORIAL APPLICATION OF CONVENTION, 3.42–3.46, 11.16

TERRITORIAL APPLICATION OF 1982 ACT, 11.16

THIRD PARTY PROCEEDINGS,
jurisdiction under Convention, 5.65–5.68
jurisdiction under inter-U.K. scheme, 9.20
jurisdiction under Scottish scheme, 10.54

TORT. *See* DELICT AND QUASI-DELICT.

TRANSITIONAL PROVISIONS. *See* COMMENCEMENT AND TRANSITIONAL PROVISIONS.

TRANSPORT,
contracts of, excluded from S.4 of Title II of the 1968 Convention, 3.35

TRAVAUX PRÉPARATOIRES, 2.17

TRESPASS TO FOREIGN LAND, 11.21

TRIBUNALS, APPEALS FROM,
excluded from inter-U.K. scheme, 9.08, 9.12
excluded from Scottish scheme, 10.08

TRUSTS,
domicile of, 5.52
jurisdiction under Convention,
availability of general rules, 5.50
court of domicile, 5.51–5.56
exclusive jurisdiction by prorogation, 7.27
jurisdiction under inter-U.K. scheme, 5.53, 9.27
jurisdiction under Scottish scheme, 10.34–10.35

TUTORY AND CURATORY PROCEEDINGS,
excluded from Scottish scheme, 10.08 (3)

UNITED STATES, 3.40

VERIFICATION OF JURISDICTION,
under Convention, 7.29–7.30
under Scottish scheme, 10.79–10.81

VERIFICATION OF SERVICE, 7.31–7.36, 8.17, 9.30

WARRANTY,
jurisdiction against warrantor, 5.65

WESER, M., 1.05, 1.10

WILLS AND SUCCESSION, MATTERS RELATING
TO,
excluded from scope of Convention, 3.19
excluded from scope of inter-U.K. scheme
of jurisdiction, 9.09

not excluded from inter-U.K. scheme for
reciprocal enforcement of judgments,
9.36 (4)
not excluded from Scottish jurisdictional
scheme, 10.09